Fodor's

WASHINGTON, D.C.

Welcome to Washington, D.C.

With its Neoclassical buildings and broad avenues, Washington, D.C., looks its part as America's capital. Majestic monuments and memorials honor our nation's history, but D.C. also lives in the present; new restaurants and bars continually emerge, upping the hipness factor from Capitol Hill to U Street. Fun museums and tree-shaded parks make it a terrific place for families. You may come for the official sites, but you'll remember D.C.'s local flavor, too. Please note that this book was produced during the COVID-19 pandemic. As you plan your visit, please confirm that places are still open and let us know when we need to make updates by writing to us at editors@fodors.com.

TOP REASONS TO GO

★ **Cherry Blossoms:** For a few weeks in spring, D.C. is awash in glorious pink blooms.

★ **The White House:** 1600 Pennsylvania may be the best-known address in the U.S.

★ **Memorials:** The lives of soldiers, presidents, and political figures are commemorated.

★ **Museums:** For every taste—whether you like spies, airplanes, history, or art.

★ **Globe-trotting Cuisine:** Diverse cultures support restaurants with authentic flavors.

★ **The Mall:** Ground zero for museums, picnics, festivals, and performances.

Contents

Fodor's Features

MAPS

IN THIS TEMPLE
AS IN THE HEARTS OF THE PEOPLE
FOR WHOM HE SAVED THE UNION
THE MEMORY OF ABRAHAM LINCOLN
IS ENSHRINED FOREVER

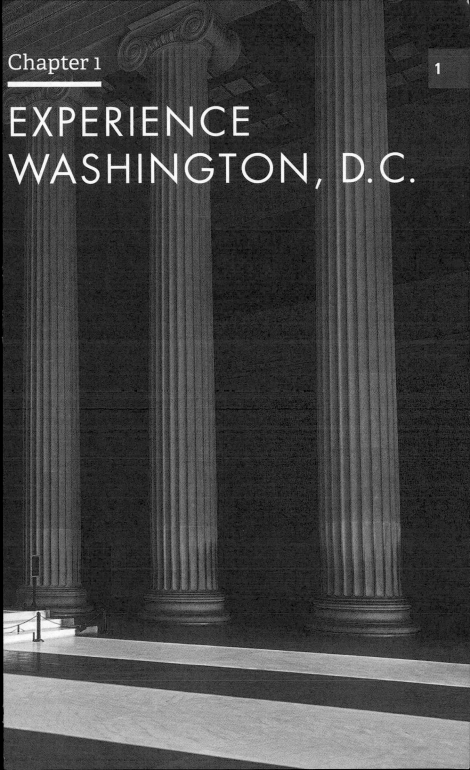

Chapter 1

EXPERIENCE WASHINGTON, D.C.

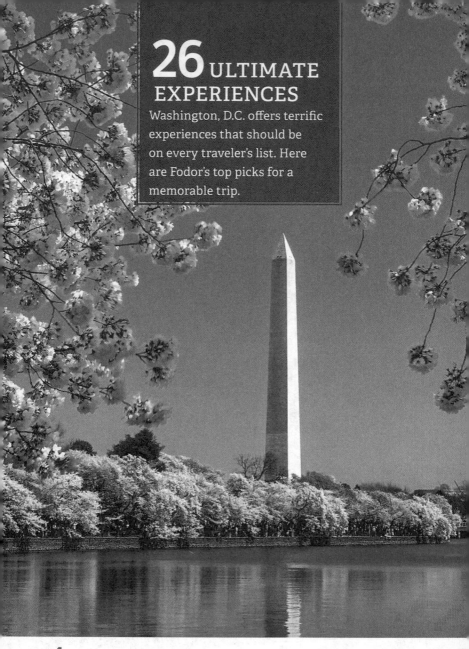

26 ULTIMATE EXPERIENCES

Washington, D.C. offers terrific experiences that should be on every traveler's list. Here are Fodor's top picks for a memorable trip.

1 Cherry Blossom Festival

Every spring Washington is blanketed with pink and white flowers, heralding the three-week-long National Cherry Blossom Festival. Many of the original trees (a gift from Japan in the early 1900s) stand around the Tidal Basin; come early to avoid the crowds. *(Ch. 3)*

2 The NMAAHC

The museum chronicles the African American experience, from the history of slavery through the Civil War to the Jim Crow era and up to today. *(Ch. 3)*

3 The White House

The White House is located at 1600 Pennsylvania Avenue; opposite nearby Jackson Square, the new Black Lives Matter Plaza reminds us to fight injustice. *(Ch. 6)*

4 National Cathedral

With a prominent spot on the city's skyline, this stone church is built in a soaring, 14th-century Gothic style and is the site of state funerals for presidents of every faith. *(Ch. 11)*

5 The Wharf

One of D.C.'s newest neighborhoods opened to acclaim in 2017, with a mix of residences and businesses along the Potomac Southwest Waterfront. The second phase should be completed in 2022. *(Ch. 12)*

6 Georgetown

One of Washington's ritziest enclaves, Georgetown marries old-world charm with upscale dining and shopping, as well as a soupçon of college nightlife via Georgetown University. *(Ch. 7)*

7 14th Street and U Street

Historically, U Street was the focal point of early-20th-century African American culture in D.C. *(Ch. 10)*

8 Smithsonian Museums

What do baby pandas, astronauts, and postage stamps have in common? They all make up the dizzying array of offerings at the Smithsonian's 19 museums. *(Ch. 3, 4, 11)*

9 Nationals Park

Even before the Nationals won the 2019 World Series, Nats games were one of the top things to do, with a waterfront setting, affordable tickets, and friendly fans. *(Ch. 12)*

10 Supreme Court

The highest court in the country—and home of the third branch of government—is housed in a Neoclassical white building a block from the U.S. Capitol. Oral arguments are open to the public. *(Ch. 5)*

11 Union Market and Eastern Market

D.C.'s markets set a high bar for discerning shoppers. Eastern Market is better known and more historic; Union Market offers high-end brands, while nearby La Cosecha celebrates Latinx culture. *(Ch. 5)*

12 Kennedy Center

The pinnacle of performing arts in Washington has a prominent perch on the banks of the Potomac. It's worth a visit just for the views—and the new state-of-the-art REACH expansion. *(Ch. 6)*

13 Mount Vernon

George Washington's colonial plantation home 10 miles south of Alexandria, is a place to learn about American history, including the lives of enslaved people in the 18th century. *(Ch. 14)*

14 Monuments and Memorials

If there's one place in Washington you need to visit, it's the National Mall. The 2-mile lawn between the Lincoln Memorial and the U.S. Capitol is home to most of the city's monuments and museums. *(Ch. 3)*

15 National Zoo

If you had to choose D.C.'s signature animal, the giant panda would win. The National Zoo is home to three (including a new baby), as well as numerous other rare animals. *(Ch. 11)*

16 Dupont Circle

Dupont has a little bit of everything: a mix of shops, restaurants, embassies, and museums, including the Phillips Collection and the Heurich House Museum. It's also a popular residential area. *(Ch. 8)*

17 Potomac River

It won't attract swimmers or win "clean water" accolades anytime soon, but the Potomac swarms with kayakers, stand-up paddleboarders, rowers, and sightseeing cruises. *(Ch. 12)*

18 Arlington National Cemetery

A quick trip across the Memorial Bridge brings you to this 624-acre plot in Virginia that is the final resting place of two presidents and about 400,000 American veterans. *(Ch. 13)*

19 Shaw

This neighborhood is booming with artisanal bars, restaurants, and boutiques. Beer drinkers have plenty to cheer about, as do foodies looking for D.C. hotspots. *(Ch. 10)*

20 U.S. Capitol

The seat of legislative power for the United States anchors one end of the Mall with a soaring dome, one of the tallest structures in the city. *(Ch. 5)*

21 The Food Scene

D.C.'s restaurants are among the nation's most vibrant and creative, embracing global flavors and Michelin-worthy flair. (Ch. 4)

22 Holocaust Museum

You can't leave here without being moved. The brilliant museum educates visitors about Nazi-era Germany and the horrific events of the Holocaust. (Ch. 3)

23 Historic Hotels

The Watergate has been restored, while the Mayflower, the Hay Adams, and the Willard InterContinental have hosted everyone from Mark Twain to Martin Luther King, Jr. (Ch. 4, 6)

24 H Street NE

It's a tad isolated, the artsy H Street corridor, also called the Atlas District, is home to many bars and restaurants. (Ch. 5)

25 Tidal Basin

One of the most photographed spots in Washington, this serene inlet lined with monuments, memorials, and cherry trees is just south of the National Mall. *(Ch. 3)*

26 Library of Congress

The world's largest library has about 540 miles of bookshelves. The catch: you can't actually check them out, but you can join a free tour of the grand building. *(Ch. 5)*

WHAT'S WHERE

1 The National Mall and Federal Triangle. The expanse of green stretching from the Capitol to the Lincoln Memorial is lined by famous museums and monuments; to the north are the National Archives and government offices.

2 Downtown, Chinatown, and Penn Quarter. The area north of the Mall has hotels, bars, restaurants, museums, and galleries, and the Capitol One Arena.

3 Capitol Hill and Northeast. The Capitol, Supreme Court, and Library of Congress dominate this area. Beyond are restaurants, bars, and a thriving outdoor market; northeast is the ever-growing H Street corridor.

4 Foggy Bottom, the West End, and the White House. The world's most famous house sits at the eastern end of this area. To the west are hotels, restaurants, museums, the Kennedy Center, and the Watergate.

5 Georgetown. One of the capital's wealthiest neighborhoods is great for strolling and shopping; the C&O Canal also starts here.

6 Dupont Circle and Kalorama. This hub of fashionable restaurants, shops, and embassies is also the capital's gayest neighborhood.

7 Adams Morgan. The ethnically diverse area has offbeat restaurants and shops, happening nightlife, and grand 19th-century apartment buildings and row houses.

8 U Street Corridor, Logan Circle, Shaw, and Columbia Heights. Revitalization has brought trendy boutiques and hip eateries to the area around 14th and U, while Shaw gets busier and trendier every year.

9 Upper Northwest. This mostly residential swath of D.C. has the National Cathedral and the National Zoo.

10 Southwest Waterfront, Southeast, and Anacostia. The newly developing Southwest Waterfront district is one of D.C.'s liveliest new areas. Southeast is the Navy Yard and historic Anacostia.

11 Arlington and Northern Virginia. Just across the Potomac, this area is also home to the Pentagon and Arlington National Cemetery.

Washington, D.C. Today

Classically majestic and stunningly beautiful, the Capitol, the White House, and the Supreme Court stand at the heart of Washington, D.C., symbols of the enduring stability and strength of the nation. In recent years, D.C. has proven it's more than just a political town, emerging as a cosmopolitan, global city with world-class restaurants, hotels, and cultural events.

POLITICS

President Trump was never popular in overwhelmingly Democratic D.C. Starting off with the historic Women's March just after his inauguration, his term saw the White House become a fenced-off fortress, with Black Lives Matter Plaza across Jackson Square standing in opposition. Top that off with the ever-present underlying discontent of Washingtonians not having voting representation in Congress—hence the display on their license plates: Taxation without Representation. Let's just say, conversation in the bars around town can be very interesting. President Joseph Biden got a much warmer welcome when he took office in January 2021.

SPORTS

First and foremost, this is a football town, as the hordes of loyal Washington Football Team (formerly known as the Redskins) fans demonstrate each fall Sunday at the city's many sports bars. Still, the team has struggled under billionaire owner Danny Snyder, who has shelled out big bucks to attract top players but has yet to return the team to the Super Bowl under his watch. Frustrated fans have noticed, and tickets are much easier to come by than they once were (though they still aren't cheap). Filling the void, the Nationals baseball team, headed by all-star talents like Max Scherzer, won the World Series in 2019 after a series of disheartening playoffs through the years. If that's not enough, the Capitals hockey team, led by perennial all-star Alex Ovechkin, finally snatched the long-evasive Stanley Cup in 2018. The DC United soccer team, spearheaded by Wayne Rooney, one of the biggest names to play in the MLS, has a sparkling new stadium. And even the Wizards basketball team has shed its once-lowly reputation, joining the playoff ranks on the wings of scoring sensation John Wall; while the Washington Mystics women's basketball team went all out and won the WNBA finals in 2019.

CANNABIS

D.C. has been on the cutting edge of the growing national movement to legalize marijuana, but with some complications. In 2014, D.C. voters overwhelmingly approved a measure permitting those over 21 to possess up to 2 ounces of marijuana, grow a small number of cannabis plants in their homes, and transfer up to an ounce of the drug to another adult—if no money accompanies the exchange. The law means you can smoke pot in private places, but you cannot buy it legally, which doesn't allow the pot tourism seen in states like Colorado. Still, that nuance has not dissuaded faithful users, and visitors should not be surprised if, on occasion, they encounter a whiff of pot smoke in the air.

DEMOGRAPHICS

Washington's prepandemic economic boom accelerated its demographic look, highlighted by several recent population milestones: an increase in residents, and a median age that has fallen below 34—almost four years younger than the country as a whole.

Hardly unrelated, the trends reveal that, after years of fleeing D.C. due to high crime rates and underperforming schools, more and more suburban families are opting to live in the city where they work. These younger professionals—mostly white, mostly drawn by the government and related industries—have helped bolster Washington's economy, but not without a price. Indeed, the gentrification—heightened by enormous stadium projects like Nationals Park—has reached deep into the traditionally Black areas of Northeast and Southeast, stirring resentment, driving up costs, and pricing many longtime residents out of their childhood homes. Indeed, D.C. has one of the widest income gaps between rich and poor in the country, leaving local officials to seek ways to strengthen commercial interests without sacrificing community and culture.

FOOD

Washington has made great culinary strides in recent years. No longer known only for stuffy steak houses catering to lobbyists, D.C. now offers options to satisfy the most eclectic tastes. And top-tier chefs from around the country have taken notice, with many descending on D.C. to catch the wave, along with young chefs who love the welcoming, innovative vibe. Most recently, 15 restaurants have been bestowed a coveted Michelin star, with two restaurants receiving two—and one (the venerable Inn at Little Washington) receiving three.

Jeremiah Langhorne aims to put mid-Atlantic cuisine back on the culinary map with The Dabney, with most of its cooking done on a central wood-burning hearth. Marjorie Meek-Bradley, a *Top Chef* alum, has made her mark with Roofers Union, featuring American fare, in Adams Morgan. It's no surprise that Italian chef Fabio Trabocchi wows with his Italian-flavored Fiola and Fiola Mare, but he has set a whole new course with the impeccable, coastal-Spain-inspired Del Mar at the District Wharf. And Johnny Monis, who won the 2013 James Beard award for the best chef in the

mid-Atlantic region, is at the helm of the Michelin-starred Komi and Little Serow.

These relative newcomers join D.C. pioneers like Robert Wiedmaier, whose Belgian roots are on full display at the award-winning Marcel's in Foggy Bottom, and James Beard Foundation Award–winning-chef turned humanitarian José Andrés, the culinary powerhouse behind Zaytinya, Oyamel, Jaleo, and the Michelin-starred minibar, all near Chinatown. He continues to expand his mini-empire with his newest endeavor, America Eats Tavern, which showcases historical takes on American favorites, including 19th-century mac and cheese and 1950s-era steak tartare.

FITNESS

The ACSM American Fitness Index recently ranked D.C. as one of the nation's top six fittest cities. Quite aside from the numerous gyms popping up all over the city—and ignoring, for a moment, the countless joggers constantly circling the Mall—residents have adopted a slew of activities to get outside and stay in shape. Like to play kickball? There are teams all over the city. Enjoy Ultimate Frisbee? There's a league for that, too. Rugby? Got it. Even bocce—the age-old Italian sport of lawn bowling—has inspired a passionate following and launched formal competitions around town. The District's many parks and green spaces cater perfectly to that game of pickup football (or *fútbol*), and the city's wild embrace of bike sharing has been complemented by the creation of bike-only lanes on some of its most traveled thoroughfares. Add a long list of burgeoning indoor crazes to the mix—everything from yoga and Pilates to Zumba and CrossFit—and you've got a city intent on shedding its wonks-only reputation.

What to Buy

A PLUSH PANDA

Perhaps there's no animal more beloved at the Smithsonian's National Zoo than the giant pandas—Mei Xiang, Tian Tian, and their new baby. Many visitors will want to take one home, even if it's a facsimile.

A UNIQUE MUSEUM GIFT

One thing the District has in abundance is spectacular museums—and along with museums come museum gift shops. These are some of the most underrated places for a shopping spree, with seriously curated wares including designer clothes, hangable art, coffee-table books, weird technology, and more.
A few singular museum shops to check out are: the Renwick Gallery (contemporary American pottery, clothing, and jewelry), National Gallery of Art (books, clothes, and housewares featuring famous artworks), National Air and Space Museum (a favorite: astronaut ice cream), and the International Spy Museum (supercool decoder rings or a pen camcorder).

LOCAL FOOD PRODUCTS

D.C. has a lively food culture based on fresh ingredients, and local producers make delicious honey, jam, granola, beer, and more. Shop Made in D.C. at the Wharf and several other locations has a fabulous selection of items (as well as art, clothing, and other locally made items) and primo signature gift boxes. Union Market in NoMa is another option. Salt & Sundry has foodie gifts as well jewelry, knits, and other works by local artists. And everywhere you go, keep an eye out for D.C.'s most iconic condiment: the sweet and tangy Capital City Mumbo Sauce.

A REAL-LIFE CHERRY TREE

Crowds flock to D.C. to view the ephemeral cherry blossoms, a traditional spring pilgrimage since the Japanese presented 3,000 of them as a gift to the capital city in 1912. If you'd like one of your own, you can order it through the DC Gift Shop; they'll spare you the trouble of having to shuffle it aboard the plane by sending it straight to your house. If a standard size cherry tree just isn't practical, what about a gemstone cherry blossom bonsai instead? The DC Gift Shop sells those, too.

LOCAL DESIGNER CLOTHING

Once upon a time (and not that long ago), the District was mostly about three-piece suits, with beach-sand tan being the most audacious color. These days, local fashion designers have quietly blossomed, creating and selling a variety of stunningly unique fashions that you won't find anywhere else. Mimi Miller, Amanda Casarez, and Maven Women by Rebecca Ballard are great places to start, but most don't have their own storefronts—yet.

BOOKS, BOOKS, AND MORE BOOKS

In a city with such integral ties to American history, you can bet your tricorn hat that you'll find a cornucopia of books covering every aspect of Americana. You'll find them in the shops of every museum and attraction—the shops at the Library of Congress, the National Building Museum, and the National Museum of American History are especially good. And while you're at it, there are several beloved independent bookstores with a local bent that are worth a peek as well, including Kramerbooks and afterwords café and the legendary Politics and Prose.

HANDCRAFTED SUNDRIES

Eastern Market on Capitol Hill has been a buzzing local market since 1873. It's still a viable food market, but these days, there's more. On weekends, artists and crafters take over the surrounding streets and the plaza, purveying colorful ceramic pitchers, aromatherapy soaps, funky fashion jewelry, cloth dolls, batik wall hangings, and a long list of other beautifully crafted items. Shop Made in

D.C. and Union Market are other places you'll find the work of local makers.

A STYLIZED, GRAPHIC PRINT OF YOUR FAVOR-ITE D.C. NEIGHBORHOOD

Washington, D.C. is a mosaic of vibrant and diverse neighborhoods. Victory Dance Creative's bold-color, hand-screen-printed neighborhood prints—50-some to choose from—are the perfect reminder to hang on your wall back home.

LOCALS SPORTS GEAR

D.C. has some serious sports teams, including the Nationals (baseball), Wizards (basketball), Capitals (ice hockey), D.C. United (soccer), and Washington Football Team. You can find good selections of caps, jerseys, T-shirts, and more at the stadiums themselves, if you happen to be there for a game or match. Or stop by any

DICK's Sporting Goods, Modell's Sporting Goods, even Target in the District.

DISTRICT-THEMED HOUSEWARES

You'll find one-of-a-kind boutiques selling super-original items for your home, including artsy tea towels with D.C. motifs, D.C.-shaped cutting boards, and printed hand-drawn maps of D.C. neighborhoods. You can even find cookie cutters in the shape of the District. Check out Cherry Blossom Creative and Hill's Kitchen for starters.

Under the Radar

LINCOLN COTTAGE

Lincoln and his family lived in this cottage during the Civil War, and it's since become a museum and cultural center. Visitors can take self-guided tours through permanent exhibits that cover the history of the Civil War and the Lincoln family as well as frequent special exhibits.

KENILWORTH AQUATIC GARDENS

Breathtaking water lilies and lotus flowers abound here. Spring and summer are the best times to visit, when the flowers and trees are in bloom. But fall at the park also has its charm, with leaves changing on cypress trees, calm waters, and lower temperatures. Stop by the gardens in early July for the annual Lotus and Water Lily Festival.

PEACOCK ROOM

Painted by American expatriate artist James McNeill Whistler, the Freer Gallery's most famous room's blue-and-gold-hued walls immediately catch visitors' eyes. Walk around the room to browse an extensive collection of Middle Eastern and Asian porcelain and to study the exquisite paintings of dueling peacocks and the "princess from the land of porcelain."

PHILLIPS COLLECTION

Most visitors flock to the National Mall for art museums, but Dupont Circle's Phillips Collection offers a nice change of pace. Tucked away on a quiet residential street, America's first modern art museum showcases more than 3,000 works, including French Impressionist paintings and American prints. Watch for blockbuster special exhibitions.

WASHINGTON NATIONAL CATHEDRAL

Take in Gothic-style architecture, stained-glass windows, and gargoyles in Northwest D.C. Book a ticket in advance to climb the cathedral's 30-story central tower, the city's highest point. A crypt level inside the cathedral holds the graves of President Woodrow Wilson, Helen Keller, and Matthew Shepard.

HILLWOOD ESTATE

Once the home of a D.C. socialite, Hillwood now holds collections of Russian imperial and French decorative art. Browse the Georgian-style mansion or roam its lush gardens. A Japanese-style garden includes trickling streams and stone paths.

U.S. BOTANIC GARDEN

Often overlooked, the inside garden is a hidden gem, one of the oldest in the United States. It's home to a variety of rare and endangered plants. Don't miss Bartholdi Park, across the street from the main conservatory—it features colorful plants, flowers, and a photogenic fountain in the middle.

MERIDIAN HILL PARK

In Columbia Heights, the park, also known as Malcolm X Park, is a good place to stop for a picnic or midafternoon stroll. Designed as an Italian garden, it has cascading water fountains, winding stone staircases, and plenty of green spaces.

SPANISH STEPS

Named for the famous staircase in Rome, D.C.'s steps, next to Embassy Row, aren't quite as grand, but they do provide a tranquil reprieve from the hustle and bustle of the city.

ROOSEVELT ISLAND

Cross Key Bridge to get to Roosevelt Island, an 88-acre oasis in the middle of the Potomac River. Lush woods and miles of hiking trails offer views of Georgetown and the harbor.

WOODROW WILSON HOUSE

Take a step back in time at the sprawling estate near Embassy Row that was home to President Wilson and his wife after they left the White House in 1921. Stately rooms include a parlor with the Wilsons' century-old Steinway piano.

Free Things to Do in D.C.

U.S. BUREAU OF ENGRAVING AND PRINTING

Everything from stamps to paper currency to military commissions is produced here. The Treasury Department prints up to 38 million notes a day. The free 40-minute tours (weekdays only, booked in advance) show you every step of currency production.

FREDERICK DOUGLASS HOUSE

One of the best views of the Capitol and the D.C. skyline can be found at this house perched on a hill in Anacostia. Douglass purchased the estate in 1877, named it Cedar Hill, and lived there until his death in 1895. You can tour the house and stroll the grounds.

U STREET

The birthplace of Duke Ellington and an important hub of African American culture is known primarily for its theaters and live-music venues. Miles Davis, Ella Fitzgerald, and Louis Armstrong all frequented the area, which is still full of popular restaurants, funky boutiques, and tons of nightlife.

SMITHSONIAN MUSEUMS

Thanks in large part to the Smithsonian Institution, Washington is absolutely stuffed with museums, 16 of which are connected with the institution endowed by James Smithson in 1846. But that's not all. Other free museums include the National Gallery of Art and the United States Holocaust Memorial Museum.

THE MEMORIALS

Forming the spine of the city, the National Mall is anchored by the Lincoln Memorial on the west, the Washington Monument in the middle, and the U.S. Capitol on the east. Other famous memorials remember Vietnam veterans, World War II, FDR, and Martin Luther King Jr.

JOHN F. KENNEDY CENTER FOR THE PERFORMING ARTS

Opened in 1971, the Kennedy Center is one of the largest U.S. performing arts facilities, staging roughly 2,000 performances a year, with the adjacent REACH expansion adding on more indoor-outdoor performance space. Free tours include a stop at an exhibit about Kennedy's life and presidency and a walk through several of the main theaters. On your way out, catch a glimpse of the famous Watergate complex, just to the north.

THE PENTAGON

A building so big it requires six zip codes, the Pentagon houses the headquarters of the Department of Defense in its astonishingly large confines. At its widest point, the Pentagon is almost as wide as the Empire State Building is tall. Construction began in September 1941 and was finished in a remarkably quick 16 months. Tours are free but require advance reservations; check the Pentagon's website for details.

OLD STONE HOUSE

This unassuming Georgetown house holds the distinction of being the oldest unaltered building in the District. Christopher and Rachel Layman purchased the property in 1764, building the house the following year. Now a museum and public garden, it was turned over to the National Park Service in 1953.

ROCK CREEK PARK

Rock Creek Park became the third national park ever created, signed into law by President Harrison in 1890. Just a 20-minute drive from the center of the city, it offers 1,754 quiet, beautiful acres for roaming, horseback riding, cycling, and inline skating.

EASTERN MARKET

Thomas Jefferson established the market in 1805, and it was moved to its current location in 1873, where it has remained for the last 148 years. Weathering the storm of competition from grocery store chains, Eastern Market has become a community staple and is a great place to stock up or simply window-shop for food, crafts, or antiques. Weekends feature live music and local artists, as well as the farmers' market.

NATIONAL ZOO

An act of Congress created the National Zoo in 1889. Designed by Frederick Law Olmsted, the 163-acre facility is home to more than 390 animal species, nearly 75 of which are endangered or vulnerable, including three giant pandas.

What to Read and Watch

MINORITY REPORT

Based on a short story by Philip K. Dick, this Steven Spielberg blockbuster takes place in the year 2054, blending genres of sci-fi, action, and thriller. It's chock-full of dramatic chase scenes throughout a futuristic D.C., as a "precrime" police force—backed by a team of surreal psychics— arrests people for crimes they're destined to commit in the future. It has all the special effects and over-the-top action sequences you could desire from a Tom Cruise protagonist and a Steven Spielberg budget.

IN THE LOOP

British filmmaker Armando Iannucci gives us the somewhat maddening, totally entertaining world of D.C. political missteps and blundered negotiations— that later inspired his HBO show *Veep*. The movie follows the political frenzy between Britain and the United States leading up to the Iraq War. Politicians and staffers race in circles around the conference rooms and hallways of D.C.'s government buildings, dropping dry gems of British humor along the way.

ALL THE PRESIDENT'S MEN

This Academy Award–winning film follows Carl Bernstein and Bob Woodward—the two young *Washington Post* journalists responsible for the incredible investigation of the Watergate scandal— through their meetings with clandestine informant Deep Throat, the discovery of President Nixon's tapes, and the process of exposing it all to the American public. While a little less studly without the young Dustin Hoffman–Robert Redford combination, the nonfiction book of the same name (written by the journalists themselves) delves deeper into the details of a political detective story almost too good for fiction.

ADVISE AND CONSENT

Allen Drury's 1959 political thriller, following the tumultuous nomination process of a secretary of state with a Communist background, was both a *New York Times* bestseller and Pulitzer prize winner—a rare occurrence for any novel. Credited with creating a realistic yet racy tale about a could-be-boring political process, the book became a series and was followed by five sequels. The 1962 movie stars Henry Fonda, with many of the scenes shot in and around key Washington landmarks.

SEVEN DAYS IN MAY

Kirk Douglas, Burt Lancaster, Frederic March, and Ava Gardner star in this 1964 film, where the Cold War hysteria of the times is condensed into a weeklong attempted takeover of the United States government. The 1962 *New York Times* best-selling book (by Fletcher Knebel and Charles W. Bailey II) served as the movie's inspiration. Both film and book follow the same structure, split into day-by-day chapters as the week's events unfurl.

MR. SMITH GOES TO WASHINGTON

In this 1939 black-and-white classic, a baby-faced, idealistic Jimmy Stewart comes to the nation's capital and is soon wrapped up in the unscrupulousness of the U.S. Senate. Stewart's scene orating against greed and corruption on the floor of the Senate is still one of the most iconic cinematic performances ever about D.C. politics.

DESIGNATED SURVIVOR

What happens when the Capitol is blown up in a terrorist attack—killing the president, vice president, his cabinet, and all of Congress? In this three-season political thriller that originally aired on ABC, Kiefer Sutherland plays the man chosen to stay away from the State of the Union and becomes the inexperienced sole survivor, suddenly responsible for piecing the government back together. It's not so easy, he finds, when shadowy forces are up to no good, threatening national—and personal—security at every turn.

WEST WING
Follow President Bartlet through his two terms in this epic political drama that delves into the lives of staffers of the White House's West Wing. On the air for seven seasons beginning in 1999, it's a feel-good reminder of what politics can be when run by good people.

VEEP
This HBO political comedy satirizes the personalities that make up American policy and power, with an Emmy-winning performance by Julia Louis-Dreyfus as the "Veep" (vice president, and on-again, off-again president hopeful) and a hilarious, hapless cast of political staffers. Scenes take you in and out of political press conferences, conspiratorial meetings in the VP's back rooms, the Oval Office, the halls of Congress, and many a limo drive through the streets of Washington.

SCANDAL
In this political thriller full of plot twists, Olivia Pope, played by Kerry Washington, is D.C.'s ultimate fixer. She is based loosely on George H.W. Bush's administrative press aide, Judy Smith, who started her own crisis management firm. The series ran seven seasons, from 2012 to 2018.

LONG DISTANCE LIFE BY MARITA GOLDEN
Marita Golden's novel centers on one family's experience living in D.C. throughout the 20th century, but she vividly fills in the background with the complex history of Black America as a whole. Naomi Johnson, the family's matriarch (and first-person narrator of many chapters) moves from North Carolina to D.C. in 1926, and the novel continues from there to tell the hardships and joys of Naomi's family throughout generations in the capital city.

THE BEAUTIFUL THINGS THAT HEAVEN BEARS BY DINAW MENGESTU
A refreshing break from the political circus of Capitol Hill, Dinaw Mengestu's novel exists instead within the stores, restaurants, and homes of Northwest D.C.'s Logan Circle neighborhood. In a city of monuments and memorials to America's (often constructed, embellished) past, and in a neighborhood on the brink of gentrification, Sepha, an Ethiopian refugee, moves through the daily grind of being an American while haunted by memories of his home country. Through Sepha's long talks and friendships with refugees from other African countries, Mengestu creates a gentle, moving portrait of the African diaspora in Washington.

CHOCOLATE CITY BY CHRIS MYERS ASCH AND DEREK MUSGROVE
This enthralling 2017 book examines the four-century history of race and democracy in Washington, D.C., from plantation society to slave trade center to the nation's first Black-majority city.

GO-GO LIVE BY NATALIE HOPKINSON
The story of Black Washington, written by activist and cultural scholar Natalie Hopkinson and published in 2012, is told against the backdrop of the rise of go-go music, the conga-drum-infused mix of blues, church, and Latino sounds that D.C. native Chuck Brown created in the '70s.

D.C. with Kids

D.C. is filled with kid-friendly attractions. These sights are sure winners:

BUREAU OF ENGRAVING AND PRINTING

Any youngster who gets an allowance will enjoy watching bills roll off the presses. Despite the lack of free samples, the self-guided, 40-minute bureau tour is one of the city's most popular attractions.

DC DUCKS

What do you get when you cross a tour bus with a boat? A duck—DC Ducks, that is. Tour the city by both land and water without leaving your seats aboard these unusual amphibious vehicles: standard 2½-ton GM trucks in watertight shells with propellers.

DISCOVERY THEATER

Within the Smithsonian's Ripley Center on the Mall, this lively theater began by offering low-key puppet shows before expanding to feature more than 300 programs a year exploring art, science, and global heritage—everything from robots to the Wright brothers to African drums.

INTERNATIONAL SPY MUSEUM

This museum takes the art of espionage to new levels for junior James Bonds and Nancy Drews. Even the most cynical preteens and teenagers are usually enthralled with all the cool gadgetry. This museum is best for older tweens and teens—if you bring along a younger sibling, you could be in for a workout: there aren't many places to sit down, and strollers aren't allowed in the museum. Also, there is an entrance fee. The museum moved to its more capacious L'Enfant Plaza in 2019.

NATIONAL AIR AND SPACE MUSEUM

There's a good reason why this place is one of the most popular museums in the world: kids love it. The 23 galleries here tell the story of aviation and space from the earliest human attempts at flight. The museum store sells ever-popular freeze-dried astronaut food—not as tasty as what we eat on Earth, but it doesn't melt or drip.

NATIONAL MUSEUM OF AMERICAN HISTORY

Oh, say, you can see … the flag that inspired "The Star-Spangled Banner," Oscar the Grouch, the ruby slippers from *The Wizard of Oz,* an impressive collection of trains, and more Americana than anyone can digest in a day.

NATIONAL MUSEUM OF NATURAL HISTORY

Say hello to Henry. One of the largest elephants ever found in the wild, this stuffed beast has greeted generations of kids in the rotunda of this huge museum dedicated to natural wonders. Take your kid to the O. Orkin Insect Zoo, home to live ants, bees, centipedes, tarantulas, roaches, and other bugs. Did we mention the dinosaurs?

NATIONAL ZOO

Known more for its political animals than its real animals, D.C. nevertheless has one of the world's foremost zoos. If your child is crazy about animals, this is an absolute must—it's huge.

NATIONAL CHILDREN'S MUSEUM

You enter this new museum in Downtown D.C. via cloud-inspired dream machine, going on to enjoy a slime pavilion, data science alley, a green screen in which body movements create weather, and more—all of which slip in STEAM educational principles.

PADDLEBOAT THE TIDAL BASIN

How better to see the Jefferson Memorial and the world-famous cherry trees—gifts from Japan—than from the waters of the Tidal Basin? The paddleboats get the kids and you off your feet and into the sun!

Chapter 2

TRAVEL SMART

Updated by
Barbara Noe Kennedy

★ **CAPITAL:**
Washington

👫 **POPULATION:**
705,749

💬 **LANGUAGE:**
English

$ **CURRENCY:**
U.S. Dollar

☎ **AREA CODE:**
202

⚠ **EMERGENCIES:**
911

🚗 **DRIVING:**
On the right

⚡ **ELECTRICITY:**
120–220 v/60 cycles; plugs
have two or three rectangu-
lar prongs

🕐 **TIME:**
Same as New York

🌐 **WEB RESOURCES:**
www.washington.org
www.nps.gov
www.si.edu

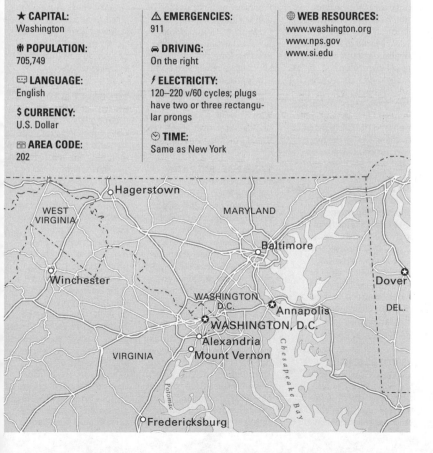

Know Before You Go

When is the best time to visit our nation's capital? What times should you avoid? Which airport should you fly into? Where should you stay? You may have some important questions before your trip to Washington, D.C. We've got the answers and a few tips to help you make the most of your visit.

BE AIRPORT SAVVY.

D.C. has three airports: Ronald Reagan Washington National (DCA), Dulles International (IAD), and Baltimore/Washington International–Thurgood Marshall Airport (BWI). DCA, located in Arlington, Virginia, about 4 miles from Downtown D.C., is the closest and most convenient; it has its own Metro stop. It only serves shorter domestic flights (and some flights to the Caribbean and Canada). IAD is the main international airport, 25 miles west of Downtown DC in Chantilly, Virginia. You can take the Silver Line as far as Wiehle–Reston East and hop on the Silver Line Express Bus from there (a Silver Line extension to IAD is expected to be completed in 2021). BWI is located just south of Baltimore, Maryland, about 30 miles north of D.C. You can take the MARC or Amtrak train from Union Station.

BE HOTEL SMART.

Hotels in Downtown D.C. are expensive, though the rates typically drop during the weekend, after the business travelers leave. Arlington, Alexandria, and Bethesda are relatively nearby and may have better deals than Downtown D.C. One thing to remember: Fairfax, Gaithersburg, and Vienna are not near Downtown D.C., as some hotel advertising will have you thinking they are. The short of it: before you book, study the map to ensure you're staying relatively near the attractions you want to visit. And be sure to book a hotel near the Metro line if you don't have a car.

TAKE PUBLIC TRANSPORT ... OR WALK.

Parking is expensive, and traffic can be frightful, so relying on your car is not the best way to see the District. However, D.C. is a very pedestrian-friendly city, with many attractions within close range, so you may be able to walk to most of what you want to see. There's also an excellent Metro system that can get you to most major sights as well (except Georgetown, Adams Morgan, and the H Street corridor). Another option is the DC Circulator bus, which is free and has several routes past tourist sights.

KNOW WHAT STUFF IS FREE ... AND WHAT'S NOT AND STILL WORTHWHILE.

One beloved aspect of D.C. is that so many of its remarkable sights are free, including the Smithsonian museums and the national monuments and memorials. Even the blockbuster shows that sometimes stop by the National Gallery of Art are free. Check Destination D.C. or individual websites for free shows, concerts, lectures, and guided tours, especially at the National Gallery of Art and Library of Congress. That said, keep in mind that some of the city's best museums do come at a price that is still well worth your while, including the Phillips Collection and International Spy Museum.

THE EARLY BIRD CATCHES THE POPULAR SIGHT TICKETS.

Get your tickets for popular sights long before your trip, including the White House, the National Museum of African American History and Culture, and the Pentagon. For the White House, you'll need to contact your member of Congress several months in advance to request a self-guided public tour (citizens of foreign countries should contact their embassy in Washington, D.C.). If you miss out on the White House, the White House Visitor Center, across the street, is a good substitute, with its videos, artifacts, and displays delving into the life and times of America's most famous house. Timed-entry passes are required for certain peak times and seasons at the National Museum of African American History and Culture; you can obtain them up to three months in advance on the museum website, on the first Wednesday of every month. For the Pentagon, you can book tours from 14 to 90 days in advance, either online or by contacting your Congressional representative (foreign residents must contact their embassy).

BE A CAPITOL VIP.
Get a VIP Capitol staff–led tour by contacting your representative or senator up to 90 days in advance. Even if you miss out on the VIP tour, you can still visit the Capitol by making your own advance reservation online or obtaining a same-day pass from the information desks located on the lower level of the U.S. Capitol Visitor Center. Note that same-day passes may have limited availability, especially during the spring, summer, and some holidays.

BEAT THE CROWDS AT STAR-STUDDED NSO PERFORMANCES.
The nation's capital celebrates July 4 and Memorial Day with world-class performances starring the National Symphony Orchestra, which air around the world on PBS. Thousands of guests are invited to sit on the West Lawn of the Capitol and enjoy these spectacular concerts in person for free (bring a picnic—no alcohol allowed). But therein lies the problem—the thousands of people all

vying to get in, requiring you to arrive hours early to stake your space on the grass (and possibly be turned away). You can see exactly the same shows (minus the fireworks) by attending the dress rehearsals in advance. A Capitol Fourth practices the evening before, normally at 6 pm, while the National Memorial Day Concert rehearsal takes place at 3:30 pm on the Sunday before Memorial Day. The host may be a tad improvisational, and might not get all the lines on the first try, but the shows are enjoyable nonetheless. There's also a Labor Day concert on the Capitol's West Lawn showcasing the NSO (which is not aired on TV).

THINK SMALL.
While the Smithsonian museums get all the glory, remember that there are scores of excellent smaller museums, including the Clara Barton Missing Soldiers Office Museum, the President Woodrow Wilson House, the Society of the Cincinnati, and the National Museum of Women in the Arts. Plan ahead to know which ones suit your interests.

SAVE AT THE THEATER BOX OFFICE.
Washington, D.C., is a theater town, with well-reviewed theaters both large (Kennedy Center, Warner Theatre, National Theatre) and small (Woolly Mammoth Theatre Company, Shakespeare Theatre Company). Save on tickets by using a discount broker such as Goldstar,

Groupon, and the TodayTix app. Also keep in mind that some theaters offer same-day tickets at a reduced price, including Arena Stage, Shakespeare Theatre Company, and Folger Shakespeare Theatre, while others offer pay-what-you-can-afford tickets, including Woolly Mammoth, Round House, and Constellation Theatre (arrive early and bring cash).

KNOW YOUR SEASONS.
Spring and fall have the best weather, with the added bonus of the famous cherry blossoms in spring and colorful changing foliage in fall. The holidays are another time when the nation's capital shines, with special events including the National Christmas Tree Lighting, ZooLights at Smithsonian's National Zoo, and the Downtown Holiday Market. House museums offer special candlelit tours that showcase colonial-era decorations, including Mount Vernon. D.C. also puts on an extravaganza of festivals, offering another reason to visit at a specific time of year. Some of the most popular include Day of Service on Martin Luther King Jr.'s birthday in January; Passport DC in May, when dozens of embassies open their doors to visitors; and St. Patrick's Day in March, with a parade down Constitution Avenue. But if you simply want to visit at a time with sunny weather and fewer crowds, early November is often prime.

Getting Here and Around

Air

A flight to D.C. from New York takes a little less than an hour. It's about 1½ hours from Chicago, 3 hours from Denver or Dallas, and 5 hours from San Francisco. Passengers flying from London should expect a trip of about 6 hours. From Sydney it's an 18-hour flight. Most major airlines fly into one of D.C.'s three major airports, but only Dulles and Baltimore airports are served by international carriers (DCA services some flights to and from Canada and the Caribbean).

AIRPORTS

Ronald Reagan Washington National Airport (DCA) is in Virginia, 4 miles south of Downtown Washington.

Dulles International Airport (IAD) is in Virginia, 25 miles west of Washington, D.C.

Baltimore/Washington International–Thurgood Marshall Airport (BWI) in Maryland, about 30 miles to the northeast.

Reagan National Airport is closest to Downtown D.C. and has a Metro stop connected to the terminal. East Coast shuttles and shorter flights tend to fly in and out of this airport. Dulles is configured primarily for long-haul flights, although as a United hub, it's also well-connected regionally. BWI offers blended service, with its many gates for Southwest Airlines, as well as international flights. Although Metro trains don't serve Dulles (expected 2021) or BWI, there is affordable and convenient public transportation to and from each airport. Be aware that the Mid-Atlantic region is prone to quirky weather that can snarl air traffic, especially on stormy summer afternoons.

AIRPORT TRANSFERS

Ronald Reagan Washington National Airport, located across the Potomac River in Arlington, Virginia, is the only regional airport reachable by the District's Metro system, a ride that takes about 20 minutes and costs between $2.25 and $6 (you must pay with a plastic SmarTrip card, available from machines in all stations). The Metro station is within easy walking distance of Terminals B and C, and a free airport bus shuttles between the station and Terminal A. Driving typically takes longer than the Metro (about 20 to 30 minutes, depending on traffic and where you start). A taxi will cost between $15 and $25 to Downtown, plus a $3 airport surcharge. Ride-share services like Uber and Lyft are allowed to pick up on the arrivals level.

Dulles International Airport is 25 miles west of Downtown; the ride takes 45 minutes but can be considerably longer when traffic is heavy. Public transit will typically take an hour or more. Take the Metro's Silver Line to the Wiehle–Reston East station (6 am to 10:20 pm); the 15-minute Silver Line Express bus ride from the station to the airport (every 15 to 20 minutes) is $5, payable with cash or credit card at the ticket counter in the Arrivals area. (The Silver Line extension directly to IAD is expected to be completed in 2021.) The Washington Metropolitan Area Transit Authority (WMATA) operates express bus service between Dulles and several stops in Downtown D.C., including the L'Enfant Plaza Metro station and Rosslyn Metro station in Arlington, Virginia, for $7.50 (every hour between 6:35 am and 10:10 pm); exact fare or a SmarTrip card is required. Taxi fare to Washington, D.C., from Dulles is about $55 to $65 plus tip, depending on traffic, and takes about 45 minutes. Ride-share services like Uber and Lyft are allowed to pick up at the arrivals level.

Baltimore/Washington International–Thurgood Marshall Airport is about 30 miles northeast of Downtown; the ride takes 50 to 60 minutes but can be considerably longer when traffic is heavy. Both Amtrak and Maryland Rail Commuter Service (MARC) trains run between BWI and Washington, D.C.'s, Union Station from around 4:30 am to 10 pm; the ride takes 30 minutes and costs between $15 and $45 on Amtrak, $7 on MARC's Penn Line. A free shuttle bus connects the airline terminals and the train station (which is in a distant parking lot). WMATA operates express bus service (Bus No. B30) between BWI and the Greenbelt Metro station from approximately 7 am to 10 pm on weekdays for $7.50. The taxi fare from Downtown to BWI is about $90 plus tip. Ride-share services like Uber and Lyft are allowed to pick up at the arrivals level.

Bus

Most of the sightseeing neighborhoods (the Mall, Capitol Hill, Downtown, Dupont Circle) are near Metro rail stations, but a few (Georgetown, Adams Morgan) are more easily reached via Metrobus ($2 per ride, exact change payable in bills or coins or with a SmarTrip card; you can also buy a seven-day pass for $15). Bus No. 42 travels from the Dupont Circle Metro stop to and through Adams Morgan.

The DC Circulator has six routes (free). The Eastern Market–L'Enfant Plaza, Woodley Park–Adams Morgan–McPherson Square, and Congress Heights–Union Station routes cut a path from north to south; the Georgetown–Union Station and Rosslyn–Georgetown–Dupont Circle routes go west to east. And the National Mall route, which operates April to September only, stops at major sightseeing destinations around the Mall.

Several bus lines run between New York City and the Washington, D.C., area, including BoltBus, BestBus, Megabus, Peter Pan Bus Lines, TripperBus, Vamoose, and Washington Deluxe. Tripper and Vamoose routes run between NYC and Metro stations in Bethesda, Maryland, and Arlington, Virginia. All the buses are clean, the service satisfactory, and the price can't be beat. Believe it or not, with advance planning, you might be able to get a round-trip ticket for just $2. Several of the bus lines offer power outlets, Wi-Fi, and a frequent-rider loyalty program.

Car

A car is often a drawback in Washington, D.C. Traffic is awful, especially at rush hour, and driving is often confusing, with many lanes and some entire streets changing direction at the beginning and end of rush hour. Most traffic lights stand at the side of intersections (instead of hanging suspended over them), and the streets often are dotted with giant potholes. The city's most popular sights are all within a short walk of a Metro station, so do yourself a favor and leave your car at the hotel. If you're visiting sights in Maryland or Virginia or need a car because of reduced mobility, time your trips to avoid D.C. rush hours, 7–10 am and 3–7 pm.

With Zipcar, an urban car-rental membership service, you can rent a car for a couple of hours or a couple of days from convenient Downtown parking lots. A one-time application fee of $25, an annual membership fee of $70 (or $7 per month with a monthly plan option), plus hourly rates starting at $7.75, or $66 per day, buys you gas, insurance, parking, and satellite radio. Reserve online or by phone.

Getting Here and Around

Another option is Free2Move, a car-sharing program featuring white Chevrolets, with a one-time registration fee of $10. Rates are $0.47 a minute, $13 an hour, or $95 a day. There is no additional cost for insurance, gas, or parking. One advantage of Free2Move is that you can pick up and end rentals in on-street public parking spots.

Like the comfort of a car but don't want to drive? Uber is your answer. You can request a ride through the mobile app or the Uber website. Drivers are available seven days a week, 24 hours a day. Once you request your ride, you'll be able to see exactly where the driver is and how long you'll have to wait. The fare for a Black (sedan) is $7 base charge, plus $3.40 per mile and $.40 per minute; the SUV fare is $14 base charge, plus $3.65 per mile and $0.45 per minute; the economy option, UberX, charges a $1.15 base rate plus $1.02 per mile and $0.17 per minute. After registering, your credit card information is kept on file and your card is charged upon completion of your ride. When demand is high due to weather, holidays, or special events, rates can be considerably higher. There's a cancellation fee of $5. Other ride-sharing apps like Lyft offer similar options.

PARKING

Parking in D.C. is a question of supply and demand—little of the former, too much of the latter. The police are quick to ticket, tow away, or boot any vehicle parked illegally, so check complicated parking signs, and feed the meter before you go. If you find you've been towed from a city street, call *311* or the Department of Public Works Customer Service Center at *202/541–6083*. Be sure you know the license-plate number, make, model, and color of the car before you call.

Most of the outlying, suburban Metro stations have parking lots, though these fill quickly with city-bound commuters. If you plan to park in one of these lots, arrive early.

Downtown private parking lots often charge around $9–$10 an hour and up to $40 or more a day. Most of the streets along the Mall have metered parking. There is no parking at the Lincoln or Roosevelt memorials. If you don't find street parking nearby, try along Ohio Drive SW and in three lots in East Potomac Park, south of the 14th Street Bridge.

RULES OF THE ROAD

You may turn right at a red light after stopping if there's no oncoming traffic and no signs indicate otherwise, but D.C. has many such signs and one-way streets. When in doubt, wait for the green. The speed limit in D.C. is 25 mph. Beware of HOV express lanes on major highways during rush hours (you need an E-ZPass to use them, and costs are high).

Ⓜ Metro/Public Transport

The Metro is a convenient way to get around the city—if you're staying near a Metro stop. It operates from 5 am weekdays, 7 am Saturday, and 8 am Sunday; it shuts down at 11:30 pm Monday through Thursday, 1 am Friday and Saturday, and 11 pm Sunday. Keep in mind that service disruptions for weekend work are common. The Metro's base fare is $2 but can be much higher depending on the time of day and the distance traveled. All rides now require a SmarTrip card, a rechargeable fare card that can be used throughout the Metro, bus, and parking system. Buy your SmarTrip card at a vending machine in any station; they accept cash and credit cards or debit cards. You can buy one-day passes for $13, three-day passes for $28, and seven-day passes for $58.

Ride-Sharing

Both Uber and Lyft operate in Washington, D.C., and may or may not be cheaper than a regular taxi depending on the time or day and distance traveled. Pooled rides are almost always cheaper for a single rider than a taxi but are almost always more expensive than the Metro. For a group of four people, however, a ride-share can be cheaper for a short trip than the Metro.

Taxi

Taxis are easy to hail in commercial districts, less so in residential ones. If you don't see one after a few minutes, walk to a busier street. If you call, make sure to have an address—not just an intersection—and be prepared to wait, especially at night. The base rate for the first one-eighth mile is $3.50. Each additional mile is $2.16, and each minute stopped or traveling less than 10 mph is $25 an hour ($0.40 per minute). A charge of $1 is tacked on for additional passengers, regardless how many. The telephone dispatch fee is $2. During D.C.-declared snow emergencies, there is an additional $15 fee. Cab rates in Virginia differ by county, but immediately surrounding D.C., riders should expect to pay $2–$3 for the first one-sixth mile and $0.36 for each additional one-sixth mile.

Train

More than 80 trains a day arrive at Washington, D.C.'s, Union Station. Amtrak's regular service runs from D.C. to New York in 3¼–3¾ hours and from D.C. to Boston in 7¾–8 hours. Acela, Amtrak's high-speed service, travels from D.C. to New York in 2¾–3 hours and from D.C. to Boston in 6½ hours, but can cost as much as a flight. Two commuter lines—Maryland Rail Commuter Service (MARC) and Virginia Railway Express (VRE)—run to the nearby suburbs. They're cheaper than Amtrak, but the VRE doesn't run on weekends or federal holidays. MARC's Penn Line does run on weekends, offering service to Baltimore for $7 each way.

Essentials

Health

COVID-19

A novel coronavirus brought all travel to a virtual standstill in 2020. Although the illness is mild in most people, some experience severe and even life-threatening complications. Once travel started up again, albeit slowly and cautiously, travelers were asked to be particularly careful about hygiene and to avoid any unnecessary travel, especially if they are sick. Older adults, especially those over 65, have a greater chance of having severe complications from COVID-19. The same is true for people with weaker immune systems or those living with some types of medical conditions, including diabetes, asthma, heart disease, cancer, HIV/AIDS, kidney disease, and liver disease. Starting two weeks before a trip, anyone planning to travel should be on the lookout for some of the following symptoms: cough, fever, chills, trouble breathing, muscle pain, sore throat, new loss of smell or taste. If you experience any of these symptoms, you should not travel at all.

And to protect yourself during travel, do your best to avoid contact with people showing symptoms. Wash your hands often with soap and water. Limit your time in public places, and, when you are out and about, wear a cloth face mask that covers your nose and mouth. Indeed, a mask may be required in some places, such as on an airplane or in a confined space like a theater, where you share the space with a lot of people. You may wish to bring extra supplies, such as disinfecting wipes, hand sanitizer (12-ounce bottles were allowed in carry-on luggage at this writing), and a first-aid kit with a thermometer.

Given how abruptly travel was curtailed in March 2020, it is wise to consider protecting yourself by purchasing a travel insurance policy that will reimburse you for any costs related to COVID-19 related cancellations. Not all travel insurance policies protect against pandemic-related cancellations, so always read the fine print.

Addresses

Although it may not appear so at first glance, there's a system to addresses in D.C., albeit one that's a bit confusing for newcomers. The city is divided into the four quadrants of a compass (NW, NE, SE, SW), with the U.S. Capitol at the center. Because the Capitol doesn't sit in the exact center of the city (and because Virginia took back its lands that originally were part of the District in 1847), Northwest is the largest quadrant. Northwest also has most of the important landmarks, although Northeast and Southwest have their fair share. The boundaries are North Capitol Street, East Capitol Street, South Capitol Street, and the National Mall.

If someone tells you to meet them at 6th and G, ask them to specify the quadrant, because there are actually four different 6th and G intersections (one per quadrant). Within each quadrant, numbered streets run north to south, and lettered streets run east to west (the letter *J* was omitted to avoid confusion with the letter *I*). The streets form a fairly simple grid—for instance, 900 G Street NW is the intersection of 9th and G Streets in the NW quadrant of the city. Likewise, if you count the letters of the alphabet, skipping *J*, you can get a good approximation of an address for a numbered street. For instance, 1600 16th Street NW is close to Q Street, Q being the 16th letter of the alphabet if you skip *J*.

As if all this weren't confusing enough, Major Pierre L'Enfant, the Frenchman who originally designed the city, threw in diagonal avenues recalling those of Paris. Most of D.C.'s avenues are named after U.S. states. You can find addresses on avenues the same way you find those on numbered streets, so 1200 Connecticut Avenue NW is close to M Street, because *M* is the 12th letter of the alphabet when you skip *J*.

Dining

D.C. has always had a wide variety of international restaurants, but in recent times, the city has come to the forefront of good eating.

DISCOUNTS AND DEALS

If you eat early or late you may be able to take advantage of prix-fixe deals not offered at peak hours. Many upscale restaurants offer great lunch deals with special menus at cut-rate prices designed to give customers a true taste of the place. At high-end restaurants, ask for tap water to avoid paying high rates for bottled water.

PAYING

Most restaurants take credit cards, but some smaller places do not. It's worth asking. Waiters expect a 20% tip at high-end restaurants; some add an automatic gratuity for groups of six or more.

RESERVATIONS AND DRESS

Always make a reservation at an upscale restaurant when you can. Some are booked weeks in advance, but some popular restaurants don't accept reservations. As unfair as it is, the way you look can influence how you're treated—and where you're seated. Generally speaking, jeans and a button-down shirt will suffice at most restaurants, but some pricier

restaurants require jackets, and some insist on ties. In reviews, we mention dress only where men are required to wear a jacket or a jacket and tie. If you have doubts, call the restaurant and ask.

MEALS AND MEALTIMES

Washington has less of an around-the-clock mentality than other big cities, with many big-name restaurants shutting down between lunch and dinner and closing by 11 pm. Many Downtown chain eateries close on weekends. For late-night dining, your best bets are restaurants near Dupont Circle and the U Street Corridor; for a late lunch, look for smaller places in Penn Quarter.

WHAT IT COSTS in U.S. Dollars			
$	$$	$$$	$$$$
AT DINNER			
under $17	$17–$26	$27–$35	over $35

Lodging

The District has some great hotels, but in general, rates are very high, especially on weekdays.

RESERVATIONS

Always make a reservation in D.C. Hotels often fill up, and rooms can be particularly hard to come by in late March or early April during the Cherry Blossom Festival, and in May, when students at the many local colleges graduate. Late October's Marine Corps Marathon also increases demand for rooms.

FACILITIES

You can assume that all rooms have private baths, phones, TVs, and air-conditioning, unless otherwise indicated. Breakfast is noted when it is included

Essentials

in the rate, but it's not a typical perk at most Washington hotels. There are a few hotels with pools, though some are indoors.

PARKING

Parking in D.C. is very expensive, and hotel parking fees can exceed $50. Independent garages may be slightly cheaper. Street parking is free after 6:30 pm and Sunday (after 10 pm in some neighborhoods), but parking rules can be confusing, and tickets are expensive.

PRICES

Rates drop in August (during the Congressional recess) and in late December and January, except around inaugurations. Weekends are also more affordable. Travelers on a budget may find cheaper lodging in Virginia and Maryland suburbs, so long as the hotel is near a Metro line.

WHAT IT COSTS in U.S. Dollars			
$	$$	$$$	$$$$
FOR TWO PEOPLE			
under $210	$210–$295	$296–$400	over $400

Shopping

Beyond the typical museum gift shops on the Mall, smaller one-of-a-kind shops, designer boutiques, and interesting specialty collections add to Washington's shopping scene alongside stores that have been part of the landscape for generations. Weekdays, Downtown street vendors add to the mix by offering funky jewelry; brightly patterned ties; buyer-beware watches; sunglasses; and African-inspired clothing, accessories, and art. Discerning shoppers will find satisfaction at upscale malls on the city's outskirts. Not surprisingly, T-shirts and Capital City souvenirs are in plentiful supply. Stores that cater to Downtown office workers may close on weekends, while stores in Georgetown, Adams Morgan, and the U Street Corridor may stay open late.

Nightlife

The District has a surprisingly busy night-life scene. Georgetown, the U Street Corridor, and Adams Morgan are popular destinations, but the Penn Quarter and Shaw are growing in popularity. Good happy hours abound during the week. Last call in D.C. is 2:30 am on weekends.

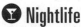 Performing Arts

Whatever you are looking for, Washington, D.C., has some of the most exciting and thought-provoking entertainment in the country. Since the opening of the John F. Kennedy Center for the Performing Arts in 1971, the city's performing arts culture has grown steadily. Washington now hosts one of the largest theater scenes in the country, as well as a rich offering of nightly music opportunities featuring local, national, and international talent, and so much more. For up-to-date information, look for the *Washington City Paper* (⊕ *www.washingtoncitypaper. com*) or the *Washington Post's Going Out Guide* ⊕ *www.washingtonpost.com/gog*).

Activities

Visitors to Washington can enjoy a wealth of outdoor attractions. Rock Creek Park is one of the city's treasures, with miles of wooded trails and paths for bikers,

Where Should I Stay?

	NEIGHBORHOOD VIBE	PROS	CONS
The West End	Pleasant residential and office area along Pennsylvania Avenue, with excellent restaurant choices. Stately early-20th-century buildings.	Safe area; close to Downtown's commercial sites and to halls of government, and the Mall.	Parking is always difficult and lots of traffic; older hotels with few budget rates.
Foggy Bottom	Bustling with college students most of the year. Its 18th- and 19th-century homes make for pleasant views.	Safe area; walking distance to Georgetown and the Kennedy Center; good Metro access.	Somewhat removed from other areas of city; paltry dining options.
Capitol Hill and Northeast D.C.	Charming residential blocks of Victorian row houses on Capitol Hill populated by members of Congress and their staffers.	Convenient to Union Station and Capitol. Stylish (if not cheap) hotels. Fine assortment of restaurants and shops.	Some streets iffy at night; parking takes some work; hotels are pricey. Blocks around Capitol and Union Station are chock-full of tourists.
Downtown	A vibrant, bustling, modern mix of commercial and residential properties, packed during the day and rowdy in places at night.	Right in the heart of the Metro system; easy access to the White House. Large selection of hotels, shops, and restaurants.	Crowded; busy; daytime street parking is nearly impossible.
Georgetown	Wealthy neighborhood bordered by the Potomac and a world-class university. Filled with students, upscale shops, and eateries.	Safe area. Historic charm on every tree-lined street. Wonderful walking paths along river.	Crowded; no nearby Metro access; lots of traffic. Almost no parking. Lodging options tend to be expensive.
Dupont Circle	Cosmopolitan, lively neighborhood filled with bars and restaurants; beautiful city sights.	Plenty of modern hotels; easy Metro access; good selection of bars and restaurants.	Few budget hotel options; very limited street parking; crowded in summer months.
Adams Morgan	The center of late-night activity; eclectic and down-to-earth; languages galore.	Fabulous selection of ethnic bars and restaurants; vibrant, hip nightlife.	Few lodging options; 10-minute walk to Metro; very hard to park.
Upper Northwest	A pleasant residential neighborhood with a lively strip of good restaurants.	Safe, quiet; easy walk to zoo, Metro, restaurants; street parking easier than Downtown.	A long ride to attractions other than the zoo; feels like an inner suburb. Few new hotels.

2

Travel Smart ESSENTIALS

Essentials

runners, and walkers that extend to almost every part of the city. The National Mall connects the Lincoln Memorial and the Capitol and is one of the most scenic green spaces in the world. Around the Tidal Basin you can run, bike, tour the monuments, and rent paddleboats. Theodore Roosevelt Island, a wildlife sanctuary, has several paths for hiking and enjoyable spots for picnics. Kayaking and stand-up paddleboarding are popular in the Potomac and Washington Channel. And these places are just a few among dozens.

BIKING

The numerous trails in the District and its surrounding areas are well maintained and clearly marked. Washington's large parks are also popular with cyclists. Plus, new bike lanes are on all major roads. The Capital Bikeshare scheme, with 400 stations around Washington, Arlington, and Alexandria, is also a great way to get around town.

SPECTATOR SPORTS

Washington, D.C., has several professional sports teams, some with world-champion status.

★ D.C. United

SOCCER | One of the best Major League Soccer teams has a huge fan base in the nation's capital, finding many of its fans in the international crowds who miss the big matches at home, as well as families whose kids play soccer. Matches are played March through October in the new, state-of-the-art, 20,000-seat Audi Field in Southwest's Buzzard Point. You can buy tickets at the ticket office or through the team's website, which offers special youth pricing. Talon, the team mascot, entertains the crowd, along with enthusiastic, horn-blowing fans. ⊠ *Audi Field, 100 Potomac Ave. SW, Southwest* ⊕ *audiofieldddc.com* ✉ *From $50* Ⓜ *Navy Yard–Ballpark or Waterfront–SEU.*

Washington Capitals

HOCKEY | Stanley Cup winners in 2018, the Washington Capitals play loud and exciting home games October through April at Capital One Arena. The team is led by one of hockey's superstars, Alex Ovechkin, and enjoys a huge, devoted fan base. Tickets are difficult to find but can be purchased at the Capital One Arena box office, Ticketmaster, or NHL Ticket Exchange. ⊠ *Capital One Arena, 601 F St. NW, Penn Quarter* ☎ *202/266–2222* ⊕ *washcaps.com* ✉ *From $50* Ⓜ *Gallery Pl.–Chinatown.*

Washington Football Team

FOOTBALL | The perennially popular Washington Football Team (formerly the Redskins) continues to play football in the Maryland suburbs at 82,000-seat FedEx Field. As an increasing number of people deem their original name insensitive to Native Americans, talks are underway to change it—unannounced as of press time. Individual game-day tickets can be hard to come by when the team is enjoying a strong season. Your best bet is to check out StubHub (*www.stubhub.com,* the official ticket marketplace of the Washington Football Team). ⊠ *FedEx Field, 1600 FedexWay, Landover* ☎ *301/276–6000 FedEx Field* ⊕ *www.washingtonfootball.com* ✉ *From $60.*

Washington Mystics

BASKETBALL | This WNBA team plays at the Capital One Arena in downtown Washington and perennially leads the WNBA in attendance, at long last capturing their first championship in 2019. The games are loud, boisterous events. You can buy Mystics tickets at the Capital One Arena box office or through Ticketmaster. The women's season runs from late May to August. ⊠ *Capital One Arena, 601 F St. NW, Penn Quarter* ☎ *202/628–3200* ⊕ *washingtonmystics.com* ✉ *From $15* Ⓜ *Gallery Pl.–Chinatown.*

★ The Washington Nationals

BASEBALL/SOFTBALL | The 2019 World Champion Nationals have taken Washingtonians on a wild ride, finally clinching the apex title after several heart-wrenching seasons. But no matter how Max Scherzer, Stephen Strasburg, and the rest are playing, it's always fun to hang out in the modern ballpark, eating some of D.C.'s most iconic foods (including half-smokes from Ben's Chili Bowl), admiring a view off to the Capitol and Washington Monument in the distance. Buy tickets directly at the ballpark or through Stub-Hub. ✉ *Nats Park, 1500 S. Capitol St. SE, Southeast* ☎ *202/675–6287* ⊕ *www.mlb. com* Ⓜ *Navy Yard–Ballpark.*

Washington Wizards

BASKETBALL | From October to April the NBA's Washington Wizards play at the Capital One Arena and feature NBA All-Star John Wall. For showtime entertainment look for G-Wiz, G-Man, the Wiz Kids, and the Wizard Dancers. Buy tickets from the Capital One Arena box office, the Wizards' online, StubHub, or Ticketmaster. ✉ *Capital One Arena, 601 F St. NW, Penn Quarter* ☎ *202/661–5100* ⊕ *www.nba.com/wizards* 🎟 *From $12 (average is $54)* Ⓜ *Gallery Pl.–Chinatown.*

⊕ Health/Safety

Washington, D.C., is a fairly safe city, but as with any major metropolitan area, it's best to stay alert. Keep an eye on purses and backpacks, and be aware of your surroundings before you use an ATM, especially one that is outdoors. Assaults are rare, but they do happen, especially late at night in Adams Morgan, Capitol Hill, Northeast D.C., and U Street Corridor. Public transportation is quite safe, but late at night, choose bus stops on busy streets over those on quiet ones. If someone threatens you with violence, it's best to hand over your money and seek help from police later. Also be careful with smartphones and other electronics, as it's not uncommon for thieves to snatch those devices straight from the hands of unsuspecting pedestrians and Metro riders.

🧳 Packing

A pair of comfortable walking shoes is your must-pack item. This is a walking town, and if you fail to pack for it, your feet will pay. Business attire tends to be fairly conservative, but around college campuses and in hip neighborhoods like U Street Corridor, H Street, NoMa, or Adams Morgan, styles are more eclectic. While you shouldn't show up at upscale restaurants in a Hawaiian shirt and flip-flops, the dress code takes in a wide range of the spectrum. Even at the Kennedy Center you'll see a mix of sparkly long dresses and jeans.

Winters are cold, with nighttime temperatures in the 20s and daytime highs in the 40s and 50s. Although the city doesn't normally get much snow, when it does, many streets won't be plowed for days, so if you're planning a visit for winter, bring a warm coat and hat and shoes that won't be ruined by snow and salt. Summers are muggy and very hot, with temperatures in the 80s and 90s and high humidity. Plan on cool, breathable fabrics, a hat for the sun, a sweater for overzealous air-conditioning, and an umbrella for afternoon thunderstorms. Fall and spring are the most enjoyable, with temperatures in the 60s and occasional showers. Pants, lightweight sweaters, and light coats are appropriate.

Essentials

$ Money

Washington is an expensive city, comparable to New York for hotels and restaurant prices. On the other hand, many attractions, including most of the museums, are free, though some can cost upward of $20 or more. Prices in this guide are given for adults. Substantially reduced fees are almost always available for children, students, and senior citizens.

$ Taxes

Washington's hotel tax is a whopping 14.95%. Maryland and Virginia charge hotel taxes of 4.3%–6% plus additional fees in some cities. The effective sales tax is 6% in D.C., Maryland, and Northern Virginia.

Tipping Guides for Washington, D.C.

Bartender	$1–$5 per round of drinks, depending on the number of drinks
Bellhop	$1–$5 per bag, depending on the level of the hotel
Coat Check	$1–$2 per coat
Hotel Concierge	$5 or more, depending on the service
Hotel Doorstaff	$1–$5 for help with bags or hailing a cab
Housekeeping	$2–$5 a day (in cash, preferably daily since cleaning staff may be different each day you stay)
Hotel Room Service Waiter	$1–$2 per delivery, even if a service charge has been added
Porter at Airport or Train Station	$1 per bag
Restroom Attendants	$1 or small change
Skycap at Airport	$1–$3 per bag checked
Spa Personnel	15%–20% of the cost of your service
Taxi Driver	15%–20%
Tour Guide	10%–15% of the cost of the tour, per person
Valet Parking Attendant	$2–$5, each time your car is brought to you
Waiter	15%–20%, with 20% being the norm at high-end restaurants; nothing additional if a service charge is added to the bill

D.C.'s Top Festivals

For a look at yearly events, visit ⊕ *www.washington.org*, the website of the tourism bureau.

WINTER
National Christmas Tree Lighting/Pageant of Peace (☎ *202/796–2500* ⊕ *www.thenationaltree.org, Dec.*). Each year in early December, the president lights the tree at dusk on the Ellipse, with a G-scale model railway running around the tree's base and smaller decorated trees representing the states and territories providing a festive setting. Concerts are held through the month.

Restaurant Week (⊕ *www.ramw.org/restaurantweek, Jan. and Aug.*). More than 200 top restaurants offer lunch and dinner menus for around $20 and $35, respectively—often a steal.

Washington Auto Show (⊕ *www.washingtonautoshow.com, Jan. and Feb.*). Held at the convention center, this yearly event showcases the latest offerings from the world of automobiles.

SPRING
National Cherry Blossom Festival (☎ *877/442–5666* ⊕ *www.nationalcherryblossomfestival.org, late Mar.–mid Apr.*). D.C.'s most eye-catching annual festival opens with an evening of world-class traditional and contemporary performances at the historic Warner Theater.

Georgetown French Market (☎ *202/298–9222* ⊕ *www.georgetownfrenchmarketdc.com, late Apr.*). Shop, eat, wander, and enjoy strolling mimes and live musicians in one of D.C.'s most beautiful neighborhoods.

National Cathedral Flower Mart (⊕ *allhallowsguild.org, late Apr.–early May*). This long-standing free event on the cathedral grounds features food, music, kids' activities and, of course, flowers.

SUMMER
Capital Pride Festival (☎ *202/719–5304* ⊕ *www.capitalpride.org, June*). This weeklong festival with a parade celebrates LGBTQ+ citizens.

Smithsonian's Folklife Festival (☎ *202/633–6440* ⊕ *www.folklife.si.edu, late June–early July*). This two-week festival on the National Mall celebrates traditional dance and music, storytelling, and food from around the world.

Independence Day Celebration (☎ *202/619–7222* ⊕ *July4thparade.com, www.nps.gov, July*). A parade sashays down Constitution Avenue, fireworks fly over the Washington Monument, and the NSO plays on the Capitol's West Lawn.

National Symphony Orchestra Labor Day Concert (☎ *202/416–8114* ⊕ *www.aoc.gov, Labor Day weekend*). This free concert is held on the grounds of the U.S. Capitol.

FALL
National Book Festival (☎ *202/707–5000* ⊕ *www.loc.gov, early Sept.*). This Saturday event attracts some of the world's top authors and poets to the convention center, where visitors can listen to readings and discussions and get books signed.

Washington International Horse Show (☎ *202/525–3679* ⊕ *www.wihs.org, late Oct.*). Held at Capital One Arena, this annual show features jumping, dressage, barrel racing, and more.

Veterans Day (☎ *877/907–8585* for Cemetery Visitor Center, ☎ *202/426–6841* for National Park Service, Nov. 11). Services are held at Arlington National Cemetery, Vietnam Veterans Memorial, and the U.S. Navy Memorial, with a wreath laying at 11 am at the Tomb of the Unknowns.

Great Itineraries

ONE DAY IN D.C.

If you have a day or less in D.C., your sightseeing strategy is simple: Take the Metro to the Smithsonian stop and explore the area around the National Mall. You'll be at the heart of the city—a beautiful setting where you'll find America's greatest collection of museums, with the city's monuments and the halls of government a stone's throw away.

Facing the Capitol, to your left are the **National Museum of African American History and Culture, National Museum of American History, National Museum of Natural History,** and the **National Gallery of Art.** To your right are the **Freer Gallery,** the **National Museum of African Art,** the **Hirshhorn Museum and Sculpture Garden,** the **National Air and Space Museum,** and more. Head in the other direction, toward the **Washington Monument,** and you're also on your way to the **National World War II Memorial,** the **Lincoln Memorial,** the **Vietnam Veterans Memorial,** and more monuments to America's presidents and its past. A lover of American history and culture could spend a thoroughly happy month, much less a day, wandering the Mall and its surroundings.

If you're here first thing in the morning: You can hit monuments and memorials early. They're open 24 hours a day and staffed beginning at 9:30 am. The sculpture garden at the Hirshhorn opens at 7:30, and the Smithsonian Institution Building ("the Castle") opens at 8:30. In the Castle, you can grab a cup of coffee, watch an 18-minute film about D.C., and see examples of objects from many of the Smithsonian's 19 museums and galleries.

If you have only a few hours in the evening: Experience the beauty of the monuments at dusk and after dark. Many people think they're even more striking when the sun goes down. National Park Service rangers staff most monuments until 10 pm.

THREE DAYS IN D.C.
DAY 1

With more time, you have a chance both to see the sights and to get to know the city. A guided bus tour is a good way to get oriented; a hop-on, hop-off tour will give you genuine insights without a lot of tourist hokum.

Because you can get on and off wherever you like, it's a good idea to use a bus tour to explore **Georgetown** and the **Washington National Cathedral,** neither of which is easily accessible by Metro. This is a good opportunity to visit **Arlington National Cemetery** as well.

In the afternoon, visit the **Smithsonian American Art Museum** and/or the **National Portrait Gallery** in Penn Quarter; the **International Spy Museum,** recently expanded at its new L'Enfant Plaza location, is another option.

DAY 2

Devote your next day to the National Mall, where you can check out the museums and monuments that were probably your prime motivation for visiting D.C. in the first place. There's no way you can do it all in one day, so just play favorites, and save the rest for next time. Try visiting the monuments in the evening: they remain open long after the museums are closed and are dramatically lit after dark.

Keep in mind that the **National Museum of Natural History** is the most visited museum in the country, while the **National Air and Space Museum,** the **National Gallery of Art,** and the **National Museum of American History** aren't far behind; plan for crowds almost any time you visit. If you visit the **United States Holocaust Memorial Museum,** plan on spending two to three hours. The **National Museum of African American History and Culture** is the newest museum on the Mall, though lines have lessened since it opened in 2016. If you're with kids on the Mall, take a break by riding the carousel.

Cafés and cafeterias within the museums are your best option for lunch. Three excellent picks are the Cascade Café at the **National Gallery of Art**; the Mitsitam Café at the **National Museum of the American Indian**, where they serve creative dishes inspired by indigenous cultures; and Sweet Water Café at the **National Museum of African American History and Culture**, showcasing the rich traditions of African American cuisine.

If the weather permits—and you're not already weary—consider the healthy walk from the **Washington Monument** to the **Lincoln Memorial** and around the **Tidal Basin**, where you can see the **Jefferson Memorial**, the **Franklin Delano Roosevelt Memorial**, and the **Martin Luther King Jr. Memorial**. Nearby, nestled north of the Mall's reflecting pool, is the **Vietnam Veterans Memorial**, "The Wall," a sobering black granite monolith commemorating the 58,318 Americans who died in service of the Vietnam War—a design that's "not so much a tombstone or a monument as a grave," in the somber words of writer Michael Ventura.

DAY 3

Start your day on **Capitol Hill**, where you'll have the option of visiting the **Capitol**, the **U.S. Botanic Garden**, the **Library of Congress**, the **Supreme Court**, and the **Folger Shakespeare Library**.

Call your senator or congressional representative (or your country's embassy, if you are a visitor from outside the United States) in advance of your trip for passes to see Congress in session. You can also venture into one of the congressional office buildings adjacent to the Capitol, where congressional hearings are almost always open to the public. (Visit ⊕ *www.house.gov* and ⊕ *www.senate.gov* for schedules.) Likewise, check the Supreme Court's website (⊕ *www.supremecourtus.gov*) for dates of oral arguments. If you arrive early enough, you might gain admission for either a short (three-minute) visit or the full morning session.

In the afternoon, hop on the Metro to bustling **Dupont Circle** for lunch, then visit the renowned **Phillips Collection** or head farther north on Connecticut Avenue to the **National Zoo** to say "hi" to the pandas.

Washington, D.C. Black History Walk

A walk along U Street and the eastern rim of Adams Morgan gives a taste of D.C. that most tourists never get. This tour through "Black Broadway" bounces from lively commercial streets brimming with hip bars, cafés, and boutiques to quiet, tree-lined, residential blocks.

"BLACK BROADWAY" —U STREET CORRIDOR

The Howard Theatre at T Street and Florida Avenue is a good place to start. Opened in 1910, this landmark of Black culture found its way onto the National Register of Historic Places for hosting some of the greatest musical acts of the last century—a list that includes such notables as Ella Fitzgerald and native son Duke Ellington in the 1930s and, more recently, Lena Horne, James Brown, and Marvin Gaye. All but destroyed in 1968, following the assassination of Martin Luther King Jr., the theater was renovated beautifully in 2012 and now features live acts almost nightly. A short hike west, at Vermont and U Streets, sits the **African American Civil War Memorial,** where the names of more than 200,000 Black soldiers who fought for their freedom are inscribed. The adjacent **African American Civil War Museum** features wonderful photographs from the era and an extensive on-site database for searching individual soldiers. A block west at 2000 11th Street is **Washington Industrial Bank,** which thrived by offering African Americans a service that others in the city wouldn't: the option to borrow money. Next, grab a half-smoke at **Ben's Chili Bowl**. This D.C. landmark refused to close its doors during the fierce riots that followed King's assassination. While most of U Street was being destroyed, Ben's fed the police officers and Black activists trying to keep order. Next door is the **Lincoln Theater,** another exceptional jazz venue and, from 1922 until

Washington, D.C. Black History Walk

HIGHLIGHTS:
U Street was the center of Black culture before Harlem was Harlem. See where Duke Ellington played, indulge in a half-smoke at Ben's Chili Bowl, and learn a bit about African American history along the way.

WHERE TO START:
Howard Theatre, just east of Metro's U Street/African American Civil War Memorial/Cardozo stop on the Green or Yellow lines

LENGTH:
About 1½ miles; 1–2 hours, with window-shopping

WHERE TO STOP:
All Souls Unitarian Church. The S2 or S4 bus lines on 16th Street will whisk you back Downtown.

BEST TIME TO GO:
While the sun is up, though the nightlife on U Street is an attraction in itself.

WORST TIME TO GO:
Avoid walking through Meridian Hill Park after dark.

SHOPPING DETOUR:
Check out the sprawling Miss Pixie's (*1626 14th St. NW*) for handpicked collectibles, vintage furniture, and fun home decor, and browse GoodWood (*1428 U St. NW between 14th and 15th Sts.*) for antique wooden furniture and estate jewelry.

desegregation, one of the largest and most elegant historically Black theaters. Two blocks north up 13th Street NW and a quick left on W Street will bring you to the **Anthony Bowen Branch YMCA,** the oldest Black Y in the country (1853), recently completely overhauled.

NORTH OF U STREET

Venture a block southwest to 15th and V to marvel at **St. Augustine's Catholic Church**—a gorgeous, two-tower cathedral now home to a Black congregation that seceded from its segregated church (St. Matthews) in 1858. Feel free to walk inside to glimpse the striking stained-glass portrait of a Black St. Augustine and St. Monica. A block north on 15th Street

awaits sprawling **Meridian Hill (or Malcolm X) Park,** where a number of civil rights marches have originated over the years. Just north of the park, you'll spot **Meridian Hill Hall,** Howard University's first coed dorm. Alumni of the elite African American school include Thurgood Marshall and Toni Morrison. Continuing north, you'll find **All Souls Unitarian Church** at 1500 Harvard Street NW. Its pastor in the 1940s, Reverend A. Powell Davies, led the push to desegregate D.C. schools.

Best Tours in D.C.

It's pretty easy to do D.C. on your own, but consider one of the following options if you're looking for chaperoned convenience.

BIKE TOURS

Bike and Roll. Based at L'Enfant Plaza, just off the National Mall, Bike and Roll offers a series of guided tours through D.C.'s top sites, including the Capitol, Supreme Court, and WWII Memorial. Bike rentals and Segway tours are also offered, and self-guided options stretch as far as Mount Vernon and even Pittsburgh. ✉ *955 L'Enfant Plaza SW, North Bldg., Southwest* ☎ *202/842–2453* ⊕ *www.bikeandrolldc.com* ✉ *From $44.*

Fat Tire Tours. Yet another option for touring the monuments, Fat Tire Tours offers guided day tours, sunset trips, Segway rentals, and packages that include entrance into the Spy Museum and other sites. A typical tour is three hours of easy peddling. ✉ *955 L'Enfant Plaza, Southwest* ☎ *866/614–6218, 202/842–2453* ⊕ *www.fattiretours.com* ✉ *From $39* Ⓜ *L'Enfant Plaza.*

BOAT TOURS

Capitol River Cruises. Sightseeing tours lasting 45 minutes are aboard the *Nightingale* and *Nightingale II*, former Great Lakes boats from the 1950s. Departures are hourly, noon to 8 pm, May through September, to 7 pm April and October. ✉ *Washington Harbor, 3050 K St. NW, Georgetown* ☎ *301/460–7447* ⊕ *www.capitolrivercruises.com* ✉ *$18.*

Odyssey III. Specially built to fit under the Potomac's bridges, the *Odyssey III* departs from the Gangplank marina near the District Wharf for daily dinner cruises, weekday lunch cruises, and weekend brunch cruises—elegant affairs with a dress code (jackets for men) at dinner. ✉ *600 Water St. SW, D.C. Waterfront*

☎ *703/684–0580, 877/511–2628* ⊕ *www.odysseycruises.com* ✉ *From $65* Ⓜ *Waterfront–SEU.*

Potomac Riverboat Company. With docks in Alexandria, Georgetown, Mount Vernon, National Harbor, and The Wharf, this company offers a monuments tour, a Mount Vernon cruise, and transportation to Washington Nationals baseball games and D.C. United soccer games. It also runs the sleek water taxi that connects The Wharf, Georgetown, Alexandria, and National Harbor. ✉ *Alexandria* ☎ *877/511–2628, 703/684–0580* ⊕ *www.potomacriverboatco.com* ✉ *From $18.*

Thompson Boat Center. Another way to see the monuments from the Potomac River is through Thompson Boat Center in Georgetown, which offers canoe, kayak, and stand-up paddleboard rentals for self-guided tours. Pack a lunch and paddle over to Roosevelt Island for a picnic. A double kayak rents for $22 per hour, while a canoe goes for $25 per hour and a stand-up paddleboard for $22 per hour. Sculls are also available for certified rowers. ✉ *2900 Virginia Ave. NW, Georgetown* ☎ *202/333–9543* ⊕ *www.thompsonboatcenter.com* ✉ *From $16 for a single kayak.*

BUS TOURS

Big Bus Tours. Brightly painted, red-and-yellow, open-top, double-decker buses provide a hop-on, hop-off service with different city loops. Discount tickets are sometimes offered online. ☎ *877/332–8689* ⊕ *www.bigbustours.com* ✉ *From $49.*

City Sights. This bus tour offers double-decker fun for those seeking to take advantage of warmer weather and get an elevated view of Washington. The group runs multiple loops around the city, some of which extend well beyond the

Mall to include Georgetown, the National Cathedral, Arlington National Cemetery, and the Pentagon. All trips offer hop-on, hop-off convenience, and several multi-day options are available for those on longer stays. City Sights also offers night tours, boat trips, and guided bike tours. ☎ 202/650–5444, 866/723–4400 ⊕ www.citysightsdc.com ✉ From $50.

DC Ducks. Ready for a unique take on Washington? DC Ducks takes the traditional jaunt through the city and adds a thrilling twist: the 90-minute guided tour ends with a splashdown in the Potomac River, where the amphibious Duckmobile gives visitors a rousing water leg to their trip. Tours, which run from mid-March to November, begin at Union Station, leaving every hour between 10 am and 4 pm. ☎ 866/754–5039 ⊕ www.dcducks.com ✉ From $45.

Gray Line. This venerable tour company specializes in lectured sightseeing tours of Washington. D.C., Mount Vernon, Gettysburg, and more. ☎ 202/779–9894 ⊕ www.graylinedc.com ✉ From $35.

Old Town Trolley Tours. D.C.'s longest-running tour company offers one of the best narrated glimpses of the city's many historic wonders, with the option of hop-on, hop-off service at 24 different stops. Two loops are available: one wraps around the Mall, the Capitol, and the Wharf; the other extends from the Lincoln Memorial to Arlington National Cemetery in Virginia. (Transfers between the loops are part of the deal.) Visitors can begin their tour at any of the stops, and buses swing by every 30 minutes beginning at 9 am; the last re-boarding is at 4:45 pm. ☎ 844/356–2603 ⊕ www.trolleytours.com/washington-dc ✉ From $57.

OnBoard D.C. Tours. The daily, six-hour "D.C. It All" tour lets you hop on and off with the guide at 12 locations, and,

from mid-March through October, the tour includes a one-hour private Potomac River cruise and stops at the Pentagon and Air Force Memorial. Several other tours are offered, including a three-hour "D.C. The Lights!" nightlife tour. ☎ 301/839–5261 ⊕ www.washingtondc-tours.onboardtours.com ✉ From $60.

SEGWAY AND SCOOTER TOURS

Rest your feet and glide by the monuments, museums, and major attractions aboard a Segway. Guided tours usually last between two and three hours. D.C. city ordinance requires that riders be at least 16 years old; some tour companies have weight restrictions of 250 pounds. Tours, limited to 6 to 10 people, begin with an instruction session.

Capital Segway. More than 25 historic sights are included on this company's Segway tours, which depart from the corner of 17th and I Street NW. ✉ 818 Connecticut Ave. NW ☎ 202/682–1980 ⊕ www.capitalsegway.com ✉ From $60 Ⓜ McPherson Sq.

Scootaround Inc. This company rents mobility scooters and wheelchairs for self-guided tours. ✉ Washington ☎ 888/441–7575 ⊕ www.scootaround.com ✉ Scooters from $32 per day; wheelchairs from $27 per day.

SPECIALTY TOURS

DC Metro Food Tours. Some 20 tours, each lasting 3½ hours and conducted on weekends year-round, explore the culinary heritage of different neighborhoods in D.C. and nearby Virginia. Private tours can be arranged. ☎ 202/851–2268 ⊕ www.dcmetrofoodtours.com ✉ From $60.

Smithsonian Associates. Experience D.C.'s art, history, and culture through the lens of the Smithsonian Associates. Tours of Arlington National Cemetery, nearby Civil

Best Tours in D.C.

War battlefields, and an Anacostia River hike are some of the excursions on offer. ☎ *202/633–3030* ⊕ *www.smithsonianassociates.org* ✉ *From $45.*

A Tour de Force. Local historian and author Jeanne Fogle will escort you via custom-designed tours, by limo or on foot, of historic homes, diplomatic buildings, and off-the-beaten-path sites. You can opt for half-day, full-day, multiday, or evening tours. ☎ *703/525–2948* ⊕ *www.atourdeforce.com.*

Washington Photo Safari. Founder E. David Luria promises opportunities for photographers of all skill levels (even camera phones are fine) on his half-day and full-day "Monuments and Memorials" workshops. Special themed tours, led by a team of professional photographers, are held on selected weekends. ☎ *202/669–8468* ⊕ *www.washingtonphotosafari.com* ✉ *From $89.*

WALKING TOURS

Capitol Historical Society. This group leads guided tours around the grounds of the Capitol weekdays at 5:30 pm, March through Memorial Day, 7 pm Memorial Day through Labor Day, and 5:30 pm Labor Day through October 31. The two-hour tour starts at Garfield Circle, at the intersection of First Street and Maryland Avenue Southwest. Reservations must be made at least 48 hours in advance. ☎ *800/887–9318, 202/543–8919* ⊕ *www.uschs.org* ✉ *$30.*

Cultural Tourism DC. This nonprofit group has 17 self-guided Neighborhood Heritage Trails, plus a citywide African American Heritage Trail, all of which are highlighted with historic markers. All the tours can be downloaded from its website. One week each fall, the group leads free guided walking tours that highlight the history and architecture of certain neighborhoods, from the Southwest

Waterfront to points much farther north. You can also check out other cultural events happening around the city, many free, on the website. ☎ *202/355–4280* ⊕ *www.culturaltourismdc.org* ✉ *Free.*

DC by Foot. Dozens of tours, including the Tidal Basin and National Mall, Arlington National Cemetery, Capitol Hill, Georgetown, and U Street, are led by guides who work for tips, guaranteeing a highly entertaining experience. Tours last two to four hours and are available year-round, but days and times vary by season, and advance reservations are required. ☎ *202/370–1830* ⊕ *www.freetoursbyfoot.com* ✉ *Guides work for tips.*

DC Walkabout. Download a tour to any mobile device, and set off in your own time and at your own pace, guided by a narration, historical recordings, and even music and sound effects. Tours, ranging from 1 to 2 miles, include "American Scandal," "Capitol Hill," "Georgetown Ghost," "Haunted History," "Lincoln Assassination," "National Mall," and "Tidal Basin." ⊕ *www.dcwalkabout.com* ✉ *$9.*

History on Foot. Relive the night of President Abraham Lincoln's assassination with Detective McDevitt on this two-hour walking tour. From Ford's Theatre you'll follow the escape route taken by assassin John Wilkes Booth on the 1½-mile trek, ending at Lafayette Park. Tours are offered March through October. ☎ *202/347–4833* ⊕ *www.fords.org* ✉ *$18.*

Washington Walks. The wide range of tours offered by Washington Walks includes "Hamilton's D.C." and "Women Who Changed America." ☎ *202/484–1565* ⊕ *www.washingtonwalks.com* ✉ *$20.*

Contacts

 ## Air

AIRLINE CONTACTS
American Airlines/American Eagle. ☎ 800/433–7300 ⊕ www.aa.com. **Delta Airlines.** ☎ 800/221–1212 ⊕ www.delta.com. **JetBlue.** ☎ 800/538–2583 ⊕ www.jetblue.com. **Southwest Airlines.** ☎ 800/435–9792 ⊕ www.southwest.com. **United Airlines.** ☎ 800/864–8331 ⊕ www.united.com.

AIRPORTS Baltimore/Washington International–Thurgood Marshall Airport. (BWI). ☎ 800/435–9294, 410/859–7111 ⊕ www.bwiairport.com. **Dulles International Airport.** ☎ 703/572–2700 ⊕ www.flydulles.com. **Ronald Reagan Washington National Airport.** (DCA). ☎ 703/417–8000 ⊕ www.flyreagan.com.

REAGAN NATIONAL (DCA) AIRPORT TRANSFERS
Taxicab Commission. ☎ 311, 202/645–6018 ⊕ www.dfhv.dc.gov. **Washington Metropolitan Area Transit Authority.** ☎ 202/637–7000, 202/962–2033 TTY ⊕ www.wmata.com.

BALTIMORE/WASHINGTON (BWI) AIRPORT TRANSFERS Amtrak. ☎ 800/872–7245 ⊕ www.amtrak.com. **Maryland Rail Commuter Service.** ☎ 410/539–5000, 410/539–3497 TTY, 866/743–3682 ⊕ www.mta.maryland.gov. **Washington Metropolitan Area Transit Authority.** ☎ 202/637–7000, 202/962–2033 TTY ⊕ www.wmata.com.

DULLES (IAD) AIRPORT TRANSFERS Washington Flyer. ☎ 703/572–8294 ⊕ www.flydulles.com. **Washington Metropolitan Area Transit Authority.** ☎ 202/637–7000, 202/962–2033 TTY ⊕ www.wmata.com.

Bus

D.C. CITY BUSES DC Circulator. ☎ 202/671–2020 ⊕ www.dccirculator.com. **Metro Center sales office.** ✉ 12th and F Sts. NW, Downtown ⊕ www.wmata.com. **Washington Metropolitan Area Transit Authority.** ☎ 202/637–7000, 202/962–2033 TTY ⊕ www.wmata.com.

REGIONAL BUSES Best-Bus. ☎ 202/332–2691, ⊕ www.bestbus.com. **BoltBus.** ☎ 877/265–8287 ⊕ www.boltbus.com. **Megabus.** ☎ 877/462–6342 ⊕ us.megabus.com. **Peter Pan Bus Lines.** ☎ 800/343–9999 ⊕ www.peterpanbus.com. **Tripper Bus.** ☎ 718/834–9214, 877/826–3874 ⊕ www.tripperbus.com. **Vamoose.** ☎ 212/695–6766, 301/718–0036 ⊕ www.vamoosebus.com. **Washington**

Deluxe. ☎ 866/287–6932 ⊕ www.washny.com.

 ## Car

CAR RENTAL COMPANIES
Alamo. ☎ 844/354–6962 reservations, 844/357–5138 customer service, 800/522–9292 TTY ⊕ www.alamo.com. **Avis.** ☎ 800/352–7900 ⊕ www.avis.com. **Budget.** ☎ 800/218–7992 ⊕ www.budget.com. **Hertz.** ☎ 800/654–3131 ⊕ www.hertz.com. **National Car Rental.** ☎ 844/393–9989 customer service, 844/382–6875 ⊕ www.nationalcar.com.

Metro/Public Transport

METRO INFORMATION
Washington Metropolitan Area Transit Authority. (WMATA). ✉ Downtown ☎ 202/637–7000, 202/962–2033 TTY, 888/762–7874 customer service ⊕ www.wmata.com.

Ride-Sharing

RIDE SHARES Lyft. ⊕ www.lyft.com. **Uber.** ⊕ www.uber.com. **Zipcar.** ☎ 866/494–7227 ⊕ www.zipcar.com.

Contacts

Taxi

**TAXI COMPANIES Bar-
wood.** ☎ *301/984–1900*
⊕ *www.barwoodtaxi.com.*
Diamond. ☎ *202/387–6200.*
Red Top Cab of Arlington.
☎ *703/522–3333* ⊕ *www.
redtopcab.com.* **Taxi Transportation.** ☎ *202/398–0500*
⊕ *www.dctaxionline.com.*
Yellow. ☎ *202/544–1212*
⊕ *dcyellowcab.com.*

Train

TRAIN CONTACTS Amtrak.
☎ *800/872–7245* ⊕ *www.
amtrak.com.* **Maryland
Rail Commuter Service.**
(*MARC*). ☎ *866/743–3682,
410/539–5000* ⊕ *www.
mta.maryland.gov.* **Union
Station.** ✉ *50 Massachusetts Ave. NE, Washington*
☎ *202/289–1908* ⊕ *www.
unionstationdc.com.*
Virginia Railway Express.
(*VRE*). ☎ *703/684–1001
customer service,
800/743–3873* ⊕ *www.
vre.org.*

● Visitor Information

**EVENTS National Park
Service.** ☎ *202/208–6843*
⊕ *www.nps.gov.* **Smith-
sonian.** ☎ *202/633–1000,
202/633–5285 TTY*
⊕ *www.si.edu.* **White
House Visitor Center.**
✉ *1450 Pennsylvania
Ave. NW, Washington*
☎ *202/208–1631* ⊕ *www.
nps.gov/whho.*

**THE DISTRICT Destination
DC.** ✉ *901 7th St. NW, 4th
fl., Downtown* ☎ *202/789–
7000, 800/422–8644*
⊕ *www.washington.org.*

**VIRGINIA AND MARY-
LAND State of Maryland.**
☎ *866/639–3526* ⊕ *www.
visitmaryland.org.* **Virginia Tourism Corporation.**
☎ *800/847–4882* ⊕ *www.
virginia.org.*

Chapter 3

THE NATIONAL MALL

WITH FEDERAL TRIANGLE AND SOUTHWEST

3

Updated by
Claire Handscombe

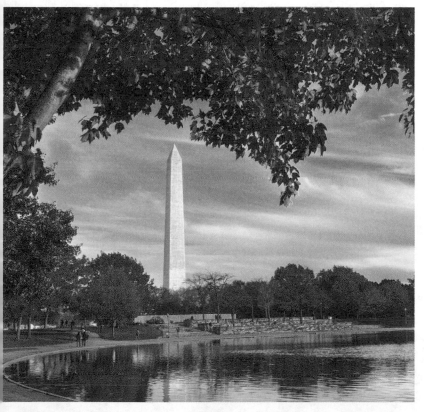

👁 Sights
★★★★★

🍴 Restaurants
★★☆☆☆

🛏 Hotels
★☆☆☆☆

🛍 Shopping
★★☆☆☆

🌙 Nightlife
★☆☆☆☆

NEIGHBORHOOD SNAPSHOT

TOP EXPERIENCES

■ **Monuments at night:** For a unique (and less crowded) historical experience, tour the many monuments after dark, when they are lit and beautiful.

■ **National Air and Space Museum:** Touch a moon rock, see the original *Spirit of St. Louis* and Apollo Lunar Module.

■ **National Archives:** Stand in awe as you read the Declaration of Independence, Constitution, Bill of Rights, and a 1297 Magna Carta.

■ **National Museum of African American History and Culture:** D.C.'s newest museum is also its most moving. Learn about when captive slaves were first brought to the New World, and celebrate the many artists, writers, actors, and cultural leaders who have contributed to our country's history.

■ **National Gallery of Art:** Two massive buildings offer an extensive collection ranging from classics to modern art. Don't miss the only Leonardo da Vinci in the United States, the renowned *Ginevra de' Benci.*

■ **The Holocaust Museum:** This museum serves as a monument to those lost in the Holocaust and offers perspective on the effects of genocide—across the world and throughout time.

GETTING HERE

Federal Triangle (Blue and Orange lines) is convenient to the Natural History and American History museums. Smithsonian (Blue and Orange lines) is close to the Holocaust Memorial Museum and Hirshhorn Museum. Archives–Navy Memorial–Penn Quarter (Yellow and Green lines) takes you to the National Gallery of Art. L'Enfant Plaza (Blue, Orange, Yellow, and Green lines) is the best stop for the Hirshhorn and Air and Space Museum. Many visitors take advantage of the DC Circulator National Mall Route buses that cost just $1 and run daily up and down the Mall.

QUICK BITES

■ **Garden Café.** After marveling at the masterpieces in the National Gallery West Building, grab a quick bite on the ground floor at this full-service, sit-down café offering salads, house-roasted meats, and European-style desserts. ✉ *National Gallery, West Bldg., 6th and Constitution* Ⓜ *Archives–Navy Memorial–Penn Quarter.*

■ **Mitsitam Cafe.** The quick-service food court offers stations with dishes from five regional Native American cuisines. The food here is meant to give visitors a deeper insight into the culinary history of indigenous peoples, including cooking techniques, ingredients, and flavors. ✉ *National Museum of the American Indian, 4th St. SW and Independence Ave.* Ⓜ *Federal Center SW.*

■ **Sweet Home Café.** This cafeteria's menu offers traditional and authentic seasonally rotating dishes that showcase the rich history of African American cuisine from four distinct geographic regions. Many ingredients are locally sourced, and everything is cooked from scratch. ✉ *Museum of African American History and Culture, 1400 Constitution Ave. NW* Ⓜ *Smithsonian or Federal Triangle.*

It could be said that the National Mall—the heart of almost every visitor's trip to Washington—has influenced life in the United States more than any other park.

The National Mall is a picnicking park, jogging path, and outdoor stage for festivals and fireworks. People come here from around the world to tour the illustrious Smithsonian museums, celebrate special events, or rally over the hot-button issues of the day.

Sights

Arthur M. Sackler Gallery
MUSEUM | The Smithsonian's second museum devoted to Asian art opened in 1987, having been inspired by the donation of 1,000 objects by Dr. Arthur M. Sackler. You can enter a dramatically lit Tibetan Buddhist shrine, complete with the sounds of chanting monks, or view a majestic life-size sculpture of a Yogini, a protective and ferocious Hindu goddess. ⊠ 1050 Independence Ave. SW, The Mall ☎ 202/633–4880 ⊕ www.freersackler. si.edu ⛝ Free Ⓜ Smithsonian.

Bureau of Engraving and Printing
GOVERNMENT BUILDING | FAMILY | Paper money has been printed here since 1914, when the bureau relocated from the redbrick-towered Auditors Building at the corner of 14th Street and Independence Avenue. In addition to paper currency, military certificates and presidential invitations are printed here, too. You can only enter the bureau on tours, which last about 40 minutes. From March through early September (dates vary each year), free, same-day, timed-entry tour passes are issued starting at 8 am (plan on being in line no later than 7 am) at the Raoul Wallenberg Place SW ticket booth. For the rest of the year, tickets are not required, and you can simply wait in line. You also can also arrange a tour through your U.S. senator or representative. ⊠ 14th and C Sts. SW, The Mall ☎ 202/874–2330, 866/874–2330 tour information ⊕ moneyfactory.gov ⛝ Free Ⓜ Smithsonian.

Constitution Gardens
GARDEN | Many ideas were proposed to develop this 52-acre site near the Reflecting Pool and the Vietnam Veterans Memorial. Paths wind through groves of trees and a 1-acre island on the lake pays tribute to the signers of the Declaration of Independence, with all of their 56 signatures carved into a low stone wall. This spot is particularly lovely in the fall, with vibrant red colors, and it's a quieter part of the Mall for picnics. At the circular snack bar just west of the lake, you can get hot dogs, potato chips, candy bars, and soft drinks. ⊠ Constitution Ave., between 17th and 23rd Sts. NW, The Mall ⊕ www.nps.gov/coga Ⓜ Farragut W or Foggy Bottom–GWU.

District of Columbia War Memorial
GARDEN | Despite its location and age, visitors often overlook this memorial on the National Mall, though it's a favorite with locals for wedding and engagement photos. President Herbert Hoover dedicated this monument in 1931, and unlike the neighboring memorials on the Mall, this relatively small structure isn't a national memorial. The 47-foot-high, circular, domed, columned temple is dedicated to the 26,000 residents from Washington, D.C., who served in the Great War and the 499 men and women (military and

The National Mall

The National Mall

Pennsylvania Ave. N.W.

Department of the Treasury

The White House

President's Park

Ellipse

G St. N.W.

F St. N.W.

E St. Expy.

E St. N.W.

E St. N.W.

D St. N.W.

Edward J. Kelly Park

Department of the Interior

Bolivar Park

C St. N.W.

C St. N.W.

Constitution Ave. N.W.

Constitution Ave. N.W.

Virginia Ave. N.W.

Constitution Gardens Pond

The National Mall

Reflecting Pool

Independence Ave. S.W.

Independence Ave. S.W.

Independence Ave. S.W.

Ohio Dr. S.W.

West Potomac Park

Tidal Basin

Potomac River

Marine Ave. S.

KEY

1 *Exploring Sights*

1 *Restaurants*

1 *Hotels*

0 — 1,000 ft
0 — 200 m

Sights ▼

1 Arthur M. Sackler Gallery **G5**

2 Bureau of Engraving and Printing **E6**

3 Constitution Gardens... **C4**

4 District of Columbia War Memorial.......... **C5**

5 East Potomac Park **F7**

6 Franklin Delano Roosevelt Memorial.... **C7**

7 Freer Gallery of Art **G5**

8 Hirshhorn Museum and Sculpture Garden.. **H5**

9 Korean War Veterans Memorial **A5**

10 Lincoln Memorial **A4**

11 Martin Luther King Jr. National Memorial...... **B6**

12 Museum of the Bible ... **J6**

13 National Archives Museum **H3**

14 National Gallery of Art, East Building **J3**

15 National Gallery of Art, West Building **I3**

16 National Museum of African American History and Culture **F3**

17 National Museum of the American Indian **J5**

18 Old Post Office Pavilion **G2**

19 Ronald Reagan Building and International Trade Center **F3**

20 Smithsonian Castle Information Center.................... **H4**

civilian) who died in service. Unofficially referred to as the "World War I Memorial" in the District, its marble structure was restored through the American Recovery and Reinvestment Act of 2009 and is now maintained by the National Park Service. ⊠ *Independence Ave. SW, The Mall* ✛ *West Potomac Park, between Reflecting Pool and Independence Ave.* ☎ *202/426–6841* ⊕ *www.nps.gov/nacc* Ⓜ *Foggy Bottom–GWU.*

East Potomac Park

CITY PARK | FAMILY | This 328-acre finger of land extends south of the Jefferson Memorial from the Tidal Basin, between the Washington Channel and the new Southwest Waterfront redevelopment neighborhood to the east and the Potomac River to the west. Locals consider the park a retreat with its playgrounds, picnic tables, tennis courts, swimming pools, driving range, one 18-hole and two 9-hole golf courses, and miniature golf. There's also a scenic riverfront trail that winds around the park's perimeter. Double-blossoming Japanese cherry trees line Ohio Drive and bloom about two weeks after the single-blossoming variety that attracts throngs to the Tidal Basin each spring. ⊠ *Ohio Dr. SW, The Mall* ☎ *202/426–6841* ⊕ *www.npca.org/parks* Ⓜ *Smithsonian.*

Franklin Delano Roosevelt Memorial

MEMORIAL | This 7.5-acre memorial to the 32nd president, on the west side of the Tidal Basin, includes waterfalls and reflecting pools, four outdoor gallery rooms—one for each of Roosevelt's presidential terms (1933 to 1945)—and 10 bronze sculptures. The granite megaliths connecting the galleries are engraved with some of Roosevelt's famous statements, including, "The only thing we have to fear is fear itself." A bronze statue of First Lady Eleanor Roosevelt stands in front of the United Nations symbol in the fourth room. She was a vocal spokesperson for human rights and one of the most influential

The FDR Memorial

Congress established the Franklin Delano Roosevelt Memorial Commission in 1955 and invited prospective designers to look to "the character and work of Roosevelt to give us the theme of a memorial." Several decades passed before Lawrence Halprin's design for a "walking environmental experience" was selected. It incorporates work by artists Leonard Baskin, Neil Estern, Robert Graham, Thomas Hardy, and George Segal, and master stone carver John Benson.

women of her time. In consideration of Roosevelt's own disability, this was the first memorial designed to be wheelchair-accessible, and several pillars include Braille lettering. The memorial was dedicated in 1997, but it wasn't until 2001 that a statue of a wheelchair-bound Roosevelt was added near the entrance after years of debate about whether to portray Roosevelt realistically or to honor his desire not to display his disability, as had been done throughout his presidency. ⊠ *400 W. Basin Dr. SW, The Mall* ☎ *202/426–6841* ⊕ *www.nps.gov/fdrm* ➲ *Free* Ⓜ *Smithsonian.*

Freer Gallery of Art

MUSEUM | The first art museum in the Smithsonian group of museums, donated by railroad tycoon Charles Lang Freer, is devoted to Asian and American art. A highlight is the Peacock Room, a jewel box of a space designed by James McNeill Whistler, with gold peacock murals on blue-green walls, and a gilded peacock-feather-pattern ceiling. At noon on the third Thursday of every month, the floor-to-ceiling shutters are opened, bathing the room in natural light.

There are also works from around Asia, including China, Korea, and India, as well as the Middle East. ⊠ *12th St. and Jefferson Dr. SW, The Mall* ☎ *202/633–4880* ⊕ *www.freersackler.si.edu* ✉ *Free* Ⓜ *Smithsonian.*

★ **Hirshhorn Museum and Sculpture Garden**
MUSEUM | Conceived as the nation's museum of modern and contemporary art, the Hirshhorn is home to nearly 12,000 works by modern masters, including Alexander Calder, Andy Warhol, and Louise Bourgeois, as well as contemporary superstars Anish Kapor and Yinka Shonibare. The art is displayed in a circular poured-concrete building, designed by Gordon Bunshaft, that was dubbed the "Doughnut on the Mall" when it was built in 1974. Most of the collection was bequeathed by the museum's founder, Joseph H. Hirshhorn, a Latvian immigrant who made his fortune in uranium mines. Within the sculpture garden stands Yoko Ono's *Wish Tree for Washington, DC.* In front of the building is Jimmie Durham's *Still Life with Spirit and Xitle,* a car crushed by a smiley-faced boulder.

Inside, the second level houses rotating exhibits devoted to particular artists or themes, while the third level is the place to see dramatic postwar art from the museum's permanent collection.

⊠ *Independence Ave. and 7th St. SW, The Mall* ☎ *202/633–4674* ⊕ *www.hirshhorn.si.edu* ✉ *Free* Ⓜ *Smithsonian or L'Enfant Plaza (Maryland Ave. exit).*

Korean War Veterans Memorial
MEMORIAL | At the west end of the Mall, this memorial to the 5.8 million United States men and women who served in the Korean War (1950–53) highlights the cost of freedom. Nearly 37,000 Americans were killed on the Korean peninsula, 8,000 were missing in action, and more than 103,000 were wounded. The privately funded memorial was dedicated on July 27, 1995, the 42nd anniversary of the Korean War Armistice. In the *Field*

The Freer|Sackler

The Smithsonian Institution has two museums of Asian art: the Freer Gallery of Art, which opened to the public in 1923, and the Arthur M. Sackler Gallery, which welcomed its first visitors in 1987. Both are physically connected by an underground passageway; ideologically linked through the study, exhibition, and sheer love of Asian art; and often referred to as the "Freer|Sackler." Free highlight tours are held regularly, as are events such as film screenings, concerts, and talks.

of Service, 19 oversize stainless-steel soldiers trudge through rugged terrain toward an American flag; look beneath the helmets to see their weary faces. Unlike many memorials, this one contains few words. The 164-foot-long granite wall etched with the faces of 2,400 unnamed servicemen and servicewomen says, "Freedom is not free." The plaque at the flagpole base reads, "Our nation honors her sons and daughters who answered the call to defend a country they never knew and a people they never met." The only other words are the names of 22 countries that volunteered forces or medical support. The adjacent circular Pool of Remembrance is a quiet spot for contemplation. ⊠ *Daniel French Dr. SW and Independence Ave. SW, The Mall* ☎ *202/426–6841* ⊕ *www.nps.gov/kwvm* ✉ *Free* Ⓜ *Foggy Bottom–GWU.*

★ Lincoln Memorial
MEMORIAL | Daniel Chester French's 19-foot statue of the seated president gazing out over the Reflecting Pool may be the most iconic on the Mall. The surrounding white Colorado-marble memorial was designed by Henry Bacon and

The view from inside the Lincoln Memorial captures its reflecting pool and the iconic Washington Monument.

completed in 1922. The 36 Doric columns represent the 36 states in the Union at the time of Lincoln's death; their names appear on the frieze above the columns. At night, the memorial is illuminated, creating a striking play of light and shadow across Lincoln's face. Two of Lincoln's great speeches—the second inaugural address and the Gettysburg Address—are carved on the north and south walls. Above each is a Jules Guerin mural: the south wall has an angel of truth freeing a slave; the unity of North and South is opposite. The memorial's powerful symbolism makes it a popular gathering place for marches in favor of peace and social justice. It may be best known, though, as the site of Martin Luther King Jr.'s "I Have a Dream" speech. ⊠ *2 Lincoln Memorial Circle NW, The Mall* ✠ *West end of Mall* ☎ *202/426–6841* ⊕ *www.nps.gov/linc* ☒ *Free* Ⓜ *Foggy Bottom–GWU.*

Martin Luther King Jr. National Memorial

MEMORIAL | A "King" now stands tall among the presidents on the National Mall. The memorial opened on August 22, 2011, 15 years after Congress approved it in 1996 and 82 years after the famed civil rights leader was born in 1929, and was dedicated by President Barack Obama on October 16. Located strategically between the Lincoln and Jefferson memorials and adjacent to the FDR Memorial, the crescent-shaped King Memorial sits on a 4-acre site on the curved bank of the Tidal Basin. You enter either from West Basin Drive (by walking through a cutout in a huge boulder, the "Mountain of Despair") or from the Tidal Basin. A 28-foot-tall granite structure (the "Stone of Hope") shows a likeness of King looking out toward Jefferson's statue. The centerpiece stone was carved by Chinese sculptor Lei Yixin. Fittingly, Yixin first read about King's "I Have a Dream" speech at age 10 while visiting the Lincoln Memorial. The themes of democracy, justice, hope, and love are reflected through quotes on the south and north walls and on the Stone of Hope. ⊠ *1964 Independence Ave. SW, The Mall* ☎ *202/426–6841* ⊕ *www.nps.gov/mlkm* ☒ *Free* Ⓜ *Smithsonian.*

Introduction to the Smithsonian

Be amazed by the history of air and space travel, then explore the 1903 *Wright Flyer* that Wilbur and Orville Wright piloted over the sands of Kitty Hawk, North Carolina, in the National Air and Space Museum. Imagine yourself as Thomas Jefferson composing documents at his "writing box" or as Julia Child cooking in her perfect kitchen—both are on display at the National Museum of American History.

Thought-provoking modern art is on view at the constantly changing Hirshhorn Museum, where you'll see Roy Lichtenstein's 32-foot yellow cartoon sculpture in the outdoor sculpture garden and Yoko Ono's *Sky TV for Washington* inside the museum, or see the only Leonardo da Vinci painting in the United States at the National Gallery of Art West Building.

Visiting the Smithsonian

Most of the 19 Smithsonian museums are open daily between 10 am and 5:30 pm (with at least four or five closed days per year for major holidays), and all are free, though there are sometimes charges for special exhibits. During the spring and summer, many of the museums offer extended hours, closing as late as 7:30 pm. To get oriented, start with a visit to the Smithsonian building—aka the "Castle," for its towers-and-turrets architecture—which has information on all the museums. The museum also has a free app to help you explore the collections and buildings, but it has limited functionality.

Special Events

Smithsonian museums regularly host an incredible spectrum of special events, from evenings of jazz and dance nights to food and wine tastings, films, lectures, and events for families and kids. A full schedule is available at ⊕ *www.si.edu/events*. Popular events include live jazz on Friday evenings in summer at the National Gallery of Art sculpture garden and Take Five performances every third Thursday at the Smithsonian American Art Museum. The National Museum of the American Indian often holds weekend festivals that showcase the history and culture of indigenous peoples from the around the world, complete with workshops, film screenings, hands-on activities for all ages, craft shows, and cooking demonstrations.

Museum of the Bible

MUSEUM | Seven floors encompassing over 430,000 square feet are all dedicated to the history, narrative, and impact of the Bible on the world. The *illumiNations* exhibit displays Bibles in more than 2,000 languages, and visitors can touch, read, and explore them and other illuminated manuscripts. The museum includes exhibits focused on modern films, speakers, fashion, and technology to tell the story of the Bible's continuing influence today. Here you can also see the papyrus featuring early copies of the New Testament, biblically inspired designer clothing, and even Elvis Presley's Bible. Stop by the Manna restaurant for biblically themed foods and other Mediterranean-inspired meals. This museum was founded and funded in part by Steve Green, CEO of the Hobby Lobby craft-store chain. ⊠ *400 4th St. SW, The Mall* ☎ *866/430–6682* ⊕ *www.museumofthebible.org* ᗒ *$25* Ⓜ *Smithsonian*.

★ National Archives Museum

LIBRARY | FAMILY | Monument, museum, and the nation's memory, the National Archives preserves more than 12 billion paper records dating from as far back as 1774, as well as billions of recent electronic records. The so-called Charters of Freedom—the Declaration of Independence, the Constitution, and the Bill of Rights—are the star attractions and are housed in the archives' cathedral-like rotunda, each on a marble platform and encased in bulletproof glass. On display at the entrance to the David M. Rubenstein Gallery is a 1297 Magna Carta, the document of English common law whose language inspired the Constitution; one of four remaining originals, it sets the stage for the gallery's interactive *Records of Rights* exhibits, which trace the civil rights struggles of African Americans, women, and immigrants. Highlights include the discharge papers of a slave who fought in the Revolutionary War to gain his freedom; the mark-up copy of the 1964 Civil Rights Act; and letters to the president from children who questioned segregation. You can also find records that give a glimpse into federal investigations, from the Lincoln assassination to Watergate. ⊠ *Constitution Ave., between 7th and 9th Sts., Washington* ☎ *866/272–6272, 877/444–6777 tours and reservations* ⊕ *www.archives.gov* ⛔ *Free; $1 fee for reservations* Ⓜ *Archives–Navy Memorial–Penn Quarter.*

National Gallery of Art, East Building

MUSEUM | The National Gallery's East Building opened in 1978 in response to the museum's changing needs, especially to house a growing collection of modern and contemporary art. The building itself is a modern masterpiece. The trapezoidal shape of the site prompted architect I.M. Pei's dramatic approach and inside the ax-blade-like southwest corner, the sunlit atrium is dominated by a colorful, 76-foot-long Alexander Calder mobile. Visitors can view a dynamic 500-piece collection of photography, paintings, sculpture, works on paper, and media arts in thought-provoking chronological, thematic, and stylistic arrangements. Don't miss Katharina Fritsch's *Hahn/Cock, 2013,* a tall blue rooster that appears to stand guard over the street and federal buildings from the roof terrace, which also offers views of the Capitol. The upper-level gallery showcases modern art from 1910 to 1980, including masterpieces by Marcel Duchamp, Henri Matisse, Joan Miró, Jackson Pollock, and Andy Warhol. Ground-level galleries are devoted to American art from 1900 to 1950, including pieces by George Bellows, Edward Hopper, and Georgia O'Keeffe. The concourse level is reserved for rotating special exhibitions. ⊠ *Constitution Ave., between 3rd and 4th Sts. NW, The Mall* ☎ *202/737–4215* ⊕ *www. nga.gov* ⛔ *Free* Ⓜ *Archives–Navy Memorial–Penn Quarter.*

National Gallery of Art, West Building

MUSEUM | The historic West Building of the National Gallery opened in 1941, a gift to the nation from treasury secretary Andrew W. Mellon. The rotunda, with marble columns surrounding a fountain, sets the stage for the masterpieces on display in more than 100 galleries. *Ginevra de' Benci,* the only painting by Leonardo da Vinci on display in the Americas, is the centerpiece of the collection's comprehensive survey of Italian Renaissance paintings and sculpture. Rembrandt van Rijn and Johannes Vermeer, masters of painting light, anchor the magnificent collection of Dutch and Flemish works. The 19th-century French Galleries house gorgeous Impressionist masterworks by such superstars as Vincent van Gogh, Paul Cézanne, Claude Monet, Auguste Renoir, and Edgar Degas. Walk beneath flowering trees in the sculpture garden on the Mall between 7th and 9th Streets. Granite walkways guide you through a shaded landscape featuring works from the gallery's growing collection, as well as loans for special exhibitions.

Continued on page 74

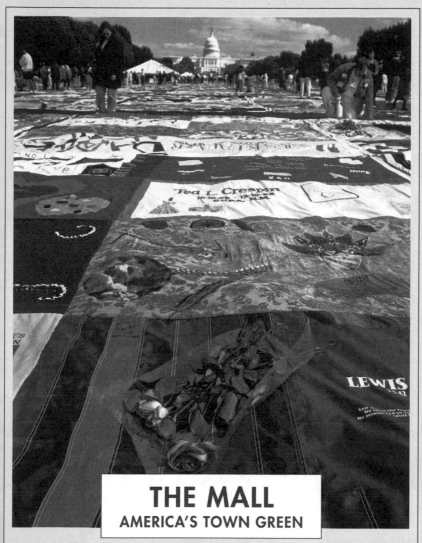

THE MALL
AMERICA'S TOWN GREEN

It could be said that the Mall—the heart of almost every visitor's trip to Washington—has influenced life in the U.S. more than any other expanse of lawn. The Mall is a picnicking park, a jogging path, and an outdoor stage for festivals and fireworks. People come here from around the globe to tour the illustrious Smithsonian museums, celebrate special events, or rally to make the world a better place.

The AIDS Memorial Quilt on the Mall in 1996.

FROM TRASH HEAP TO TOURIST ATTRACTION: A BRIEF HISTORY OF THE MALL

Even before becoming the birthplace of American political protest, the Mall was a hotly contested piece of real estate. More than a century of setbacks and debate resulted not in Pierre L'Enfant's vision of a house-lined boulevard, but rather the premier green space you see today.

In 1791, Pierre Charles L'Enfant designed Washington, D.C., with a mile-long Grand Avenue running west from the Congress building. According to his plan, the boulevard would be lined with homes for statesmen and open green spaces, including a central garden bordered by a dense grove of trees.

L'Enfant's grandiose plan took more than 100 years to become a reality. By 1850, the area we now know as the Mall had not become a park, but was used instead as a storage area for lumber, firewood, and trash. With President Fillmore's permission, a group of businessmen hired landscape designer Andrew Jackson Downing to plan a national park featuring natural-style gardening. Sadly, Downing was killed in 1852, and his plan was never fully implemented.

Despite this setback, progress continued. The first Smithsonian museum on the Mall, the National Museum (now the Arts and Industries Building), opened to the public in 1881, and after 35 years of construction, the Washington Monument was completed in 1884.

A victory for the Mall occurred in 1901, when the Senate Park Commission, or McMillan Commission, was created to redesign the Mall as the city's ceremonial center. The McMillan plan embraced L'Enfant's vision of formal, public spaces and civic art, but replaced his Grand Avenue with a 300-foot expanse of grass bordered by American elms. It also called for cultural and educational institutions to line the Mall. Finally, a modified version of L'Enfant's great open space would become a reality.

The National Park Service assumed management of the Mall in 1933. In the latter half of the twentieth century and into the twenty-first, new museums and monuments have opened on the Mall to create the public gathering place, tourist attraction, and tribute to our nation's heroes that we know today.

Top, Martin Luther King Jr. delivers his "I Have a Dream" speech. Center, Vietnam War Veterans protest. Bottom, Million Man March.

HISTORIC RALLIES ON THE MALL

1894: Coxey's Army, a group of unemployed workers from Ohio, stage the first-ever protest march on Washington.

1939: Contralto Marian Anderson gives an Easter Sunday concert on the grounds of the Lincoln Memorial after the Daughters of the American Revolution bar her from performing at their headquarters.

1963: The Lincoln Memorial is the site of Martin Luther King Jr.'s inspirational I Have a Dream speech.

1971: The Vietnam Veterans Against the War camp out on the Mall to persuade Congress to end military actions in Southeast Asia.

1972: The first Earth Day is celebrated on April 22.

1987: The AIDS Memorial Quilt is displayed for the first time in its entirety. It returns to the Mall in 1988, 1989, 1992, and 1996.

1995: Nearly 400,000 African-American men fill the Mall, from the Capitol to the Washington Monument, during the Million Man March.

2009: The inauguration of President Barack Obama brings a record two million onlookers to the Mall.

2017: The Women's March on January 21, 2017, the day after President Donald Trump's inauguration, was the largest single-day protest in U.S. history.

WHAT ABOUT THE MONUMENTS?

Visitors often confuse the Mall with the similarly named National Mall. The Mall is the expanse of lawn between 3rd and 14th Streets, while the National Mall is the national park that spans from the Capitol to the Potomac, including the Mall, the monuments, and the Tidal Basin. To reach the monuments, head west from the Mall or south from the White House and be prepared for a long walk. To visit all the monuments in one day requires marathon-level stamina and good walking shoes. You're better off choosing your top priorities. Better may be to take a guided coach tour, or one at night.

TOP 15 THINGS
TO DO ON THE MALL

1. Ride the old-fashioned carousel in front of the Smithsonian Castle.

2. Watch the fireworks on the Fourth of July.

3. See the original Spirit of St. Louis, and then learn how things fly at the National Air and Space Museum.

4. Gross out your friends at the Natural History Museum's Insect Zoo.

5. Gawk at Dorothy's ruby slippers, Julia Child's kitchen, Abraham Lincoln's top hat, and Lewis and Clark's compass at the American History Museum.

6. Twirl around the ice skating rink in the National Gallery of Art's sculpture garden.

7. View astonishing wooden masks at the Museum of African Art.

8. Taste North, South, and Central American dishes at the National Museum of the American Indian's Mitsitam Café.

9. Exercise your First Amendment rights by joining a rally or protest.

10. Peek at the many-armed and elephant-headed statues of Hindu gods at the Sackler Gallery.

11. Pose with sculptures by Auguste Rodin and Henry Moore at the Hirshhorn Sculpture Garden.

12. Learn how to make money—literally—at the Bureau of Engraving and Printing.

13. Follow the lives of the people who lived and died in Nazi Germany at the Holocaust Memorial Museum.

14. Visit the newest museum, the National Museum of African American History and Culture.

15. Picnic and people-watch on the lawn after a hard day of sightseeing.

Stop the racist war on Arabs and Muslims
socialistworker.org

VISITING THE MUSEUMS ON THE MALL

MAKE THE MOST OF YOUR TIME

With 13 museums spread out along 11 city blocks, you can't expect to see everything in one day. Few people have the stamina for more than half a day of museum- or gallery-hopping at a time; children definitely don't. To avoid mental and physical exhaustion, try to devote at least two days to the Mall and use these itineraries to make the best use of your time.

Historical Appeal: For a day devoted to history and culture, start with the **National Archives,** grabbing lunch at its café. After refueling, the next stop is the **National Museum of American History.** Or, visit the **National Museum of the American Indian** or the **United States Holocaust Memorial Museum.** It takes planning, but a trip to the **National Museum of African American History and Culture** is a don't-miss experience.

Art Start: To fill a day with paintings and sculptures, begin at the **National Gallery of Art.** Enjoy the museum's sculptures while you dine in the garden's outdoor café. You'll find a second sculpture garden directly across the Mall at the **Hirshhorn.** If you like the avant-garde, visit the Hirshhorn's indoor galleries; for a cosmopolitan collection of Asian and African art and artifacts, head instead to the **Sackler Gallery** and **Museum of African Art.**

Taking the Kids: The most kid-friendly museum of them all, the **National Air and Space Museum** is a must-see for the young and young-at-heart. There's only fast food in the museum, but the **Museum of the American Indian** next door has healthier options. If your young bunch can handle two museums in a day, cross the lawn to the **Natural History Museum.** This itinerary works well for science buffs, too.

THE BEST IN A DAY

Got one day and want to see the best of the Smithsonian? Start at the **Air and Space Museum,** then skip to the side-by-side **Natural History** and **American History Museums.** Picnic on the Mall or hit the museum cafeterias.

NOT ANOTHER HOT DOG! A Survival Guide to Eating Well on the Mall

Even locals wonder where to grab a decent bite to eat when touring the Smithsonian Museums. Hot dogs, soft pretzels, and ice cream from a cart don't make for a nutritious lunch. On a weekday, the streets north of Constitution Avenue offer easy-to-find lunch spots, but virtually all are closed on weekends.

Here are some places for better dining by the Mall, though several require a few blocks' walk.

On the Fly food carts offer eco-friendly, often organic snacks. Find one by the Sackler Gallery.

Museum of the American Indian: The Mitsitam Café—the name means "let's eat" in the language of the Delaware and Piscataway people—is one of the best museum cafeterias on the Mall. Food stations serve native-inspired sandwiches, entrees, soups, and desserts from five regions of the western hemisphere.

Pavilion Café: Located in the **National Gallery's Sculpture Garden,** this eatery offers indoor and outdoor seating with views of the artwork and fountain/ice rink outside. The menu includes salads, sandwiches, and pizzas. You'll also find more food options inside the National Gallery.

Pennsylvania Avenue SE: If lunchtime finds you on the east end of the Mall, head past the Capitol to Pennsylvania Avenue SE. Between Second and Fourth Streets, you'll find plenty of pubs, cafés, and sandwich shops. It's a bit of a hike, but well worth the shoe leather.

National Museum of Natural History: Three high-quality restaurants focus on healthy, seasonal food, drinks, and desserts.

National Museum of African American History and Culture: Sweet Home Cafe, which serves diverse regional American cuisine, is among the best places to eat on the Mall.

ANNUAL EVENTS

The Mall's spacious lawn is ideal for all kinds of outdoor festivals. These annual events are local favorites and definitely worth a stop if you're in town while they're happening.

St. Patrick's Day Parade

WINTER

Ice Skating: Whirl and twirl at the outdoor ice rink in the National Gallery of Art's Sculpture Garden. *Mid-November through mid-March.*

St. Patrick's Day Parade: Dancers, bands, and bagpipes celebrate all things Irish along Constitution Avenue. *Mid-March.*

SPRING

National Cherry Blossom Festival: When the cherry trees burst into bloom, you know that spring has arrived. Fly a kite, watch a parade, and learn about Japanese culture in a setting sprinkled with pink and white flowers. *Late March through early April.*

Cherry Blossom Festival

SUMMER

Smithsonian Folklife Festival: Performers, cooks, farmers, and craftsmen demonstrate cultural traditions from around the world. *Around July 4.*

Independence Day: What better place to celebrate the birth of our nation than in the capital city? Enjoy concerts and parades on the Mall, then watch the fireworks explode over the Washington Monument. *July 4.*

Smithsonian Folklife Festival

Screen on the Green: Film favorites are shown on a gigantic movie screen on Monday nights. Bring a blanket and picnic dinner to better enjoy the warm summer evenings. *Mid-July through mid-August.*

FALL

Black Family Reunion: D.C. celebrates African-American family values. Pavilions showcase businesses owned by African-Americans and events and performances feature black entertainers, celebrities, and experts. *September.*

Independence Day Reenactment

National Book Festival: Meet your favorite author in person at the Library of Congress' annual literary festival. Over 70 writers and illustrators participate in readings, live interviews, and events for kids. *September.*

Marine Corps Marathon: The "Marathon of the Monuments" starts in Virginia but winds its way around the entire National Mall. It's as fun to cheer as it is to run. *Late October.*

Marine Corps Marathon

PLANNING YOUR VISIT

National Cherry Blossom Festival Parade

KEEP IN MIND

■ All of the museums on the Mall are free to the public.

■ Since September 11, 2001 security has increased, and visitors will need to go through screenings and bag checks, which create long lines during peak tourist season.

■ Two museums require timed-entry passes: the Holocaust Museum from March through August, and the Bureau of Printing and Engraving. If you've got a jam-packed day planned, it's best to get your tickets early in the morning or in advance.

GETTING HERE AND AROUND

Metro: You can access the Mall from several Metro stations. On the Blue and Orange lines, the Federal Triangle stop is convenient to the Natural History and American History museums, and the Smithsonian stop is close to the Holocaust Memorial Museum and Sackler Gallery. On the Yellow and Green lines, Archives/Navy Memorial takes you to the National Gallery of Art. The L'Enfant Plaza stop, accessible from the Blue, Orange, Yellow, and Green lines, is the best exit for the Hirshhorn and Air and Space Museum.

Bus: Walking from the Holocaust Memorial Museum to the National Gallery of Art is quite a trek. Many visitors take advantage of the D.C. Circulator National Mall Route buses that cost just $1 and run daily.

Car: Parking is hard to find along the Mall. You can find private parking garages north of the Mall in the Downtown area, where you'll have to pay to leave your car. If you're willing to walk, limited free parking is available on Ohio Drive SW near the Jefferson Memorial and East Potomac Park.

HELP, THERE'S A PROTEST ON THE MALL!

Since the 1890s, protesters have gathered on the Mall to make their opinions known. If you're not in a rallying mood, you don't have to let First Amendment activities prevent you from visiting the Smithsonian museums or enjoying a visit to the Mall.

■ **Use the back door:** All of the Smithsonian museums have entrances on Constitution or Independence Avenues, which do not border the Mall's lawn. Use these doors to gain admission without crossing the Mall itself.

■ **Know you're protected:** The Mall is a national park, just like Yosemite or Yellowstone. The National Park Service has a responsibility to visitors to make sure they can safely view park attractions. To this end, demonstrators are often required to keep main streets open.

■ **Avoid the crowds:** Even the biggest rallies don't cover the entire National Mall. If the crowd is by the Capitol, head west to visit the Lincoln Memorial. If protestors are gathered around the Washington Monument, visit the Jefferson Memorial on the opposite side of the Tidal Basin. There's plenty to see.

⊠ *4th St. and Constitution Ave. NW, The Mall* 🕿 *202/737–4215* ⊕ *www.nga.gov* 🎫 *Free* Ⓜ *Archives–Navy Memorial–Penn Quarter.*

★ National Museum of African American History and Culture

MUSEUM | Washington's newest and most powerful museum may also be the most recognized structure on the Mall, with its bronze corona and filigree design. Spanning six floors, the museum's 12 exhibitions display nearly 3,000 objects. Sixty percent of the museum is underground, while 40% is aboveground. Underground exhibits showcase a somber and wrenching historical time line from slavery through the civil rights movement and modern political change. Aboveground, galleries celebrate the cultural contributions of African Americans. To best experience this museum, start at the underground Concourse History Galleries. There's a 350-seat theater in the main concourse and a Center for African American Media Arts on the second floor. Among the memorabilia are Michael Jackson's sequined jacket, Muhammad Ali's robe, Gabby Douglas's leotard, and Louis Armstrong's trumpet. You must have a timed pass to enter the museum; same-day passes are available online daily beginning at 6:30 am, and a limited number of walk-up passes are given out weekdays beginning at 1 pm, but they go fast. Otherwise reserve a spot months in advance. Download the helpful app. ⊠ *1400 Constitution Ave. NW, The Mall* ✛ *14th and Constitution Ave. NW* 🕿 *202/633–1000, 844/750–3012 for timed-entry passes only* ⊕ *www. nmaahc.si.edu* 🎫 *Free* Ⓜ *Smithsonian or Federal Triangle.*

National Museum of the American Indian

MUSEUM | Visually and conceptually, the National Museum of the American Indian stands apart from the other cultural institutions on the Mall. The exterior, clad in Minnesota limestone, evokes a sense that the building was carved by wind and water. Inside, four floors of galleries cover 10,000 years of history of the western hemisphere's indigenous tribes. However, only 5% of the museum's holdings are on display at any one time. Touring with one of the "cultural interpreters" helps bring the history and legends to life. Live music, dance, theater, and storytelling are central to experiencing this museum. Tribal groups stage performances in the Rasmuson Theater and sunlit Potomac atrium. Visit between 11 and 2 on a sunny day to see the Potomac atrium awash in rainbows created by the light refracted through prisms in the southern wall. Free tours are offered weekdays at 1:30, and the museum's family-friendly imagiNATIONS Activity Center includes hands-on activities throughout the year. ⊠ *4th St. and Independence Ave. SW, The Mall* 🕿 *202/633–1000* ⊕ *www.americanindian. si.edu* 🎫 *Free* Ⓜ *L'Enfant Plaza.*

Old Post Office Pavilion

CLOCK | Although the building is now the Trump International Hotel, the Old Post Office Tower (which is within the hotel) is still open for public tours through the National Park Service. The building, a symbol of the modern American spirit when it was constructed in 1899, was the first government edifice to have its own electric power plant. Now, tourists can see the 360-degree view from the top of the tower, the second-tallest building in D.C. Tours (from 9 to 5 daily with the last entry at 4:30) are free, but tour guests must enter through a specified entrance for the general public. ⊠ *Trump International Hotel, 1100 Pennsylvania Ave. NW, The Mall* 🕿 *202/289–4224* ⊕ *www.nps.gov* Ⓜ *Federal Triangle.*

Ronald Reagan Building and International Trade Center

GOVERNMENT BUILDING | At more than 3 million square feet, this is the largest federal building in Washington, and the only property dedicated to both government and private entities. A blend of classical

Did You Know?

Within the National Museum of African American History and Culture you'll find a collection of the country's most moving and powerful exhibits. If necessary, you can take time to emotionally recharge within the Reflection Room, where a glass structure called the oculus allows light in from above and a waterfall effect offers a quiet space for contemplation.

and modern architecture, the center welcomes over a million visitors annually and is officially the World Trade Center, Washington, D.C. The Reagan Building, which hosts special events throughout the year, is home to a permanent art collection—one that includes a section of the Berlin Wall—and the Woodrow Wilson Presidential Memorial Exhibit and Learning Center. It's also a popular place to get married, thanks to its great views over the city. If you're hungry, pick up something from one of the 20 eateries in the spacious food court on the concourse level. In summer, check out Live!, a free concert series, performed daily from noon to 1:30. A farmers' market takes over the plaza on Friday from the spring to the fall. ⊠ *1300 Pennsylvania Ave. NW, Washington* ☎ *202/312–1300* ⊕ *www. itcdc.com* ⊠ *Free* Ⓜ *Federal Triangle.*

Smithsonian Castle Information Center

MUSEUM | The original home of the Smithsonian Institution is an excellent first stop on the Mall to get your bearings and plan your exploration of the museums. Built of red sandstone, this Medieval Revival–style building, better known as the "Castle," was designed by James Renwick Jr., architect of St. Patrick's Cathedral in New York City. British scientist and founder James Smithson left his entire fortune "to found at Washington, under the name of the Smithsonian Institution, an establishment for the increase and diffusion of knowledge," resulting in the many museums lining the Mall. A 10-minute video gives an overview of the museums and the National Zoo, and *The Smithsonian Institution: America's Treasure Chest* exhibition features objects representing all the museums, revealing the breadth and depth of the collections. Outside the north entrance stands the historic carousel, while the Haupt Garden surrounds the south entrance. ⊠ *1000 Jefferson Dr. SW, The Mall* ☎ *202/633–1000* ⊕ *www. si.edu* ⊠ *Free* Ⓜ *Smithsonian.*

★ Smithsonian National Air and Space Museum

MUSEUM | The country's second-most-visited museum has the world's largest collection of historic aircraft and spacecraft. The 23 galleries tell the story of aviation from the earliest human attempts at flight to supersonic jets and spacecraft. Among the most notable artifacts is the 1903 *Wright Flyer* that Wilbur and Orville Wright piloted over the sands of Kitty Hawk, North Carolina, and the *Spirit of Saint Louis,* which was flown across the Atlantic by Charles Lindbergh. You can even climb into one of the museum's six motion simulators, or immerse yourself in space by taking in an IMAX film. Free docent-led tours leave daily at 10:30 am and 1 pm from the museum's welcome center. Although the museum has begun a multiyear renovation to update and redesign all of its galleries by 2025, it will remain open throughout the whole process, closing only construction areas. ⊠ *Independence Ave. at 6th St. SW, The Mall* ☎ *202/633–1000, 866/868–7774 movie information* ⊕ *www.airandspace. si.edu* ⊠ *Free; IMAX or planetarium $9; IMAX feature film $15; flight simulators from $7* Ⓜ *Smithsonian.*

Smithsonian National Museum of African Art

MUSEUM | FAMILY | This unique underground building houses stunning galleries, a library, photographic archives, and educational facilities that are dedicated to collecting, conserving, and studying Africa's arts and culture from a wide variety of media and eras. The rotating exhibits illuminate African visual arts, including sculpture, textiles, photography, archaeology, and modern art. *Currents: Water in African Art* showcases the power of art through pieces like intricately carved wooden masks and figures paying tribute to water spirits and deities. In *Heroes: Principles of African Greatness,* artists tells the stories of key figures in Africa's art and history, making explicit a core value that their life embodied. The museum's educational programs for both children and adults include films with contemporary perspectives on African life, storytelling programs, and festivals including Community Day. The hands-on workshops, such as traditional basket weaving, bring Africa's oral and cultural traditions to life. Workshops and demonstrations by African and African American artists offer a chance to meet and talk to practicing artists. ⊠ *950 Independence Ave. SW, The Mall* ☎ *202/633–4600* ⊕ *africa.si.edu* ✉ *Free* Ⓜ *Smithsonian.*

★ Smithsonian National Museum of American History

MUSEUM | FAMILY | The 3 million artifacts and archival materials in the country's largest American history museum explore America's cultural, political and scientific past. The centerpiece of the **Star-Spangled Banner** gallery is the banner that in 1814 was hoisted to show that Fort McHenry had survived 25 hours of British rocket attacks and inspired Francis Scott Key to write the lyrics that became the national anthem. Exhibits showcasing modern America include *Girlhood (It's Complicated)* and an exploration of the suffrage movement. From April 1, 2021, there will also be an exhibit on Latinos and baseball. ⊠ *Constitution Ave. and 14th St. NW, The Mall* ☎ *202/633–1000* ⊕ *www.americanhistory.si.edu* ✉ *Free* Ⓜ *Smithsonian or Federal Triangle.*

Smithsonian National Museum of Natural History

MUSEUM | FAMILY | One of the world's great natural history museums offers 18 exhibition halls—including a fully renovated Dinosaur and Fossil Hall, which opened in June 2019—filled with not only fossils, but also glittering gems, creepy-crawly insects, and other natural wonders. There are more than 145 million specimens in the collection. Marvel at the enormous African bush elephant, which greets you in the rotunda, and learn about elephant behavior and conservation efforts. Discover **Q?RIUS,**

a state-of-the-art, discovery space for all ages featuring 6,000 objects, on-site experts, and an array of digital tools that focus on the natural world. Walk among hundreds of live butterflies in the **Butterfly Pavilion** ($7.50). Check out giant millipedes and furry tarantulas in the **O. Orkin Insect Zoo** (don't miss the daily live tarantula feedings). See perfectly preserved giant squids, a jaw-dropping replica of a whale, and the ecosystem of a living coral reef in the **Sant Ocean Hall**. Watch as paleobiologists study some of the museum's collection of 46 million fossils, which includes the nation's T. rex found in Montana in 1988. ⊠ *Constitution Ave. and 10th St. NW, The Mall* ☎ *202/633–1000* ⊕ *www.mnh.si.edu* ✉ *Free; Butterfly Pavilion $6 (free Tues.)* Ⓜ *Smithsonian or Federal Triangle.*

★ Thomas Jefferson Memorial

MEMORIAL | In the 1930s, Congress decided to build a monument to Thomas Jefferson as prominent as the Washington and Lincoln memorials. Workers scooped and moved tons of the river bottom to create dry land for the spot due south of the White House where the monument was built. Jefferson had always admired the Pantheon in Rome, so the memorial's architect, John Russell Pope, drew on it for inspiration. His finished work was dedicated on April 13, 1943, the bicentennial of Jefferson's birth. The bronze statue of Jefferson stands on a 6-foot granite pedestal. Surrounding the statue are his writings about freedom, which have since come under scrutiny for their inherent hypocrisy, as Jefferson owned many slaves in his lifetime. The Smithsonian National Museum of African American History and Culture delves into Jefferson's transgressions in its Monticello exhibit, *Paradox of Liberty.* ⊠ *Tidal Basin, south bank, off Ohio Dr. SW, The Mall* ☎ *202/426–6841* ⊕ *www.nps.gov/thje* ✉ *Free* Ⓜ *Smithsonian.*

The United States Holocaust Memorial Museum is the country's official memorial remembering those lost in the Holocaust.

★ Tidal Basin

NATIONAL/STATE PARK | FAMILY | The Tidal Basin, a partially man-made reservoir between the Potomac and the Washington Channel, is part of West Potomac Park, adjacent to the Mall. It's the setting for memorials to Thomas Jefferson, Franklin Delano Roosevelt, Martin Luther King Jr., and George Mason. Two gargoyles on the sides of the Inlet Bridge can be seen as you walk along the sidewalk that hugs the basin. The inside walls of the bridge also feature two other sculptures: bronze, human-headed fish that once spouted water from their mouths. Sculptor Constantin Sephralis, who also worked on the National Cathedral, made them in honor of John Fish, the chief of the park, who was retiring at the time. Once you cross the bridge, continue along the Tidal Basin to the right. This route is especially scenic when the famous cherry trees are in bloom. The trees, a gift from the Japanese during the administration of William Howard Taft, are perhaps the Tidal Basin's most iconic feature beyond the memorials.

✉ *Bordered by Independence and Maine Aves., The Mall* Ⓜ *Smithsonian.*

★ United States Holocaust Memorial Museum

MUSEUM | This "living museum" asks you to consider how the Holocaust was made possible by the choices of individuals, institutions, and governments, as it presents the histories of some 6 million Jews and millions of others who died under Nazi Germany. The permanent exhibition spans over three floors to chronicle the rise of Nazi power and offer a chronological narrative of the Holocaust through artifacts, photographs, and film. Two places of remembrance challenge you to reflect on the relevance of the Holocaust today. The Wexner Center has exhibitions on genocide throughout the world, and the special exhibition *Americans & the Holocaust* is a portrait of the responses to the Holocaust in America. Timed-entry passes (distributed on a first-come, first-served basis at the 14th Street entrance starting at 9:45 or in advance through the museum's website)

DC's Famed Cherry Blossoms

The first batch of ornamental cherry trees arrived from Japan in 1909, but they were infected with insects and fungus, and the Department of Agriculture ordered them destroyed. A diplomatic crisis was averted when the United States politely asked the Japanese for another batch, and, in 1912, First Lady Helen Taft planted the first tree. The second was planted by the wife of the Japanese ambassador, Viscountess Chinda. There are 3,750 total trees around the Tidal Basin, some of which are considered original from 1912.

The trees are now the centerpiece of Washington's three-week **National Cherry Blossom Festival**, held each spring since 1935. The festivities are kicked off by the lighting of a ceremonial Japanese lantern, which rests on the north shore of the Tidal Basin, not far from where the first tree was planted. The celebration has grown over the years to include concerts, a running race, a kite festival, and a parade. The trees are usually in bloom for about 12 days in late March or early April. When winter will not release its grip, parade and festival take place without the presence of blossoms.

are necessary for the permanent exhibition from March through August, but allow extra time for lines in the spring and summer. No passes are required from September through February. ✉ *100 Raoul Wallenberg Pl. SW, at 14th St. SW, The Mall* ☎ *202/488–0400, 800/400–9373 for tickets* ⊕ *www.ushmm.org* 🎟 *Free; $1 per ticket service fee for advance online reservations* Ⓜ *Smithsonian.*

★ Vietnam Veterans Memorial

MEMORIAL | "The Wall," as it's commonly called, is one of the most visited sites in Washington. The names of more than 58,000 Americans who died in the Vietnam War are etched in its black granite panels. The memorial was conceived by Jan Scruggs, a corporal who served in Vietnam, and designed by Maya Lin, a then 21-year-old architecture student at Yale. In 1984, Frederick Hart's statue of three soldiers and a flagpole was erected to the south of the wall, and in 2004, a plaque was added to honor veterans who died after the war as a direct result of injuries in Vietnam. The Vietnam Women's Memorial, dedicated in 1993, consists of a bronze sculpture created by Glenna Goodacre. Names on the wall are

ordered by date of death. To find a name, consult the lists found at either end or ask at the white kiosk near the entrance. At the wall, rangers and volunteers wearing yellow caps can look up the names and supply you with paper and pencils for making rubbings. ✉ *Constitution Gardens, 23rd St. NW and Constitution Ave. NW, The Mall* ☎ *202/426–6841* ⊕ *www.nps.gov/vive* 🎟 *Free* Ⓜ *Foggy Bottom–GWU.*

Washington Monument

MEMORIAL | The top of the Washington Monument is perhaps the best, most breathtaking place to see the city and get a good idea of its layout.

The 555-foot, 5⅛-inch monument, which punctuates the capital like a huge exclamation point, was part of Pierre L'Enfant's plan for Washington, but his intended location proved to be so marshy that the structure was moved 100 yards southeast. Construction began in 1848 and continued until 1884. Upon completion, the monument was the world's tallest structure and weighed more than 81,000 tons. Six years into construction, members of the anti-Catholic

Every Memorial Day, thousands flock to the Vietnam Veterans Memorial to pay their respects to those lost in the conflict.

Know-Nothing Party stole and smashed a block of marble donated by Pope Pius IX. This action, combined with funding shortages and the onset of the Civil War, brought construction to a halt. After the war, building finally resumed, and though the new marble came from the same Maryland quarry as the old, it was taken from a different stratum with a slightly different shade. Inserted into the walls of the monument are 193 memorial stones from around the world. The monument reopened in spring 2019 after an elevator modernization project. Up to six tickets can be requested for just $1 per person at recreation.gov. ⊠ *15th St. NW, between Constitution Ave. NW and Independence Ave. SW, The Mall* ☎ *202/426–6841, 877/444–6777 for reservations* ⊕ *www.nps.gov/wamo* Ⓜ *Smithsonian.*

West Potomac Park
CITY PARK | FAMILY | Between the Potomac and the Tidal Basin, this park is known for its flowering cherry trees, which bloom for two weeks in late March or

early April, and for a slew of memorials, including those honoring Abraham Lincoln, Martin Luther King Jr., Franklin Delano Roosevelt, Thomas Jefferson, and George Mason, as well as the World War II, Korean War, and Vietnam War Veterans memorials. It's a nice place to play ball, picnic, or just relax while admiring the water views. ⊠ *Bounded by Constitution Ave., 17th St., and Independence Ave., The Mall* ⊕ *www.npca.org.*

World War II Memorial
MEMORIAL | This symmetrically designed monument, in a parklike setting between the Washington Monument and Lincoln Memorial, honors the 16 million Americans who served in the armed forces, the more than 400,000 who died, and all who supported the war effort at home. An imposing circle of 56 granite pillars, each bearing a bronze wreath, represents the United States and its territories of 1941–45. Four bronze eagles, a bronze garland, and two 43-foot-tall arches inscribed with "Atlantic" and "Pacific," representing victory on both fronts,

surround the large circular plaza. The roar of the water comes from the Rainbow Pool, here since the 1920s and renovated to form the centerpiece of the memorial. There are also two fountains and two waterfalls. The Field of Stars, a wall of over 4,000 gold stars, commemorates the more than 400,000 Americans who lost their lives in the war. Bas-relief panels depict women in the military, medics, the bond drive, and V-J Day, all telling the story of how World War II affected Americans daily. ⊠ 17th St. SW and Home Front Dr. SW, between Independence Ave. SW and Constitution Ave. NW, The Mall ☎ 202/426–6841 ⊕ www.nps.gov/nwwm 🎫 Free Ⓜ Smithsonian.

🍴 Restaurants

Dining on the Mall is not what it used to be, with museums constantly upping the game. The National Museum of African American History and Culture, the National Gallery of Art, and the National Museum of the American Indian are leading the charge for dining experiences on the Mall. For a quick bite, stop at one of the many food trucks sprinkled around the Mall, or head over to L'Enfant Plaza for fast food. If you are on the northeastern end of the Mall, it may be closer to walk north to the Penn Quarter.

Garden Café

$$ | AMERICAN | After marveling at the masterpieces in the National Gallery West Building, sit down in a lovely open courtyard, complete with a fountain. The Garden Café features a hybrid counter service offering breakfast, lunch, and late-day bites, including sandwiches, salads, and cheese and charcuterie plates. **Known for:** cheese and charcuterie plates; a lovely setting; locally crafted beer. Ⓢ Average main: $12 ⊠ National Gallery of Art, West Building, 6th and Constitution Ave. NW, The Mall ♣ Enter at 6th St. ☎ 202/842–6716, 202/712–7453 reservations ⊕ www.nga.gov/visit/cafes/garden-cafe.html 🕙 No

dinner Ⓜ Archives–Navy Memorial–Penn Quarter.

Manna

$$ | **MEDITERRANEAN** | This museum restaurant is a foray into the past with a menu full of dishes with biblically inspired names like A Taste of Canaan, Revelations, and Exodus. The reality is that chef Todd Gray has created a menu filled with traditional falafel, lamb meatballs, and roasted eggplant over sides of marinated chickpeas and tabbouleh with pistachios and dates. **Known for:** Mediterranean-inspired cuisine with biblical names; Sunday gospel brunch; open-seating concept. Ⓢ Average main: $19 ⊠ Museum of the Bible, 400 4th St. SW, The Mall ☎ 855/554–5300 ⊕ www.museumofthebible.org/museum/dining 🕙 No dinner Ⓜ Federal Center SW.

Mitsitam Native Foods Cafe

$$ | **AMERICAN** | The food stations here offer both traditional and contemporary Native American dishes from throughout the western hemisphere. Executive chef Freddie Bitsoie offers seasonal menus from five regional cuisines, expanding the museum experience with insight into indigenous culinary history, cooking techniques, ingredients, and flavors. **Known for:** seasonal cuisine from different indigenous cultures; fry bread and corn totopos; cafeteria-style food stations. Ⓢ Average main: $17 ⊠ National Museum of the American Indian, 4th St. SW and Independence Ave. SW, The Mall ☎ 202/868–7774 ⊕ www.mitsitamcafe.com 🕙 No dinner Ⓜ Federal Center SW.

Pavilion Café

$ | **CAFÉ** | At the edge of the National Gallery of Art's Sculpture Garden, you can sidle up to the counter and feast your eyes on the menu items before deciding what you'll order at this casual, sit-down eatery. From pastries to anything-but-ordinary salads to hot and cold sandwiches with Southwestern or East Asian flavors, you'll have an array of choices. **Known for:** summer barbecue during Jazz in the Garden; boozy beverages during winter; pastries made fresh in-house. ⑤ *Average main: $11* ✉ *National Gallery Sculpture Garden, Constitution Ave. NW and 7th St., The Mall* ⊕ *At far end of National Gallery of Art Sculpture Garden* ☎ *202/289–3361* ⊕ *www.nga.gov/visit/cafes/pavilion-cafe.html* ☉ *No dinner* Ⓜ *Archives–Navy Memorial–Penn Quarter or L'Enfant Plaza.*

★ Sweet Home Café
$ | AMERICAN | The Mall's newest museum restaurant offers traditional and authentic dishes that rotate based on the seasons. Executive chef Jerome Grant uses locally sourced ingredients and a from-scratch cooking style to showcase the rich history of African American cuisine from four distinct geographic regions. **Known for:** regional food stations; local ingredients; rotating seasonal menus. ⑤ *Average main: $13* ✉ *National Museum of African American History, 1400 Constitution Ave. NW, The Mall* ☎ *202/633–6174* ⊕ *www.nmaahc.si.edu* ☉ *No dinner* Ⓜ *Smithsonian or Federal Triangle.*

Hotels

The Mandarin Oriental stands out in luxury and experience for lodging near the Mall. However, other conveniently located chain hotels can be found in the area around L'Enfant Plaza, immediately south of the Mall, including a Hilton, Hyatt Place, and a Residence Inn.

Hilton Washington DC National Mall
$$$ | HOTEL | A stay at this newly renovated, LEED-certified hotel puts you close to the National Mall, with spectacular river and monument views from certain rooms—all of which have floor-to-ceiling windows. **Pros:** short walk to Smithsonian; nice pool and fitness center; pet-friendly. **Cons:** must use valet parking; area is sleepy at night; few nearby restaurants. ⑤ *Rooms from: $350* ✉ *480 L'Enfant Plaza SW, The*

Mall ☎ *202/484–1000, 202/869–1952* ⊕ *www3.hilton.com* ⮑ *367 rooms* ꣠ *Free Breakfast* Ⓜ *L'Enfant Plaza.*

Holiday Inn Washington-Capitol
$ | HOTEL | FAMILY | One block from the National Air and Space Museum, this family-friendly hotel is in a great location for those bound for the Smithsonian museums. **Pros:** rooftop pool and large deck area; kids eat for free; close to the best museums in town. **Cons:** limited dining options nearby; not much going on in the neighborhood at night; self-parking is available, but expensive. ⑤ *Rooms from: $199* ✉ *550 C St. SW, The Mall* ☎ *202/479–4000* ⊕ *www.hicapitoldc.com* ⮑ *536 rooms* ꣠ *No meals* Ⓜ *L'Enfant Plaza.*

Mandarin Oriental, Washington DC
$$$$ | HOTEL | Offering the maximum in creature comforts on the Mall, the Mandarin is perfect for luxury-seekers who want to visit not only the museums but also the Navy Yard and the Wharf along the southwest waterfront. **Pros:** plenty of luxury; reasonably close to both the Mall and waterfront; fantastic spa, pool, and fitness area. **Cons:** few nearby dining options outside the hotel itself; you'll need to take a car or taxi to get here; rates can be very high during much of the year. ⑤ *Rooms from: $495* ✉ *1330 Maryland Ave. SW, The Mall* ☎ *202/554–8588* ⊕ *www.mandarinoriental.com* ⮑ *397 rooms* ꣠ *No meals* Ⓜ *L'Enfant Plaza.*

Performing Arts

CONCERTS
Armed Forces Concert Series
MUSIC | In a Washington tradition, bands from the four branches of the armed services perform from June through August on weekday evenings on the U.S. Capitol West Front steps. Concerts usually include marches, patriotic numbers, and some classical music. Setup begins

at 4 pm, with the concerts beginning at 8 pm, but look out for scheduling changes or notices on individual bands' social media accounts. Food is permitted, but glass bottles and alcohol are not allowed. ⊠ *U.S. Capitol, Capitol Hill* ⊕ *www.aoc. gov/news/2018-military-bands-sum-mer-concert-series* Ⓜ *Capitol S.*

★ National Gallery of Art Concert Series
CONCERTS | FAMILY | On Friday from 5 to 8:30 pm from mid-May through the end of August, jazz groups from all over the country perform to packed crowds at the Pavilion Café in the Sculpture Garden. Listeners dip their feet in the fountain, sip sangria, and let the week wash away. From October to May, free concerts by the National Gallery Orchestra and performances by visiting recitalists and ensembles are held in the West Build-ing's West Garden Court on Sunday after-noons. Entry is first come, first served, with doors opening at 6 pm and concerts starting at 3:30 pm. Also be sure to check out the gallery's film series. ⊠ *6th St. and Constitution Ave. NW, The Mall* ☎ *202/842–6941* ⊕ *www.nga.gov* Ⓜ *Ar-chives–Navy Memorial–Penn Quarter.*

★ Smithsonian Institution Concert Series
CONCERTS | Throughout the year, the Smithsonian Associates sponsor programs that offer everything from a cappella groups to Cajun zydeco bands; all events require tickets, and locations vary. For an especially memorable musical experience, catch a performance of the Smithsonian Jazz Masterworks Orchestra in residence at the Nation-al Museum of American History. The Smithsonian's annual summer Folklife Festival, held on the Mall, highlights the cuisine, crafts, and day-to-day life of several different cultures. ⊠ *1000 Jeffer-son Dr. SW, The Mall* ☎ *202/357–2700, 202/633–1000 recording, 202/357–3030 Smithsonian Associates* ⊕ *www.si.edu* Ⓜ *Smithsonian.*

FILM
★ National Archives Film Series
FILM | Historical films, usually documenta-ries, are shown here regularly. Screen-ings range from Robert Flaherty's 1942 coverage of the plight of migrant workers to archival footage of Charles Lindbergh's solo flight from New York to Paris. Stroll by and inspect the Constitution and other world-changing documents in this solemn and impressive venue, pop out for dinner, and come back to catch a documentary. ⊠ *Constitution Ave. between 7th and 9th Sts. NW, Washington* ☎ *202/501–5000* ⊕ *www.archives.gov* Ⓜ *Archives–Navy Memorial–Penn Quarter.*

National Gallery of Art Film Series
FILM | Free classic, international, and art films—from Steven Spielberg's first feature-length film, *Duel,* to Béla Tarr's *Macbeth,* which was filmed inside a Budapest castle—as well as classic video art are usually shown in this museum's large auditorium each weekend. Some-times films complement the exhibitions. For more information, pick up a film calendar at the museum or visit their website. ⊠ *National Gallery of Art, East Bldg., Constitution Ave. between 3rd and 4th Sts. NW, The Mall* ☎ *202/842–6799* ⊕ *www.nga.gov* Ⓜ *Archives–Navy Memorial–Penn Quarter.*

🛍 Shopping

Museum Store in the United States Holo-caust Memorial Museum
BOOKS/STATIONERY | This unique museum store offers a slew of books, including memoirs, to further your knowledge of the Holocaust and the plight of other persecuted peoples throughout history. It's also a great place to buy mezuzah scrolls, menorahs, kiddush cups, seder plates, and other Jewish heritage items, as well as secular souvenirs. ⊠ *100 Raoul Wallenberg Pl. SW, The Mall* ☎ *202/488–0400* ⊕ *www.ushmm.org/museum-shop* Ⓜ *Smithsonian.*

★ National Archives Store and Gift Shop

CRAFTS | In a town full of museum shops, this store at the National Archives Museum stands out, with exclusive memorabilia, reproductions, apparel, books, gifts, and plenty of Founding Fathers gear that let you own a piece of history. Authentic-looking copies of the Constitution and other historical documents are printed in Pennsylvania. The popular "red tape" paperweights are crafted in the United States with real red tape that once bound government documents: hence the phrase "cut through the red tape." Other popular products feature Rosie the Riveter and Stars and Stripes bags; Teddy in Hat items for young children; and apparel featuring Franklin, Hamilton, and other Founding Fathers. Throughout the store, interactive games associated with special exhibits provide entertaining insight on U.S. and even personal history: enter your last name into the computer to see how many Americans share your name and where in the country they live. ⊠ Constitution Ave. NW between 7th and 9th Sts., Washington ☎ 202/357–5271 ⊕ www.nationalarchivesstore.org Ⓜ Archives–Navy Memorial–Penn Quarter.

National Gallery of Art West Building Shop

BOOKS/STATIONERY | This expansive shop, one of four in the National Gallery, offers a vast series of books, paper goods, apparel, fine jewelry, and knickknacks that all relate to or reflect the museum's art collection. Prices range from little over a dollar for a pencil to well over $100 for designer jewelry. Some items were created by the museum; the rest are specially curated and sourced by museum buyers. Grab a Monet umbrella on a rainy day or some Andy Warhol pop-art crayons to pair with your favorite artist-themed coloring book. Here you can find whatever you need—and many things you didn't even realize you wanted.

⊠ National Gallery of Art, West Bldg., 4th St. and Constitution Ave. NW, The Mall ☎ 800/697–9350 ⊕ shop.nga.gov Ⓜ Archives–Navy Memorial–Penn Quarter or L'Enfant Plaza.

Pop-up Shop in the National Museum of African American History and Culture

GIFTS/SOUVENIRS | After traversing the many floors of the museum, shop here for a mug, a T-shirt, or a model of the museum building to commemorate your trip. Some of the merchandise is traditional and/or handmade, including sweetgrass baskets, jewelry, scarves, and even food items. ⊠ National Museum of African American History and Culture, 1400 Constitution Ave. NW, The Mall ☎ 844/750–3012 ⊕ nmaahc.si.edu Ⓜ Smithsonian.

USDA Farmers' Market

OUTDOOR/FLEA/GREEN MARKETS | Blueberry popcorn anyone? On Friday from May through October from 9 to 2, you can pick up fresh fruits, vegetables, breads, and other baked goods (and that flavored popcorn) across from the Smithsonian Metro station. Appropriately, the market is in the parking lot of the U.S. Department of Agriculture building. ⊠ 12th St. and Independence Ave. SW, The Mall ☎ 202/708–0082 ⊕ www.usda.gov/farmersmarket Ⓜ Smithsonian.

Chapter 4

DOWNTOWN

WITH CHINATOWN AND PENN QUARTER

4

Updated by
Bob Carden

⊙ Sights   🍴 Restaurants   🛏 Hotels   🛍 Shopping   🍸 Nightlife

★★★★☆   ★★★★☆   ★★★★☆   ★★★☆☆   ★★★★☆

NEIGHBORHOOD SNAPSHOT

GREAT EXPERIENCES DOWNTOWN

■ **CityCentre:** This high-end, open-air shopping district also has some good restaurants including the acclaimed Fig & Olive.

■ **International Spy Museum:** Indulge your inner James Bond with a look at 007's Aston Martin, along with more serious toys used by real spies.

■ **Dining:** Penn Quarter is one of the city's best areas for dining, where José Andrés opened his first restaurant, Jaleo.

■ **National Portrait Gallery and Smithsonian American Art Museum:** These masterful museums have something for everyone.

■ **Theater District:** Performances ranging from Shakespeare to contemporary dramas and musicals are mounted in Penn Quarter's theaters.

GETTING HERE

The Federal Triangle or Archives–Navy Memorial–Penn Quarter Metro stops serve the government buildings along Pennsylvania Avenue. Gallery Place–Chinatown gives direct access to the Capital One Arena, Chinatown, and the nearby museums. Judiciary Square has its own stop, and Metro Center is the best choice for the National Theatre and Penn Quarter. Bus routes crisscross the area as well. Street parking on nights and weekends is limited.

PLANNING YOUR TIME

Downtown is densely packed with major attractions. Art lovers might focus on the **National Portrait Gallery** and **Smithsonian American Art Museum**; history buffs will enjoy the **National Building Museum**; families with kids may prefer the **International Spy Museum**. Come back at night to enjoy the many restaurants.

QUICK BITES

■ **Nando's Peri-Peri.** For a quick lunch after visiting the National Portrait Gallery, this spicy Portuguese chicken restaurant can't be beat. ⊠ *819 7th St. NW* ⊕ *www.nandosperiperi.com* Ⓜ *Gallery Pl.–Chinatown.*

■ **Teaism.** The District's favorite Asian tearoom chain has a big location in Penn Quarter near the National Archives for tea, pastries, or a bento box or sandwich. ⊠ *400 8th St. NW* ⊕ *www.teaism.com* Ⓜ *Archives–Navy Memorial–Penn Quarter.*

SAFETY

■ Downtown's blocks of government and office buildings still become a bit of a ghost town when the working day is done, but a revitalized Penn Quarter remains energized late into the evenings, especially when there are events at the Capital One Arena.

Downtown, Penn Quarter, and Chinatown are a tale of three cities. Washington, D.C.'s Downtown is staid, compact, and home to some wonderful hotels, though pretty quiet at night. Chinatown and the Penn Quarter jump at night with their many shops, bars, and restaurants.

The Capital One Arena sits in the middle, and the nights are supercharged when the Capitals or Wizards are in town. There are also many great museums and theaters, including Ford's and the Warner.

◉ Sights

There are loads of good museums and theaters here, most of them in Downtown, including the National Theater, the Warner, and Ford's, as well as most major museums. Chinatown and the Penn Quarter have the wonderful National Portrait Gallery.

American Veterans Disabled for Life Memorial

MEMORIAL | Located on a 2.4-acre tract adjacent to the Mall and within full view of the U.S. Capitol, this memorial illustrates the journey of veterans with disabilities, from injury and healing to rediscovery of purpose. The plaza, with a star-shape fountain and low triangular reflecting pool, features bronze sculptures, glass panels, and granite walls engraved with quotations from 18 veterans describing their experiences. With its single ceremonial flame, the fountain is the focal point, a powerful icon, expressing the healing, cleansing properties of

water and the enlightenment, power, and eternal nature of fire. The needs of those with disabilities are front and center in the memorial's design. The low fountain can easily be surveyed by someone in a wheelchair, there are numerous benches in front of text panels, and unobtrusive metal bars are placed strategically to help visitors who need assistance to sit or stand. Designed by Michael Vergason Landscape Architects, of Alexandria, Virginia, the memorial is a fitting reminder of the cost of human conflict. ✉ 150 Washington Ave. SW, Downtown ⊕ www.avdlm.org 🎫 Free Ⓜ Federal Center SW.

Capital One Arena

SPORTS VENUE | One of the country's top-grossing sports and entertainment venues, the 20,000-seat Capital One Arena averages more than 200 events each year and has helped to turn the surrounding area into the most vibrant part of Downtown, where you'll find several of the city's best restaurants. But there are also decent food and beverage options inside the arena that go beyond the standard stadium fare of hot dogs, chicken fingers, and beer, including good local chili from Hard Times Café and Chesapeake Bay crab cakes, paired with craft beers and Angry Orchard Gluten-Free Hard Cider. Sporting events include hockey featuring the Stanley Cup champion Washington Capitals; basketball with the Washington Wizards, Washington Mystics, and Georgetown Hoyas; and figure-skating events. Outside, street musicians of all kinds and styles add to the experience. The Metro station is directly below the arena. ✉ *601 F St. NW, between 6th and 7th Sts., Chinatown* ☎ *202/628–3200* ⊕ *capitalonearena.view-lift.com* Ⓜ *Gallery Pl.–Chinatown.*

The FBI Experience

INFO CENTER | There have been no formal tours of FBI headquarters since September 11, 2001. Rather, visits can be arranged to see The FBI Experience. Located within the FBI headquarters building, it features interactive multimedia exhibits, artifacts from well-known cases, and large posters providing a history of the bureau. The tour takes about 90 minutes and is self-guided, but there are typically both retired and active FBI agents on hand to offer information and answer questions. The Experience is open until 3 pm on weekdays, but you can't simply come in off the street. All visitors must arrange for tickets through their congressperson or senator. You can request a visit up to five months in advance but no less than four weeks before the desired date. You are generally notified two weeks prior to your date if you have been cleared for the visit, and you must arrive 30 minutes before your designated start time. ✉ *935 Pennsylvania Ave. NW, Downtown* ☎ *202/324–3447* ⊕ *www.fbi.gov/contact-us/fbi-headquarters/the-fbi-experience* ⊘ *Closed weekends* Ⓜ *Archives–Navy Memorial–Penn Quarter.*

★ Ford's Theatre

HISTORIC SITE | **FAMILY** | April 14, 1865, shocked the nation: during a performance of *Our American Cousin,* John Wilkes Booth entered the Presidential Box at Ford's Theatre and shot Abraham Lincoln in the back of the head; the president died later that night. This block-long, Lincoln-centered, cultural campus encompasses four sites. In the **Museum,** you'll explore Lincoln's presidency and Civil War milestones and learn about Booth and those who joined his conspiracy to topple the government. Artifacts include Lincoln's clothing and weapons used by Booth. The **Theatre,** which stages performances throughout the year, is restored to look as it did when Lincoln attended, including the Presidential Box draped with flags as it was on the night he was shot. In the restored **Petersen House,** you can see the room where Lincoln died and the parlor where his wife, Mary Todd Lincoln, waited in anguish through the night. The centerpiece of the **Aftermaths Exhibits at the Center for Education and Leadership** is a jaw-dropping, three-story tower of 6,800 books written about Lincoln. Here, visitors take an immersive step back in time, entering a 19th-century street scene where they find a reproduction of Lincoln's funeral train car. Pick up free timed tickets beginning at 8:30 am or reserve one online for a fee. ✉ *511 10th St. NW, Downtown* ☎ *202/347–4833* ⊕ *www.fords.org* 🎫 *Free; ticket reservations $3* Ⓜ *Metro Center or Gallery Pl.–Chinatown.*

★ International Spy Museum

MUSEUM | **FAMILY** | Fun for kids of all ages, the museum displays the world's largest collection of spy artifacts. *The Secret History of History* takes you behind the headlines, from Moses' use of spies in Canaan and Abraham Lincoln's employment of the Pinkerton National Detective Agency as a full-scale secret service in the Civil War to the birth of WWII's OSS. Check out the spy gadgets, weapons, vehicles, and disguises, and then see if you have what it takes to be a spy in *School for Spies. Exquisitely Evil: 50 Years of Bond Villains* brings you face-to-face with 007's archenemies. *Operation Spy,* a one-hour immersive experience,

Kids love the International Spy Museum, where they can adopt a cover identity and try out being a spy in an interactive mission.

works like a live-action game, dropping you in the middle of a foreign intelligence mission. Each step—which includes decrypting secret audio files, a car chase, and interrogating a suspect agent—is taken from actual intelligence operations. Advance tickets (purchased at the museum or on its website) are highly recommended. All tickets are date- and time-specific. Tickets are most likely available on Tuesday, Wednesday, and Thursday or daily after 2 pm. ⊠ *700 L'Enfant Plaza, Downtown* ☎ *202/393–7798* ⊕ *www.spymuseum.org* ▨ *Permanent exhibition $21; combo Museum and Operation $30 (when purchased online)* Ⓜ *L'Enfant Plaza.*

Madame Tussauds Washington DC
MUSEUM | This branch of the famous London-based waxworks franchise focuses on U.S. presidential history. You can see and pose for pictures (some for a small fee) with uncanny likenesses of the Founding Fathers or any of the presidents, including Barack Obama and his wife, or sit inside the Oval Office,

painstakingly re-created in wax. The Civil Rights room features Martin Luther King Jr. and Rosa Parks. There are cultural icons, sports figures, and a behind-the-scenes exhibit where experts demonstrate wax sculpting. The Glamour Room is populated with waxen re-creations of George Clooney, Beyoncé, Zac Efron, and Taylor Swift, among others. ⊠ *1025 F St. NW, Downtown* ☎ *202/942–7300, 866/823–9565 to confirm hrs* ⊕ *www. madametussaudsdc.com* ▨ *$22, with many extra additions possible* Ⓜ *Metro Center or Gallery Pl.–Chinatown.*

National Building Museum
MUSEUM | FAMILY | Architecture, design, landscaping, and urban planning are the themes of this museum, the nation's premier cultural organization devoted to the built environment. The open interior of the mammoth redbrick edifice is one of the city's great spaces and has been the site of many presidential inaugural balls. The eight central Corinthian columns are among the largest in the world, rising to a height of 75 feet. Although they

Downtown

KEY
1 Exploring Sights
1 Restaurants
1 Hotels

0   1,000 ft

0   200 m

Sights ▼

1 American Veterans
  Disabled for Life
  Memorial I9

2 National Geographic
  Museum B2

3 National Museum of
  Women in the Arts....... E4

4 WWI Memorial/
  Pershing Park D6

Restaurants ▼

1 Bombay Club C4

2 Brasserie Beck F3

3 Centrolina................ G4

4 City Tap House G4

5 DBGB Kitchen
  and Bar G4

6 Del Frisco's Double Eagle
  Steak House.............. G4

7 District Taco.............. E5

8 The Fourth Estate....... E5

9 The Hamilton D5

10 Joe's Seafood, Prime
   Steak & Stone Crab D4

11 Kaz Sushi Bistro A4

12 Kinship H3

13 Modena................... F4

14 Old Ebbitt Grill........... D5

15 The Oval Room.......... B4

16 P.J. Clarke's DC C3

17 Proper 21 .... E5

18 Rare Steakhouse
   and Tavern................ C4

19 Siroc Restaurant........ D3

Hotels ▼

1 AC Hotel
  Washington DC A2

2 Capital Hilton............ C3

3 Comfort Inn Downtown
  DC/Convention Center .. E2

4 Conrad
  Washington DC G4

5 Eaton Hotel,
  Washington, DC.......... F3

6 Hamilton Hotel
  Washington, D.C. E3

7 The Hay-Adams.......... C4

8 Henley Park Hotel G3

9 InterContinental
  The Willard
  Washington D.C......... D6

10 The Jefferson C2

11 JW Marriott
   Washington, DC.......... E6

12 The Madison
   Washington, DC,
   A Hilton Hotel D2

13 Marriott Marquis
   Washington, DC......... G3

14 The Mayflower Hotel,
   Autograph Collection.....B2

15 Morrison-Clark
   Historic Inn F2

16 Renaissance
   Washington, D.C.
   Downtown Hotel........ G4

17 The St. Regis
   Washington, D.C. C3

18 Sofitel Washington, D.C.
   Lafayette Square D4

19 W Washington, D.C.....D6

20 Washington Marriott
   at Metro Center......... F5

resemble Siena marble, each is made of 70,000 bricks that have been covered with plaster and painted. The long-term exhibition *House and Home* features a kaleidoscopic array of photographs, objects, models, and films that takes visitors on a tour of houses both surprising and familiar, through past and present, exploring American domestic life and residential architecture. Among the most popular permanent exhibits is the hands-on *Building Zone,* where children ages two to six can construct a tower, explore a kid-size playhouse, or play with bulldozers and construction trucks. ⊠ *401 F St. NW, between 4th and 5th Sts., Downtown* ☎ *202/272–2448* ⊕ *www.nbm.org* ⊟ *$10; tool kits from $3; docent-led tour of building and entrance to Great Hall, shop, and café free* Ⓜ *Judiciary Sq. or Gallery Pl.–Chinatown.*

★ **National Geographic Museum**
MUSEUM | FAMILY | Founded in 1888, the National Geographic Society is best known for its magazine, and entering this welcoming, 13,000-square-foot exhibition space feels like stepping into its pages. The compact museum offers family-friendly, if pricey, interactive exhibitions delving into the historical, cultural, and scientific research that distinguishes National Geographic Magazine. There are items from the permanent collections—cultural, historical, and scientific—as well as traveling exhibitions. It also has a virtual-reality theater experience introduced in 2018. Nat Geo Nights—presentations by explorers with interactive activities, music, and food and drink specials—are held the third Thursday of every month. The M Street Lobby photography exhibit, as well as the outdoor photo display around the perimeter of the museum, are free. ⊠ *1145 17th St. NW, Downtown* ☎ *800/647–5463* ⊕ *www.nationalgeographic.com* ⊟ *$15; M Street Photographic Gallery free* Ⓜ *Farragut N.*

National Law Enforcement Officers Memorial
MEMORIAL | These 3-foot-high walls bear the names of more than 21,000 American police officers killed in the line of duty since 1791. On the third line of Panel 13W are the names of six officers killed by William Bonney, better known as Billy the Kid. J.D. Tippit, the Dallas policeman killed by Lee Harvey Oswald, is honored on the ninth line of Panel 63E. Other names include the 72 officers who died due to the events of 9/11. Directories here allow you to look up officers by name, date of death, state, and department. Call to arrange for a free tour. A National Law Enforcement Museum is in the works; until then, a small visitor center (*400 7th St.*) has a computer for looking up names, a display on the history of law enforcement, and a small gift shop. ⊠ *400 block of E St. NW, Penn Quarter* ☎ *202/737–3400* ⊕ *www. lawmemorial.org* ⊟ *Free* Ⓜ *Judiciary Sq.*

National Museum of Women in the Arts
MUSEUM | This museum—in a beautifully restored, 1907, Renaissance Revival building designed by Waddy B. Wood—brings to light remarkable female artists of the past, while promoting the best female artists working today. Founded in 1987, this is the only major museum in the world solely dedicated to recognizing women's creative contributions. In addition to hosting special exhibitions, the museum holds a collection of 5,000 artworks including paintings, drawings, sculpture, prints, videos, and photographs by Frida Kahlo, Camille Claudel, Mary Cassatt, Alma Thomas, Judy Chicago, Magdalena Abakanowicz, Nan Goldin, Louise Dahl-Wolfe, Helen Frankenthaler, and Élisabeth Vigée-Lebrun, among others. The installations highlight connections between historical and contemporary artworks. Gallery and artist talks, hands-on art workshops, and concerts are held regularly; check the museum's website for the calendar

Visitation has doubled at the National Portrait Gallery since Kehinde Wiley's portrait of President Barack Obama was unveiled in 2018. Amy Sherald's portrait of First Lady Michelle Obama is equally popular.

of events. ✉ *1250 New York Ave. NW, Downtown* ☎ *202/783–5000* ⊕ *www. nmwa.org* ✉ *$10* Ⓜ *Metro Center.*

★ National Portrait Gallery

MUSEUM | FAMILY | The intersection of art, biography, and history is illustrated here through images of people who have shaped U.S. history. There are prints, paintings, photos, and sculptures of subjects from George Washington to Madonna. The stunning building has been deemed one of the country's best examples of Greek Revival architecture. America's Presidents shares the stories of the country's leaders and the times in which they governed. In this gallery, you'll see the only complete collection of presidential portraits outside the White House. From portraits of generals Eisenhower and Patton to Andy Warhol's *Time* magazine cover of Michael Jackson, the third-floor gallery, Twentieth-Century Americans, offers a vibrant tour of the people who shaped the country and culture of today. Free docent-led tours depart weekdays at noon and 2:30 and most weekends at 11:45, 1:30, 3:15, and 4:30. Check the website to confirm times. At the Lunder Conservation Center on the third and fourth floors, you can watch conservators at work. ✉ *8th and F Sts. NW, Downtown* ☎ *202/633–8300* ⊕ *www.npg.si.edu* ✉ *Free* Ⓜ *Gallery Pl.–Chinatown.*

Smithsonian American Art Museum

MUSEUM | From Childe Hassam's *The South Ledges, Appledore* to Nelson Shanks's *The Four Justices,* the Smithsonian American Art Museum features one of the world's largest collections of American art that spans more than four centuries. Over the past few decades, the museum has broadened its collection to include modern and contemporary art, too. Among the artists represented are Benny Andrews, José Campechi, Robert Indiana, Roy Lichtenstein, Isamu Noguchi, Robert Rauschenberg, Mickalene Thomas, and Charlie Willeto. On the first floor, you'll discover an enormous tinfoil altarpiece by James Hampton and more than 60 sculptures and paintings by Emery Blagdon that represent his thought-provoking and constantly changing *Healing Machine*. Art from the Colonial period to the dawn of Modernism is displayed throughout the galleries on the second floor. Discover masterpieces by Mary Cassatt, Frederick Carl Frieseke, Thomas Moran, Harriett Whitney Frishmuth, George Catlin, Albert Bierstadt, Winslow Homer, and John Singer Sargent, to name just a few. Free docent-led tours of the museum are available every day at 12:30 and 2. ✉ *8th and G Sts. NW, Downtown* ☎ *202/633–7970* ⊕ *www.americanart.si.edu* ✉ *Free* Ⓜ *Gallery Pl.–Chinatown.*

United States Navy Memorial

MEMORIAL | Although Pierre L'Enfant included a Navy Memorial in his plans for Washington, D.C., it wasn't until 1987 that one was built. The main attraction here is a 100-foot-diameter granite map of the world, known as the Granite Sea. It's surrounded by fountains, benches, and six ship masts. The *Lone Sailor*, a 7-foot-tall statue, stands on the map in the Pacific Ocean between the United States and Japan. The Naval Heritage Center, next to the memorial in the Market Square East Building, displays videos and exhibits of uniforms, medals, and other aspects of navy life. If you've served in the navy, you can enter your record of service into the log here. Bronze relief panels on the Pennsylvania Avenue side of the memorial depict 26 scenes commemorating events in the nation's naval history and honoring naval communities. ✉ *701 Pennsylvania Ave. NW, Downtown* ☎ *202/737–2300* ⊕ *www.navymemorial.org* ✉ *Free* Ⓜ *Archives–Navy Memorial–Penn Quarter.*

WWI Memorial/Pershing Park

MEMORIAL | In late 2014, Congress redesignated this quiet, sunken garden, to honor General John J. "Black Jack" Pershing, the first—a century ago—to hold the title General of the Armies. An official unit of the National Park System,

the memorial currently includes engravings on the stone walls recounting pivotal campaigns from World War I, when Pershing commanded the American expeditionary force and conducted other military exploits. Steps and small tables surround a fountain and duck pond, making for a pleasant midday respite. A $46 million renovation of the memorial is currently underway and is expected to be completed in 2021. ✉ *15th St. and Pennsylvania Ave., Downtown* Ⓜ *McPherson Sq.*

🍴 Restaurants

Until recently, tourists who trekked north from the Mall hungry for something more than Smithsonian cafeteria food were stranded Downtown with little but high-end options. Now, young Washingtonians are taking advantage of residential development and moving off Capitol Hill to Downtown, Penn Quarter, and Chinatown, where nothing short of a restaurant revolution has taken shape in the last decade.

Bombay Club

$$ | INDIAN | One block from the White House, the beautiful Bombay Club tries to re-create the refined aura of British private clubs in colonial India. On the menu are unusual seafood specialties and a large number of vegetarian dishes, but the real standouts are the aromatic curries. **Known for:** great Indian curries; British colonial club vibe; upscale Sunday buffet brunch. ⑤ *Average main: $24* ✉ *815 Connecticut Ave. NW, Downtown* ☎ *202/659–3727* ⊕ *www.bombayclubdc. com* ⊗ *No lunch Sat.* Ⓜ *Farragut W.*

Brasserie Beck

$$$ | BELGIAN | FAMILY | Give in to sensory overload at this homage to the railway dining rooms that catered to the prewar European elite. The food is just as rich as you'd expect: entrée-size salads with Belgian frites, *fruits de mer* platters with enough shellfish for a small army,

and a dizzying lineup of artisanal beers. **Known for:** luxurious vintage-inspired interiors; excellent brunch that includes Belgian waffles and unlimited mimosas; great outdoor patio. ⑤ *Average main: $32* ⊠ *1101 K St. NW, Downtown* ☎ *202/408–1717* ⊕ *www.brasseriebeck. com* Ⓜ *McPherson Sq.*

★ Cafe Riggs

$$ | **BRASSERIE** | **FAMILY** | This spacious restaurant is on the ground floor of the 130 year old Riggs Bank Building, which was recently converted to a luxury hotel. The café boasts huge Corinthian columns, original stone floors, a sky-high ceiling, and Palladian windows. **Known for:** vegan options; $98 grilled cheese and caviar sandwich; luxury feel. ⑤ *Average main: $26* ⊠ *900 F St, Penn Quarter* ✛ *Near Gallery Pl., heart of Penn Quarter* ☎ *202 /788–2800* ⊕ *www.caferiggs.com* Ⓜ *Gallery Pl. Red and Yellow.*

Centrolina

$$$ | **ITALIAN** | This bright, airy Italian osteria has an adjoining market and a daily changing menu that is all about locally sourced meats and produce, as well as sustainable fish. Authentic and innovative, pastas and sauces are made fresh daily, and the specials change regularly. **Known for:** innovative pasta dishes; daily changing menu; fun option in CityCentre development. ⑤ *Average main: $32* ⊠ *974 Palmer Alley NW, Chinatown* ✛ *Near convention center* ☎ *202/898–2426* ⊕ *centrolinadc.com* Ⓜ *Gallery Pl.–Chinatown.*

China Chilcano

$$ | **PERUVIAN** | The José Andrés formula is pleasantly familiar to D.C. diners who have visited his ever-growing empire of endlessly kicky, small-plate restaurants since Jaleo first opened in 1993. This hybrid of Peruvian and Chinese-Japanese styles, inspired by a 19th-century wave of migration to South America, is one of the newer additions to the stylish family. **Known for:** part of chef José Andrés's empire; Peruvian-inspired shareable small plates; pisco fruit cocktails. ⑤ *Average main: $20* ⊠ *418 7th St. NW, Penn Quarter* ☎ *202/783–0941* ⊕ *chinachilcano.com* ⊘ *No lunch* Ⓜ *Gallery Pl.–Chinatown.*

★ City Tap House

$$ | **AMERICAN** | **FAMILY** | This upscale gastropub chain just a block from the convention center offers more than 40 beers on tap and loads of bottles. The high ceilings, reclaimed wood walls, and copper bar give the large spot a warm, rustic feel. **Known for:** standard American pub fare; great selection of beers; communal tables and big-screen TVs. ⑤ *Average main: $18* ⊠ *901 9th St. NW, Penn Quarter* ☎ *202/733–5333* ⊕ *pennquarter. citytap.com* Ⓜ *Gallery Pl.–Chinatown.*

★ Crimson Diner + Whiskey Bar

$ | **AMERICAN** | **FAMILY** | An upscale, Southern-influenced diner with an open kitchen and lively bar, Crimson offers seating in booths to convey that diner feel. A huge breakfast menu is available all day, and dinner plates include shrimp and grits, rainbow trout, and, yes, meat loaf. **Known for:** Southern cooking; fine whiskey; great views. ⑤ *Average main: $15* ⊠ *627 H St. NW, Chinatown* ☎ *202/847–4459* ⊕ *www.crimson-dc.com* Ⓜ *Gallery Pl.–Chinatown.*

Daikaya

$ | **RAMEN** | This intimate, no-reservations, Sapporo-style ramen shop is one of the city's best bets for the tasty Japanese noodle soup. It offers five excellent types of ramen, with the vegan version a welcome option. **Known for:** expect a wait; loud, local-friendly vibe; fancier Izakaya upstairs. ⑤ *Average main: $14* ⊠ *705 6th St. NW, Chinatown* ☎ *202/589–1600* ⊕ *www.daikaya.com* Ⓜ *Gallery Pl.–Chinatown.*

DBGB Kitchen and Bar

$$$ | **FRENCH** | After leaving D.C. in 1982, famed chef Daniel Boulud finally returned 32 years and 18 restaurants later to open this interpretation of a classic French brasserie in Downtown D.C. The small plates of house-made sausage, coq au vin, and baked Alaska for dessert demonstrate the impressive culinary chops he picked up while away. **Known for:** world-famous chef's return home; variety of house-made sausages; fun cocktail menu. ⑤ *Average main: $28* ✉ *931 H St. NW, Downtown* ☎ *202/695–7660* ⊕ *www.dbgb.com/dc* Ⓜ *Gallery Pl.–Chinatown.*

Del Frisco's Double Eagle Steak House

$$$$ | **STEAKHOUSE** | Del Frisco's is yet another upscale steak house in a city bursting with them. Like many others, the cuts of meat are tasty, generous, and pricey, but the overall atmosphere here is nicer—or at least brighter. **Known for:** big, juicy steaks; floor-to-ceiling windows; large courtyard. ⑤ *Average main: $45* ✉ *950 I St. NW, Chinatown* ☎ *202/289–0201* ⊕ *www.delfriscos.com* Ⓜ *Gallery Pl.–Chinatown or McPherson Sq.*

Dirty Habit

$$$ | **FUSION** | Inside trendy Hotel Monaco, Dirty Habit woos diners with a towering skylit space that until 1901 was the general post office. Homing in on globally inspired shared plates, the chef conjures up such satisfying dishes as poached hen dumplings and smoked Chilean sea bass. **Known for:** alfresco dining (and drinking) in the courtyard; popular happy hour; small plates in a historic space. ⑤ *Average main: $30* ✉ *Hotel Monaco, 555 8th St. NW, Penn Quarter* ☎ *202/783–6060* ⊕ *www.dirtyhabitdc.com* Ⓜ *Gallery Pl.–Chinatown.*

District Taco

$ | **MEXICAN** | **FAMILY** | The line out the door at lunchtime is a dead giveaway that D.C.er's have taken to this fast-casual, Yucatán-style Mexican restaurant that got its start as a food truck in 2009. While you can customize the toppings of your tacos or burritos, ordering them the Mexican way (with cilantro and onion) is a sure bet. **Known for:** food truck origins; all-day breakfast tacos; extensive salsa bar. ⑤ *Average main: $8* ✉ *1309 F St. NW,* Downtown ☎ *202/347–7359* ⊕ *www. districttaco.com* Ⓜ *Metro Center.*

Fiola

$$$$ | **MODERN ITALIAN** | Chef Fabio Trabocchi's flights of fancy—such as oysters with granita and caviar or Nova Scotia lobster ravioli—delight many area foodies but come with a hefty price tag. Happy hour and lunch menus offer more affordable small plates to go with inventive cocktails (head to the bar or patio for these à la carte options). **Known for:** upscale and innovative Italian dishes; date-night crowd; encyclopedic beverage list. ⑤ *Average main: $47* ✉ *601 Pennsylvania Ave. NW, Penn Quarter* ✛ *Enter at 678 Indiana Ave.* ☎ *202/628–2888* ⊕ *www.fioladc.com* Ⓜ *Archives–Navy Memorial–Penn Quarter.*

★ The Fourth Estate

$$ | **AMERICAN** | A hidden gem atop the National Press Building offers classic American cuisine (strong on seafood), beautifully prepared and presented in an elegant setting at surprisingly affordable prices. Although part of the National Press Club, which is private, the restaurant is open to the public. **Known for:** fresh seafood; great spot for pretheater dinner; opportunity to view National Press Club photos. ⑤ *Average main: $26* ✉ *529 14th St., Downtown* ☎ *202/662–7638* ⊕ *www.press.org/fourthestate* ☾ *No dinner Mon. Closed Sun.* Ⓜ *Metro Center.*

Full Kee

$ | **CHINESE** | Many locals swear that amid the slew of mediocre Chinese joints in the area this one is a standout. The style-free interior—reminiscent of the fluorescent-lit dives of Manhattan's Chinatown—can be off-putting, but the cuisine is better than most similar options within the city limits. **Known for:** rare good spot for Chinese food in Chinatown; Cantonese-style roasted meats; no-frills decor. ⑤ *Average main: $14* ✉ *509 H St. NW, Chinatown* ☎ *202/371–2233* Ⓜ *Gallery Pl.–Chinatown.*

The Hamilton

$$ | ECLECTIC | Formerly a Borders bookstore, the Hamilton (no relation to the hit musical) is now an enormous multiroom restaurant (38,000 sq feet) that includes a subterranean live-music hall capable of accommodating almost 1,000 people. The menu is just as ambitious as the venue, offering burgers, sushi, pasta, steaks, salads, seafood, and one solitary vegetarian entrée. **Known for:** all-encompassing menu; huge space with live music; happy hour deals. ⑤ *Average main: $26* ✉ *600 14th St. NW, Downtown* ☎ *202/787–1000* ⊕ *www.thehamiltondc.com* Ⓜ *Metro Center.*

Hill Country Barbecue Market

$$ | BARBECUE | FAMILY | Few who stop by this bustling hive of smoky brisket and gooey ribs can deny that it does Texas meat right. This is evident down to the pay-by-the-pound ethos that lets you sample one slice of lean beef and one scoop of gooey white shoepeg corn pudding alongside a succulent turkey breast. **Known for:** Texas-style brisket—with the rub; cafeteria-style, pay-by-the-pound ordering; country western karaoke night every Wednesday. ⑤ *Average main: $18* ✉ *410 7th St. NW, Penn Quarter* ☎ *202/556–2050* ⊕ *www.hillcountrywdc.com* Ⓜ *Archives–Navy Memorial–Penn Quarter.*

Jaleo

$$ | SPANISH | Make a meal of the long list of tapas at celebrity chef José Andrés's lively Spanish bistro, although the five types of handcrafted paella are the stars of the ample entrée menu. Tapas highlights include the *gambas al ajillo* (sautéed garlic shrimp), tender piquillo peppers stuffed with goat cheese, and the grilled homemade chorizo, which also comes draped in creamy mashed potatoes. **Known for:** José Andrés original tapas eatery; sangria by the pitcher; different paella options. ⑤ *Average main: $25* ✉ *480 7th St. NW, Penn Quarter*

☎ *202/628–7949* ⊕ *www.jaleo.com* Ⓜ *Gallery Pl.–Chinatown.*

Joe's Seafood, Prime Steak & Stone Crab

$$$$ | STEAKHOUSE | Just a couple of blocks from the White House, this gargantuan space (a century-old bank building), with a towering second-floor terrace, centers on a huge black granite bar adorned with marble columns and leather stools. Affiliated with the legendary Joe's Stone Crab in Miami, the D.C. Joe's distinguishes itself with steaks; sure they have seafood, but this is a steak house. **Known for:** primarily prime steaks but also fresh seafood; everything big: place, portions, prices; fun happy hour. ⑤ *Average main: $52* ✉ *750 15th St. NW, Downtown* ✛ *On 15th St., a block from Treasury Bldg.* ☎ *202/489–0140* ⊕ *joes.net* Ⓜ *Metro Center.*

Kaz Sushi Bistro

$$ | JAPANESE | Traditional Japanese cooking is combined with often inspired improvisations ("freestyle Japanese cuisine," in the words of chef-owner Kaz Okochi) at this serene location. For a first-rate experience, sit at the sushi bar and ask for whatever is best—you're in good hands. **Known for:** one of D.C.'s original sushi spots; unique Japanese dishes and small plates. ⑤ *Average main: $26* ✉ *1915 I St. NW, Downtown* ☎ *202/530–5500* ⊕ *www.kazsushibistro.com* ☾ *Closed Sun. No lunch Sat.* Ⓜ *Farragut W.*

Kinship

$$$$ | MODERN AMERICAN | The unique menu divides Kinship's offerings into four categories; first there's craft, honoring a particular cooking technique, and then history, which offers a different take on a classic dish. The ingredients menu explores a certain product while the indulgence section is where you'll find dishes like caviar with potato chips or lobster French toast. **Known for:** excellent wine list and pairing suggestions; Chesapeake Bay soft-shell crabs (when in season); warm yet chic ambience.

$ Average main: $50 ⊠ 1015 7th St. NW, Chinatown ☎ 202/737-7700 ⊕ www. kinshipdc.com Ⓜ Mt. Vernon Sq. 7th St.–Convention Center.

★ minibar by José Andrés

$$$$ | CONTEMPORARY | For food fanatics who can afford it, a visit to chef José Andrés's cutting-edge culinary counter is a must. Here, Andrés showcases his molecular-gastronomy techniques with the 20 or so courses in the tasting menu that vary regularly (no à la carte ordering allowed). **Known for:** hard-to-get reservations required; chocolate-covered foie gras; experimental cocktails. $ Average main: $275 ⊠ 855 E. St. NW, Penn Quarter ☎ 202/393-0812 ⊕ www.minibarbyjoseandres.oom/minibar.

★ Modena

$$$ | ITALIAN | Buzzy, trendy Modena has one of the area's more inventive menus, featuring very good modern Italian fare. Dinner starts with an antipasti trolley that stops at each table so diners can choose their favorite starters, from braised artichokes to panzella salad; entrées include seafood, duck, and pastas. **Known for:** local ingredients; sidewalk patio for alfresco dining; wood-fired pizza. $ Average main: $30 ⊠ 1100 New York Ave. NW, Washington ✛ Actual entrance is at 12th and H Sts. ☎ 202/216-9550 ⊕ www.modenadc.com Ⓜ McPherson Sq.

Old Ebbitt Grill

$$$ | AMERICAN | People flock here to drink at the several bars, which seem to go on for miles, and to enjoy well-prepared buffalo wings, hamburgers, and hearty sandwiches (the Reuben is a must). A 160-year-old institution (it claims Teddy Roosevelt may have "bagged animal heads" at the main bar), Old Ebbitt also has one of Washington's best raw bars. **Known for:** one of D.C.'s oldest bars; standard bar menu, including great oysters; an institution that shouldn't be missed. $ Average main: $27 ⊠ 675 15th St. NW, Downtown ☎ 202/347-4800 ⊕ www.ebbitt.com Ⓜ Metro Center.

The Oval Room

$$$ | CONTEMPORARY | The city is full of established restaurants that cater to lobbyists and the government officials they're wining and dining, but the Oval Room is a rare example of one that also has great food. The menu is largely split between Southern-influenced dishes, like shrimp and grits, and Mediterranean-inspired ones, such as smoked yellowfin potato agnolotti. **Known for:** clientele of D.C. insiders; classy and intimate dining room; modern American cuisine like yellowfin tuna crudo. $ Average main: $28 ⊠ 800 Connecticut Ave. NW, Downtown ☎ 202/463-8700 ⊕ www.ovalroom.com ☉ Closed Sun. No lunch weekends Ⓜ Farragut W.

Oyamel Cocina Mexicana

$$ | MEXICAN | The specialty at chef José Andrés's Mexican stunner is *antojitos*, literally translated as "little dishes from the streets." But the high ceilings, gracious service, and gorgeous Frida Kahlo–inspired interior are anything but street, and even the smallest of dishes is larger than life when doused with chocolate mole poblano sauce or piquant lime-cilantro dressing. **Known for:** street-inspired Mexican small plates; grasshopper tacos; affordable lunch deals. $ Average main: $23 ⊠ 401 7th St. NW, Penn Quarter ☎ 202/628-1005 ⊕ www.oyamel.com Ⓜ Archives–Navy Memorial–Penn Quarter.

The Partisan

$$$ | MODERN AMERICAN | Charcuterie is more than just salami at this wood-paneled homage to all parts of the pig. Sample servings of meat under headings like rich + earthy, herbal + floral, and boozy, and complement the taste with one of the vibrant small plates like grilled octopus and Brussels-sprout slaw. **Known for:** pig-focused charcuterie menu; late-night hot spot; great dessert menu including hazelnut mudpies. $ Average main: $30 ⊠ 709 D St. NW, Penn Quarter

D.C. Food Trucks

The nation's capital celebrates celebrity chefs and pricey bistros, but it also loves affordable and accessible dining, as evidenced by its many food trucks. The mobile-food rush reached its peak several years ago when local brick-and-mortar restaurateurs attempted to fight the trucks' appeal by passing an ordinance to keep them from staying too long in one place. That battle continues, but visitors keen to try the best D.C. trucks can always take advantage of Twitter. Even those without a Twitter account are free to visit the trucks' pages to track their locations—and in many cases, check out menus to see whether chicken vindaloo or red-velvet cupcakes are on the docket at these favorite spots.

Arepa Zone (⊕ www.twitter.com/ arepazone) is a celebration of Venezuelan cuisine; arepas, *cachapas* (cheese sticks), and *cachapas* (tacolike sweet corn pancakes) all feature heavily.

PhoWheels (⊕ www.twitter.com/ PhoWheels) makes pho so delicious you'll want a cup even on a hot D.C. day (go for the eye-round steak). Soup can be a bit difficult to eat when sitting on a curb or park bench, but luckily PhoWheels also offers impressive bánh mì sandwiches and Vietnamese-style tacos.

Red Hook Lobster Pound (⊕ twitter. com/lobstertruckdc) is the Washington outpost of the popular Brooklyn, New York, spot that purveys rolls filled with uberfresh shellfish from Maine (tossed with light mayo) and Connecticut (kissed by creamy butter) variations—or try the equally good shrimp roll for $7 less. Add a decadent chocolate homemade whoopie pie for dessert.

☎ 202/524–5322 ⊕ thepartisandc.com Ⓜ Gallery Pl.–Chinatown.

PAUL

$ | **FRENCH** | **FAMILY** | This Parisian-style café is fast and casual yet sophisticated. The puff of its cheese *gougeres*, the heft of its salty-sweet croque monsieur sandwiches, and the delicate crunch of its almond-flour macaron cookies will leave you craving more. **Known for:** Parisian-style, fast-casual chain; huge pastry selection; big crowds during lunch. Ⓢ Average main: $10 ✉ 801 Pennsylvania Ave. NW, Downtown ☎ 202/524–4500 ⊕ www.paul-usa.com ⊘ No dinner Ⓜ Archives–Navy Memorial–Penn Quarter.

P.J. Clarke's DC

$$ | **BURGER** | **FAMILY** | The D.C. branch of the venerable New York institution focuses on classic American comfort food, including burgers, oysters, rotisserie chicken, and steaks. The checkered tablecloths, rich woods, and relaxed service make it clear that this is an old-fashioned saloon. **Known for:** excellent burgers; great raw bar; energetic happy hour. Ⓢ Average main: $26 ✉ 1600 K St. NW, Downtown ☎ 202/463–6610 ⊕ pj-clarkes.com Ⓜ Farragut N or Farragut W.

Proper 21

$$ | **AMERICAN** | Proper 21 bills itself as an upscale sports bar (think: low light, sleek black tables, and big screens mounted behind the bar). Indeed, amid standard fare like burgers, the menu also features elevated dishes like grilled halloumi, a Brussels salad, and nachos graced with hi tuna. **Known for:** high-end sports bar; spacious; perfect for game nights or

dates. ⑤ *Average main: $22 ⊠ 1319 F St. NW, Downtown ⊹ A block from Metro Center subway ☎ 202/847–3674 ⊕ www. propersocial.com* Ⓜ *Metro Center.*

Rare Steakhouse and Tavern

$$$ | **STEAKHOUSE** | **FAMILY** | Rare is two restaurants in one: a casual street-level tavern that will appeal to most diners and an upstairs high-end steak house. The Tavern is most accessible, with a large bar decorated with colorful murals, perfect if you are meeting friends for happy hour, and its menu takes pub grub to another level. **Known for:** dry-aged steaks; long, airy bar; upscale tavern downstairs, high-end steak house upstairs. ⑤ *Average main: $27 ⊠ 1595 I St. NW, Downtown ☎ 202/800–9994 ⊕ www.raresteaks. com* ⊗ *No lunch weekends* Ⓜ *Farragut N, Farragut W, or McPherson Sq.*

★ Rasika

$$ | **INDIAN** | Adventurous wine lists, stellar service, inventive presentations that don't scrimp on the spice—this Indian kitchen is a local legend. A sceney, romantic atmosphere means couples snatch up reservations weeks in advance. **Known for:** upscale Indian with unique dishes; plenty of options for vegetarians; tables that book up weeks in advance. ⑤ *Average main: $25 ⊠ 633 D St. NW, Penn Quarter ☎ 202/637–1222 ⊕ www.rasikarestaurant.com* ⊗ *Closed Sun. No lunch Sat.* Ⓜ *Archives–Navy Memorial–Penn Quarter.*

Rosa Mexicano

$$ | **MEXICAN** | Big and vibrant, this Mexican restaurant and bar (a branch of the New York City original) sits directly across the street from Verizon Center. The menu focuses on authentic Mexican food, and prides itself on the tableside guacamole presentation. **Known for:** fresh guacamole prepared tableside; inventive margaritas; bustling happy hour. ⑤ *Average main: $25 ⊠ 575 7th St. NW, Penn Quarter ☎ 202/783–5522 ⊕ rosamexicano.com* Ⓜ *Gallery Pl.–Chinatown.*

★ Shake Shack

$ | **AMERICAN** | **FAMILY** | Yes, it's a chain made most famous in Manhattan, but if you're craving a burger, there's no better place to address that problem than its D.C. Chinatown outpost. Juicy burgers with a special sauce, classic fries (get them with cheese), and tasty shakes make it worth the short wait—especially if you're looking for a tasty, reasonably priced lunch between visits to Downtown attractions. **Known for:** classic Shack Burger (and that sauce!); vanilla milk shakes; long lines that go fast. ⑤ *Average main: $9 ⊠ 800 F St. NW, Penn Quarter ☎ 202/800–9930 ⊕ www.shakeshack. com/location/f-street-dc* Ⓜ *Gallery Pl.–Chinatown.*

★ Siroc Restaurant

$$ | **ITALIAN** | This wonderfully intimate, Italian-Mediterranean restaurant sits in the heart of Downtown D.C. Family owned and run, a rarity in this neighborhood, it delivers top-notch food at very reasonable prices. **Known for:** fresh pasta made in-house; Italian-style seafood presentations; intimate, candlelit dining. ⑤ *Average main: $23 ⊠ 915 15th St. NW, Downtown ☎ 202/628–2220 ⊕ www. sirocrestaurant.com* ⊗ *No lunch weekends* Ⓜ *Farragut N or Farragut W.*

The Smith

$$ | **AMERICAN** | **FAMILY** | Bright, loud, raucous, and fun, with a brightly lit bar and long, communal tables, this branch of the New York City original makes it hard not to meet people. An "American" brasserie, it's a large space with an even bigger menu, so if you can't find something you like here, it might not exist. **Known for:** great bar scene; eclectic international menu; all-day breakfast. ⑤ *Average main: $26 ⊠ 901 F St. NW, Downtown ☎ 202/868–4900 ⊕ thesmithrestaurant. com* Ⓜ *Gallery Pl.–Chinatown or Metro Center.*

Teaism Penn Quarter

$ | ASIAN | FAMILY | This informal teahouse stocks more than 50 imported teas (black, white, and green) and also serves healthy and delicious Japanese, Indian, and Thai food. You can mix small dishes—like udon noodle salad and grilled avocado—to create meals or snacks. **Known for:** impressive selection of teas; lunch dishes spanning several Asian cuisines; chocolate salty oat cookies. ⑤ *Average main: $12* ✉ *400 8th St. NW, Downtown* ☎ *202/638–6010* ⊕ *www. teaism.com* Ⓜ *Archives–Navy Memorial– Penn Quarter.*

★ Zaytinya

$$ | MIDDLE EASTERN | This sophisticated urban dining room with soaring ceilings is a local favorite for meeting friends or dining with a group (and popular enough that reservations can still be difficult to get). Here chef José Andrés devotes practically the entire menu to Turkish, Greek, and Lebanese small plates, known as meze. **Known for:** variety of meze; roasted lamb shoulder to share; vegetarian-friendly options. ⑤ *Average main: $26* ✉ *701 9th St. NW, Penn Quarter* ☎ *202/638–0800* ⊕ *www.zaytinya. com* Ⓜ *Gallery Pl.–Chinatown.*

 Hotels

For those who have not stayed in Washington for a decade or so, throw away your expectations. Cutting-edge hotels like Monaco in Penn Quarter and Donovan and Eaton Workshop closer to Downtown, have joined the traditional luxury names like St. Regis and the Jefferson, with the trustworthy Marriotts and Hiltons still visible and growing.

★ AC Hotel Washington DC

$$$ | HOTEL | The AC Hotel by Marriott is minimalist and elegant, with a European flare (the brand started in Spain and Italy), and occupies the former Smith and Wollensky steak house in the Golden Triangle business district. **Pros:** in the heart of downtown; great lobby bar; close to many restaurants. **Cons:** can get noisy; $45 for valet parking; far from monuments. ⑤ *Rooms from: $350* ✉ *1112 19th St. NW, Downtown* ✢ *Just 2 blocks to Metro Red and Blue lines* ☎ *202/303– 0190* ⊕ *www.marriott.com* ⋗ *219 rooms* ⊠ *No meals* Ⓜ *Farragut N.*

Capital Hilton

$$$ | HOTEL | The choice of many celebrities and dignitaries since it opened in 1943, the Hilton has modern perks like a health club and spa and is well located for shopping and eating out. **Pros:** nice guest rooms; desirable location; great gym, however, there's a daily fee unless you're a silver, gold, or diamond Hilton Honors member. **Cons:** expensive valet parking; reports of street noise; fee for Wi-Fi. ⑤ *Rooms from: $400* ✉ *1001 16th St. NW, Downtown* ☎ *202/393–1000* ⊕ *www.capital.hilton.com* ⋗ *576 rooms* ⊠ *No meals* Ⓜ *Farragut N.*

Comfort Inn Downtown DC/Convention Center

$ | HOTEL | There's nothing fancy at this hotel, and rooms tend to be on the small side, but the location, price, and daily hot breakfast buffet all add up to a good value. **Pros:** freshly baked afternoon cookies and popcorn, and all-day coffee and tea; pleasant staff; decent hot breakfast. **Cons:** some street noise at night; a bit out of the way; valet parking is $30 per day. ⑤ *Rooms from: $185* ✉ *1201 13th St. NW, Downtown* ☎ *202/682–5300* ⊕ *www.dcdowntownhotel.com* ⋗ *100 rooms* ⊠ *Free Breakfast* Ⓜ *Mt. Vernon Sq. 7th St.–Convention Center.*

Conrad Washington DC

$$$ | HOTEL | The Conrad, a modern hotel at CityCentreDC near the convention center, features an enormous, light-filled atrium and verdant outdoor terraces. **Pros:** part of Hilton's luxury collection; large rooms with floor-to-ceiling windows; rooftop terraces and 24-hour gym. **Cons:** pricey; some might prefer a more

Did You Know?

The National Building Museum was originally built to house the United States Pension Bureau. A renovation of its Great Hall—with its soaring, 75-foot-tall Corinthian columns—was completed in March 2020.

intimate setting. ⑤ *Rooms from: $395*
⌧ *950 New York Ave. NW, Downtown*
✛ *CityCentreDC* ☎ *202 /844–5900* ⊕ *con-
radhotels3@hilton.com* ⤶ *360 rooms*
⑪ *No meals* Ⓜ *Red, Blue, Yellow.*

Eaton Hotel, Washington, DC

$ | HOTEL | Eaton is a politically progres-
sive hotel that offers retro-cool and comfortable rooms, as well as digital content
on hot-button issues, including climate
change and immigration. **Pros:** commu-
nal space designed for discussions and
festivals; makes a political statement;
wellness center and bar on-site. **Cons:**
you may not agree with the hotel's
politics; valet parking only (costs extra);
not particularly family-friendly. ⑤ *Rooms
from: $200* ⌧ *1201 K St. NW, Downtown*
☎ *202/289–7600* ⊕ *eatonworkshop.com*
⤶ *209 rooms* ⑪ *No meals* Ⓜ *Metro
Center or McPherson Sq.*

Fairfield Inn & Suites Washington DC/ Downtown

$ | HOTEL | Bold, contemporary design
provides a soothing retreat in a busy part
of town, near many of the top attractions like the Capital One Arena, the
National Portrait Gallery, and the Mall.
Pros: complimentary hot breakfast buffet;
lots of restaurants, entertainment, and
attractions nearby; authentic Irish pub
on-site. **Cons:** some complaints about
street noise; small gym; part of town
not for everyone. ⑤ *Rooms from: $195*
⌧ *500 H St. NW, Chinatown* ☎ *202/289–
5959* ⊕ *www.marriott.com* ⤶ *198
rooms* ⑪ *Free Breakfast* Ⓜ *Gallery
Pl.–Chinatown.*

Grand Hyatt Washington

$$$ | HOTEL | A city within the city is what
greets you as you step inside the Hyatt's
doors and gaze upward to the balconies
overlooking the blue lagoon and the
many conveniences within the atrium.
Pros: great location for sightseeing and
shopping; often has weekend deals;
nice gym and indoor pool. **Cons:** often
filled with conventioneers; chain-hotel

feel; expensive valet parking. ⑤ *Rooms
from: $319* ⌧ *1000 H St. NW, Downtown*
☎ *202/582–1234, 800/233–1234* ⊕ *www.
hyatt.com* ⤶ *897 rooms* ⑪ *No meals*
Ⓜ *Metro Center.*

Hamilton Hotel Washington, D.C.

$$$$ | HOTEL | A short walk from the White
House and the Mall, this appealing Art
Deco hotel, on the National Register of
Historic Places, is a good choice for visi-
tors doing the sights, as well as business
guests who come for top-notch meeting
rooms and the nearby convention
center. **Pros:** central location near White
House; well-equipped fitness center;
two restaurants and deluxe microbar.
Cons: some street noise; small rooms;
expensive valet parking. ⑤ *Rooms from:
$440* ⌧ *1001 14th St. NW, Downtown*
☎ *202/682–0111* ⊕ *www.hamiltonho-
teldc.com* ⤶ *318 rooms* ⑪ *No meals*
Ⓜ *McPherson Sq.*

★ The Hay-Adams

$$$$ | HOTEL | Given the elegant charm
and refined style, with guest rooms
decorated in a class above the rest, it's
no wonder this impressive Washington
landmark continues to earn international
accolades for its guest experience. **Pros:**
impeccable service; basically next door
to the White House; complimentary
bikes, helmets, locks, and cycling maps.
Cons: expensive parking; no pool; small
bathrooms for this price point. ⑤ *Rooms
from: $450* ⌧ *800 16th St. NW, Down-
town* ☎ *202/638–6600, 800/424–5054*
⊕ *www.hayadams.com* ▭ *No credit
cards* ⤶ *145 rooms* ⑪ *No meals*
Ⓜ *McPherson Sq. or Farragut N.*

Henley Park Hotel

$ | HOTEL | A Tudor-style building adorned
with gargoyles, this National Historic
Trust property has the cozy feel of an
English country house, and the atmos-
phere extends to charming rooms that
were once the choice of senators and
notables from Washington society.
Pros: centrally located; historic building;

welcoming staff. **Cons:** some rooms are small with very tiny bathrooms; rooms can be noisy and not all have views; expensive valet parking. $ *Rooms from: $175 ✉ 926 Massachusetts Ave. NW, Penn Quarter ☎ 202/638–5200, 800/222–8474 ⊕ www.henleypark.com ❖ 96 rooms ❍❍ No meals Ⓜ Mt. Vernon Sq. 7th St.–Convention Center.*

★ **InterContinental The Willard Washington D.C.**

$$$ | HOTEL | FAMILY | Favored by American presidents and other news makers, this Washington landmark only two blocks from the White House only offers superb service, a wealth of amenities, and guest rooms filled with period detail and Federal-style furniture. **Pros:** great on-site dining, high tea, and happy hour; impeccable service; exudes a real sense of history. **Cons:** expensive valet parking; no pool; street-facing rooms can be noisy. $ *Rooms from: $299 ✉ 1401 Pennsylvania Ave. NW, Downtown ☎ 202/628–9100, 800/827–1747 ⊕ www.washington. intercontinental.com ❖ 376 rooms ❍❍ No meals Ⓜ Metro Center.*

★ **The Jefferson**

$$$$ | HOTEL | Every inch of this 1923, Beaux Arts landmark exudes refined elegance, from the intimate seating areas that take the place of a traditional check-in counter to the delicate blooms and glass atrium at the entryway to Plume, the fine-dining restaurant. **Pros:** exquisite historic hotel in a great location; impeccable service; the Quill is about the best hotel bar in the city. **Cons:** expensive; some rooms have views of other buildings; not at all family-friendly. $ *Rooms from: $500 ✉ 1200 16th St. NW, Downtown ☎ 202/448–2300 ⊕ www.jeffersondc.com ❖ 119 rooms ❍❍ No meals Ⓜ Farragut N.*

JW Marriott Washington, DC

$$$$ | HOTEL | From the location near the White House to the views from the top floors, it's hard to forget you are in the nation's capital when you stay in one of the beautifully furnished rooms here. **Pros:** in the heart of town; lovely rooms with a luxurious, traditional feel; good views from top floors. **Cons:** very busy; charge for in-room Wi-Fi; pricey in-house restaurants. $ *Rooms from: $449 ✉ 1331 Pennsylvania Ave. NW, Downtown ☎ 202/393–2000, 800/393–2503 ⊕ www. jwmarriottdc.com ❖ 772 rooms ❍❍ No meals Ⓜ Metro Center.*

★ **Kimpton Hotel Monaco Washington DC**

$$$ | HOTEL | Elegance and whimsy are in perfect harmony at this popular boutique Kimpton hotel—Washington's first all-marble building—in the heart of the Penn Quarter. **Pros:** all the Kimpton extras like a nightly wine hour; amazing design throughout; historic charm. **Cons:** noisy part of town; no pool; expensive valet parking. $ *Rooms from: $325 ✉ 700 F St. NW, Penn Quarter ☎ 202/628–7177, 800/649–1202 ⊕ www.monaco-dc.com ❖ 183 rooms ❍❍ No meals Ⓜ Gallery Pl.–Chinatown.*

The Madison Washington DC, A Hilton Hotel

$$ | HOTEL | The signatures of presidents, prime ministers, sultans, and kings fill the guest register at this classic Washington address, noted for polite service and stylish comfort and now rebranded as a Hilton. **Pros:** central location; pretty guest rooms with plush furnishings and linens; staff goes the extra mile. **Cons:** 20-minute walk from the Mall; many rooms are a bit dark with no views; not enough plugs in the room for electronic devices. $ *Rooms from: $225 ✉ 1177 15th St. NW, Downtown ☎ 202/862–1600 ⊕ www.hilton.com ❖ 356 rooms ❍❍ No meals Ⓜ McPherson Sq.*

Marriott Marquis Washington, D.C

$$$ | HOTEL | This eco-friendly hotel, directly adjacent to the Washington Convention Center, spans an entire city block, and is capped with an enormous atrium skylight that accentuates the dramatic lobby sculpture. **Pros:** location near

4

Downtown

Metro; nicely designed building; within walking distance of great restaurants. **Cons:** rooms overlooking atrium have less privacy and can be noisy; expensive fee for in-room Wi-Fi; big and impersonal. ⑤ *Rooms from: $325* ✉ *901 Massachusetts Ave. NW, Downtown* ☎ *202/824–9200* ⊕ *www.marriott.com* ⮌ *1224 rooms* ⦿ *No meals* Ⓜ *Mt. Vernon Sq. 7th St.–Convention Center.*

★ The Mayflower Hotel, Autograph Collection

$$$ | HOTEL | FAMILY | With its magnificent block-long lobby filled with antique crystal chandeliers, layers of gold trim, and gilded columns, there's little wonder that this luxurious landmark has hosted presidential balls since its opening in 1925, as well as historic news conferences and even, for a short time, the Chinese Embassy. **Pros:** near dozens of restaurants; a few steps from Metro; the setting of plenty of political history and scandal. **Cons:** rooms vary greatly in size; expensive parking and pet fees; charge for in-room Wi-Fi unless you're a Marriott rewards member. ⑤ *Rooms from: $325* ✉ *1127 Connecticut Ave. NW, Downtown* ☎ *202/347–3000, 800/228–7697* ⊕ *www.marriott.com* ⮌ *731 rooms* ⦿ *No meals* Ⓜ *Farragut N.*

★ Morrison-Clark Historic Inn

$$ | HOTEL | A fascinating history makes these beautiful, 1864, Victorian town houses interesting, as well as comfortable and well-located, choices. **Pros:** charming alternative to cookie-cutter hotels; historic feel throughout; near convention center. **Cons:** some street noise; room size and style vary considerably; some bathrooms are pretty small. ⑤ *Rooms from: $199* ✉ *1011 L St. NW, Downtown* ☎ *202/898–1200, 800/332–7898* ⊕ *www.morrisonclark.com* ⮌ *114 rooms* ⦿ *No meals* Ⓜ *Metro Center.*

Renaissance Washington, D.C. Downtown Hotel

$ | HOTEL | Large rooms with views and fine linens, extensive business services, and such amenities as a lavish fitness center and spa elevate this chain hotel into the luxury realm. **Pros:** convenient to Convention Center and Metro; nice lobby and rooftop terrace; great fitness center and spa. **Cons:** convention crowds; chain-hotel feel; expensive parking. ⑤ *Rooms from: $199* ✉ *999 9th St. NW, Chinatown* ☎ *202/898–9000, 800/228–9898* ⊕ *www.marriott.com* ⮌ *807 rooms* ⦿ *No meals* Ⓜ *Gallery Pl.–Chinatown.*

★ Sofitel Washington, D.C. Lafayette Square

$$$ | HOTEL | Only a minute's walk from the White House, the French luxury chain could not have landed a better location, and its caring, multilingual staff offers a warm welcome and great service. **Pros:** prestigious location; highly rated restaurant; lovely rooms. **Cons:** lobby on the small side; expensive parking; many rooms have internal views. ⑤ *Rooms from: $360* ✉ *806 15th St. NW, Downtown* ☎ *202/730–8800* ⊕ *www.sofitel.com* ▭ *No credit cards* ⮌ *237 rooms* ⦿ *No meals* Ⓜ *McPherson Sq.*

The St. Regis Washington, D.C

$$$$ | HOTEL | Just two blocks from the White House, this gorgeous, 1926, Italian Renaissance–style landmark attracts a business and diplomatic crowd. **Pros:** close to White House; historic property; exceptional service. **Cons:** most rooms don't have great views; very expensive; some rooms noisy and in need of upgrading. ⑤ *Rooms from: $500* ✉ *923 16th St. NW, Downtown* ☎ *202/638–2626* ⊕ *www.stregiswashingtondc.com* ⮌ *172 rooms* ⦿ *No meals* Ⓜ *Farragut N or McPherson Sq.*

★ W Washington, D.C

$$$$ | HOTEL | Just steps from the White House, this hip property has a living room–style lobby that blends Italian

Renaissance with stylish swank, while rooms contain ultramodern furnishings. **Pros:** trendy ambience; individualized and attentive service; popular rooftop bar. **Cons:** pricey; might be too modern for some; no pool. $ *Rooms from: $499 ⊠ 515 15th St. NW, Downtown ☎ 202/661–2400 ⊕ www.starwoodhotels.com/whotels ⊸ 349 rooms* ⦿ *No meals* Ⓜ *McPherson Sq.*

Washington Marriott at Metro Center

$$$ | **HOTEL** | The big-chain feel is offset by a good location just steps away from the monuments and museums; attractive, comfortable guest rooms; and an indoor pool and health club. **Pros:** great location; Starbucks on property with outdoor patio; Metro Center subway station is right under hotel. **Cons:** generic decor; charge for in-room Wi-Fi; big and impersonal. $ *Rooms from: $379 ⊠ 775 12th St. NW, Downtown ☎ 202/737–2200, 800/393–2100 ⊕ www.marriott.com/wasmc ⊸ 459 rooms* ⦿ *No meals* Ⓜ *Metro Center.*

Ⓨ Nightlife

You'll find plenty of bars and lounges in the Downtown area, which has been wonderfully revitalized. Development around Chinatown and the Capital One Arena has turned this into a lively neighborhood, especially when there's a sports or musical event at the arena. A few blocks south, the formerly quiet Penn Quarter is seeing larger evening crowds, thanks to the opening of several terrific new restaurants, cafés, bars, and a world-class theater scene. Conveniently, especially if you plan to imbibe, you can easily get to Downtown on the Metro, exiting at the Archives–Navy Memorial–Penn Quarter station (Green and Yellow lines) or at the Gallery Place–Chinatown stop (Green, Yellow, and Red lines).

BARS AND LOUNGES
Barmini

BARS/PUBS | Only a small plaque on a bland concrete wall in a nondescript block of Penn Quarter identifies one of Washington's most sophisticated experiences. Step inside to see José Andrés's cocktail lab for his acclaimed chain of restaurants that looks the part, with white-on-white furnishings and mixologists in lab attire often seen pouring smoking libations out of beakers. A metal notebook features a menu of more than 100 alcohol-centered liquid experiments, grouped by spirit. Make it a show with drinks such as the tequila-based Cedar and Agave, in which a glass and block of ice are infused with the smell of burning wood, table-side, or the Floral Cloud, a fruity gin-based beverage delivered in a hibiscus haze. Soak up the chemical reactions with snacks such as savory miniwaffles. Behind the bar you can peer through a framed glass window to see a handful of foodies at the sister minibar taking a similarly science-inspired culinary tour. It all comes at a cost (between $18 and $25). ⊠ *501 9th St. NW, Penn Quarter ☎ 202/393–4451 ⊕ www.minibarbyjoseandres.com/barmini* Ⓜ *Archives–Navy Memorial–Penn Quarter.*

The Dignitary

BARS/PUBS | Inside the shell of an Art Deco–inspired edifice that once housed a labor union is one of the newest and most comfortably elegant bars in D.C., the corner spot of the Marriott Marquis. Deeper inside the hotel, you'll find a bustling lobby bar as well as a large, noisy sports bar with 48 beers on tap. But the Dignitary attracts a more refined crowd with its focus on more than 50 types of bourbons and ryes poured by a crew of bartenders as experienced as they are friendly. This Dignitary also features an outdoor patio in the warmer months. ⊠ *901 Massachusetts Ave. NW, Downtown ☎ 202/824–9681 ⊕ www.marriott.com* Ⓜ *Mt. Vernon Sq. 7th St.–Convention Center.*

The Hamilton

MUSIC CLUBS | From the street, it looks like a swanky Downtown D.C. restaurant with a high-ceilinged power bar to match. The magic really happens, however, with live shows in The Hamilton's cavernous basement space. Care in equal parts has focused on acoustics, comfort, and tiered seating that makes it hard to find a bad seat. There is secondary space above the bar–restaurant where the venue regularly hosts more intimate acts and "Free Late Night Music in the Loft." ⊠ 600 14th St. NW, Downtown ☎ 202/787–1000 ⊕ live. thehamiltondc.com Ⓜ Metro Center.

★ P.O.V.

BARS/PUBS | For decades, the perfect way to end a night out in Washington was a trip up to the Sky Tavern on the Hotel Washington's 11th-floor rooftop. The W Hotel has replaced the Hotel Washington, and the Sky Tavern has been reincarnated as P.O.V. ("Point of View"), a trendy, hipster indoor lounge with an outdoor terrace offering tremendous vistas of D.C.'s low skyline. Enjoy the unique view of the Washington Monument and the White House while savoring a pan-Mediterranean array of cocktails, appetizers, and small plates. While the panoramas here are no secret, meaning waits are common, P.O.V. does take reservations. Popping by in the late afternoon may be a more relaxed option. ■ TIP→ After 5 pm, the venue only allows 21 and older. ⊠ 515 15 St. NW, Downtown ☎ 202/661–2400 ⊕ www.povrooftop.com Ⓜ McPherson Sq.

Quill

PIANO BARS/LOUNGES | At this *Mad Men* flashback fantasy bar tucked inside the Jefferson Hotel, the drinks are stiff and complex, and the mood is a quiet celebration of all things civilized. The dimly lit, two-room, wood-paneled, Art Deco space provides an intimate atmosphere made even more welcoming by the friendly and expert service of the bartenders. A pianist quietly serenades patrons throughout the evening. Pricey, but worth it. ⊠ *The Jefferson, 1200 16th St. NW, Downtown* ☎ *202/448–2300* ⊕ *www.jeffersondc.com/dining/quill* Ⓜ *Farragut N.*

COMEDY CLUBS
★ Capitol Steps

COMEDY CLUBS | Putting the "mock" in democracy, the musical political satire of this group—many of whom are current or former Hill staffers—is presented in the amphitheater of the Ronald Reagan Building every Friday and Saturday at 7:30 pm and occasionally at other spots around town. This Washington classic is fun for the whole family, no matter on which side of the aisle you sit. Tickets are around $40 and available through Ticketmaster and online. ⊠ *Ronald Reagan Bldg. and International Trade Center, 1300 Pennsylvania Ave. NW, Downtown* ☎ *703/683–8330* ⊕ *www.capsteps.com* Ⓜ *Federal Triangle.*

DC Improv

COMEDY CLUBS | The city's main spot for comedy offers a steady menu of well-known and promising stand-up headliners—recent acts have included Judah Friedlander—as well as a bevy of funny amateurs. Tickets vary depending on the act. Typically, there's a two-item minimum from a full food and drink menu. ⊠ *1140 Connecticut Ave. NW, Downtown* ☎ *202/296–7008* ⊕ *www.dcimprov.com* Ⓜ *Farragut N.*

DANCE CLUBS
The Park at Fourteenth

DANCE CLUBS | A high-end crowd includes visiting basketball players and R&B stars, who dance on four levels. The fancy and formal dress code is strictly enforced by the bouncers. Pricey perks include your own bottle service. You can arrange in advance to get a table or brave the long lines that develop later in the night. This is definitely a place to see and be seen. ⊠ *920 14th St. NW, Downtown* ☎ *202/737–7275* ⊕ *www.park14.com* Ⓜ *McPherson Sq.*

⭐ Performing Arts

Several of Washington's most prestigious performance centers can be found in Downtown D.C. Woolly Mammoth Theater, the Shakespeare Theatre's Sidney Harmon Hall, and other venues are surrounded by a bustling nightlife, where visitors have their choice of cuisines and after-performance conversation. You'll also be entertained by a host of street performers and musicians.

FILM

⭐ Landmark's E Street Cinema

FILM | Specializing in independent, foreign, and documentary films, this theater is beloved by D.C. movie enthusiasts both for its selection and its state-of-the-art facilities. The *Washington Post* has often declared it D.C.'s best movie theater, its concession stand is fabulous, and it is one of the city's few movie theaters that serves alcohol. ⊠ *555 11th St. NW, Downtown* ☎ *202/452-7672* ⊕ *www.landmarktheatres.com* Ⓜ *Metro Center*.

MAJOR VENUES

Capital One Arena

CONCERTS | In addition to being the home of the NHL Stanley Cup champion Washington Capitals and Washington Wizards basketball teams, this 19,000-seat arena also hosts D.C.'s biggest concerts and other major events. Drivers need to park in one of the many underground garages close by, but there are several convenient Metro lines, too. During warmer months, be sure to check out the frequent street concerts on the intersections surrounding the arena. ⊠ *601 F St. NW, Chinatown* ☎ *202/661-5000* ⊕ *capitalonearena.viewlift.com* Ⓜ *Gallery Pl.–Chinatown*.

THEATER AND PERFORMANCE ART

Ford's Theatre

THEATER | FAMILY | Looking much as it did before President Lincoln was shot at a performance of *Our American Cousin,* Ford's hosts musicals as well as dramas with historical connections, and it stages *A Christmas Carol* every year.

The historic theater is now maintained by the National Park Service. Tours of the venue and accompanying museum are free, but timed-entry tickets are required. Tickets to shows can range from $20 to $70 ⊠ *511 10th St. NW, Downtown* ☎ *202/426-6925* ⊕ *www.fords.org* Ⓜ *Metro Center*.

National Theatre

THEATER | FAMILY | Though rebuilt several times, the National Theatre has operated in the same location since 1835. It now hosts touring Broadway shows, from classics like *Porgy and Bess* and *Chicago,* to contemporary punk like *American Idiot.* Ticket prices vary with each show. ⊠ *1321 Pennsylvania Ave. NW, Downtown* ☎ *800/447-7400* ⊕ *thenationaldc.org* Ⓜ *Metro Center*.

⭐ Shakespeare Theatre

THEATER | This acclaimed troupe crafts fantastically staged and acted performances of works by Shakespeare and other significant playwrights, offering traditional renditions but also some with a modern twist. Complementing the stage in the Lansburgh Theatre is Sidney Harman Hall, which provides a state-of-the-art, midsize venue for an outstanding variety of performances—from Shakespeare's *Much Ado About Nothing* to Racine's tragic *Phèdre*—by visiting companies like South Africa's Baxter Theatre, which staged a production of *Mies Julie.* ⊠ *450 7th St. NW, Downtown* ☎ *202/547-1122* ⊕ *shakespearetheatre.org* Ⓜ *Gallery Pl.–Chinatown or Archives–Navy Memorial–Penn Quarter*.

Sixth & I Historic Synagogue

MUSIC | Known for its author readings and its comedy, with guests ranging from comedian Tina Fey to Nancy Pelosi, the Sixth & I Historic Synagogue has been named one of the most vibrant congregations in the nation. The intimate space, founded in 1852, hosts religious events as well. ⊠ *600 I St. NW, Chinatown* ☎ *202/408-3100* ⊕ *www.sixthandi.org* Ⓜ *Gallery Pl.–Chinatown*.

Warner Theatre

DANCE | One of Washington's grand theaters, the Warner hosts Broadway road shows, dance recitals, high-profile pop-music acts, and comedians in a majestic Art Deco performance space with wonderful acoustics. ⊠ *513 13th St. NW, Downtown* ☎ *202/783–4000* ⊕ *warnertheatredc.com* Ⓜ *Metro Center.*

★ Woolly Mammoth

THEATER | Unusual cutting-edge shows with solid acting have earned this company top reviews and 35 Helen Hayes Awards. The theater performs works for a decidedly urban audience that challenge the status quo. In recent years, they have welcomed Chicago's The Second City for an annual political comedy show as well as the works of Mike Daisey, the author of *The Agony and Ecstasy of Steve Jobs.* The troupe's talent is accentuated by its modern, 265-seat theater in bustling Downtown D.C. The Woollies also create a unique lobby experience for each show; bring your iPhone, and share the experience. ⊠ *641 D St. NW, Downtown* ☎ *202/393–3939* ⊕ *www.woollymammoth.net* Ⓜ *Gallery Pl.–Chinatown or Archives–Navy Memorial–Penn Quarter.*

🛍 Shopping

Downtown D.C. is spread out and sprinkled with federal buildings and museums. Shopping options run the gamut from the upscale CityCenterDC complex and Gallery Place shopping center to small art galleries and bookstores. Gallery Place houses familiar chain stores like Urban Outfitters, Bed Bath & Beyond, and Ann Taylor Loft; it also has a movie theater and a bowling alley. Other big names in the Downtown area include Macy's and chain stores like H&M, Target, and Banana Republic. With its many offices, Downtown tends to shut down at 5 pm sharp, with the exception of the department stores and larger chain stores. A jolly happy-hour

crowd springs up after work, and families and fans fill the streets during weekend sporting events at the Capital One Arena. The revitalized Penn Quarter has some of the best restaurants in town peppered among its galleries and specialty stores.

The worthwhile shops are not concentrated in one area, however. The Gallery Place–Chinatown Metro stop provides the most central starting point—you can walk south to the galleries and design shops or west toward the Metro Center and Farragut North, though this trek is only for the ambitious. Although Gallery Place is a nightlife hot spot, the Metro Center and the Farragut area are largely silent after working hours.

CLOTHING

Coup de Foudre

CLOTHING | The name translates to "love at first sight," and that may be the case when you step into this inviting, elegant boutique. All the upscale lingerie hails from France, England, Belgium, and Italy, and the specialty is friendly, personalized bra fittings. Appointments are accepted. ⊠ *1001 Pennsylvania Ave. NW, Downtown* ☎ *202/393–0878* ⊕ *www.shopcdf.com* Ⓜ *Metro Center.*

J. Press

CLOTHING | Like its flagship store (founded in Connecticut in 1902 as a custom shop for Yale University), this Washington outlet keeps with the Ivy League traditions. Harris tweed and classic navy blazers are the best sellers. ⊠ *1801 L St. NW, Downtown* ☎ *202/857–0120* ⊕ *www.jpressonline.com* Ⓜ *Farragut N.*

Rizik's

CLOTHING | This tony, patrician Washington institution offers women's designer clothing, accessories, outerwear, bridal fashions, and expert advice. The sales staff will help you find just the right style from the store's extensive inventory from worldwide designers. If you're looking for a one-of-kind cocktail or evening dress, this is the place to get it. Take the elevator up from the northwest corner of Connecticut Avenue and L Street. ✉ *1100 Connecticut Ave. NW, Downtown* ☎ *202/223–4050* ⊕ *www.riziks.com* Ⓜ *Farragut N.*

CRAFTS AND GIFTS
★ Fahrney's Pens

CRAFTS | What began in 1929 as a repair shop and a pen bar—a place to fill your fountain pen before setting out for work—is now a wonderland for anyone who loves a good writing instrument. You'll find pens in silver, gold, and lacquer by the world's leading manufacturers. If you want to improve your handwriting, the store offers classes in calligraphy and cursive. And yes, the store still offers repair services for all writing instruments—in this digital age Fahrneys' endures. ✉ *1317 F St. NW, Downtown* ☎ *202/628–9525* ⊕ *www.fahrneyspens. com* Ⓜ *Metro Center.*

JEWELRY
★ Capitol Coin & Stamp Co

ANTIQUES/COLLECTIBLES | Searching for a William Howard Taft candy dish? How about a William McKinley 1896 campaign button? It's all here, whether you need it or not. Capitol Coin is a charming political memorabilia and coin shop (they don't sell stamps, despite the name) just a hop and skip from the White House. In the basement of a building next to the Secret Service, it's not easy to find, but for political junkies it's worth the effort. It's been in operation at various locations for more than 40 years. The priciest political artifact is a medallion of George Washington's presidency that goes for about $2,000, but most offerings are fairly modest. For mementos, Capitol Coin beats the airport gift shops by a long shot. ✉ *1616 H St. NW , Suite B-1, Downtown* ✛ *Enter at 1616 and take elevator to basement* ☎ *202/296–0400* ⊕ *www.capitolcoin.com* Ⓜ *Farragut W.*

★ Tiny Jewel Box

JEWELRY/ACCESSORIES | Despite its name, this venerable D.C. favorite contains six floors of precious and semiprecious wares, including unique gifts, home accessories, vintage pieces, and works by such well-known designers as David Yurman, Penny Preville, and Alex Sepkus. The Federal Collection on the sixth floor features handmade boxes and paper-weights with decoupages of vintage prints of Washington commissioned by the Tiny Jewel Box. *InStore Magazine* has named this family-run store "America's Coolest Jewelry Store." Even if you're not buying, come in and look around. It's like a shopping museum. ✉ *1147 Connecticut Ave. NW, Downtown* ☎ *202/393–2747* ⊕ *www.tinyjewelbox.com* Ⓜ *Farragut N.*

SHOPPING MALLS
CityCenterDC

SHOPPING CENTERS/MALLS | Downtown's newest complex is an upscale gathering of high-end boutiques, restaurants, res-idential and office buildings, a park, and an open-air plaza, bordered by New York Avenue, 9th, 11th, and H Streets NW. It's all too easy to spend several hundred dollars in just a few minutes here, with leather goods from Longchamp, Louis Vuitton, and Salvatore Ferragamo; designer fashions and accessories from Burberry, Canali, CH Carolina Herrera, Kate Spade, Loro Piana, Paul Stuart, Zadig & Voltaire; outdoor clothing and sporting goods from Arc'teryx; Tumi luggage; and David Yurman jewelry. For a break from shopping or browsing, grab an indulgent treat from Rare Sweets or a scrumptious gelato from Dolcezza, and relax in the plaza with its benches, tables, and fountains. ✉ *825 10th St. NW, Downtown* ☎ *202/347–6337* ⊕ *www. citycenterdc.com* Ⓜ *Metro Center or Gallery Pl.–Chinatown.*

SPAS
Andre Chreky
SPA/BEAUTY | Housed in an elegantly ren-
ovated Victorian town house, this salon
offers complete services—hair, nails,
facials, waxing, and makeup. Because
it's a favorite of the Washington elite,
you might just overhear a tidbit or two
on who's going to what black-tie function
with whom. Adjacent whirlpool pedicure
chairs allow two friends to get pampered simultaneously. ⊠ *1604 K St. NW,
Downtown* ☎ *202/293–9393* ⊕ *www.
andrechreky.com* Ⓜ *Farragut N.*

The Grooming Lounge
SPA/BEAUTY | Get pampered with
old-fashioned hot-lather shaves, haircuts,
massages, and business manicures
and pedicures. The hair- and skin-care
products—from Kiehl's, Billy Jealousy,
and Malin+Goetz, to name just a few—
make this a worthy stop even if you don't
have time for a service. ⊠ *1745 L St. NW,
Downtown* ☎ *202/466–8900* ⊕ *www.
groominglounge.com* Ⓜ *Farragut N.*

Chapter 5

CAPITOL HILL AND NORTHEAST

Updated by
Sabrina Medora

☻ Sights	🍴 Restaurants	🛏 Hotels	🛍 Shopping	🍸 Nightlife
★★★★☆	★★★☆☆	★★★☆☆	★★★☆☆	★★★★☆

NEIGHBORHOOD SNAPSHOT

TOP EXPERIENCES

■ **The Capitol:** See where democracy is put into action. Start your tour at the visitor center, then walk among marble American heroes and gape at the soaring Rotunda.

■ **The Markets:** Eastern Market is the more traditional market, offering fresh produce, baked goods, and locally made crafts. Union Market is an upscale version, featuring oyster bars and chic coffee shops. Both are beloved weekend destinations.

■ **The Library of Congress and Supreme Court:** Flanking the Capitol, both are architectural wonders offering a must-see window into the nation's history and the workings of government.

■ **Union Station:** More than a train station, it's a stunning gem of classical architecture, where the vaulted ceiling soars almost 100 feet above the massive marble floor. Shops and restaurants also await.

■ **Strolling and Dining:** The area has three lively commercial corridors: Pennsylvania Avenue, H Street, and Barracks Row, one of the city's oldest neighborhoods and a vital bulwark in wars past. All feature a wide array of bars, restaurants, and shops.

■ **United States Botanic Garden:** Wrinkle your nose at the corpse flower, explore the jungle, gawk at the orchids or stroll the paths of the National Garden.

GETTING HERE

From the Red Line's Union Station, you can walk to most destinations on Capitol Hill. A new streetcar runs from behind the station along the full length of H Street—a good option for accessing the street's spirited nightlife. From the Blue and Orange lines, the Capitol South stop is close to the Capitol and Library of Congress, and the Eastern Market stop leads to the market and the Marine Corps Barracks. Bus Nos. 31, 32, 36 and Circulator buses run from Friendship Heights through Georgetown and Downtown to Independence Avenue, the Capitol, and Eastern Market.

SAFETY

■ Although crime is rare around Capitol Hill, it does occur, particularly in fast-changing neighborhoods like the H Street corridor. You can limit the risk with commonsense steps like keeping to well-populated areas and traveling with companions after dark. In short, stay alert—D.C. is relatively safe, but it's still a city.

QUICK BITES

■ **Library of Congress's Madison Building Cafeteria.** Steps from the Capitol, it gets rave reviews for its varied breakfasts and lunches (weekdays only). ⊠ *Madison Bldg., Library of Congress, Independence Ave. SE, between 1st and 2nd Sts.* ⊕ *www.loc.gov* Ⓜ *Capitol S.*

■ **Union Station.** No matter the time of day or dining moods of your group, you'll find everything you might want here. ⊠ *50 Massachusetts Ave. NE* ⊕ *www.union-stationdc.com/restaurants* Ⓜ *Union Station.*

■ **We, the Pizza.** *Top Chef's* Spike Mendelsohn flips specialty pies with creative ingredients every day but Sunday. ⊠ *305 Pennsylvania Ave. SE* ⊕ *www.wethepizza.com* Ⓜ *Capitol S.*

The people who live and work on "the Hill" do so in the shadow of the edifice that lends the neighborhood its name: the gleaming white U.S. Capitol.

But beyond the area's grand buildings lies a vibrant and diverse group of neighborhoods with charming residential blocks lined with Victorian row houses and a fine assortment of restaurants, shops, and bars, where senators, members of Congress, and lobbyists come to unwind or to continue their deal making. This area includes the Eastern Market, the Atlas District (also known as the H Street corridor), Union Station, and Union Market.

Sights

Belmont-Paul Women's Equality National Monument

HISTORIC SITE | Standing strong on Capitol Hill for more than 200 years, this house witnessed the construction of the U.S. Capitol and Supreme Court, and its early occupants participated in the formation of Congress. In 1929, the National Woman's Party (NWP), founded by Alice Paul, an outspoken suffragist and feminist, purchased the house, and it soon evolved into a center for feminist education and social change. For more than 60 years, the trailblazing NWP utilized its strategic location, steps from the U.S. Capitol and its Congressional offices, to lobby for women's political, social, and economic equality. Today, an expansive collection of artifacts from the suffrage and equal rights campaigns brings the story of the women's rights movement to life. The innovative tactics and strategies these women devised became the blueprint for women's progress throughout the 20th century. In 2016, President Obama designated the home as a national monument. ⊠ 144 Constitution Ave. NE, Capitol Hill ⊹ Entrance on 2nd St., next to Hart Senate Office Bldg. ☎ 202/543–2240 ⊕ www.nps.gov/bepa ⊠ Free ⊘ Closed Mon. and Tues. Ⓜ Union Station (Red Line) is the closest station to the north. To the south, Capitol South (Blue, Orange, Silver) is the next closest.

Folger Shakespeare Library

LIBRARY | Housing the world's largest collection of Shakespeare memorabilia, this Tudor-style institution is a combination museum, library, theater, and architectural wonder. The Great Hall is simply stunning and holds rotating exhibits from the library's collection. Henry Clay Folger, the Library's founder, personally selected the inscriptions by and about Shakespeare that are found throughout the property, and the First Folio of Shakespeare is always on view. Visitors are greeted at the entrance to the Elizabethan Theatre—a reproduction of a 16th-century inn-yard playhouse—by a marble statue of Puck from A Midsummer Night's Dream. This is where you can see performances of Shakespearean plays, chamber music, readings, lectures, and family programs; check the website for a calendar of events. Two wings of the library—the Paster and New Reading Rooms—are devoted to scholarly research. On Saturday at noon, you can tour both rooms, though reservations are required. A manicured Elizabethan garden on the grounds is open to the public, and the gift shop contains many collectibles featuring the Bard and

Sights ▼

1 Belmont-Paul Women's
Equality National Monument..... **D4**

2 Folger Shakespeare Library...... **D5**

3 Library of Congress................ **D6**

4 Marine Barracks.................... **G9**

5 Smithsonian National Postal
Museum **C2**

6 Supreme Court
of the United States **D5**

7 United States Botanic Garden ... **A6**

8 United States Capitol.............. **B5**

9 United States
National Arboretum **J1**

Restaurants ▼

1 Ambar Capitol Hill **G8**

2 Belga Café.......................... **G8**

3 Bistro Bis **B2**

4 Cava Mezze **G8**

5 Ethiopic Restaurant **E1**

6 Good Stuff Eatery.................. **E6**

7 Granville Moore's.................. **I1**

8 IMM Thai on H **J1**

9 Jimmy T's Place.................... **F5**

10 Le Grenier **F1**

11 The Market Lunch **G6**

12 Pineapple and Pearls **G9**

13 Rose's Luxury **G9**

14 Seventh Hill Pizza................. **G7**

15 Sonoma Restaurant and
Wine Bar............................ **E6**

16 Ted's Bulletin **G8**

17 Tune Inn............................. **E7**

Hotels ▼

1 Capitol Hill Hotel **D7**

2 City House Hostel
Washington DC **F1**

3 Hilton Garden Inn
Washington DC/U.S. Capitol....... **C1**

4 Hyatt Regency Washington on
Capitol Hill **A3**

5 Kimpton George Hotel............. **B2**

6 Phoenix Park Hotel **B2**

7 Washington Court Hotel **B2**

English theater. ⊠ *201 E. Capitol St. SE, Capitol Hill* ☎ *202/544–4600* ⊕ *www. folger.edu* ✉ *Free* Ⓜ *Capitol S.*

★ **Library of Congress**
LIBRARY | Founded in 1800, the largest library in the world has more than 167 million items on approximately 838 miles of bookshelves. Only 39 million of its holdings are books—the library also has millions of maps, recordings, photographs, and other materials. Built in 1897, the copper-domed Thomas Jefferson Building is the oldest of the library's three structures. The building's Great Hall is richly adorned with mosaics, paintings, and curving marble stairways. The octagonal Main Reading Room, its central desk surrounded by mahogany readers' tables under a 160-foot-high domed ceiling, inspires researchers and readers alike. Computer terminals have replaced card catalogs, but books are still retrieved and dispersed the same way: readers (16 years or older) give request slips to librarians and await the hand-delivery of the materials. Items from the library's collection—which includes one of only three perfect Gutenberg Bibles in the world—are on display in the Jefferson Building. ■**TIP→ To get a sense of the library's grandeur, one of the free hourly tours is highly recommended.** ⊠ *Jefferson Bldg., 1st St. and Independence Ave. SE, Capitol Hill* ☎ *202/707–9779* ⊕ *www.loc. gov* ✉ *Free* ⊘ *Closed Sun.* Ⓜ *Capitol S.*

Marine Barracks
HISTORIC SITE | In early 1801, President Thomas Jefferson and the second commandant of the Marine Corps, Lt. Col. William Ward Burrows, made a horseback tour through Washington, D.C., looking for a proper site for the Marine Barracks. They selected "Square 927," and the commandant's house was completed in 1806, followed by the barracks in 1808. It was among the few buildings left standing when the British burned much of the Capitol in 1814. After years of renovations and additions, the

Georgian-Federalist-style home now has 15,000 square feet of space and more than 30 rooms. Still used for its original purpose, the Home of the Commandants on 8th and I Streets is said to be the oldest continuously occupied public building in Washington, D.C. "Square 927," now the block surrounded by 8th, I, 9th, and G Streets SE, was designated a National Historic Landmark in 1976. Although you can't tour the home, you can see the outside of this impressive home for the commandant of the Marine Corps and the historic Marine Barracks. ⊠ *801 G St. SE, Eastern Market* ☎ *202/433–6040* ⊕ *www.barracks.marines.mil* Ⓜ *Eastern Market or Potomac Ave.*

Smithsonian National Postal Museum
MUSEUM | **FAMILY** | The National Museum of Natural History has the Hope Diamond, but the National Postal Museum has the envelope wrapping used to mail the gem to the Smithsonian—part of a collection that consists of more than 6 million stamps. Exhibits, underscoring the important part the mail has played in America's development, include horse-drawn mail coaches, railroad mail cars, airmail planes, and a collection of philatelic rarities. Learn about stamp collecting, and tour *Systems at Work,* an exhibit that demonstrates how mail has gone from the mailbox to its destination for the past 200 years and features a high-def film highlighting amazing technologies. The **William Gross Stamp Gallery**, the largest of its kind in the world, has an additional 20,000 objects never before on public display, showing how closely stamps have intertwined with American history. The museum is next to Union Station in the old Washington City Post Office, designed by Daniel Burnham and completed in 1914. ⊠ *2 Massachusetts Ave. NE, Capitol Hill* ☎ *202/633–5555* ⊕ *www.postalmuseum.si.edu* ✉ *Free* Ⓜ *Union Station.*

Continued on page 127

ON THE HILL, UNDER THE DOME: EXPERIENCING THE CAPITOL

In Washington, the Capitol literally stands above it all: by law, no other building in the city can reach the height of the dome's peak.

Beneath its magnificent dome, the day-to-day business of American democracy takes place: senators and representatives debate, coax, and cajole, and ultimately determine the law of the land.

For many visitors, the Capitol is the most exhilarating experience Washington has to offer. It wins them over with a three-pronged appeal:

■ It's the city's most impressive work of architecture.

■ It has on display documents, art, and artifacts from 400 years of American history.

■ Its legislative chambers are open to the public. You can actually see your lawmakers at work, shaping the history of tomorrow.

THE CAPITOL THROUGH THE CENTURIES

(Clockwise from top left) Moving into the new Capitol circa 1800; 19th–century print by R. Brandard; Thornton sketch circa 1797; the Capitol before the dome.

1792 - 1807
A Man with a Plan

William Thornton, a physician and amateur architect from the West Indies, wins the competition to design the Capitol. His plan, with its central rotunda and dome, draws inspiration from Rome's Pantheon. On September 18, 1793, George Washington lays the Capitol's cornerstone. In November 1800, Congress moves from Philadelphia to take up residence in the first completed section, the boxlike area between the central rotunda and today's north wing. In 1807, the House wing is completed, just to the south of the rotunda; a covered wooden walkway joins the two wings.

1814 - 1826
Washington Burns

In 1814, British troops march on Washington and set fire to the Capitol, the White House, and other government buildings. The wooden walkway is destroyed and the two wings gutted, but the walls remain standing after a violent rainstorm douses the flames. Fearful that Congress might leave Washington, residents fund a temporary "Brick Capitol" on the spot where the Supreme Court is today. By 1826, reconstruction is completed under the guidance of architects Benjamin Henry Latrobe and Charles Bulfinch; a low dome is made of wood sheathed in copper.

1850s - 1880s
Domed if You Do

North and south wings are added through the 1850s and '60s to accommodate the growing government of a growing country. To maintain scale with the enlarged building, work begins in 1885 on a taller, cast-iron dome. President Lincoln would be criticized for continuing the expensive project during the Civil War, but he calls the construction "a sign we intend the Union shall go on."

(Clockwise from top left)
The east front circa 1861;
today the Capitol is a
tourist mecca with its
own visitor center;
Freedom statue.

1960s - Today

Expanding the Capitol

The east front is extended 33½ feet, creating 100 additional offices. In 1983 preservationists fight to keep the west front, the last remaining section of the Capitol's original facade, from being extended; in a compromise the facade's crumbling sandstone blocks are replaced with stronger limestone. In 2000 the ground is broken on the subterranean Capitol Visitor Center, to be located beneath the grounds to the building's east side. The extensive facility, three-fourths the size of the Capitol itself, was finally completed on December 2, 2008 to the tune of $621 million.

Freedom atop the Capitol Dome

The twin-shelled Capitol dome, a marvel of 19th-century engineering, rises 285 feet above the ground and weighs 4,500 tons. It can expand and contract as much as 4 inches in a day, depending on the outside temperature.

The allegorical figure on top of the dome is *Freedom*. Sculpted in 1857 by Thomas Crawford, *Freedom* was cast with help from Philip Reid, a slave. Crawford had first planned for the 19½-foot-tall bronze statue to wear the cloth liberty cap of a freed Roman slave, but Southern lawmakers, led by Jefferson Davis, objected. An "American" headdress composed of a star-encircled helmet surmounted with an eagle's head and feathers was substituted. A light just below the statue burns whenever Congress is in session.

Before the visitor center opened, the best way to see the details on the *Freedom* statue atop the Capitol dome was with a good set of binoculars. Now, you can see the original plaster model of this classical female figure up close. Her right hand rests on a sheathed sword, while her left carries a victory wreath and a shield of the United States with 13 stripes. She also wears a brooch with "U.S." on her chest.

THE CAPITOL VISITOR CENTER

The enormous and sunlit Capitol Visitor Center (CVC) is the start for all Capitol tours, and brings a new depth to the Capitol experience with orientation theaters, an interactive museum, and live video feeds from the House and Senate. It also provides weary travelers with welcome creature comforts, including a 530-seat restaurant.

DESIGN

At 580,000 square feet, the visitor center is approximately three-quarters the size of the 775,000-square-foot Capitol. The center's belowground location preserves the historic landscape and views designed by Frederick Law Olmsted in 1874. Inside, skylights provide natural light and views of the majestic Capitol dome. The center opened in December 2008, three years late and $356 million over budget.

EMANCIPATION HALL

The center's largest space is a gorgeous sunlit atrium called Emancipation Hall in honor of the slaves who helped to build the Capitol in the 1800s. The plaster model of the *Freedom* statue, which tops the Capitol's dome, anchors the hall. Part of the Capitol's National Statuary Hall collection is also on display here.

MUSEUM

Other attractions include exhibits about the Capitol, historical artifacts, and documents. A marble wall displays historic speeches and decisions by Congress, like President John F. Kennedy's famous 1961 "Man on the Moon" speech and a letter Thomas Jefferson wrote to Congress in 1803 urging the funding of the Lewis and Clark Expedition.

KIDS AT THE CVC

The Capitol Visitor Center is a great place for families with children who may be too young or too wiggly for a tour of the Capitol. In the Exhibition Hall, the 11-foot tall touchable model of the Capitol, touch screen computers, and architectural replicas welcome hands-on exploration.

Challenge younger kids to find statues of a person carrying a spear, a helmet, a book, and a baby.

Tweens can look for statues of the person who invented television, a king, a physician, and a representative who said, "I cannot vote for war."

PLANNING YOUR CAPITOL DAY

LOGISTICS

To tour the Capitol, you can book free, advance passes at ⊕ *www.visitthecapitol.gov* or through your representative's or senator's offices. In addition, a limited number of same-day passes are available at the Public Walk-Up line on the lower level of the visitor center. Tours run every 15 minutes; the first tour begins at 8:50 and the last at 3:20, Monday through Saturday. The center is closed on Sunday.

Plan on two to four hours to tour the Capitol and see the visitor center. You should arrive at least 30 minutes before your scheduled tour to allow time to pass through security. Tours, which include a viewing of the orientation film *Out of Many, One,* last about one hour.

If you can't get a pass to tour the Capitol, the Capitol Visitor Center is still worth a visit. You can also take one of the free guided tours that do not require reservations.

To get passes to the chambers of the House and Senate, contact your representative's or senator's office. Many will also arrange for a staff member to give you a tour of the Capitol or set you up with a time for a Capitol Guide Service tour. When they're in session, some members even have time set aside to meet with constituents. You can link to the e-mail of your representative at ⊕ *www.house.gov* and of your senators at ⊕ *www.senate.gov.*

SECURITY

Expect at least a 30-minute wait going through security when you enter the Capitol Visitor Center. Bags can be no larger than 14 inches wide, 13 inches high, and 4 inches deep. View the list of prohibited items on ⊕ *www.visitthecapitol.gov.* (There are no facilities for storing prohibited belongings.) For more information, call ☎ *202/226–8000, 202/224–4049 TTY.*

BEAN SOUP AND MORE

A favorite with legislators, the Senate bean soup has been served every day for more than 100 years in the exclusive Senate Dining Room. It's available to the general public in the restaurant of the CVC (◷ Open 7:30 AM–4 PM) on a rotating basis. You can also try making your own with the recipe on the Senate's Web site (⊕ www.senate.gov).

GETTING HERE— WITHOUT GETTING VOTED IN

The Union Station, Capitol South and Federal Center, SW Metro stops are all within walking distance of the Capitol. Follow the people wearing business suits—chances are they're headed your way. Street parking is extremely limited, but Union Station to the north of the Capitol has a public garage and there is some metered street parking along the Mall to the west of the Capitol.

RENOVATION

A complete renovation of the Capitol Dome was completed in late 2016, just before the presidential inauguration in January 2017.

TOURING THE CAPITOL

National Statuary Hall

Your 30- to 40-minute tour conducted by the Capitol Guide Service includes stops at the Rotunda, followed by the National Statuary Hall, the Hall of Columns, the old Supreme Court Chamber, the crypt (where there are exhibits on the history of the Capitol), and the gift shop. Note that you *don't* see the Senate or House chambers on the tour. (Turn the page to learn about visiting the chambers.) The highlights of the tour are the first two stops. . . .

THE ROTUNDA

You start off here, under the Capitol's dome. Look up and you'll see *Apotheosis of Washington,* a fresco painted in 1865 by Constantino Brumidi. The figures in the inner circle represent the 13 original states; those in the outer ring symbolize arts, sciences, and industry. Further down, around the Rotunda's rim, a frieze depicts 400 years of American history. The work was started by Brumidi in 1877 and continued by another Italian, Filippo Costaggini. American Allyn Cox added the final touches in 1953.

NATIONAL STATUARY HALL

South of the Rotunda is Statuary Hall, which was once the chamber of the House of Representatives. When the House moved out, Congress invited each state to send statues of two great deceased residents for placement in the hall. Because the weight of the statues threatened to make the floor cave in, and to keep the room from being cluttered, more than half of the sculptures have ended up in other spots in the Capitol. Ask your guide for help finding your state's statues.

ARTIST OF THE CAPITOL
Constantino Brumidi (1805-80) devoted his last 25 years to frescoing the Capitol; his work dominates the Rotunda and the Western Corridor. While painting the section depicting William Penn's treaty with the Indians for the Rotunda's frieze *(pictured above),* a 74-year-old Brumidi slipped from the 58-foot scaffold, hanging on until help arrived. He would continue work for another four months, before succumbing to kidney failure.

TRY THIS
Because of Statuary Hall's perfectly elliptical ceiling, a whisper uttered along the wall can be heard at the point directly opposite on the other side of the room. Try it when you're there—if it's not noisy, the trick should work.

ONE BIG HAWAIIAN
With a solid granite base weighing six tons, Hawaii's Kamehameha I in Statuary Hall is among the heaviest objects in the collection. On Kamehameha Day (June 11, a state holiday in Hawai'i), the statue is draped with leis.

United States Capitol

Marble Room
(Senators' Retiring
Room)

Ceremonial Office
of the Vice President

President's
Room

Senators'
Reception
Room

Senate
Chamber

Democratic
Cloakrooms

Republican
Cloakrooms

Senators'
Conference
Room

Old Senate
Chamber

West Front

Rotunda

Prayer
Room

Congresswomen's
Suite

House
Document
Room

Statuary
Hall

House
Reception
Room

Republican
Cloakrooms

Democratic
Cloakrooms

House
Chamber

Representatives'
Retiring Room

C St. NE

Constitution Ave.

1st St.

1st St.

U.S. Capitol
Visitor Center
(Underground)
◀ ENTRANCE

United States
Capitol

New Jersey Ave.

1st St.

Canal St.

0   30 yards
0   30 meters

GOING TO THE FLOOR

ONE IF BY LAND . . . ?
When flags fly over their respective wings of the Capitol, you'll know the House and Senate are in session. The House is on the south side, the Senate on the north.

A tour of the Capitol is impressive, but the best part of a visit for many people is witnessing the legislators in action. Free gallery passes into the House and Senate chambers have to be obtained from your representative's or senator's office. They aren't hard to come by, but getting them takes some planning ahead. Once you have a pass, it's good for any time the chambers are open to public, for as long as the current Congress is sitting. Senate chambers are closed when the Senate is not in session, but the House is open.

HOUSE CHAMBER

The larger of two chambers may look familiar: it's here that the president delivers the annual State of the Union. When you visit, you sit in the same balcony from which the First Family and guests watch the address.

Look carefully at the panels above the platform where the Speaker of the House sits. They're blue (rather than green like the rest of the panels in the room), and when the House conducts a vote, they light up with the names of the representatives and their votes in green and red.

SENATE CHAMBER

With 100 members elected to six-year terms, the Senate is the smaller and ostensibly more dignified of Congress's two houses. Desks of the senators are arranged in an arc, with Republicans and Democrats divided by the center aisle. The vice president of the United States is officially the "president of the Senate," charged with presiding over the Senate's procedures. Usually, though, the senior member of the majority party oversees day-to-day operations, and is addressed as "Mr. President" or "Madam President."

Judiciary Committee

House session

SWEET SPOT IN THE SENATE
In the sixth desk from the right in the back row of the Senate chamber, a drawer has been filled with candy since 1968. Whoever occupies the desk maintains the stash.

Visiting Government Buildings

You can visit many of Washington's government offices, but you have to do some advance planning in many cases. Here's a rundown of how far ahead you should make arrangements.

No Advance Planning Required

Two of the most impressive places in Washington don't require reservations. The **Library of Congress** and the **U.S. Supreme Court** are architectural and political treasures.

With its murals, paintings, sculptures and statues, and, of course, millions of books and manuscripts, the Library of Congress is truly spectacular. Even if you're not a bookworm, the free docent-led tour is one of the best things going in the city. Revolving exhibits prevent the experience from ever getting stale. The Supreme Court does not offer guided tours, but visitors are welcome to amble through its public spaces, which include the courtroom itself. Other features include the John Marshall statue, a visitor film, and ever-rotating court-related exhibits. Court sessions are also open to the public on a first-come, first-served basis.

Capitol Visitor Center

One of the most visited attractions, the **Capitol Visitor Center** is the starting point for tours of the Capitol and where you'll discover a plethora of historical treasures, including a table used by Abraham Lincoln during his 1865 inaugural address. Crowds in spring and summer can number in the thousands, so plan for at least three hours here. The five-football-fields-size underground complex is a destination in itself, with the model of the statue of *Freedom*, a 530-seat dining room that serves the famous Senate bean soup, and exhibits on the Capitol. A 13-minute orientation film lends some footing. The visitor center is open until 4:30 pm, Monday through Saturday, but the last Capitol tour is at 3:20. Allow extra time to go through security.

To visit the Capitol, you can reserve tickets online at ⊕ *www.visitthecapitol.gov*, contact your representative or senator, or gamble for a limited number of same-day passes.

★ **Supreme Court of the United States**
GOVERNMENT BUILDING | Completed in 1935, the Supreme Court is a white-marble temple with twin rows of Corinthian columns—a must-see even if you decide not to go in. The court convenes on the first Monday in October and hears cases until April (though court is in session through June). The case calendar is displayed on the court's website a month in advance, and the public is welcome to watch, though you'll need to line up early to see the most contentious cases. When the court is in session, two lines form: the "three-to-five-minute" line shuttles you through, giving you a quick impression of the court at work; the full-session line gets you in for the whole show (be in line by 8:30). Electronics are prohibited in the courtroom, but you can store them in coin-operated lockers. Regardless of whether the court is in session, there's plenty to do and see, including revolving exhibits, lectures from experts, a film about the court, a gift shop, and a larger-than-life statue of John Marshall, the longest-serving chief justice in Supreme Court history. ⊠ *1 1st St. NE, Capitol Hill* ☎ *202/479–3030* ⊕ *www.*

The Supreme Court officially began meeting in this Corinthian-column-lined building in 1935.

supremecourt.gov ✉ *Free* ⊘ *Closed weekends* Ⓜ *Union Station or Capitol S.*

★ United States Botanic Garden

GARDEN | FAMILY | Established by Congress in 1820, this is the oldest continually operating botanic garden in North America. The conservatory sits at the foot of Capitol Hill and offers an escape from the stone-and-marble federal office buildings that surround it. Inside are exotic rain-forest species, desert flora, and trees from all parts of the world. Walkways suspended 24 feet above the ground provide a fascinating view of the plants. Established in 2006, the National Garden emphasizes educational exhibits and features a Rose Garden, Butterfly Garden, Lawn Terrace, First Ladies' Water Garden, and Regional Garden. ✉ *1st St. at 100 Maryland Ave. SW, Capitol Hill* ☎ *202/225–8333* ⊕ *www.usbg.gov* ✉ *Free* Ⓜ *Federal Center SW.*

★ United States Capitol

GOVERNMENT BUILDING | Beneath the Capitol's magnificent dome, the day-to-day business of American democracy transpires: Congress debates, cajoles, and crafts the laws of the land. It's an exhilarating experience with a three-pronged appeal: it's the city's most impressive architectural work; it displays documents, art, and artifacts from 400 years of American history; and its legislative chambers are open to the public, allowing you to witness your lawmakers at work. The easiest way to see the Capitol is through the visitor center, where free 90-minute tours are conducted Monday through Saturday from 8:40 am to 3:20 pm. Same-day tours are available, but spots can fill quickly, so advance booking is recommended. Security lines can be long, so an early arrival is also suggested. Visit the website for more details and to make your free reservations. Tours, as well as passes to watch Congress in session, are also available through the office of your local lawmaker, but you can't enter the visitors gallery without a pass. International visitors may request both from the appointment desks in the visitor center. ✉ *East end of The Mall, Capitol Hill* ☎ *202/226–8000*

Inside Congress: How Laws Are Made

Amid the grand halls of the Capitol building, members of Congress and their aides are busy crafting the laws of our land. It's not a pretty process; as congressional commentators have quipped, laws are like sausages—it's best not to know how they're made. But for iron stomachs, here's a brief tour through Washington's sausage factory.

The Idea Stage

Most laws begin as proposals that any of Congress's 535 members may offer in the form of bills. Many are trivial, such as renaming post-office branches. Others are vital, like funding the federal government. Once introduced, all proposals move to a relevant congressional committee.

Congressional Committees and Committee Hearings

Although thousands of proposals are introduced each year, almost all die in committee. Congress never has enough time to entertain each bill, so committee leaders prioritize. Some bills are dismissed for ideological reasons.

Others simply lack urgency. Efforts to rein in fuel costs, for instance, are popular when gas prices are high. Lobbying and special-interest money are other major factors influencing the content and even success or failure of individual bills.

For bills that advance, merits and drawbacks are debated in committee hearings. These hearings—staged in the congressional office buildings adjacent to the Capitol—are usually open to the public; check ⊕ www.house.gov and ⊕ www.senate.gov under the "committee" headings for schedules. Committee members then vote on whether to move bills to the chamber floor.

Passing the House, Senate, and White House

A bill approved by committee still faces three formidable tests before becoming a law: it must pass the full House, the full Senate, and usually the White House.

Each legislative chamber has different rules for approving bills. In the House, proposals that clear a committee and have the blessing of House leaders need only a simple majority. In the Senate, legislation can be delayed by filibustering—a time-honored process of talking nonstop on the Senate floor—until at least 60 senators vote to end the delay. If the House and Senate pass different versions of the same proposal, then those differences are reconciled in a joint conference committee before returning to the respective floors for another round of voting.

A bill passed by both the House and Senate then proceeds to the White House. The president can either sign it—in which case it becomes law—or veto it, in which case it returns to Congress. Lawmakers can override a veto, but two-thirds of each chamber must support the override to transform a vetoed bill into law. When President George W. Bush twice vetoed a popular children's health care proposal, House supporters couldn't rally the two-thirds majority to override it. The bill enjoyed President Obama's support and became law after he took office.

The United States Botanic Garden, founded in 1820, is the oldest in North America.

⊕ www.visitthecapitol.gov 🖾 Free
⊙ Closed Sun. Ⓜ Capitol S or Union
Station.

★ United States National Arboretum

GARDEN | During azalea season (mid-April through May), this 446-acre oasis operated by the U.S. Department of Agriculture is a blaze of color. In early summer, clematis, peonies, rhododendrons, and roses bloom. At any time of year, the 22 original Corinthian columns from the U.S. Capitol, re-erected here in 1990, are striking. All 50 states are represented by a state tree or flower. Since 2014, a pair of American bald eagles have made a home near the azaleas, and the nest can be seen via an unobstructed viewing scope. The arboretum has guided hikes throughout the year, including a Full Moon Hike, and dogs are allowed on the grounds as long as they're on a leash at all times. Check the website for schedules and to register. Visit the Cryptomeria Walk and Japanese Stroll Garden, which are part of the Bonsai and Penjing Museum. On weekends, a tram tours the arboretum's curving roadways at 11:30 and on the hour 1–4. 🖾 3501 New York Ave. NE, Northeast 🕾 202/245–2726 ⊕ www.usna usda.gov 🖾 Free Ⓜ Weekends: Union Station, then X6 bus (runs every 40 mins); weekdays: Stadium–Armory, then B2 bus to Bladensburg Rd. and R St.

🍴 Restaurants

"The Hill," as locals know it, was once an enclave of congressional boardinghouses in the shadow of the Capitol building but is now D.C.'s largest historic district, with an eclectic mix of restaurants. Around the Capitol South Metro station, government offices end, and neighborhood dining begins. Here, along tree-lined streets, some of the city's most acclaimed restaurants have joined the local bars and eateries that have long catered to lunch and happy-hour crowds during the week.

Neighborhood establishments and all-American pubs line historic Barracks Row, with Eastern Market anchoring the homey House side of the Hill; the Senate end is given a more hustle-and-bustle vibe with the chain dining and upscale boîtes of Union Station. The Atlas District, also known as the H Street corridor, overflows with great restaurants, and a few blocks north is Union Market, where dozens of local food and beverage purveyors sell everything from arepas to Zinfandels.

Ambar Capitol Hill

$$ | EASTERN EUROPEAN | Ambar, a handsome, noisy, two-story restaurant–bar at the heart of Barracks Row is your spot for Balkan comfort food. The Belgrade-inspired menu is full of hearty novelties like lamb medallions with pomegranate syrup, almond-crusted chicken with green apple, drunken mussels with capers and lemon, savory pies, a host of rich sausages, and all flavor of kebabs. **Known for:** reservations highly recommended; all-you-can-eat small plates; attentive and enthusiastic servers. $ *Average main: $20* ⊠ *523 8th St. SE, Eastern Market* ☎ *202/813–3039* ⊕ *www.ambarrestaurant.com* Ⓜ *Eastern Market.*

Belga Café

$$$ | BELGIAN | Belgium culture aficionados can go traditional with mussels and the crispiest of French fries or dabble in what the chef calls Eurofusion at this sleek café done up with dark wood and exposed brick. Classic dishes such as Flemish beef stew made with Corsendonk Brune beer sauce help capture that Belgian charm. **Known for:** 10 styles of mussels; 12-page beer menu; waffle-centric brunch menu. $ *Average main: $28* ⊠ *514 8th St. SE, Eastern Market* ☎ *202/544–0100* ⊕ *www.belgacafe.com* Ⓜ *Eastern Market.*

Bistro Bis

$$$ | FRENCH | The zinc bar, cherrywood interior, and white tablecloths create great expectations at Bistro Bis, where the seasonal menu offers modern takes on French bistro fare. Thanks to its prime location, acclaimed menu, deep wine

list, and classic cocktails, it's a popular spot for Washington power brokers and insiders. **Known for:** excellent steak frites and steak tartare; sophisticated ambience that attracts a powerful clientele; an elegant apple tart. $ *Average main: $29* ⊠ *Hotel George, 15 E St. NW, Capitol Hill* ☎ *202/661–2700* ⊕ *www.bistrobis.com* Ⓜ *Union Station.*

★ Cava Mezze

$$ | GREEK | This modern mecca for mezes (small plates for sharing) delivers delicious, chic Mediterranean cuisine without the whiz-bang conceits of its pricier cousins. There are few surprises on the menu, save for the feta hush puppies, but the wood-and-brick interior and gallant service make the traditional dishes feel new again. **Known for:** crazy feta hush puppies and spicy lamb sliders; lots of vegan and gluten-free options; all-you-can-eat brunch with 25¢ mimosas. $ *Average main: $24* ⊠ *527 8th St. SE, Eastern Market* ☎ *202/543–9090* ⊕ *www.cavamezze.com* ☾ *No lunch Mon.* Ⓜ *Eastern Market.*

Ethiopic Restaurant

$$ | ETHIOPIAN | FAMILY | The spongy rolls of sourdough *injera* bread (ubiquitous on Ethiopian plates) used in place of utensils can make traditional Ethiopian feel decidedly indelicate, but the bright surroundings and friendly service here make for a downright romantic experience. Venture off the well-beaten path of spicy lamb and lentils to try the spicy chickpea dumplings or fragrant simmered split peas, laden with garlic and served in a clay pot. **Known for:** minimalist yet friendly atmosphere; Ethiopian standards like beef tibs and injera; great Ethiopian coffee and beer options. $ *Average main: $23* ⊠ *401 H St. NE, Capitol Hill* ☎ *202/675–2066* ⊕ *www.ethiopicrestaurant.com* ☾ *Closed Mon. No lunch Tues.–Thurs.* Ⓜ *Union Station.*

★ Good Stuff Eatery

$ | AMERICAN | FAMILY | Fans of Bravo's *Top Chef* will first visit this brightly colored burgers-and-shakes joint hoping to spy charismatic celebrity chef Spike Mendelsohn, but they will return for the comfort-food favorites. The lines can be long, as it's a favorite lunch spot of congressional aides, but Spike's inventive beef dishes are worth the wait. **Known for:** fun burgers like the "Prez Obama" (with bacon, onion marmalade, and Roquefort cheese); thick malted milk shakes; variety of dipping sauces for hand-cut skinny fries. ⑤ *Average main: $8* ✉ *303 Pennsylvania Ave. SE, Capitol Hill* ☎ *202/543–8222* ⊕ *www.good-stuffeatery.com* ⊗ *Closed Sun.* Ⓜ *Eastern Market.*

Granville Moore's

$$ | BELGIAN | This Belgian beer hall with a gourmet soul is worth a visit for both its intense beer list and mussels and frites, plus a few other unique salads and burgers. Snag a seat at the bar or at one of the first-come, first-served tables, and linger over unfiltered artisanal brews that range from Chimay to obscure options from the reserve and limited-stock beer selection. **Known for:** steamed mussels served in five unique sauces; wide-ranging Belgian beer list; crunchy frites and homemade dipping sauces. ⑤ *Average main: $20* ✉ *1238 H St. NE, Capitol Hill* ☎ *202/399–2546* ⊕ *www.granvillemoor-es.com* ⊗ *No lunch Mon.–Thurs.* Ⓜ *Union Station.*

IMM Thai on H

$$ | THAI | "IMM" in Thai means "pleasantly full," and this tiny newcomer at the eastern edge of the H Street corridor will get you there happily. The spicy curries and other traditional entrées like pad Thai come in heaping servings, all but ensuring you'll have leftovers for tomorrow's lunch. **Known for:** intimate dining with attentive service; heaping curries, spiced hot as you like; happy hour sushi deals. ⑤ *Average main: $18* ✉ *1360 H St.*

NE, Capitol Hill ☎ *202/748–5536* ⊕ *www.immthai.com* Ⓜ *Union Station.*

Jimmy T's Place

$ | AMERICAN | Known for its boisterous owner and throngs of talkative regulars, this D.C. institution is tucked into the first floor of an old row house only five blocks from the Capitol. Enjoy favorites like eggs Benedict made with a toasted English muffin, a huge piece of ham, and lots of hollandaise sauce. **Known for:** classic greasy-spoon atmosphere; breakfast combos like grits and pumpkin pancakes; absolutely no substitutions and cash only. ⑤ *Average main: $7* ✉ *501 E. Capitol St. SE, Capitol Hill* ☎ *202/546–3646* ▭ *No credit cards* ⊗ *Closed Mon. No dinner* Ⓜ *Capitol S.*

Le Grenier

$$ | FRENCH | Le Grenier's slogan is "the French on H," and it's no joke: this cozy spot near Union Station has every bit the feel of a Parisian neighborhood bistro, with a menu of traditional favorites to match. The wonderful assortment of cheeses and charcuterie plates—featuring a delectable pâté and fig chutney sides, as well as heaping bowls of mussels—never disappoints. **Known for:** traditional French comfort food in a cozy setting; signature cocktails like the "H for Hipster"; affordable brunch with a superb Bloody Mary. ⑤ *Average main: $20* ✉ *502 H St. NE, Capitol Hill* ☎ *202/544–4999* ⊕ *www.legrenierdc.com* ⊗ *Closed Mon.* Ⓜ *Union Station.*

The Market Lunch

$ | AMERICAN | FAMILY | Digging into a hefty pile of pancakes from this casual counter in Eastern Market makes for the perfect end to a stroll around the Capitol. Morning favorites include not only pancakes but also eggs and grits; crab cakes, fried shrimp, and fish are popular at lunch. **Known for:** blueberry buckwheat pancakes; long lines and lots of kids; cash-only policy. ⑤ *Average main. $14* ✉ *225 7th St. SE, Eastern Market*

☎ 202/547–8444 ⊕ www.marketlunchdc.
com ▭ No credit cards ⊗ Closed Mon.
No dinner Ⓜ Eastern Market.

★ Pineapple and Pearls

$$$$ | CONTEMPORARY | For his follow-up to
the smash hit Rose's Luxury, chef Aaron
Silverman opened this reservation-only
dining room next door that offers only an
expensive 12-course (give or take) tasting
menu (the price includes beverages
and tips). Bar seating is also available
for a lower price that doesn't include
the drinks. **Known for:** expensive (but
all-inclusive) tasting menu; fun and low-
key dishes with zero pretension; intense
reservation process. ⑤ Average main:
$325 ⊠ 715 8th St. SE, Eastern Market
☎ 202/595–7375 ⊕ www.pineapplean-
dpearls.com ⊗ Closed Sun., Mon., and
(usually) Sat. Ⓜ Eastern Market.

★ Rose's Luxury

$$ | MODERN AMERICAN | A darling of both
diners and the media, Rose's Luxury
lives up to the hype as one of the city's
most welcoming and groundbreaking
dining destinations. The dishes are as
delightful as they are shocking, and
cause visitors to wait in line for hours to
visit the supremely stylish re-creation
of a hipster's dream dinner party. **Known
for:** innovative small plates; the sausage,
lychee, and habanero salad; long waits
for a table (with reservations only for big
groups). ⑤ Average main: $20 ⊠ 717 8th
St. SE, Eastern Market ☎ 202/580–8889
⊕ www.rosesluxury.com ⊗ No lunch
Ⓜ Eastern Market.

Seventh Hill Pizza

$ | PIZZA | Breezy charm and a casual
ambience helped to vault this pizzeria to
the top of the list of D.C.'s best. Each pie
is named for a nearby neighborhood—the
zesty mating of basil and anchovies on
the "Southwest Waterfront" is matched
only by the creamy goat cheese of the
"Eastern Market." Pizzas pair well with
the small lineup of bottled beers. **Known
for:** locally named wood-fired pizzas;

bright and welcoming atmosphere; Nute-
lla calzone for dessert. ⑤ Average main:
$16 ⊠ 327 7th St. SE, Eastern Market
☎ 202/544–1911 ⊕ www.montmartredc.
com/seventhhill ⊗ Closed Mon. Ⓜ Eastern Market.

Sonoma Restaurant and Wine Bar

$$ | WINE BAR | This chic, multilevel wine
bar has pours aplenty (in both tasting
portions and full glasses) along with
well-thought-out charcuterie boards piled
with prosciutto and fluffy, grill-charred
focaccia. There's more-filling fare, too,
like potato gnocchi with mushrooms.
Known for: hip and vast wine menu;
happy hour catering to a congressional
crowd; house-made charcuterie and
thin-crust pizzas. ⑤ Average main: $22
⊠ 223 Pennsylvania Ave. SE, Capitol Hill
☎ 202/544–8088 ⊕ www.sonomadc.com
⊗ No lunch Sat. Ⓜ Capitol S.

Ted's Bulletin

$$ | DINER | FAMILY | This cheeky homage
to mid-20th-century diners is styled
after a newspaper office, with menus
printed in broadsheet format and specials
mounted on the wall in mismatched
plastic lettering. But one bite of the
grilled cheese with tomato soup or the
house pastrami, will convince you that
the kitchen's skills are no joke. **Known for:**
fun newsroom-meets-diner ambience;
milk shakes with clever names (with or
without alcohol); homemade Pop-Tarts.
⑤ Average main: $17 ⊠ 505 8th St.
SE, Eastern Market ☎ 202/544–8337
⊕ www.tedsbulletin.com Ⓜ Eastern
Market.

Tune Inn

$ | DINER | Part bar, part diner, part hap-
py-hour haunt for Hill staffers, this Capitol
Hill tradition is one of the neighborhood's
last great dives. Opened in 1947, and still
run by the same family, the space was
upgraded after a fire in 2011 but retains
its lodgelike decor, including a healthy
display of taxidermied animals staring
down from the walls. **Known for:** cheap

beer and greasy grub; an utter absence of pretension; breakfast served all day. $ *Average main: $8* ✉ *331 Pennsylvania Ave. SE, Capitol Hill* ☎ *202/543–2725* ⊕ *tuneinndc.com* Ⓜ *Capitol S.*

 # Hotels

To be sure, politics and commerce, like oil and water, don't mix, but they sure make for a great neighborhood in which to spend a few nights. Fortunately, there's no lack of options when it comes to lodging on Capitol Hill. From modernist luxury suites to comfy boutique settings—there's even a hideaway hostel for the most thrifty travelers—the neighborhood offers plenty of choices to base your visit at the hub of some of Washington's best political, commercial, and cultural sights.

Capitol Hill Hotel

$$ | HOTEL | FAMILY | A great choice if you want to stay on the Hill and need some extra room to spread out: all Federalist-chic-style units are suites, with kitchenettes, large work desks, flat-screen TVs, and spacious closets. **Pros:** close to Metro and sights; access to on-site bikes; eco-friendly. **Cons:** expensive valet parking; hotel is spread out in two buildings, which can be inconvenient; extra fee to access certain amenities. $ *Rooms from: $271* ✉ *200 C St. SE, Capitol Hill* ☎ *202/543–6000* ⊕ *www.capitolhillhotel-dc.com* ⇆ *153 suites* ⦿❚ *Free Breakfast* Ⓜ *Capitol S.*

City House Hostel Washington DC

$ | HOTEL | It looks like a hole-in-the-wall, but this hostel is a clean, comfortable oasis—in the heart of the bustling H Street corridor and near public transit—that's perfect for backpackers and other cost-conscious travelers. **Pros:** smack in the center of a lively strip of bars, restaurants, and grocery stores; good chance to meet fellow travelers; by far the cheapest option close to the Capitol. **Cons:** H Street can be noisy; cramped

accommodations; very few private rooms. $ *Rooms from: $25* ✉ *506 H St. NE, Capitol Hill* ☎ *202/370–6390* ⊕ *www.cityhousehostels.com/washington-dc-hostel* ⇆ *14 rooms* ⦿❚ *No meals* Ⓜ *Union Station.*

Hilton Garden Inn Washington DC/U.S. Capitol

$ | HOTEL | Just a block from a Metro stop, this hotel, though a bit off the beaten path, is convenient for getting around the city. **Pros:** great views; indoor pool; business-friendly, including free Wi-Fi and printing. **Cons:** no pets allowed; not in the center of town; no self-parking, and valet parking is pricey. $ *Rooms from: $138* ✉ *1225 1st St. NE, Capitol Hill* ☎ *202/408–4870* ⊕ *www.hiltongardeninn.com* ⇆ *204 rooms* ⦿❚ *No meals* Ⓜ *NoMa–Gallaudet U.*

Hyatt Regency Washington on Capitol Hill

$ | HOTEL | A favorite for political events, fund-raising dinners, and networking meetings, this standard-issue business hotel is a solid choice if you plan to spend a lot of time on the Hill. **Pros:** beautiful sky-lit, heated indoor pool and outdoor sundeck; quick walk to Union Station; Old Town Trolley Tours stop at hotel. **Cons:** always very busy; expensive parking; anonymous feel. $ *Rooms from: $109* ✉ *400 New Jersey Ave. NW, Capitol Hill* ☎ *202/737–1234, 800/233–1234* ⊕ *www.hyatt.com* ⇆ *838 rooms* ⦿❚ *No meals* Ⓜ *Union Station.*

★ Kimpton George Hotel

$$$ | HOTEL | We cannot tell a lie—D.C.'s first contemporary boutique hotel is still one of its best, with a convenient location near Union Station and with public areas and stylishly soothing guest quarters that make it a fun, funky alternative to cookie-cutter chains. **Pros:** complimentary wine hour nightly; popular in-house restaurant; free access to bikes for touring. **Cons:** small closets; some reports of street noise; ultramodern feel not everyone's cup of tea. $ *Rooms*

from: $328 ✉ *15 E St. NW, Capitol Hill* ☎ *202/347–4200, 800/576–8331* ⊕ *www. hotelgeorge.com* ⇋ *139 rooms* ⏐◯⏐ *No meals* Ⓜ *Union Station.*

Phoenix Park Hotel

$ | **HOTEL** | If you prefer to be near the Hill but not in a convention hotel, this family-owned, European-style inn—which offers small but beautifully appointed and comfortable guest rooms across the street from Union Station—may fit the bill. **Pros:** comfy beds with good linens; live Dubliner Restaurant and Pub next-door; free Wi-Fi. **Cons:** no swimming pool; small rooms; some rooms are noisy. ⑤ *Rooms from: $129* ✉ *520 N. Capitol St. NW, Capitol Hill* ☎ *202/638–6900, 855/371–6824* ⊕ *www.phoenixparkhotel. com* ⇋ *149 rooms* ⏐◯⏐ *No meals* Ⓜ *Union Station.*

Washington Court Hotel

$ | **HOTEL** | This may not be the city's newest "It" hotel, but soothing guest rooms, done in soft grays and browns, and a location that's convenient to the Metro and sights make it a reliable, comfortable place to stay. **Pros:** Capitol views from many rooms; executive king rooms have sofa beds; 24-hour fitness and business centers. **Cons:** some reports of mixed service; complaints of hidden fees; expensive valet parking. ⑤ *Rooms from: $202* ✉ *525 New Jersey Ave. NW, Capitol Hill* ☎ *202/628–2100* ⊕ *www. washingtoncourthotel.com* ⇋ *265 rooms* ⏐◯⏐ *No meals* Ⓜ *Union Station.*

Nightlife

BARS AND LOUNGES

Biergarten Haus

BREWPUBS/BEER GARDENS | Step off H Street and into a boisterous bit of Bavaria. There might be football on TV, but that's not enough to break the spell of a place so genuinely Germanic. With about a dozen German drafts on offer, along with other authentic specialties—apfel

schnapps?—and a full bar, there's something for everyone, including a variety of spaces. Get cozy inside, or head for the courtyard, which is heated in winter. In pleasant weather, the second-story terrace also packs in visitors. ✉ *1355 H St. NE, Capitol Hill* ☎ *202/388–4085* ⊕ *www. biergartenhaus.com.*

Dubliner

BARS/PUBS | A short walk from Union Station and Capitol Hill, this Washington institution in Phoenix Park Hotel offers cozy paneled rooms, rich pints of Guinness, and other authentic fare. It's especially popular with Hill staffers and Georgetown law students. While offering live Irish music seven nights a week, this charming spot never charges a cover, save for St. Patrick's Day. ✉ *4 F St. NW, Capitol Hill* ☎ *202/737–3773* ⊕ *www. dublinerdc.com* Ⓜ *Union Station.*

Granville Moore's

BARS/PUBS | Beer and mussels: the appeal is that simple, and they're that satisfying. But the narrow, rustic bars on two floors are as popular with drinkers as diners. The Belgian-themed gastropub has one of the largest selections of beer, from pilsners to Flemish reds, in D.C. If you are hungry, offerings in this cozy spot go beyond mussels, and include steak au poivre, Liège waffles, and a hearty brunch selection. ✉ *1238 H St. NE, Capitol Hill* ☎ *202/399–2546* ⊕ *www. granvillemoores.com* Ⓜ *Union Station.*

H Street Country Club

BARS/PUBS | The only D.C. bar to offer indoor miniature golf, shuffleboard, and Skee-Ball has a friendly, laid-back vibe. Fish tacos and an impressive margarita list round out the fun mix at this popular nightspot. Big-screen sports line the walls downstairs, but you can usually catch a breath of fresh air on the roof deck. ✉ *1335 H St. NE, Capitol Hill* ☎ *202/399–4722* ⊕ *www.hstcountryclub. com* Ⓜ *Union Station.*

Harold Black

BARS/PUBS | Step back in time at this hideaway speakeasy, a relative newcomer to D.C.'s hipster scene near Eastern Market. Be aware, there are rules here: phones are discouraged, reservations are required (book online), and your seats are secured for only two hours. But those willing to play along are rewarded with a unique taste of the Roaring '20s in a wonderfully quiet space that's perfect for catching up with friends and sampling delicious signature cocktails. A limited menu features a handful of munchies, small plates, and desserts, including a light artichoke hummus, fish tacos, beef short ribs, and a rich chocolate-hazelnut cake. ⊠ *212 7th St. SE, Eastern Market* ⊕ *www.haroldblackdc.com.*

Little Miss Whiskey's

BARS/PUBS | A purple light at the door marks the spot of this eclectic, New Orleans–themed watering hole–dance club at the center of H Street. The dark interior, illuminated in black lights, features old concert posters from cult favorites like Pantera and Iggy Pop. The bar downstairs offers an enormous list of bottled beers and a signature adult slushee—the "Awesomeness"—that packs a real punch. The upstairs bar hosts DJs every Friday and Saturday night, when the space heaves with dancers packed wall-to-wall. The bar's cheeky slogan—"a lousy bar for lousy people"— isn't quite right. The service here is great. ⊠ *1104 H St. NE, Capitol Hill* ⊕ *www.littlemisswhiskeys.com* Ⓜ *Union Station.*

MUSIC CLUBS

Echostage

MUSIC CLUBS | This sprawling complex of more than 30,000 square feet effectively re-creates the vibe of an otherwise bygone era in D.C.—one of mega-nightclubs in retrofitted warehouses in derelict neighborhoods. With unobstructed sight lines to the stage and a German-imported sound system, it's the place for club kids to dance to the biggest names in E.D.M.,

from Calvin Harris to David Guetta to Tiesto. Catch your breath at one of the two 60-foot bars lining either side of the dance floor. ∎TIP➜ **With no Metro stops nearby, driving or taking a cab/rideshare is required.** ⊠ *2135 Queens Chapel Rd. NE, Northeast* ☎ *202/503–2330* ⊕ *www. echostage.com.*

Mr. Henry's

MUSIC CLUBS | Opened in 1966, this laid-back club is the last holdout of a once-thriving live-music scene on Capitol Hill. Roberta Flack got her start in the upstairs performance space, where a dozen or so tables are scattered around the wood-paneled room. There's never a cover. Check the website for upcoming acts. ⊠ *601 Pennsylvania Ave. SE, Capitol Hill* ☎ *202/546–8412* ⊕ *www.mrhenrysdc.com* Ⓜ *Eastern Market.*

🎭 Performing Arts

The arts scene in Capitol Hill and Northeast D.C. has blossomed in recent years with the opening of several performance venues and the explosion of restaurants, bars, and stages along the emerging H Street corridor. Leading the charge is the Atlas Performing Arts Center, at the cutting edge of dance, music, and drama. For classical drama, you will discover great performances and an intimate atmosphere at the Folger Theatre near the Capitol.

DANCE

Dance Place

DANCE | This studio theater showcases an eclectic array of local, national, and international dance and performance art talent in an assortment of modern and ethnic shows. Performances take place most weekends, and drop-in dance classes are held daily. The company is a bit of a trek from Capitol Hill (about 3 miles north of the Capitol), but it's quite close to the Brookland–CUA Metro station on the Red Line, just three stops from Union Station. ⊠ *3225 8th St. NE, Northeast*

☎ 202/269–1600 ⊕ www.danceplace.org
Ⓜ Brookland–CUA.

Joy of Motion

DANCE | Resident companies include El
Teatro de Danza Contemporanea El Salva-
dor, Furia Flamenca, and Silk Road Dance
Company (traditional Middle Eastern and
Central Asian), among others. They offer
drop-in classes in three locations: the
Atlas Performing Arts Center; the studio's
Jack Guidone Theatre in Upper North-
west; and in Bethesda, Maryland. There
are weekly performances in the Atlas
Performing Arts Center. ⊠ 1333 H St.
NE, Capitol Hill ☎ 202/362–3042 ⊕ www.
joyofmotion.org Ⓜ Friendship Heights.

MAJOR VENUES
Atlas Performing Arts Center

ARTS CENTERS | Known as the "People's
Kennedy Center," this performance
venue occupies a restored historic
movie theater in one of Washington's
up-and-coming neighborhoods. The
Atlas's four theaters and three dance
studios house a diverse group of resident
arts organizations, including the Mosaic
Theater Company of D.C., the Joy of
Motion Dance Center, Step Afrika!, and
the Capital City Symphony. Street parking
can be difficult, but you can now take the
DC Streetcar here from the Metro stop at
Union Station. ⊠ 1333 H St. NE, Capitol
Hill ☎ 202/399–7993 ⊕ www.atlasarts.
org Ⓜ Union Station.

MUSIC
CHAMBER MUSIC
Coolidge Auditorium at the Library of Congress

CONCERTS | Since its first concert, in
1925, the Coolidge has hosted most of
the 20th and 21st centuries' greatest
performers and composers, including
Copland and Stravinsky. Today, the
theater draws musicians from all genres,
including classical, jazz, and gospel,
and the hall continues to wow audienc-
es with its near-perfect acoustics and
sight lines. Concert tickets are free but
must be ordered in advance through

Ticketmaster. ■TIP→ **Because of the
Library's security procedures, patrons are
urged to arrive 30 minutes before the start of
each event.** ⊠ Library of Congress, Jefferson Building, 101 Independence Ave. SE,
Capitol Hill ☎ 800/551–7328 ⊕ www.loc.
gov Ⓜ Capitol S.

Folger Shakespeare Library

CONCERTS | The library's internationally
acclaimed resident chamber music
ensemble, the Folger Consort, regularly
presents Medieval, Renaissance, and
Baroque pieces performed on period
instruments. The season runs from
October to May. ⊠ 201 E. Capitol St. SE,
Capitol Hill ☎ 202/544–7077 ⊕ www.
folger.edu Ⓜ Union Station or Capitol S.

CHORAL MUSIC
★ Basilica of the National Shrine of the Immaculate Conception

CONCERTS | Choral and church groups
occasionally perform at the largest
Catholic church in the Americas, and,
every summer, recitals featuring the
massive pipe organ are offered. While
you are there, be sure to go down to
the crypt to experience the mysteries
of the world's many Madonnas. See the
website for times and visiting performers. ⊠ 400 Michigan Ave. NE, Northeast
☎ 202/526–8300 ⊕ www.nationalshrine.
com Ⓜ Brookland–CUA.

THEATER AND PERFORMANCE ART
Capital Fringe Festival

ARTS FESTIVALS | Since its founding
in 2005, the Capital Fringe Festival
has grown each year, and it currently
offers no fewer than 125 productions
over a three-week period in July. Local
and national performers display the
strange, the political, the surreal, and
the avant-garde to eclectic crowds at all
times of the day in venues throughout
the city. With tickets around $17, this
is an affordable theater experience.
■TIP→ **Don't forget your Fringe Button,
a pin that grants the holder access to all
festival events and benefits from local
retailers.** Be ready to party at the Fringe

Arts Bar, just north of H Street, where performers, musicians, and patrons rock into the wee hours. ✉ *1358 Florida Ave. NE., Capitol Hill* ☎ *866/811–4111* ⊕ *www. capfringe.org.*

★ Folger Theatre

THEATER | The theater at the Folger Shake-speare Library, an intimate 250-seat re-creation of the inn-yard theaters of Shakespeare's time, hosts three to four productions each year of Shakespear-ean or Shakespeare-influenced works. Although the stage is a throwback, the sharp acting and inspired direction con-sistently challenge and delight audienc-es. ✉ *Folger Shakespeare Library, 201 E. Capitol St. SE, Capitol Hill* ☎ *202/544–7077* ⊕ *www.folger.edu* Ⓜ *Union Station or Capitol S.*

Rorschach Theatre

THEATER | This company's intimate and passionate performances on the stages of H Street's Atlas Performing Arts Center highlight some of the most off-beat plays in Washington. The company offers lesser-known works by such play-wrights as Fengar Gael, Jennifer Maisel, and José Rivera, as well as imaginative revivals of classics like Thornton Wilder's *The Skin of our Teeth.* ✉ *1333 H St. NE, Capitol Hill* ☎ *202/452–5538* ⊕ *www. rorschachtheatre.com* Ⓜ *Union Station.*

👜 Shopping

Capitol Hill is surprisingly good territory for shopping. Eastern Market and the unique shops and boutiques clustered around the historic redbrick building are great for browsing. Inside Eastern Market are produce and meat counters, plus places to buy flowers and sweets. ■**TIP→ The flea market, held on weekends outdoors, presents nostalgia and local crafts by the crateful. There's also a farmers' market on Saturday.** Along 7th Street, you can find a number of small shops selling such specialties as art books, handwoven rugs, and antiques. Cross Pennsylvania

Avenue, and head south on 8th Street for historic Barracks Row, where shops, bars, and restaurants inhabit the charming row houses leading toward the Anacostia River. The other shopping lures near the Hill are Union Market and Union Station, D.C.'s gorgeous train station, these days actually a shopping mall that happens to also accommodate Amtrak and commuter trains.

Keep in mind that Union Station and Union Market are north of the Capitol, while Eastern Market is to the south. You can certainly walk between these sights, but be aware that, from Eastern Market, Union Station is roughly a mile away, and Union Market is another mile beyond that—trekking that might prove taxing after time already spent on your feet in the shops.

BOOKS
Capitol Hill Books

BOOKS/STATIONERY | Pop into this two-story maze of used books, where the volumes are piled floor to ceiling, and no flat surface is left bare. (Even the bathroom is stacked high.) The knowledgeable staff will help you browse through a won-derful collection of out-of-print history titles, political and fiction writings, and mysteries. On the second Saturday of every month, this cozy bookstore hosts a free wine-and-cheese reception from 4 to 7, and all purchases are discounted 10%. ✉ *657 C St. SE, Eastern Market* ☎ *202/544–1621* ⊕ *www.capitolhill-books-dc.com* Ⓜ *Eastern Market.*

★ East City Bookshop

BOOKS/STATIONERY | A gathering spot for residents and visitors alike, East City stocks a wide selection of books, as well as art supplies, gifts, and toys. Check out the calendar of events, too—there's everything from story time for children to author-led book discussions to musical performances. ✉ *645 Pennsylvania Ave. SE, Suite 100, Capitol Hill* ☎ *202/290–1636* ⊕ *www.eastcitybookshop.com* ☽ *Closed Sun. and Mon.* Ⓜ *Eastern Market.*

Solid State Books

BOOKS/STATIONERY | Opened in 2017, this new addition to D.C.'s independent bookseller scene lies smack in the middle of the H Street corridor. The bright, spacious shop features a generous selection of fiction, history, and the latest political reads. An on-site coffee bar also offers beer and wine. ⊠ *600 H St. NE, Capitol Hill ⊹ A 10-minute walk from Union Station* ☎ *202/897–4201* ⊕ *www.solidstatebooksdc.com* Ⓜ *Union Station.*

CRAFTS AND GIFTS
Woven History/Silk Road

CRAFTS | Landmarks in this bohemian neighborhood, these connected stores sell gorgeous, handmade treasures from the mountain communities in India, Nepal, Turkey, Iran, Pakistan, and Tibet. You'll find everything from colorful weavings, pillows, and embroidered quilts to exotic jewelry and bags, as well as antique furniture. Woven History's rugs are made the old-fashioned way, with vegetable dyes and hand-spun wool, and sizes range from 3-by-5 feet to 8-by-10 feet. ⊠ *311–315 7th St. SE, Eastern Market* ☎ *202/543–1705* ⊕ *www.wovenhistory.com* Ⓜ *Eastern Market.*

FOOD
Hill's Kitchen

FOOD/CANDY | If you're a cook or looking for a gift for someone who is, pop into this small shop next to the Eastern Market. You'll find cookbooks, baking pans, aprons, towels and potholders, cookie cutters, barware, grilling tools, specialty foods, and much more. The shop is closed on Monday. ⊠ *713 D St. SE, Eastern Market* ☎ *202/543–1997* ⊕ *www.hillskitchen.com* Ⓜ *Eastern Market.*

MARKETS
★ Eastern Market

OUTDOOR/FLEA/GREEN MARKETS | For nearly 145 years, this has been the hub of the Capitol Hill community. Vibrantly colored produce and flowers, freshly caught fish, fragrant cheeses, and tempting sweets are sold at the market by independent vendors. On weekends year-round, local farmers sell fresh fruits and vegetables, and artists and exhibitors sell handmade arts and crafts, jewelry, antiques, collectibles, and furniture from around the world. The city's oldest continuously operating public market continues to be a vibrant and lively gathering place, complete with entertainment, art showings, and a pottery studio for residents and visitors alike. ⊠ *225 7th St. SE, Eastern Market ⊹ 7th St. and North Carolina Ave. SE* ☎ *202/698–5253* ⊕ *www.easternmarket-dc.com* Ⓜ *Eastern Market.*

Radici

FOOD/CANDY | The name means "roots" in Italian, and this little shop has quickly settled its roots into the Capitol Hill neighborhood. The charming owners have created a warm and inviting gathering spot and store with its brick walls, Venetian glass light fixtures, terra-cotta tiles, beautiful food, and handmade Italian gift displays and tables both inside and out. This is a lovely spot for an afternoon pick-me-up of espresso and cannoli or an end-of-day glass of wine and *cicchetti Veneziani* (small bites). You'll also find everything you need for an Italian-themed picnic. Wine tastings are held on Thursday evening. ⊠ *303 7th St. SE, Eastern Market* ☎ *202/758–0086* ⊕ *www.radici-market.com* Ⓜ *Eastern Market.*

Union Market

LOCAL SPECIALTIES | **FAMILY** | Arriving in 2012, this sprawling one-room market is a feast for the senses that's quickly made it a destination for locals and out-of-town visitors alike. The space offers a smorgasbord of food and drink options, from freshly shucked oysters and piping hot empanadas to Bloody Marys and fish-and-chips. There are butchers and bakers and candles (though not candlestick makers—yet), as well as cheese vendors, hand-made gelato, and a spice shop offering seasonings you've never heard of. Other features include Politics and Prose, a famed D.C. bookseller, and District Cutlery, which offers an incredible selection of German and Japanese knives (sharpening available). It's all made the market enormously popular, particularly on weekends, when parents descend to sip espresso while the youngsters bound around a generous outdoor seating area, which features a host of lawn games. Directly behind the market is a pop-up movie theater, the Angelika, which shows new releases and classic favorites alike. ⊠ *1309 5th St. NE, Capitol Hill* ⊕ *www.unionmarketdc.com* Ⓜ *NoMA–Gallaudet U.*

Union Station

SHOPPING CENTERS/MALLS | Resplendent with marble floors and vaulted ceilings, Union Station is a shopping mall as well as a train terminal. It also has restaurants and a food court with everything from sushi and smoothies to scones. The east hall is filled with vendors of expensive domestic and international wares who sell from open stalls. From April through October, an outdoor market is held Monday to Saturday with dozens of vendors selling fresh produce, baked goods and quick snacks, and arts and crafts. The Christmas season brings lights, a train display, and seasonal gift shops. ⊠ *50 Massachusetts Ave. NE, Capitol Hill* ☎ *202/289–1908* ⊕ *www.unionstationdc. com* Ⓜ *Union Station.*

TOYS
Labyrinth Games & Puzzles

TOYS | You won't find any video games in this gem, rather you'll discover an outstanding selection of handmade wooden puzzles and mazes, collectible card and travel games, board games, and brainteasers. A bonus to stopping in are the dozens of activities and games for all ages you can play. ⊠ *645 Pennsylvania Ave. SE, Eastern Market* ☎ *202/544–1059* ⊕ *www.labyrinthgameshop.com* Ⓜ *Eastern Market.*

Chapter 6

FOGGY BOTTOM

WITH THE WEST END AND THE WHITE HOUSE

Updated by
Barbara Noe Kennedy

Sights	Restaurants	Hotels	Shopping	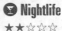 Nightlife
★★★★★	★★★☆☆	★★★☆☆	★☆☆☆☆	★★☆☆☆

NEIGHBORHOOD SNAPSHOT

TOP EXPERIENCES

■ **Department of State Diplomatic Reception Rooms:** One of D.C.'s best-kept secrets, this suite of rooms is filled with museum-quality art and historical treasures inspired by the country's founding years. You must reserve well in advance.

■ **John F. Kennedy Center for the Performing Arts:** See popular live bands on the Millennium Stage, daily at 6 pm.

■ **Thompson Boat Center:** Take in Washington's marble monuments, lush Roosevelt Island, and the Virginia coastline with a kayak ride down the Potomac.

■ **Touring the White House:** The White House website has up-to-date information on White House tours.

GETTING HERE

The White House can be reached by the Red Line's Farragut North stop or the Silver, Blue, and Orange lines' McPherson Square and Farragut West stops. Foggy Bottom has its own Metro stop, also on the Silver, Blue, and Orange lines. A free shuttle runs from the station to the Kennedy Center. Many of the other attractions are a considerable distance from the nearest Metro stop. If you don't relish long walks or if time is limited, check the map to see if you need to make alternate travel arrangements to visit specific sights.

PLANNING YOUR TIME

Touring the area around the White House could easily take a day or even two. If you enjoy history, you may be most interested in the buildings in the Lafayette Square Historic District, **DAR Museum,** and **State Department.** Save the **Kennedy Center** for the evening. You'll find some notable restaurants here as well, including the West End's Blue Duck Tavern.

QUICK BITES

■ **Burger Tap & Shake.** This GWU campus favorite serves burgers with house-made toppings, hand-cut fries, shakes, and craft beers on tap. ⊠ *2200 Pennsylvania Ave. NW* ⊕ *www.burgertapshake.com* Ⓜ *Foggy Bottom–GWU.*

■ **Flower Child.** Yummy, made-from-scratch vegetarian, vegan, and paleo bowls, salads, and wraps are served in a cheery space. ⊠ *2112 Pennsylvania Ave. NW* ⊕ *www.burgertapshake.com* Ⓜ *Foggy Bottom–GWU.*

■ **Immigrant Food.** Star chef Enrique Limardo creates fusion bowls mixing the diverse flavors brought to America by immigrants, with a devoted mission of engaging with and helping immigrants. ⊠ *1701 Pennsylvania Ave. NW* ⊕ *www.gstreetfood.com* Ⓜ *Farragut W.*

The neighborhood comprising Foggy Bottom, the West End, and the White House includes some of D.C.'s most iconic attractions, the biggest being the White House itself, the home of every U.S. president but George Washington.

But there are also some excellent smaller museums, including the Octagon House, Renwick Gallery, Decatur House, and the Department of Interior Museum. You will find the Kennedy Center along the Potomac River and George Washington University's campus. The area has a strong residential character as well, and is home to some of D.C.'s oldest houses.

◎ Sights

The White House is, of course, the primo sight in these parts. You'll need to reserve far in advance (weeks, if not months) if you want to take a tour. If you miss out, be sure to stop by the nearby White House Visitor Center, which provides a good overview of the Executive Mansion's life and times. That said, the neighborhood also boasts a selection of smaller sights that are definitely worth your while, including the Museum of the Americas at the Organization of American States, Smithsonian's Renwick Gallery, and Decatur House. There isn't tons of nightlife, but you'll discover some headline restaurants that have made waves in the foodie world. The Kennedy Center always provides good evening entertainment.

American Red Cross
BUILDING | The national headquarters for the American Red Cross, a National Historic Landmark since 1965, is composed of three buildings. Guided tours show off the oldest, a Beaux Arts structure of blinding-white marble built in 1917 to commemorate women who cared for the wounded on both sides during the Civil War. Three stained-glass windows designed by Louis Comfort Tiffany illustrate the values of the Red Cross: faith, hope, love, and charity. Other holdings you'll see on the 60-minute tour include an original N.C. Wyeth painting, sculptures, and artifacts that belonged to Clara Barton. Weather permitting, the tour includes a visit to the memorial garden. Reservations are required for the free tour, offered 10 am and 2 pm on Wednesday and Friday; schedule via email at tours@redcross.org. ⊠ 430 17th St. NW, Foggy Bottom ☎ 202/303–4233 ⊕ www. redcross.org ≊ Free ⊘ No tours Thurs. and Sat.–Tues. Ⓜ Farragut W.

Art Museum of the Americas
MUSEUM | Changing exhibits highlight modern and contemporary Latin American and Caribbean artists in this small gallery, part of the Organization of American States (OAS). The collection has 2,000 objects reflecting the diversity of expression found in the region. ⊠ 201 18th St. NW, Foggy Bottom ☎ 202/370–0147 ⊕ www.museum.oas.org ≊ Free ⊘ Closed Mon. Ⓜ Farragut W.

Black Lives Matter Plaza
LOCAL INTEREST | After President Trump held up a Bible on June 1, 2020, for a photo op in front of historic St. John's

2 Founding Farmers DC **F4**	**Hotels** ▼	**5** Hotel Lombardy **F3**	**10** The Ritz-Carlton, Washington, D.C. **A2**
3 Immigrant Food **H4**	**1** Avenue Suites Georgetown **D2**	**6** Hyatt Place Washington DC/Georgetown/ West End **E1**	**11** The St. Gregory Hotel Dupont Circle **F1**
4 Marcel's by Robert Wiedmaier **D2**	**2** Embassy Suites Washington, D.C. Georgetown **E1**	**7** Melrose Georgetown Hotel **D2**	**12** State Plaza Hotel **F5**
5 Rasika West End **E2**	**3** The Fairmont, Washington, D.C. Georgetown **D1**	**8** Park Hyatt Washington **E1**	**13** The Watergate Hotel **C4**
6 RIS **E2**	**4** Hotel Hive **E5**	**9** Residence Inn Washington, DC/ Foggy Bottom **D3**	**14** Westin Georgetown, Washington D.C **E2**
7 Westend Bistro **E2**			

Church, calling out the national guard to waylay peaceful protestors for his safe passage, D.C. mayor Muriel Bowser had the words "Black Lives Matter" painted in yellow, 35-foot-long capital letters along a two-block-long section of 16th Street NW, in front of the church and within plain view of the White House. She also renamed the plaza Black Lives Matter Plaza, which has remained a focal point of peaceful protests, weddings, and more. ⊠ *16th St. NW between H and K Sts., Foggy Bottom.*

Corcoran School of the Arts + Design at GW

MUSEUM | The Corcoran School, a prestigious art school since 1878, is now in partnership with George Washington University. As part of that collaboration, the work of students and visiting artists is put on display in shows and performances throughout the year. The iconic, beautifully restored Beaux Arts Flagg Building, which started life as the historic Corcoran Gallery of Art in 1890, shuttered its doors in 2014. There are plans for part of its collection, which was transferred to the National Gallery of Art, to return to the Flagg Building as the NGA becomes a tenant of the Corcoran School on its second floor. Don't miss the first-floor Luther W. Brady Art Gallery, which showcases temporary exhibits by renowned artists. ⊠ *500 17th St. NW, Foggy Bottom* ☎ *202/994–1700* ⊕ *go.gwu.edu/atcorcoran* Ⓜ *Farragut W or Farragut N.*

Daughters of the American Revolution (DAR) Museum

MUSEUM | FAMILY | The Beaux Arts Memorial Continental Hall, built in 1929 as the headquarters for the Daughters of the Revolution (DAR), is home to Washington, D.C.'s only decorative arts museum. The enormous collection encompasses furniture, textiles, quilts, silver, china, porcelain, stoneware, earthenware, glass, and other items made and used in the daily lives of Americans from the Colonial era through the early 20th century. Thirty-one period rooms reflect more than two centuries of American interiors, including a 1690s New England hall, an 1860s Texas bedroom, and a 1920s Ohio parlor. Two galleries feature changing exhibitions of decorative arts, and a study gallery allows researchers close access to the collection. Docent tours of the period rooms are available weekdays, depending on docent availability. The museum also hosts special events for children and adults; check the website for details. ⊠ *1776 D St. NW, Foggy Bottom* ☎ *202/628–1776* ⊕ *www. dar.org/museum* ▦ *Free* ⊘ *Closed Sun.* Ⓜ *Farragut W.*

Decatur House

HOUSE | Decatur House was built in 1818–19 on Lafayette Square, just across from the White House, for naval hero Stephen Decatur and his wife, Susan. Designed by Benjamin Henry Latrobe, the country's first professional architect, it's one of Washington's oldest surviving homes. Decatur didn't have long to enjoy it, however, since he died tragically 14 months later after a duel with Commodore James Barron. Wealthy hotel and tavern owner John Gadsby purchased the distinguished Federal-style house as a retirement home in 1836. The large two-story dependency was used as quarters for numerous enslaved individuals in his household—Washington's only extant slave quarters. Tours—offered Monday at 11 am, 12:30 pm, and 2 pm—feature these historic quarters and the house's first and second floors, much of which represent the taste of a later owner, Marie Beale, beloved for her salons with ambassadors and politicians. The White House Historical Society operates one of its three retail shops here, and you'll find a wonderful selection of White House history–themed products including the annual Christmas ornament. ⊠ *748 Jackson Pl. NW, Foggy Bottom* ☎ *202/218–4337* ⊕ *www.whha. org/programs/decatur-house-tours.html* ▦ *Free* Ⓜ *Farragut W.*

Federal Reserve Building

GOVERNMENT BUILDING | This imposing marble edifice, its bronze entryway topped by a massive eagle, was designed by Folger Shakespeare Library architect Paul Cret. Its appearance seems to say, "Your money's safe with us." Even so, there's no money here, as the Fed's mission is to set interest rates and keep the economy on track. The stately facade belies a friendlier interior, with a varied collection of art and several special art exhibitions every year. Tours of the building are available for groups of 10 or more, all aged 18 years or older; they must be booked at least two weeks in advance via email. ✉ *20th St. and Constitution Ave. NW, Foggy Bottom* ☎ *202/452–3324* ✎ *SECY-VisitorServices@frb.gov* ⊕ *www.federalreserve.gov* ✉ *Free* ⊘ *Closed weekends* Ⓜ *Foggy Bottom–GWU.*

The George Washington University Museum and The Textile Museum

MUSEUM | Designed to celebrate the creative achievements of people in the capital city and around the world, this 46,000-square-foot, LEED Gold–certified museum facility is on the campus of George Washington University. Rotating exhibits highlight global textiles and cultural traditions—ranging from handmade rugs and historical costumes to contemporary art and fashion—as well as displays on local D.C. history. The museum offers a dynamic range of free screenings, talks, and other public programs throughout the week in person and online. It's also home to a research library and two study centers, and you can find digital resources on textile creation and care on the website, along with highlights of the museum's collections. ✉ *701 21st St. NW, Foggy Bottom* ☎ *202/994–5200* ⊕ *www.museum.gwu. edu* ✉ *$8 suggested donation* ⊘ *Closed Tues.* Ⓜ *Foggy Bottom–GWU.*

The Octagon Museum of the Architects Foundation

HOUSE | FAMILY | Designed by Dr. William Thornton (original architect of the U.S. Capitol), the Octagon House was built by enslaved workers for John Tayloe III, a wealthy plantation owner, and was completed in 1801. Thornton chose the unusual shape to conform to the acute angle formed by L'Enfant's intersection of New York Avenue and 18th Street. After the British burned the White House in 1814, Thornton convinced the Tayloes to allow James and Dolley Madison to stay in the Octagon. From September 1814 until March 1815, the Octagon thereby became the temporary White House. It was in the second-floor study that the Treaty of Ghent, which ended the War of 1812, was ratified. The American Institute of Architects (AIA) established their national headquarters at the Octagon in 1898 and renovated the building as one of the country's first preservation projects. AIA stayed there for 70 years, before moving into new modern headquarters directly behind. Self-guided tours take in historically furnished rooms; second-floor gallery spaces hold rotating exhibits on architecture, design, and history. ✉ *1799 New York Ave. NW, Foggy Bottom* ☎ *202/626–7439* ⊕ *www. octagonmuseum.org* ✉ *Free* ⊘ *Closed Sun.–Wed.* Ⓜ *Farragut W or Farragut N.*

★ Renwick Gallery of the Smithsonian American Art Museum

MUSEUM | This luscious French Second Empire–style building rises across the street from the White House and the Eisenhower Executive Office Building, and even with such lofty neighbors, it is still the most appealing structure on the block. This was the country's first purpose-built art museum, and it was known then as "the American Louvre." Designed by James Renwick Jr. in 1858 to hold the art collection of Washington merchant and banker William Wilson Corcoran, the National Historic Landmark building has been a branch of the Smithsonian

Directly across the street from the White House, the Renwick Gallery was the first purpose-built art museum in the United States. It's now a branch of the Smithsonian.

American Art Museum dedicated to American crafts and decorative arts since 1972. The Renwick's exhibits are showcased in a captivating, interactive environment designed to illustrate not only the history of craft in America, but also its future. Exhibits highlight exciting contemporary artists who are using materials in innovative ways, redefining what craft is and taking it in bold new directions. Recent shows, for example, have included *No Spectators: The Art of Burning Man* and *WONDER*, featuring nine artists who created jaw-dropping site-specific installations in the museum's galleries. ⌧ *Pennsylvania Ave. at 17th St. NW, Foggy Bottom* ☎ *202/633–7970* ⊕ *americanart.si.edu* ✉ *Free* Ⓜ *Farragut W and Farragut N.*

★ Theodore Roosevelt Island
NATIONAL/STATE PARK | Designed as a living memorial to the environmentally minded 26th U.S. President, this wildlife sanctuary is off the George Washington Parkway near the Virginia side of the Potomac—close to Foggy Bottom,

Georgetown, East Potomac Park, and the Kennedy Center. Hikers and bicyclists can reach the island by crossing the Theodore Roosevelt Memorial Bridge or walking for 15 minutes from the Rosslyn Metro, but bikes are not allowed on the island and must be docked instead near the footbridge. Many birds and other animals live in the island's marsh and forests, which can be seen on a ranger-led Island Safari. A statue of Teddy greets you with his arm raised stands at the island's heart. ⌧ *Washington* ☎ *703/289–2500* ⊕ *www.nps.gov/this* Ⓜ *Rosslyn.*

U.S. Department of State Diplomatic Reception Rooms
GOVERNMENT BUILDING | U.S. foreign policy is administered by battalions of brainy analysts in the huge Department of State building (often referred to as the State Department). All is presided over by the secretary of state, who is fourth in line for the presidency (after the vice president, speaker of the House, and president pro tempore of the Senate). On the top floor are the opulent Diplomatic

Reception Rooms, decorated like the great halls of Europe and the rooms of wealthy Colonial American plantations, and where the business of diplomacy takes place to this day. Furnishings include a Portsmouth high chest and dressing table, Paul Revere silver, and the desk on which the Treaty of Paris, ending the Revolutionary War, was signed in 1783. ■TIP➔ To visit the reception rooms, register online for a tour three months in advance. ⊠ 2201 C St. NW, Foggy Bottom ☎ 202/647–3241 ⊕ receptiontours. state.gov ⊠ Free ⊗ No tours weekends Ⓜ Foggy Bottom–GWU.

U.S. Department of the Interior Museum

MUSEUM | The outside of the building is plain, but inside a wealth of art, contained in two separate collections, reflects the department's work. The **Office of the Secretary Art Collection**, featuring heroic oil paintings of dam construction, gold panning, and cattle drives, is found throughout the building's hallways, offices, and meeting rooms. The **Department of the Interior Museum Collection** outlines the work of the Bureau of Land Management, the U.S. Geological Survey, the Bureau of Indian Affairs, the National Park Service, and other department branches. On Tuesday and Thursday at 2 pm, you can view 26 photographic murals by Ansel Adams and many of the more than 40 dramatic murals painted by Maynard Dixon, John Steuart Curry, and other artists. Reservations are required for the Murals Tour; call at least two weeks in advance. The **Indian Craft Shop** across the hall from the museum sells Native American pottery, dolls, carvings, jewelry, baskets, and books. ⊠ Stewart Lee Udall Department of the Interior Bldg., 1849 C St. NW, Foggy Bottom ☎ 202/208–4743 ⊕ www. doi.gov/interiormuseum ⊠ Free ⊗ Closed weekends ☞ Visitors 18 and older must show a government-issued ID to enter the Stewart Lee Udall Department of the Interior Bldg. Ⓜ Farragut W.

U.S. Department of the Treasury

GOVERNMENT BUILDING | Once used to store currency, this is the largest Greek Revival edifice in Washington. Robert Mills, the architect responsible for the Washington Monument and the Smithsonian American Art Museum, designed the colonnade on 15th Street. After the death of President Lincoln, the Andrew Johnson Suite was used as the executive office while Mrs. Lincoln moved out of the White House. Tours must be arranged through your Congressional representative or senator; participants must be U.S. citizens or legal residents. ⊠ 1500 Pennsylvania Ave. NW, Foggy Bottom ☎ 202/622–2000 general info ⊕ home. treasury.gov/services/tours-and-library/ tours-of-the-historic-treasury-building ⊠ Free Ⓜ McPherson Sq. or Metro Center.

The White House

GOVERNMENT BUILDING | Irish architect James Hoban designed America's most famous house in 1792. It was known officially as the Executive Mansion until 1902, when President Theodore Roosevelt renamed it the White House, long its informal name. The house has undergone many structural changes, including Harry Truman's addition of a second-story porch to the south portico. First Lady Jacqueline Kennedy undertook an extensive restoration in 1961 to preserve and showcase its historical and architectural significance. The self-guided tour includes rooms on the ground floor, but the State Floor has the highlights. The East Room is the White House's largest room, the site of ceremonies and press conferences; this is also where one of Abraham Lincoln's sons harnessed a pet goat to a chair and went for a ride. The portrait of George Washington that Dolley Madison saved from torch-carrying British soldiers in 1814 hangs in the room. Grover Cleveland, the only president to marry in the White House, wed in the Blue Room. The Red Room, decorated in early-19th-century American Empire

A statue of Andrew Jackson during the battle of New Orleans presides over Lafayette Square.

style, has long been a first lady favorite. ✉ *1600 Pennsylvania Ave. NW, Foggy Bottom* ☎ *202/208–1631 White House Visitor Center, 202/456–7041 24-hr info line* ⊕ *www.whitehouse.gov* ✉ *Free* ⊘ *Closed Sun. and Mon.* Ⓜ *Federal Triangle, Metro Center, or McPherson Sq.*

White House Visitor Center

INFO CENTER | FAMILY | If you aren't able to obtain tickets to visit the White House (or even if you have), visiting the White House Visitor Center is an excellent Plan B. Displays, artifacts, photos, videos, and interactive exhibits recount the life and times of America's most famous house, providing behind-the-scenes insight into everything from the Oval Office's commitment to honoring presidential food preferences to the integral ballet of moving day, when one president must be moved out and the next moved in, in a matter of hours. ✉ *1450 Pennsylvania Ave. NW, Foggy Bottom* ☎ *202/208–1631* ⊕ *www.nps.gov* Ⓜ *Metro Center or Federal Triangle.*

Restaurants

The history-steeped Foggy Bottom area boasts architectural landmarks like the Watergate Hotel. Around George Washington University there's cheaper, college-friendly fare in burrito joints and coffee shops. Nearby, the Kennedy Center draws a more mature crowd with tastes that have evolved past burgers and nachos. North of Foggy Bottom, the West End has become a popular dining destination.

Blue Duck Tavern

$$$$ | MODERN AMERICAN | With an open kitchen firmly committed to artistically crafted American cuisine, this high-end neighborhood tavern, located in the Park Hyatt Washington D.C. hotel, uses the region's freshest seasonal ingredients to create rustic dishes such as wood oven-roasted bone marrow and roasted Rohan duck breast. Don't pass up the apple pie if it's on the seasonal menu. **Known for:** pork belly Benedict; wood oven-roasted bone marrow; intimate chef's table with tasting menu. $ *Average main: $38* ⊠ *Park Hyatt Washington D.C., 1201 24th St. NW, Washington* ☎ *202/419–6755* ⊕ *www.blueducktavern. com* Ⓜ *Foggy Bottom–GWU.*

Founding Farmers DC

$$ | MODERN AMERICAN | Inside this ultramodern take on the old-school farmhouse, affordable eco-chic is the mantra—though the sheer number of offerings can be a tad overwhelming (with categories ranging from homemade pastas to signatures to today's fish to burgers and sandwiches). Farms from all over the country provide most of the fresh vegetables, beef, and poultry, and sustainable practices are used to catch every type of fish on the menu. **Known for:** kernal-speckled cornbread, served piping hot in a cast-iron skillet; throwback sodas, such as the daily rickey and lem-on-lime ginger; the vegan-friendly array of meat- and egg-free options. $ *Average main: $18* ⊠ *1924 Pennsylvania Ave. NW, Foggy Bottom* ☎ *202/822–8783* ⊕ *www. wearefoundingfarmers.com* Ⓜ *Foggy Bottom–GWU.*

Immigrant Food

$ | INTERNATIONAL | A global menu representing the different flavors brought to D.C. by immigrants is the motif behind this casual eatery near the White House. Headed by star Venezuelan chef Enrique Limardo, its bowls offer an unexpected blending of cultures: Vietnamese spicy noodles with German-style pickled bananas; Filipino adobo spiced chicken with Sub-Sarahan-African pork rind sprin-kles; Greek-style spice-rubbed steak with pumpkin spaghetti and pesto. **Known for:** globally inspired fusion bowls; serves as an activist hub; very broad menu. $ *Average main: $13* ⊠ *1701 Pennsylvania Ave. NW, Foggy Bottom* ☎ *202/681–3848* ⊕ *immigrantfood.com* ⊗ *Closed Sun. and Mon.*

Marcel's by Robert Wiedmaier

$$$$ | FRENCH | Served in a warmly lit, elegant setting, the award-winning, Flemish-inspired French menu at Marcel's—the flagship restaurant of acclaimed chef Robert Wiedmaier—often includes multiple seafood choices (like perfectly seared diver scallops and Blue Bay mussels), succulent duck breast, and a selection of foie gras. In season, be sure to order the mixed-melon mine-strone with yogurt sorbet and cream for dessert. **Known for:** very upscale multi-course menus that change daily; flavorful Blue Bay mussels; affordable pretheater menu. $ *Average main: $125* ⊠ *2401 Pennsylvania Ave. NW, Washington* ☎ *202/296–1166* ⊕ *www.marcelsdc.com* ⊗ *No lunch* Ⓜ *Foggy Bottom–GWU.*

Rasika West End

$$$$ | INDIAN | You may think you know Indian food, but the dishes at this upscale escape to India takes Indian cooking to the next level of modern deliciousness. From popular dishes like chicken tikka masala to creative inspirations like silky glazed cod and truffled minced-lamb kebabs, chef Vikram Sunderam will make you forget all other Indian food you've ever tasted. **Known for:** upscale Indian cuisine; chef-driven. $ *Average main: $65* ⊠ *1190 New Hampshire Ave. NW, West End* ☎ *202/466–2500* ⊕ *www.rasikarestaurant.com.*

RIS

$$$ | MODERN AMERICAN | The brainchild of veteran chef Ris Lacoste, RIS serves elevated but comforting seasonal new American fare in an earthy-chic, light-filled space—the sort of place you'll find locals, the after-work crowd, and even a celebrity or two. You should definitely try the daily and seasonal specials, but you can always count on the mainstays, including onion soup, mussels, and RIS's "famous meatloaf." **Known for:** signature scallop margaritas and a gin mill featuring over 75 varieties; a great "marquee menu" for pretheater diners, available 5

to 6:30 pm; daily specials featuring the chef's take on classic dishes and fresh-from-the-market produce. ⑤ *Average main: $32* ✉ *2275 L St. NW, West End* ☎ *202/730–2500* ⊕ *risdc.com* Ⓜ *Foggy Bottom–GWU.*

Westend Bistro

$$$ | MODERN AMERICAN | The culinary team focuses on Americanized versions of bistro classics created from regional ingredients in this modern-style West End restaurant in the Ritz-Carlton Washington D.C. In warmer months, the patio is popular with guests and locals alike, and innovative cocktails please the happy hour crowd. **Known for:** a chef's table that diners can customize; weekday happy hour featuring a special cocktail of the day. ⑤ *Average main: $29* ✉ *The Ritz-Carlton Washington D.C., 1190 22nd St. NW, Washington* ☎ *202/974–5566* ⊕ *www.westendbistrodc.com* ⊟ *No credit cards* ☾ *No lunch weekends* Ⓜ *Foggy Bottom–GWU.*

 Hotels

With the Kennedy Center for the Performing Arts anchoring its southwestern side and the George Washington University campus to the north, this D.C. community is lively and energetic, even though most of its residents are longtime Washingtonians and most of its homes hearken back to the 18th and 19th centuries. And nothing beats the early-morning views of the Potomac River, where sculls and shells skim along the surface as crews prepare for upcoming races.

Avenue Suites Georgetown

$$$ | HOTEL | FAMILY | Luxurious and practical at the same time, this is a great choice for families and groups because all the suites have separate bedrooms and full kitchens, and some have views of the city and the Potomac River. **Pros:** small gym on site; complimentary Saturday-morning yoga; "Stock the Fridge"

service with Trader Joe's. **Cons:** a long walk to the Mall (but close to Georgetown); expensive valet parking; there's a gym, but it's tiny. ⑤ *Rooms from: $296* ✉ *2500 Pennsylvania Ave. NW, Foggy Bottom* ☎ *202/333–8060* ⊕ *www.avenuesuites.com* ⟿ *124 rooms* ⦿| *No meals* Ⓜ *Foggy Bottom–GWU.*

Embassy Suites Washington, D.C. Georgetown

$$$ | HOTEL | FAMILY | All accommodations at this convenient hotel within walking distance of Georgetown and Dupont Circle have a living room and bedroom and surround an atrium filled with comfortable seating areas and the hotel's dining options. **Pros:** family-friendly; reception with complimentary drinks and apps every night; pool to keep the little ones—and sweaty tourists—happy. **Cons:** museums not in walking distance; four blocks from Metro; expensive parking (not valet). ⑤ *Rooms from: $319* ✉ *1250 22nd St. NW, Foggy Bottom* ☎ *202/857–3388, 800/362–2779 customer support* ⊕ *www.embassysuites.com* ⟿ *318 rooms* ⦿| *Free Breakfast* Ⓜ *Foggy Bottom–GWU or Dupont Circle.*

★ The Fairmont, Washington, D.C., Georgetown

$ | HOTEL | FAMILY | Great for exploring Georgetown, this hotel centers on an elegant central courtyard and gardens, overlooked by the large glassed-in lobby and half of the bright, spacious rooms. **Pros:** fitness fanatics will love the gym and 50-foot indoor pool; great no-charge pet program includes homemade treats for dogs; good family amenities. **Cons:** expensive parking; far from most major attractions; some rooms can be noisy. ⑤ *Rooms from: $199* ✉ *2401 M St. NW, Foggy Bottom* ☎ *202/429–2400, 866/540–4505* ⊕ *www.fairmont.com* ⟿ *413 rooms* ⦿| *No meals* Ⓜ *Foggy Bottom–GWU.*

Hotel Hive

$$ | **HOTEL** | Hip and trendy, D.C.'s first microhotel is designed for travelers who care more about exploring and socializing than spending much time in their room. It features 83 "hives" ranging from 125 to 250 square feet with a choice of king, queen, twin, or bunk beds. **Pros:** great prices; on-site restaurant offers all-day dining; plenty of amenities including free Wi-Fi, Bluetooth music, and individual thermostats. **Cons:** occupancy limited to two people (usually with one bed); rooms on lower floors are noisy; very, very small rooms. *$ Rooms from: $239 ⌗ 2224 F St. NW, Foggy Bottom ☎ 202/849–8499 ⊕ www.hotelhive.com ↩ 83 rooms ☉ No meals.*

Hotel Lombardy

$$$ | **HOTEL** | This romantic property near the White House is an idyllic urban retreat—one where European antiques, Asian rugs, and original oil paintings lend a 1929 Art Deco building old-world charm and where guest rooms feature plush bedding, work desks, and steel-and-chrome bathrooms. **Pros:** homey rooms; beautiful lounge; complimentary Wi-Fi. **Cons:** old-fashioned decor; expensive valet parking; on busy street. *$ Rooms from: $300 ⌗ 2019 Pennsylvania Ave. NW, Foggy Bottom ☎ 202/828–2600 ⊕ www.hotellombardy.com ↩ 140 rooms ☉ No meals ⓂFoggy Bottom–GWU.*

Hyatt Place Washington DC/Georgetown/West End

$$$ | **HOTEL** | Families and business travelers will appreciate this modern hotel conveniently located in the West End neighborhood just a few blocks from the Foggy Bottom–GWU Metro. **Pros:** complimentary daily breakfast buffet; fitness center and heated indoor pool; free Wi-Fi. **Cons:** decor is not very distinctive; expensive valet parking; relatively far from major sights. *$ Rooms from: $382 ⌗ 2121 M St. NW, Foggy Bottom ☎ 202/838–2222 ⊕ www.hyatt.com*

↩ *168 rooms* ☉ *Free Breakfast* Ⓜ *Foggy Bottom–GWU.*

Melrose Georgetown Hotel

$ | **HOTEL** | **FAMILY** | Gracious, traditional rooms done in a soothing palette of creams and grays with splashes of green, blue, and red all have oversize bathrooms and mini-refrigerators, and many have pullout sofa beds, making this boutique hotel a good choice for families and a good alternative to the District's many chain hotels. **Pros:** nice fitness center; closest Georgetown hotel to a Metro stop; walk to dining and shopping. **Cons:** street noise; no pool; fee for in-room Wi-Fi. *$ Rooms from: $179 ⌗ 2430 Pennsylvania Ave. NW, Georgetown ☎ 202/955–6400, 800/635–7673 ⊕ www.melrosehoteldc.com ↩ 240 rooms ☉ No meals Ⓜ Foggy Bottom–GWU.*

★ Park Hyatt Washington

$$$$ | **HOTEL** | **FAMILY** | Understated elegance and refined service can be found at this soothing city getaway, where the guest rooms—designer Tony Chi's minimalist tribute to the American experience—feature walnut floors, hard-covered books, and folk-art accents. **Pros:** spacious and luxurious rooms; in-house restaurant serves fresh product-driven menu in contemporary, cozy setting; beautiful indoor saltwater pool. **Cons:** expensive valet parking; 10-minute walk to the Metro; many rooms lack good views. *$ Rooms from: $629 ⌗ 1201 24th St. NW, Foggy Bottom ☎ 202/789–1234 ⊕ www.hyatt.com ↩ 220 rooms ☉ No meals Ⓜ Foggy Bottom–GWU.*

Residence Inn Washington, DC/Foggy Bottom

$$$ | **HOTEL** | This all-suites hotel is close to the Kennedy Center, George Washington University, and Georgetown. **Pros:** near Metro; rooftop pool overlooks the Watergate Hotel; friendly and helpful staff. **Cons:** far from the museums; too quiet for some; small fitness room. *$ Rooms from: $379 ⌗ 801 New*

Hampshire Ave. NW, Foggy Bottom ☎ 202/785–2000 ⊕ www.marriott.com ⊷ 103 suites ⦿ Free Breakfast Ⓜ Foggy Bottom–GWU.

★ The Ritz-Carlton Washington, D.C

$$$$ | HOTEL | Luxury radiates from every polished marble surface at one of Washington's most upscale hostelries, and personalized service makes you feel pampered. **Pros:** attentive service; convenient to several parts of town; attached to fabulous health club, spa, and pool. **Cons:** pricey room rates, especially during peak times; expensive valet parking; sleepy neighborhood. Ⓢ Rooms from: $430 ✉ 1150 22nd St. NW, Foggy Bottom ☎ 202/835–0500, 800/241–3333 ⊕ www. ritzcarlton.com ⊷ 300 rooms ⦿ No meals Ⓜ Foggy Bottom–GWU.

The St. Gregory Hotel Dupont Circle

$$ | HOTEL | This sophisticated and very chic boutique hotel offers the ideal accommodations for business and leisure travelers, thanks to rooms that feature fully stocked kitchens and sofa beds. **Pros:** big rooms; central location near business district of K Street; 24-hour fitness center. **Cons:** far from museums; expensive valet parking; area is quiet at night. Ⓢ Rooms from: $269 ✉ 2033 M St. NW ☎ 202/530–3600 ⊕ www.stgregory-hotelwdc.com ⊷ 155 rooms ⦿ No meals Ⓜ Foggy Bottom–GWU or Farragut N.

State Plaza Hotel

$$ | HOTEL | Just two blocks from the National Mall's west end and across the street from the State Department, this hotel is the perfect blend of elegance and comfort, with its full-size kitchens and eating areas; large bathrooms with separate dressing areas; and sleek furnishings in shades of gray, cream, and gold. **Pros:** free Internet access; walk to Metro and close to GWU; safe neighborhood at night. **Cons:** far from museums; expensive valet parking; small fitness center. Ⓢ Rooms from: $239 ✉ 2117 E St. NW, Foggy Bottom ☎ 202/861–8200, 800/424–2859 ⊕ www.stateplaza.com

⊟ No credit cards ⊷ 230 suites ⦿ No meals Ⓜ Foggy Bottom–GWU.

★ The Watergate Hotel

$$$$ | HOTEL | Beautifully situated along the Potomac River, the legendary Watergate radiates sophistication and glamour, both embracing its infamous past and celebrating its Mid-Century Modernist style. **Pros:** beautiful mosaic-tiled saltwater pool; fun, cheeky historical touches; gorgeously designed bars and restaurant with excellent menus. **Cons:** some rooms are small; elevators are a bit complicated to use; 1960s style not for everyone. Ⓢ Rooms from: $450 ✉ 2650 Virginia Ave. NW, Foggy Bottom ☎ 202/827–1600, 844/617–1972 reservations ⊕ www.thewatergatehotel. com ⊷ 336 rooms ⦿ No meals Ⓜ Foggy Bottom–GWU.

Westin Georgetown, Washington D.C.

$ | HOTEL | FAMILY | Although not truly in Georgetown (but nearby), this Westin's location in a busy part of the West End makes it popular with both business and leisure travelers—all of whom appreciate the stately, comfortable rooms and spalike bathrooms with sunken tubs and separate glassed-in showers. **Pros:** quiet neighborhood; comfortable rooms; outdoor pool open seasonally. **Cons:** 10-minute walk to Metro; a bit out of the way for sightseeing; expensive parking. Ⓢ Rooms from: $199 ✉ 2350 M St. NW, Foggy Bottom ☎ 202/429–0100 ⊕ www. westingeorgetown.com ⊷ 248 rooms ⦿ No meals Ⓜ Foggy Bottom–GWU.

🍸 Nightlife

The area near the White House and Foggy Bottom once offered a less frantic nightlife environment as the city center emptied out during the weekends. Today, some interesting clubs and restaurants have reenergized the area. Many are near—or in—major hotels, making the area more attractive to the going-out crowd.

DANCE CLUBS
Eden

DANCE CLUBS | This four-floor hot spot near the White House attracts Washington celebrities, foreign visitors, and the sophisticated elite. The club hosts a variety of local and big-name DJs and is famous for its rooftop deck, attracting big crowds in the summer. Bottle service is available. ⊠ *1716 I St. NW, Foggy Bottom* ☎ *202/785–0270* ⊕ *www.edendc.com* Ⓜ *Farragut W.*

🔖 Performing Arts

A wealth of venues offering concerts, film screenings, music, and dance surround the president's home and the adjacent Foggy Bottom neighborhood. Here you'll find the John F. Kennedy Center for Performing Arts and George Washington University's Lisner Auditorium—two great venues that present drama, dance, and music and offer a platform for some of the most famous American and international performers. Hungry and thirsty Kennedy Center visitors can dine and drink at the Roof Terrace Restaurant.

DANCE
The Washington Ballet

DANCE | The company's classical and contemporary dances are performed from September through June, with works by choreographers like George Balanchine, Paul Taylor, Marius Petipa, Sir Frederick Ashton, Annabelle Lopez Ochoa, and more. The main shows are mounted at the Kennedy Center, Harman Center for the Arts, Warner Theatre, and THEARC in Southeast D.C. Each December, the company also performs *The Nutcracker* at the Warner Theatre. ⊠ *Washington* ☎ *202/362–3606* ⊕ *www.washingtonballet.org*.

MAJOR VENUES
DAR Constitution Hall

ARTS CENTERS | Acts ranging from the Bolshoi Ballet to U2 to B.B. King have performed at this 3,702-seat venue, one of Washington's grand old halls. It's well worth a visit for both the excellent performers it attracts and for its awesome architecture and acoustics. ⊠ *1776 D St. NW, Foggy Bottom* ☎ *202/628–4780* ⊕ *www.dar.org/constitution-hall* Ⓜ *Farragut W.*

★ John F. Kennedy Center for the Performing Arts

ARTS CENTERS | Overlooking the Potomac River, the gem of the Washington, D.C., performing arts scene is home to the National Symphony Orchestra and the Washington National Opera. The best out-of-town acts perform at one of three performance spaces—the Concert Hall, the Opera House, or the Eisenhower Theater. An eclectic range of performances is staged at the center's smaller venues, which showcase chamber groups, experimental works, cabaret-style performances, and the KC Jazz Club. But that's not all. On the Millennium Stage in the center's Grand Foyer, you can catch free performances almost any day at 6 pm. And the REACH, a major indoor-outdoor, state-of-the-art expansion designed by Steven Holl and completed in 2019, provides a dynamic, open-air, collaborative space and a pedestrian bridge that connects with the other presidential memorials on the National Mall. ■ TIP→ On performance days, a free shuttle bus runs between the Kennedy Center and the Foggy Bottom–GWU Metro stop. ⊠ *2700 F St. NW, Foggy Bottom* ☎ *202/416–8000 general, 800/444–1324 toll-free* ⊕ *www.kennedy-center.org* Ⓜ *Foggy Bottom–GWU.*

Lisner Auditorium

ARTS CENTERS | A nearly 1,500-seat theater on the campus of George Washington University attracts students and outsiders alike to its pop, classical, and choral music shows; modern dance performances; musical theater; and lectures by high-profile political and celebrity speakers. ⊠ *730 21st St. NW, Foggy*

Bottom ☎ 202/994–6800 ⊕ lisner.gwu.
edu Ⓜ Foggy Bottom–GWU.

MUSIC
Choral Arts Society of Washington
MUSIC | From fall to late spring, this
200-voice choir, founded in 1965 by
Norman Scribner, performs a musical
array, ranging from classical to tango to
Broadway hits, at the Kennedy Center
Concert Hall and other venues. Three
Christmas concerts are also scheduled
each December, and in January or
February there's a popular choral tribute
to Martin Luther King Jr. ⊠ Washington
☎ 202/244–3669 ⊕ www.choralarts.org.

Washington Performing Arts
MUSIC | One of the city's oldest arts
organizations stages high-quality classical
music, jazz, gospel, world music, modern
dance, and performance art in major
venues around the city. Past shows have
featured the Alvin Ailey American Dance
Theater, Yo-Yo Ma, the Chieftains, Herbie
Hancock, and Savion Glover. ⊠ Foggy
Bottom ☎ 202/833–9800 ⊕ www.wash-
ingtonperformingarts.org.

OPERA
Washington National Opera
OPERA | Founded in 1956, the Washington
National Opera presents a diverse reper-
tory of grand opera plus world premieres,
international tours, live recordings, and
radio broadcasts, as well as innovative
education and community-engagement
programs. The operas are performed
across three main venues of the Kennedy Center in their original languages
with English subtitles. In 2012, the WNO
created the American Opera Initiative,
which commissions young composers
and librettists to write short chamber
operas. In 2002, the WNO also started
the Cafritz Young Artists of Washington
National Opera, one of the nation's most
competitive professional training programs, providing two years of intensive
study to a carefully selected cadre of
young singers and collaborative pianists.
⊠ John F. Kennedy Center for the

Performing Arts, 2700 F St. NW, Foggy
Bottom ☎ 202/467–4600, 800/444–1324
⊕ www.kennedy-center.org/wno.

ORCHESTRA
National Symphony Orchestra
MUSIC | Under the leadership of music
director Gianandrea Noseda, the
orchestra performs classic works
by repertoire including classical and
popular concerts, commissioned work,
and genre-mixing collaborations at the
Kennedy Center, Wolf Trap National Park
in summer, and on the lawn of the U.S.
Capitol (Memorial Day, Labor Day, and
July 4) with some of the world's most
renowned talent appearing as guest
artists. ⊠ John F. Kennedy Center for
the Performing Arts, 2700 F St. NW,
Foggy Bottom ☎ 202/467–4600 tickets
and information, 800/444–1324 toll-free
⊕ www.kennedy-center.org/nso Ⓜ Foggy
Bottom–GWU.

Shopping

In the area best known for the nation's
most famous house, you can also shop
for official White House Christmas
ornaments and Easter eggs, jewelry
inspired by Jackie Kennedy, and crafts
made by living Native American artists
and artisans. If you're looking for a tasty
treat, grab the fixings for a picnic lunch
at the FRESHFARM market held every
Thursday, April through mid-November,
near Lafayette Square—the produce
that's sold here is said to be as fresh as
food grown in the White House garden.
Otherwise, it's a good spot for people-watching and fine dining, but alas
there's very little shopping in this area.

CRAFTS AND GIFTS
★ Indian Craft Shop
CRAFTS | Jewelry, pottery, sand paintings,
weavings, and baskets from more than
45 Native American tribes, including Nav-
ajo, Zuni, Cherokee, and Mohawk, are at
your fingertips here—as long as you have
a photo ID to enter the federal building.

Five Great Arts Experiences

■ **Arena Stage:** Housed in the audience-friendly Mead Center for American Theatre in the Southwest Waterfront, Arena Stage offers innovative new American plays as well as classic plays and musicals.

■ **John F. Kennedy Center for the Performing Arts:** The gem of the D.C. arts scene, this beautiful venue on the banks of the Potomac in Foggy Bottom is the one performance venue you might take with you if you were stranded on a desert island. The new REACH expansion adds ever more to its appeal.

■ **Shakespeare Theatre Company:** Among the top Shakespeare companies in the world, this troupe, which performs in a couple of venues in Penn Quarter, excels at both classical and contemporary interpretations and doesn't limit itself to the works of the Bard.

■ **Studio Theatre:** With its four intimate theaters and its hip urban locale, this 14th Street landmark provides the best in contemporary dramas and comedies.

■ **Woolly Mammoth Theatre Company:** This remarkable theater company headquartered in the heart of the Penn Quarter stages some of the most creative and entertaining new plays from the nation's best playwrights.

Items range from jewelry costing as little as $5 on up to collector-quality art pieces selling for more than $10,000. This shop has been open since 1938. ⊠ *U.S. Department of the Interior, 1849 C St. NW, Room 1023, Foggy Bottom* ☎ *202/208–4056* ⊕ *www.indiancraftshop. com* ⊙ *Closed Sat.–Mon. (except 3rd Sat. of each month) and federal holidays,* Ⓜ *Farragut W or Farragut N.*

White House Historical Association Retail Shops

GIFTS/SOUVENIRS | The White House Historical Association operates two shops: The flagship store is in the White House Visitor Center, adjacent to the White House at 1450 Pennsylvania Avenue NW, and the smaller History Shop is in the historic Decatur House on Lafayette Square at 1610 H Street NW. Both shops sell the association's historic and official merchandise, all of it carefully crafted. Highlights include official White House Christmas ornaments (from 1981 to present day), jewelry inspired by First Ladies, ties with architectural motifs, and beautifully made porcelain. ⊠ *White House Visitor Center Flagship Store, 1450 Pennsylvania Ave. NW, Foggy Bottom* ☎ *202/208–7031* ⊕ *shop.whitehousehistory.org* Ⓜ *Farragut W or Federal Triangle.*

MARKETS
FRESHFARM Foggy Bottom Market

OUTDOOR/FLEA/GREEN MARKETS | Pick up a crab cake, Belgian waffle, or small-batch craft spirit at this farmers' market on Wednesday from 3 to 7 in early April through November. Similar fare is available near Lafayette Square (810 Vermont Avenue NW) on Thursday 11–2, April–mid-November. Other FRESHFARM markets are in the Capitol Riverfront (Sunday 9–1, May–September), Dupont Circle (Sunday 8:30–1:30, year-round), H Street NE (Saturday 9–12:30, April–mid-December), Penn Quarter (Thursday 3–7, June–mid-November), and elsewhere. All locations sell local fruits and vegetables. ⊠ *901 23rd St. NW, Foggy Bottom* ☎ *202/362–8889* ⊕ *www.freshfarmmarkets.org* Ⓜ *Foggy Bottom–GWU.*

Activities

BOATING

Thompson Boat Center

BICYCLING | The center rents nonmotorized watercraft, including canoes, kayaks, and stand-up paddleboards (from $16 per hour). Rowing sculls are also available (from $22 per hour), but you must be certified and validated for rental. Bikes are also available for rent ($11 per hour). The location provides a nice launching point into the Potomac, right in the center of the city and close to the monuments. In addition to its access to the river, Thompson is conveniently sited for getting onto the Rock Creek Trail and the C&O Towpath. Note: Thompson closes from Halloween through mid-April, based on the water's temperature. ⊠ *2900 Virginia Ave. NW, Foggy Bottom* ☎ *202/333–9543* ⊕ *www.boatingindc.com* Ⓜ *Foggy Bottom–GWU.*

Chapter 7

GEORGETOWN

7

Updated by
Sabrina Medora

👁 Sights
★★★☆☆

🍴 Restaurants
★★★★☆

🛏 Hotels
★★★★☆

🛍 Shopping
★★★★★

🍸 Nightlife
★★★★☆

NEIGHBORHOOD SNAPSHOT

TOP EXPERIENCES

■ **C&O Canal:** Walk or bike along the canal-side path, which offers bucolic scenery from the heart of Georgetown across Maryland.

■ **Dumbarton Oaks:** Stroll through the 10 acres of formal gardens—Washington's loveliest oasis.

■ **M Street:** Indulge in some serious designer retail therapy (or just window-shopping). Finish at Georgetown University by the base of the famously steep staircase that appeared in the film *The Exorcist*—and climb it, if you dare.

■ **Tudor Place:** Step into Georgetown's past with a visit to the grand home of the Custis-Peter family. On view are antiques from George and Martha Washington's home at Mount Vernon and a 1919 Pierce-Arrow roadster.

■ **Washington Harbour and Waterfront Park:** Come on a warm evening to enjoy sunset drinks and fine dining while overlooking the Watergate, Kennedy Center, and Potomac River. Board a sightseeing cruise at the dock.

GETTING HERE

There's no Metro stop in Georgetown, so you have to take a bus or taxi or walk to this part of Washington. It's about a 20-minute walk from Dupont Circle and the Foggy Bottom Metro stations. Perhaps the best transportation deal in Georgetown is the Circulator (⊕ *www.dccirculator.com*). For a buck you can ride daily from Union Station, Dupont Circle, or the Rosslyn Metro to the heart of Georgetown.

PLANNING YOUR TIME

■ Georgetown is known for its shopping, but you can also spend a pleasant day here enjoying the sights. Main attractions (**C&O Canal, Georgetown University, Tudor Place, Dumbarton Oaks, Oak Hill Cemetery,** and **Dumbarton House**) are somewhat removed from one another, and the street scene, with its shops and people-watching, invites you to linger.

QUICK BITES

■ **Chaia Tacos.** The artful creations here are locally sourced, vegetarian (think: kale and potatoes), and served on a grilled corn tortilla. ⊠ *3207 Grace St. NW* ⊕ *www.bluebottlecoffee.com.*

■ **Ching Ching Cha.** You'll feel like you've entered another world at this cozy tea shop with friendly service and artisanal brewed teas. ⊠ *1063 Wisconsin Ave. NW* ⊕ *www.bluebottlecoffee.com.*

■ **Georgetown Cupcake.** Satisfy a sweet tooth at the shop made famous on TLC's *DC Cupcakes.* The line is long but moves quickly. ⊠ *3301 M St. NW* ⊕ *www.georgetowncupcake.com.*

At first glance, Washington's oldest and wealthiest neighborhood may look genteel and staid, but don't be fooled: this is a lively part of town.

Georgetown is D.C.'s top high-end shopping destination, with everything from eclectic antiques and housewares to shoes and upscale jeans. At night, particularly on weekends, revelers along M Street and Wisconsin Avenue eat, drink, and make merry. Although the coveted brick homes north of M Street are the province of Washington's high society, the rest of the neighborhood offers ample entertainment for everyone.

⊙ Sights

C&O Canal

BODY OF WATER | FAMILY | George Washington was one of the first to advance the idea of a canal linking the Potomac with the Ohio River across the Appalachians. Work started on the Chesapeake & Ohio Canal in 1828, and, when it opened in 1850, its 74 locks linked Georgetown with Cumberland, Maryland, 185 miles to the northwest (still short of its intended destination). Lumber, coal, iron, wheat, and flour moved up and down the canal, but it was never as successful as its planners had hoped due to damaging floods and competition from the Baltimore & Ohio Railroad. Today, the canal is part of the National Park System; walkers and cyclists follow the towpath once used by mules, while canoeists paddle the canal's calm waters. Ongoing construction to repair and restore locks can often result in towpath closures. The Georgetown Visitor Center is also closed until further notice. ⊠ 1057 Thomas Jefferson St. NW, Georgetown ☎ 301/767-3714 Great Falls Tavern Visitor's Center ⊕ www.nps.gov/choh ⊠ The park is free to visit except the Great Falls Tavern area in Potomac, MD. Visit the website for updated fee information.

Dumbarton House

HOUSE | Not to be confused with the Dumbarton Oaks museum, a beautiful garden and research center a few blocks away, this circa-1799 brick mansion was once the home of the first Register of the U.S. Treasury, Joseph Nourse. Today, it's the headquarters for The Colonial Dames of America. Visitors can tour the antiques-filled Federalist home, which often hosts concerts, theatrical performances, and other community events. Docent-led tours are available on the weekend, and the house is open for self-guided tours Thursday–Sunday. Timed tickets are required. ⊠ 2715 Q St. NW, Georgetown ☎ 202/337-2288 ⊕ dumbartonhouse.org ⊠ $10 ⊙ Closed Mon. Ⓜ Dupont Circle.

★ Dumbarton Oaks Museum

GARDEN | Career diplomat Robert Woods Bliss and his wife, Mildred, bought the property in 1920 and tamed the sprawling grounds into 10 acres of splendid gardens designed by Beatrix Farrand. In 1940, the Blisses gave the estate to Harvard University as a study center, library, museum, and garden. The museum holds a small but world-renowned collection of Byzantine and pre-Columbian art, reflecting the enormous skill and creativity developed at roughly the same time in two very different parts of the

A History of Georgetown

The area that would come to be known as George (after George II), then George Towne, and finally Georgetown, was part of Maryland when it was settled in the early 1700s by Scottish immigrants, many of whom were attracted by the region's tolerant religious climate.

Georgetown's position—at the farthest point up the Potomac that's accessible by ship—made it an ideal transit and inspection point for farmers who grew tobacco in Maryland's interior. In 1789, the state granted the town a charter, but two years later, Georgetown—along with Alexandria, its counterpart in Virginia—was included by George Washington in the Territory of Columbia, site of the new capital.

While Washington struggled, Georgetown thrived. Wealthy traders built their mansions on the hills overlooking the river; merchants and the working class lived in modest homes closer to the water's edge.

In 1810, a third of Georgetown's population was African American—both free people and slaves. The Mt. Zion United Methodist Church on 29th Street is the oldest organized Black congregation in the city, and when the church stood at 27th and P Streets it was a stop on the Underground Railroad (the original building burned down in the mid-1800s).

Georgetown's rich history and success instilled in all its residents a feeling of pride that persists today. When Georgetowners thought the capital was dragging them down, they asked to be given back to Maryland, the way Alexandria was given back to Virginia in 1845.

Tobacco's star eventually fell, and Georgetown became a milling center, using waterpower from the Potomac. When the Chesapeake & Ohio (C&O) Canal was completed in 1850, the city intensified its milling operations and became the eastern end of a waterway that stretched 184 miles to the west.

The C&O took up some of the slack when Georgetown's harbor began to fill with silt and the port lost business to Alexandria and Baltimore, but the canal never became the success that George Washington had envisioned.

In the years that followed, Georgetown was a malodorous industrial district, a far cry from the fashionable spot it is today. Clustered near the water were a foundry, a fish market, paper and cotton mills, and a power station for the city's streetcar system.

Georgetown still had its Georgian, Federal, and Victorian homes, though, and, when the New Deal and World War II brought a flood of newcomers to Washington, Georgetown's tree-shaded streets and handsome brick houses were rediscovered. Pushed out in the process were many of Georgetown's renters, including many of its Black residents.

In modern times, some of Washington's most famous residents have called Georgetown home, including former *Washington Post* executive editor Ben Bradlee; political pundit George Stephanopoulos; Congresswoman Nancy Pelosi; Secretaries of State John Kerry, Henry Kissinger, and Madeleine Albright; Senator John Warner and his wife at the time, Elizabeth Taylor; and *New York Times* op-ed doyenne Maureen Dowd.

Healy Hall, one of the most historic and prominent buildings of Georgetown University, houses the Riggs Library and is a National Historic Landmark.

world. The Byzantine collection includes beautiful examples of both religious and secular items executed in mosaic, metal, enamel, stone, textile, and ivory. Pre-Columbian works—artifacts and textiles from Mexico and Central and South America by peoples such as the Aztec, Maya, Inca, and Olmec—are arranged in an enclosed glass pavilion. Especially beautiful in the spring but worth visiting in any season, the gardens feature an orangery and a green terrace filled with iron furniture emblazoned with astrological motifs. ⌧ *1703 32nd St. NW, Georgetown* ☎ *202/339-6401, 202/339-6400 tours* ⊕ *www.doaks.org* ✉ *Admission to museum is free; admission to gardens is from $5* ☯ *Closed Mon.* Ⓜ *Dupont Circle.*

Georgetown University

COLLEGE | The country's oldest Catholic university (founded in 1789) does not offer architectural tours, but visitors can download a self-guided campus tour from the university's website. The 100-acre campus features a mix of architectural styles with the most striking building being Healy Hall, a Victorian Gothic masterpiece whose construction nearly bankrupted the institution. Architects oriented its front toward the city, and not the Potomac River, as a way to signal its educational stature. Old North, which was modeled after Princeton's main hall, has played host to more than a dozen U.S. presidents. Also worth a peek is the turn-of-the-century Riggs Library, which boasts impressive cast-iron railings. At the southern end of campus, between M and Prospect Streets, a set of 75 super-steep steps were immortalized in the 1973 film *The Exorcist.* When the sun rises, less sinister beings can be seen racing up and down them—Georgetown's many joggers. ⌧ *3700 O St. NW, Georgetown* ☎ *202/687-0100* ⊕ *www. georgetown.edu* Ⓜ *Foggy Bottom–GWU.*

Oak Hill Cemetery

BUILDING | Considered a best-kept secret of Washington, D.C.'s attractions, Oak Hill Cemetery functions as a public outdoor

KEY

1 Exploring Sights

1 Restaurants

1 Hotels

Rock Creek
Park

Dumbarton
Oaks Park

Montrose
Park

Dumbarton Oaks Park

Rock Creek

12

I St. N.W.

S St. N.W.

36th St. N.W.

35th St. N.W.

34th St. N.W.

37th St. N.W.

R St. N.W.

Wisconsin Ave. N.W.

Reservoir Rd. N.W.

1

3

R St. N.W.

5

Dent Pl. N.W.

Cambridge Pl.

Dent Pl. N.W.

32nd St. N.W.

31st St. N.W.

Avon Ln.

7

2

Dent Pl. N.W.

29th St. N.W.

O St. N.W.

30th St. N.W.

29th St. N.W.

28th St. N.W.

34th St. N.W.

35th St. N.W.

Volta Pl. N.W.

P St. N.W.

O St. N.W.

Wisconsin Ave. N.W.

P St. N.W.

4

O St. N.W.

33rd St. N.W.

Potomac St. N.W.

31st St. N.W.

Dumbarton St. N.W.

N St. N.W.

N St. N.W.

Georgetown

Olive St. N.W.

9 **5**

13

37th St. N.W.

36th St. N.W.

35th St. N.W.

N St. N.W.

Prospect St. N.W.

3

10 **6**

8

M St. N.W.

M St. N.W.

Wisconsin Ave. N.W.

2

31st St. N.W.

30th St. N.W.

3

Thomas Jefferson St. N.W.

29th St. N.W.

2

2

1

Grace St. N.W.

Cecil Pl.

11

5

1

4

South St.

Georgetown
Waterfront Park

4

Whitehurst Fwy.

7

6

Rock Creek & Potomac Parkway N.W.

66

District of
Columbia
↓

Francis Scott Key Bridge

Virginia

66

Potomac   River

Rock
Creek
Park

Thompson's
Boat House
Park

1

Virginia Ave.

Georgetown

0   1,000 ft

0   200 m

Sights ▼

1 C&O Canal **F9**
2 Dumbarton House **F4**
3 Dumbarton Oaks
  Museum **D3**
4 Georgetown
  University **A5**
5 Oak Hill Cemetery **F3**
6 Old Stone House **E6**
7 Tudor Place **D4**

Restaurants ▼

1 Bistrot Lepic &
  Wine Bar **B2**
2 Bourbon Steak **F7**
3 Cafe Milano **D6**
4 Chez Billy Sud **E7**
5 Das Ethiopian
  Cuisine **F6**
6 Farmers Fishers
  Bakers **E8**
7 Fiola Mare **E8**
8 Kafe Leopold **C6**
9 La Chaumière **F6**
10 Miss Saigon **E6**
11 Reverie **D7**
12 Rocklands Barbeque
  and Grilling
  Company **A1**
13 1789 Restaurant **A6**

Quick Bites ▼

1 Baked & Wired **E7**
2 Moby Dick House
  of Kabob **D7**

Hotels ▼

1 Four Seasons Hotel,
  Washington, D.C. **F7**
2 Georgetown Suites **F7**
3 The Graham
  Washington DC
  Georgetown,
  Tapestry Collection
  by Hilton **E6**
4 The Ritz-Carlton
  Georgetown,
  Washington, D.C. **D7**
5 Rosewood
  Washington D.C. **D7**

museum. Fans of George Saunders's best-selling novel *Lincoln in the Bardo* trek to this hillside corner of Georgetown near Rock Creek. Notable sights include a Gothic Revival chapel designed by James Renwick and the Carroll Family mausoleum, which, during the Civil War, briefly interred Abraham Lincoln's son, Willie, who died in childhood from typhoid fever. In addition to visiting the places where notable figures reside, visitors will discover cenotaphs, sculptures, monuments, and inscriptions. Stop by the office for a free self-guided map. ⊠ *3001 R St. NW, Georgetown* ☎ *202/337–2835* ⊕ *www.oakhillcemeterydc.org* Ⓜ *Dupont Circle.*

Old Stone House

BUILDING | FAMILY | Washington's oldest surviving building, this fieldstone house in the heart of Georgetown was built in 1765 by a cabinetmaker named Christopher Layman. It was used as both a residence and place of business by a succession of occupants until 1953, when it was purchased by the National Park Service. Over the next seven years, it underwent an extensive restoration that has preserved the building's Revolutionary War–era architecture and design. Five of the house's rooms are furnished with the simple, sturdy artifacts—plain tables, spinning wheels, and so forth—of 18th-century middle-class life. You can take a self-guided tour of the house and its lovely English-style gardens. ⊠ *3051 M St. NW, Georgetown* ☎ *202/895–6070* ⊕ *www.nps.gov/olst* ⧉ *Free* Ⓜ *Foggy Bottom–GWU.*

Tudor Place

HOUSE | Stop at Q Street between 31st and 32nd Streets, and look through the trees to the north, to the top of a sloping lawn, to see the Neoclassical Tudor Place, designed by Capitol architect Dr. William Thornton for one of Martha Washington's granddaughters. Completed in 1816, the house remained in the family for six generations, hosting countless politicians, dignitaries, and military leaders. On the house tour you can see the largest collection of George and Martha Washington items on public display outside Mount Vernon, Francis Scott Key's law desk, and spurs belonging to soldiers who were executed as spies in the Civil War. You can only visit the house by guided tour (given hourly; last tour at 3), but before and afterward, until 4 pm, you can wander freely, with a map, through the formal garden full of roses and boxwoods, many of which are more than a century old. Admission to the garden grounds is free, but reserved time tickets are required. ⊠ *1644 31st St. NW, Georgetown* ☎ *202/965–0400* ⊕ *www.tudorplace.org* ⧉ *Free* ☾ *Closed Mon. and Jan.* Ⓜ *Dupont Circle.*

🍴 Restaurants

Georgetown's picturesque Victorian streetscapes make it D.C.'s most famous neighborhood, with five-star restaurants in historic row houses and casual cafés sandwiched between large national chain stores.

At its beginnings in the mid-1700s, Georgetown was a Maryland tobacco port. Today, the neighborhood is one of D.C.'s premier shopping districts, as well as a tourist and architectural attraction. And while recent additions to the neighborhood seem more apt to be chains, there are some standout local restaurants that cater to the budgets of college students, middle-income travelers, and D.C.'s well-heeled elite.

Bistrot Lepic & Wine Bar

$$$ | FRENCH | Relaxed and upbeat, this neighborhood bistro serves twists on old classics such as potato-crusted salmon served with cherry and Pernod sauce, but some standards, including braised veal cheeks, remain. The wine is all French, with many available by the glass.

MAYDAN

LE DIPLOMATE

BARCELONA

ZAYTINYA

JALEO

Known for: busy neighborhood bistro; all-French wine list; upstairs wine bar with small plates. ⑤ *Average main: $29* ✉ *1736 Wisconsin Ave. NW, Georgetown* ☏ *202/333–0111* ⊕ *www.bistrotlepic.com* Ⓜ *Foggy Bottom–GWU.*

Bourbon Steak

$$$$ | **STEAKHOUSE** | In a city full of steak houses catering to business travelers on expense accounts, Bourbon Steak has made a name for itself as one of the best. Tucked away within the Four Seasons Hotel, the restaurant has an impressive cocktail list; a signature whiskey cart; and renowned, expertly prepared, all-natural meats and decadent sides. **Known for:** one of the top steak houses in town; lively bar scene full of locals; more affordable menu in the lounge. ⑤ *Average main: $55* ✉ *Four Seasons Washington, DC, 2800 Pennsylvania Ave. NW, Georgetown* ☏ *202/944–2026* ⊕ *www.bourbonsteakdc.com* ⊙ *No lunch weekends* Ⓜ *Foggy Bottom–GWU.*

Cafe Milano

$$$$ | **ITALIAN** | Expect authentic, sophisticated Italian cooking and a pricey wine list at this upscale Georgetown hot spot that has been around for over 25 years. Specialties are butter lettuce salad with lemon vinaigrette and crostini, thin-crust pizzas anchored by Naples-controlled San Marzano tomato sauce, and sumptuous pasta dishes in pesto or fresh vegetable sauces. **Known for:** regulars include local socialites, lobbyists, and diplomats; a patio for people-watching; the front wall of windows opens onto the street in nice weather. ⑤ *Average main: $42* ✉ *3251 Prospect St. NW, Georgetown* ☏ *202/333–6183* ⊕ *www.cafemilano.net.*

Chez Billy Sud

$$ | **FRENCH** | A favorite for an elegant working lunch, this cozy gem spotlights southern French cooking and serves lunch, dinner, and weekend brunch. If it's a nice day, request a table on the brick patio. **Known for:** chicken liver mousse

appetizer; elegant atmosphere; fine selection of French wines. ⑤ *Average main: $26* ✉ *1039 31st St. NW, Georgetown* ☏ *202/965–2606* ⊕ *www.chezbillysud.com* ⊙ *No lunch Mon.*

Das Ethiopian Cuisine

$$ | **ETHIOPIAN** | At this award-winning spot in Georgetown's historic shopping district, the delightful chicken-and-beef sampler and the harvest vegetable specialty provide a taste of Ethiopian fare at its upscale best. And don't worry about running out of the pancakelike injera bread used in place of utensils—your server will keep bringing it. **Known for:** rare Ethiopian fine dining; spicy sauces; patio dining in nice weather. ⑤ *Average main: $18* ✉ *1201 28th St. NW, Georgetown* ☏ *202/333–4710* ⊕ *www.dasethiopian.com* ⊙ *No lunch Mon. and Tues.* Ⓜ *Foggy Bottom–GWU.*

★ **Farmers Fishers Bakers**

$$ | **AMERICAN** | **FAMILY** | This restaurant near the Washington Harbour, on the banks of the Potomac River, is owned by a collective of farmers and emphasizes sustainable ingredients. The menu runs the gamut—from fresh-baked bread (there's an on-site bakery) to sushi rolls, burgers to pizza, vegetarian options and wild-caught salmon to locally raised chicken and beef—and mixologists shake up tasty tiki drinks. **Known for:** weekend brunch buffet; fried-chicken jambalaya; extensive menu that satisfies even picky eaters. ⑤ *Average main: $26* ✉ *3000 K St. NW, Georgetown* ☏ *202/298–8783* ⊕ *www.farmersfishersbakers.com* Ⓜ *Foggy Bottom–GWU.*

Fiola Mare

$$$$ | **ITALIAN** | The harborside setting for Fabio Trabocchi's ode to Italian-style seafood is one of the most sought-after spots in town. Dine alfresco, and watch the water taxis float by, or sip an Aperol spritz on a banquette by the open kitchen and raw bar: you may think you've traded D.C. for Venice. **Known for:** lobster

168

ravioli; well-priced, three-course, prix-fixe lunch; mouthwatering Italian desserts. ⑤ *Average main: $60* ✉ *3050 K St. NW, Georgetown* ☎ *202/525–1402* ⊕ *www.fiolamaredc.com* Ⓜ *Foggy Bottom–GWU.*

Kafe Leopold

$$ | AUSTRIAN | As Euro-trendy as it gets, Leopold has an all-day coffee and drinks bar, olive-and-onion tarts, crisp schnitzel paired with arugula, and a to-die for assortment of pastries. The setting is an architecturally hip dining space, with roll-up window walls and a patio complete with a fountain. **Known for:** hearty Austrian fare; arty crowd great for people-watching; great weekend brunch and daily breakfast served until 4. ⑤ *Average main: $18* ✉ *3315 Cady's Alley NW, Georgetown* ☎ *202/965–6005* ⊕ *www.kafeleopolds.com.*

La Chaumière

$$ | FRENCH | A rustic and unpretentious atmosphere meets traditional French cuisine at this Georgetown stalwart with many devoted local fans. Dishes like the boudin blanc and pike dumplings baked in lobster sauce will warm you on the inside just like the large central stone fireplace does on the outside. **Known for:** French country-style dishes and ambience; cassoulet with duck confit, lamb stew, and sausage; great wine list with lots of French options. ⑤ *Average main: $23* ✉ *2813 M St. NW, Georgetown* ☎ *202/338–1784* ⊕ *www.lachaumieredc.com* ☾ *Closed Sun.* Ⓜ *Foggy Bottom–GWU.*

Miss Saigon

$ | VIETNAMESE | Shades of mauve and green, black Art Deco accents, and potted palms decorate this Vietnamese gem in an often overpriced and overhyped neighborhood. Appearances count here, but on the plate and not in the clientele— and you'll be grateful for that when you tuck into the crisp spring rolls or refreshing salad of shredded green papaya, cucumber, and basil, topped with shrimp or chicken. ⑤ *Average main: $17* ✉ *3057 M St. NW, Georgetown* ☎ *202/333–5545* ⊕ *www.ms-saigonus.com* ▤ *No credit cards* Ⓜ *Foggy Bottom/GWU.*

Reverie

$$$$ | AMERICAN | FAMILY | Tucked away in an alley, Reverie is a New American restaurant that puts a playful spin on the traditional fine-dining experience. The roasted duck for two is renowned, but the "cheese course" (a decadent take on the McDonald's cheeseburger) might be the biggest crowd pleaser. **Known for:** fine dining; hidden gem; innovative American cuisine. ⑤ *Average main: $80* ✉ *3201 Cherry Hill La. NW, Georgetown* ⊹ *Best to approach from Wisconsin Ave., the restaurant is just off Grace St. NW in alley directly across from Chaia Tacos* ☎ *202/808–2952.*

Rocklands Barbeque and Grilling Company

$ | BARBECUE | FAMILY | The original branch of the popular local barbecue chain now has a dining room, so you can sit and enjoy the baby back ribs and tender smoked chicken. Additional locations can be found in Arlington and Alexandria, as well as inside the Capital One Arena. **Known for:** beef and pork ribs; delicious sides like cornbread, mac and cheese, and baked beans; hardwood grill. ⑤ *Average main: $14* ✉ *2418 Wisconsin Ave. NW, Georgetown* ☎ *202/333–2558* ⊕ *www.rocklands.com.*

1789 Restaurant

$$$$ | AMERICAN | This dining room with early American paintings and a fireplace could easily be a room in the White House. But all the gentility of this 19th-century town-house restaurant is offset by a daily-changing menu of down-to-earth food dressed up in effervescent presentations. **Known for:** rack of lamb; upscale, historic setting; several prix-fixe options. ⑤ *Average main: $49* ✉ *1226 36th St. NW, Georgetown* ☎ *202/965–1789* ⊕ *www.1789restaurant.com* ⋔ *Jacket required.*

☕ Coffee and Quick Bites

Baked & Wired

$ | **BAKERY** | **FAMILY** | Considered to be one of D.C.'s most essential coffee shops, Baked & Wired is the perfect place for a cup of tea or coffee and a generously sized baked good. Don't miss out on the chocolate chip cookies. **Known for:** chocolate chip cookies; big portions; signature granola. ⑤ *Average main: $5* ⊠ *1052 Thomas Jefferson St., Georgetown* ☎ *703/663–8727* Ⓜ *Foggy Bottom–GWU Station.*

Moby Dick House of Kabob

$ | **MIDDLE EASTERN** | **FAMILY** | This casual spot with Persian fare and a focus on high-quality ingredients will steal your heart. Whether you're craving kebabs, falafel, baklava, or gyros, you cannot go wrong (although we do strongly recommend the baklava and the salmon kabobs). **Known for:** baklava and salmon kebabs; authentic Persian cuisine; fresh-baked pita with every order. ⑤ *Average main: $8* ⊠ *1070 31st St., Georgetown* ☎ *202/333–4400* ⊕ *www.mobyskabob.com/stores/moby-dick-georgetown.*

🛏 Hotels

Even to other native Washingtonians, this high-end neighborhood—home to Washington's elite—is a tourist destination. Historic homes on quiet streets with plenty of trees and a canal make this area ideal for strolling. M Street and Wisconsin Avenue restaurants and shops also make it the hottest spot in town for those with money to burn. Georgetown University students keep this area bustling into the early hours.

Four Seasons Hotel, Washington, D.C

$$$$ | **HOTEL** | **FAMILY** | This favorite with celebrities, hotel connoisseurs, and families is on the edge of Georgetown and offers luxurious, ultramodern rooms outfitted in calming neutrals and featuring heavenly beds and French limestone or marble baths with separate showers and sunken tubs. **Pros:** impeccable service; excellent fitness center and spa; gorgeous saltwater lap pool. **Cons:** pricey; challenging street parking; far from Metro. ⑤ *Rooms from: $795* ⊠ *2800 Pennsylvania Ave. NW, Georgetown* ☎ *202/342–0444, 800/332–3442* ⊕ *www.fourseasons.com/washington* ⏎ *222 rooms* ❍ *No meals* Ⓜ *Foggy Bottom–GWU.*

Georgetown Suites

$ | **HOTEL** | **FAMILY** | Though they vary in size, the suites at this property—spread over two buildings a block apart in a top location—all have fully equipped kitchens and separate sitting rooms and come with perks like a continental breakfast, free Wi-Fi, a free gym, and a discount card for nearby restaurants. **Pros:** spacious suites; good choice for a family that wants to spread out; laundry facilities. **Cons:** limited underground garage parking is expensive; no pool; street noise. ⑤ *Rooms from: $155* ⊠ *1111 30th St. NW, Georgetown* ☎ *202/298–7800, 800/348–7203* ⊕ *www.georgetownsuites.com* ⏎ *221 suites* ❍ *Free Breakfast* Ⓜ *Foggy Bottom–GWU.*

The Graham Washington DC Georgetown, Tapestry Collection by Hilton

$$$ | **HOTEL** | Named after Alexander Graham Bell, the inventor who once lived in Georgetown, this upscale boutique hotel is on a residential street just steps from M Street's shops and eateries. **Pros:** quiet and spacious accommodations; nice water and city views; free Wi-Fi. **Cons:** expensive parking; no pool; small fitness room. ⑤ *Rooms from: $309* ⊠ *1075 Thomas Jefferson St. NW, Georgetown* ☎ *202/337–0900* ⊕ *www.thegrahamgeorgetown.com* ⏎ *57 rooms* ❍ *No meals* Ⓜ *Foggy Bottom–GWU.*

Hot Hotel Bars and Lounges

Some of the most iconic examples of power bars, where inside-the-Beltway decision makers talk shop and rub elbows, are housed in many of this town's historic hotels. So grab a snifter of single malt, and begin your people-watching at these classic D.C. hotel bars.

Quill at **The Jefferson** is a hidden gem in Downtown with live piano music, an outdoor terrace, and cocktail menus that change monthly. Ask for a basic drink, and the bartenders will add their creative touches to your handcrafted cocktail, all while providing great service. Plus the nibbles of olives and nuts are simply divine.

The **Off the Record** bar at Downtown's **Hay-Adams Hotel** advertises itself as the place to be seen and not heard. And while it's just steps from the White House, that couldn't be more true. It's tucked away in the historic hotel's basement, and you really never know who you might run into here.

Although they don't boast the same old-world, dark-wood-and-red-leather charm of the bars at the historic hotels, the **Dirty Habit**, at the decidedly more modern **Hotel Monaco**, and **P.O.V.**, on the roof of the **W Washington, D.C.** (both Downtown), hold their own as stops on the see-and-be-seen hotel bar scene.

The Ritz-Carlton Georgetown, Washington, D.C.

$$$ | HOTEL | FAMILY | Once an incinerator dating from the 1920s, this building still topped with a smokestack might seem the most unlikely of places for a luxury hotel, but settle into one of the large and chicly designed guest rooms (upper-level suites overlook the river), and you'll agree the concept works. **Pros:** excellent new spa and fitness center; soaking tubs in all room categories; personalized service. **Cons:** far from the Metro; pricey; expensive parking. $ *Rooms from: $325* ✉ *3100 South St. NW, Georgetown* ☎ *202/912–4200* ⊕ *www.ritzcarlton.com* ⤳ *86 rooms* ⓘ *No meals* Ⓜ *Foggy Bottom–GWU.*

★ Rosewood Washington D.C.

$$$ | HOTEL | Highlights here include the rooftop infinity pool and bar—with views of the Washington Monument, Kennedy Center, and the Potoma—and the personalized attention each guest receives, even before check-in. **Pros:** easy walking distance to both M Street shops and Washington Harbour; showstopping onyx bar in the Rye Bar; D.C.'s only luxury hotel with a rooftop pool. **Cons:** expensive; far from Metro and Mall; expensive valet parking. $ *Rooms from: $398* ✉ *1050 31st St. NW, Georgetown* ☎ *202/617–2400* ⊕ *www.rosewoodhotels.com/en/washington-dc* ⤳ *61 rooms* ⓘ *No meals* Ⓜ *Foggy Bottom–GWU.*

▼ Nightlife

Due to its proximity to the university, weekends (and even weeknights) are a happening affair in Georgetown. A number of bars serve as restaurants by day, until the college and intern crowds take over at night. Although most venues here tend to attract a younger set, the neighborhood still offers many options for patrons over thirty, such as the legendary Blues Alley. There's little parking here, and no easy Metro access, so if you're not staying nearby your best bet is a taxi. In late spring and summer, head to the Washington Harbour for drinks and a riverside stroll.

BARS AND LOUNGES

Degrees

BARS/PUBS | Hidden away inside the Ritz-Carlton hotel, in what was once the Georgetown Incinerator, this modern bar is a breath of fresh air in the neighborhood's rather monotone scene. There's an extensive wine and cocktail selection behind the black granite bar and a hip, well-dressed set of patrons in front of it. When the weather's nice, head out to the multilevel brick patio and sit by the fireplace. ⊠ The Ritz-Carlton Georgetown, 3100 South St. NW, Georgetown ☎ 202/912–4146 ⊕ www.ritzcarlton.com.

Eno Wine Bar

$ | |WINE BARS—NIGHTLIFE | Start your night at this casual, cozy Georgetown hot spot—or even make it an evening in and of itself. Although Eno offers wine by the bottle and glass, it's the wine-tasting flights of three 2.5-ounce pours where it really excels. You can also munch on cheese, charcuterie, and chocolate boards—many of the ingredients are locally sourced. Guests get two hours of free valet parking at the Four Seasons next door; the hotel manages the bar, so you can expect great service. ⊠ Four Seasons Hotel, 2810 Pennsylvania Ave. NW, Georgetown ☎ 202/342–0444 ⊕ www.fourseasons.com ⊗ Closed Mon. Ⓜ Foggy Bottom–GWU.

J Paul's

BARS/PUBS | Located in a historic building that's more than 100 years old, this neighborhood saloon is a festive place to go for a beer and a game. The menu is extensive, but stick to the great hamburgers and seafood dishes. J Paul's attracts a diverse crowd, from students to lobbyists to politicians. ⊠ 3218 M St. NW, Georgetown ☎ 202/333–3450 ⊕ www.jpaulsdc.com.

Nick's Riverside Grill

BARS/PUBS | This perch on the Georgetown waterfront offers fantastic views of the Potomac and a wintertime ice-skating rink. When the weather's nice, crowds of college students flock to the outdoor tables. The food is standard bar fare—the real draw is location, location, location. ⊠ 3050 K St. NW, Georgetown ☎ 202/342–3535 ⊕ www.nicksriverside-grill.com.

The Sovereign

BARS/PUBS | With two bars serving 50 beers on tap and another 350 in bottles, the Sovereign's devotion to suds is not in doubt. Ask your bartender or waiter for help to try a new brew without the risk of drinking a dud. If you're hungry, too, the menu focuses on tasty Belgian fare like mussels with herbed mayonnaise. ⊠ 1206 Wisconsin Ave. NW, Georgetown ✛ Entrance is off alley next to Abercrombie & Fitch ☎ 202/774–5875 ⊕ www.thesovereigndc.com Ⓜ Foggy Bottom–GWU.

The Tombs

BARS/PUBS | Visitors to Georgetown University looking for a pint or some pub grub head down the stairs below 1789 restaurant to this traditional, half-century-old, collegiate watering hole adorned with rowing paraphernalia and steeped in charming Georgetown boosterism. One block from the main gate, it's the closest bar to campus, so it gets crowded with students at night. ⊠ 1226 36th St. NW, Georgetown ☎ 202/337–6668 ⊕ www.tombs.com.

Tony and Joe's

BARS/PUBS | Right on Georgetown's waterfront, this seafood restaurant has a large outdoor patio where you can enjoy a drink al fresco on a spring or summer evening. The cocktails are a little pricey, but you can't beat the view of the Potomac River and Kennedy Center at night. ⊠ 3000 K St. NW, Georgetown ☎ 202/944–4545 ⊕ www.tonyandjoes.com.

MUSIC CLUBS
★ Blues Alley

MUSIC CLUBS | Head here for a classy evening in an intimate setting, complete with great blues, jazz, and R&B from well-known performers such as Mose Allison and Wynton Marsalis and outstanding New Orleans–style grub. Expect to pay a cover charge as well as a food or drink minimum. ■TIP→ **You can come for just the show, but those who enjoy a meal get better seats.** ✉ *1073 Wisconsin Ave. NW, near M St., Georgetown* ☎ *202/337–4141* ⊕ *www.bluesalley.com* Ⓜ *Foggy Bottom–GWU.*

🎭 Performing Arts

Georgetown entertainment goes far beyond barhopping on a Saturday night. Smaller drama groups stage productions in several of Georgetown's larger churches; check local publications for the latest offerings.

MUSIC
CHAMBER MUSIC
Dumbarton Concerts

CONCERTS | A fixture in Georgetown since 1772 (in its current location since 1850), Dumbarton United Methodist Church sponsors a concert series that has featured the Harlem Quartet, the Smithsonian Jazz Masterworks, the St. Petersburg String Quartet, plus a multigenerational community of emerging artists. It's also home to Inner City-Inner Child, Inc., a music, arts, and education organization. The program promotes diversity and accessibility to music throughout greater D.C. ■TIP→ **Before or after a performance, stroll through the nearby Dumbarton Oaks estate and park.** ✉ *Dumbarton United Methodist Church, 3133 Dumbarton Ave. NW, Georgetown* ☎ *202/965–2000* ⊕ *dumbartonconcerts.org* Ⓜ *Foggy Bottom–GWU.*

🛍 Shopping

Although Georgetown, the capital's center for famous residents, is not on a Metro line, and street parking is tough to find, people still flock here to shop.

National chains and designer shops now stand side by side with the specialty shops that first gave the district its allure, but the historic neighborhood is still charming and its street scene lively. Most stores lie east and west on M Street and to the north on Wisconsin Avenue. The intersection of M and Wisconsin is the nexus for chain stores and big-name designer shops. The farther you venture in any direction from this intersection, the more eclectic and interesting the shops become. Some of the big-name stores are worth a look for their architecture alone; several shops blend traditional Georgetown town-house exteriors with airy, modern showroom interiors.

Shopping in Georgetown can be expensive, but you don't have to add expensive parking lot fees. ■TIP→ **The DC Circulator is your best bet for getting into and out of Georgetown, especially if it's hot, or if you are laden down with many purchases. This $1 bus runs along M Street and up Wisconsin Avenue, the major shopping strips.** The nearest Metro station, Foggy Bottom–GWU, is a 10- to 15-minute walk from the shops.

ANTIQUES AND COLLECTIBLES
Marston Luce

ANTIQUES/COLLECTIBLES | House and garden accessories are in the mix here, but the emphasis is on 18th- and 19th-century French and Swedish painted furniture, sourced by the owner on yearly buying trips in Europe. ✉ *1651 Wisconsin Ave. NW, Georgetown* ☎ *202/333–6800* ⊕ *www.marstonluce.com* Ⓜ *Foggy Bottom–GWU.*

★ Opportunity Shop of the Christ Child Society

ANTIQUES/COLLECTIBLES | This gem of a consignment–thrift store has been a Georgetown landmark since 1954, with volunteers who have been with the store for over 40 years. You'll find gorgeous fine jewelry, antiques, crystal, silver, and porcelain. Prices are moderate, and profits go to a good cause—the Christ Child Society provides for the needs of local children. It's closed Sunday. ✉ 1427 Wisconsin Ave. NW, Georgetown ☎ 202/333-6635 ⊕ www.christchilddc. org Ⓜ Foggy Bottom–GWU.

ART GALLERIES
Addison Ripley

ART GALLERIES | Stunning, large-scale contemporary work by national and local artists, including painters Manon Cleary and Wolf Kahn and photographer Frank Hallam Day, is exhibited at this well-respected gallery, which is closed both Sunday and Monday. ✉ 1670 Wisconsin Ave. NW, Georgetown ☎ 202/338-5180 ⊕ www.addisonripleyfineart.com Ⓜ Foggy Bottom–GWU.

Maurine Littleton Gallery

ART GALLERIES | This gallery is devoted to glass, metal, and ceramics, and it's worth a look to see work by some of the world's finest contemporary artists. The intimate, bright space is owned and managed by the daughter of Harvey K. Littleton, founder of the American Studio Glass movement. The gallery is open by appointment only. ✉ 1667 Wisconsin Ave. NW, Georgetown ☎ 202/494-2666 ⊕ www.littletongallery.com Ⓜ Foggy Bottom–GWU.

Susan Calloway Fine Arts

ART GALLERIES | Stunning art draws people into this two-floor gallery where a mix of vintage, contemporary, and classical paintings are hung salon-style. You'll find large abstract oils and a lovely selection of landscapes, but don't miss the box full of small original paintings in the back,

most priced under $100. The gallery is closed Monday. ✉ 1643 Wisconsin Ave., Georgetown ☎ 202/965-4601 ⊕ www. callowayart.com Ⓜ Foggy Bottom–GWU or Dupont Circle.

BOOKS
Bridge Street Books

BOOKS/STATIONERY | This charming independent store focuses on politics, history, philosophy, poetry, literature, music, film, and Judaica. ✉ 2814 Pennsylvania Ave., NW, Georgetown ☎ 202/965-5200 ⊕ www.bridgestreetbooks.com Ⓜ Foggy Bottom–GWU.

CHILDREN'S TOYS
Tugooh Toys

TOYS | FAMILY | You might have a difficult time getting your children to leave this fun toy store filled with educational and eco-friendly toys. From puzzles, games, and building toys to dolls, puppets, and dress-up clothes, you are bound to find the perfect gift for youngsters. ✉ 1426 Wisconsin Ave. NW, Georgetown ☎ 202/338-9476 ⊕ www.tugoohtoys. com Ⓜ Foggy Bottom–GWU.

HOME FURNISHINGS
★ A Mano

HOUSEHOLD ITEMS/FURNITURE | The name is Italian for "by hand," and it lives up to this moniker, stocking colorful hand-painted ceramics, hand-dyed tablecloths, blown-glass stemware, hand-embroidered bed linens, and other home and garden accessories by American, English, Italian, and French artisans. Some of the jewelry pieces are simply stunning, and the kids' gifts are adorable. ✉ 1677 Wisconsin Ave. NW, Georgetown ☎ 202/298-7200 ⊕ www.amano.bz.

Random Harvest

ANTIQUES/COLLECTIBLES | Whether you're looking for something that's decorative or functional (or a combination of both), you'll find it here. Random Harvest sells new and antique treasures for the home, including pillows, mirrors, glassware, barware, and lamps. There's also a nice selection of American and European vintage furniture. ⊠ *1313 Wisconsin Ave. NW, Georgetown* ☎ *202/333–5569* ⊕ *www.randomharvesthome.com* Ⓜ *Foggy Bottom–GWU.*

JEWELRY
Ann Hand
JEWELRY/ACCESSORIES | Catering to Washington's powerful and prestigious, this jewelry and gift shop specializing in patriotic pins may seem intimidating, but prices begin at $35. Hand's signature pin, the Liberty Eagle, is $200. Photos on the walls above brightly lit display cases show who's who in Washington wearing you-know-who's designs, making this a worthwhile visit while shopping in Georgetown, though it's closed on weekends. ⊠ *3236 Prospect St. NW, Georgetown* ☎ *202/333–2979* ⊕ *www. annhand.com.*

Brilliant Earth
JEWELRY/ACCESSORIES | This Cady's Alley jeweler uses ethically sourced diamonds and gemstones in unique new and vintage settings. Create your own design, or choose from a selection by master craftsmen. By appointment only. ⊠ *3332 Cady's Alley, NW, Georgetown* ☎ *202/448–9055* ⊕ *www.brilliantearth. com* Ⓜ *Foggy Bottom–GWU.*

lou lou
JEWELRY/ACCESSORIES | A rainbow array of statement necklaces, scarves, and earrings can be found here (most under $30). Vegan leather handbags, hats, and a small selection of clothing from designers like Free People are also on offer from this family-owned, Virginia-based boutique. ⊠ *1304 Wisconsin Ave. NW, Georgetown* ☎ *202/333–3574* ⊕ *www. loulouboutiques.com* ◷ *Closed Mon.* Ⓜ *Foggy Bottom–GWU.*

SHOES
Hu's Shoes and Hu's Wear
SHOES/LUGGAGE/LEATHER GOODS | This cutting-edge selection would shine in Paris, Tokyo, or New York. Luckily for Washingtonians, Hu's brings ballet flats, heels, and boots from designers like Chloé, Fendi, Manolo Blahnik, Proenza Schouler, and Valentino right to Georgetown. You'll also find clothing designs by The Row, Isabel Marant, and Stella McCartney. ⊠ *2906 M St. NW, Georgetown* ☎ *202/342–0202* ⊕ *www.husonline.com* Ⓜ *Foggy Bottom–GWU.*

SHOPPING MALLS
Georgetown Park
SHOPPING CENTERS/MALLS | FAMILY | There's a good mix of retailers at this mall in the center of Georgetown, including Anthropologie & Co. (which has floors devoted to housewares and bridal), H&M, J. Crew, and T.J. Maxx. Stop at the Georgetown Visitor Center inside the main entrance to learn about what's happening in the neighborhood. You can even try your hand at bocce or bowling at Pinstripes, a bistro and entertainment spot with a wonderful patio. Be sure to check ahead on individual store hours as they all vary. ⊠ *3222 M St. NW, Georgetown* ☎ *202/965–1280* ⊕ *www.georgetownpark.com* Ⓜ *Foggy Bottom–GWU.*

SPAS AND BEAUTY SALONS
Bluemercury
SPA/BEAUTY | Hard-to-find skin-care lines—La Mer and Trish McEvoy, among others—are what set this homegrown, now national, chain apart. The retail space up front sells soaps, lotions, perfumes, cosmetics, and skin- and hair-care products. Behind the glass door is the "skin gym," where you can treat yourself to facials, waxing, and oxygen treatments. You'll also find branches in Dupont Circle, Downtown, and Union Station. ⊠ *3059 M St. NW, Georgetown* ☎ *202/965–1300* ⊕ *www.bluemercury.com* Ⓜ *Foggy Bottom–GWU.*

WOMEN'S CLOTHING

Ella-Rue

CLOTHING | Although it's a small shop, you'll find a wonderful selection of high-end consignment clothing, shoes, and handbags here. On any given day, you might discover pieces by designers like Carolina Herrera, Gucci, Stella McCartney, or Zac Posen. The staff is especially helpful and works hard to help you find the perfect ensemble for your next special event or important meeting. ⊠ *3231 P St. NW, Georgetown* ☏ *202/333–1598* ⊕ *www.ella-rue.com.*

★ The Phoenix

CLOTHING | All under one roof (with 30 solar panels) in a delightful shop owned and operated by the Hays family since 1955, you can find contemporary clothing in natural fibers by designers such as Eileen Fisher, OSKA, White+Warren, Michael Stars, and Lilla P. There's also a stunning selection of jewelry from Germany, Turkey, Israel, and Italy; gorgeous leather handbags by Annabel Ingall; floral arrangements from a sustainable farm in Virginia; and fine- and folk-art pieces from Mexico. ⊠ *1514 Wisconsin Ave. NW, Georgetown* ☏ *202/338–4404* ⊕ *www.thephoenixdc.com* Ⓜ *Foggy Bottom–GWU.*

★ Reddz Trading

CLOTHING | You can't miss the bright red storefront of this consignment shop, which sells clothing, accessories, jewelry, and shoes. Unlike traditional consignment stores, Reddz buys its merchandise for cash or trade so inventory is added regularly. It's not uncommon to find pieces with the price tags still attached. ⊠ *1413 Wisconsin Ave. NW, Georgetown* ☏ *202/506–2789* ⊕ *www.reddztrading. com.*

relish

CLOTHING | In fashionable Cady's Alley, this dramatic space holds a women's collection handpicked seasonally by the owner. Modern, elegant, and practical selections include European classics and well-tailored modern designers, such as Marc Jacobs, Pierre Hardy, Thom Browne, Uma Wang, and Dries Van Noten. It's closed Sunday. ⊠ *3312 Cady's Alley NW, Georgetown* ☏ *202/333–5343* ⊕ *www.relishdc.com* Ⓜ *Foggy Bottom–GWU.*

Activities

BIKING

The numerous trails in the District and its surrounding areas are well maintained and clearly marked, including those along the C&O Canal segment in Georgetown. Washington's large parks are also popular with cyclists. Plus, with new bike lanes on all major roads and the Capital Bikeshare scheme (and other rental outlets), it's also a great way to get around town.

Big Wheel Bikes

BICYCLING | **FAMILY** | This 45-year-old company near the C&O Canal Towpath rents multispeed and other types of bikes hourly or for the day. Rates begin at $35 per day for an adult bike with a three-hour minimum. Tandem bikes, kids' bikes, and bikes with baby carriers are also available. Other locations are in Bethesda, near the Capital Crescent Trail, and Alexandria, if you want to ride the Mount Vernon Trail. ⊠ *1034 33rd St. NW, Georgetown* ☏ *202/337–0254* ⊕ *www. bigwheelbikes.com.*

Capital Crescent Trail

BICYCLING | Suited for bicyclists, walkers, rollerbladers, and strollers, this paved trail stretches along the old Georgetown Branch, a B&O Railroad line that was completed in 1910 and was in operation until 1985. The 7.5-mile route's first leg runs from Georgetown near Key Bridge to central Bethesda at Bethesda and Woodmont Avenues. At Bethesda and Woodmont, the trail heads through a well-lighted tunnel near the heart of Bethesda's lively business area and

continues into Silver Spring. The 3.5-
mile stretch from Bethesda to Silver
Spring is gravel, though the all-volunteer
Coalition for the Capital Crescent Trail
is spearheading efforts to pave it. The
Georgetown Branch Trail, as this section
is officially named, connects with the
Rock Creek Trail, which goes to Rockville
in the north and Memorial Bridge past
the Washington Monument in the south.
On weekends when the weather's nice,
all sections of the trails are crowded.
✉ *Georgetown* ✛ *From intersection of
Wisconsin Ave. and M St., go down Wisconsin Ave. to its end under Whitehurst
Freeway at bottom of hill, and turn right
onto Water St. The CCT begins at end of
Water St.* ☎ *202/234–4874 Coalition for
the Capital Crescent Trail* ⊕ *www.cctrail.
org.*

Chapter 8

DUPONT CIRCLE AND KALORAMA

8

Updated by
Jessica van Dop DeJesús

👁 **Sights**
★★★☆☆

🍴 **Restaurants**
★★★★★

🛏 **Hotels**
★★★★☆

🛍 **Shopping**
★★★★☆

🍸 **Nightlife**
★★★★☆

NEIGHBORHOOD SNAPSHOT

TOP EXPERIENCES

■ **Dupont Circle:** Grab a cup of coffee and a newspaper, and soak up the always-buzzing scene around the fountain.

■ **Phillips Collection:** Admire masterpieces such as Renoir's *Luncheon of the Boating Party* and Degas's *Dancers at the Barre* at the country's first museum of modern art.

■ **Woodrow Wilson House:** Glimpse the life of the 28th American president, who lived here during his retirement, surrounded by all the modern luxuries of the early 1900s.

GETTING HERE

Dupont Circle has its own stop on the Metro's Red Line. Exit on Q Street for the Phillips Collection, Anderson House, and Kalorama attractions. On-street parking in residential areas is becoming increasingly difficult to find, especially on weekend evenings.

PLANNING YOUR TIME

The Dupont Circle neighborhood charms whatever the time or season. By day, there is the Phillips Collection's impressive Impressionist art, the historic Woodrow Wilson House, and Kramerbooks & Afterwords for browsing. Evenings, the neighborhood's restaurants, bars, nightclubs, and its own adult game room keep things hopping. Locals prize the FRESH-FARM market, open Sunday mornings year-round.

SAFETY

Dupont Circle is one of the safer areas in Washington, but muggings still occur here from time to time. Avoid dark, empty areas between bars late at night; stay sober; and avoid crowds on sidewalks, where you might encounter pickpockets.

QUICK BITES

■ **Greek Deli.** South of Dupont Circle, owner Kostas Fostieris has been wowing office workers for more than 30 years with his meatballs, spinach pie, and rack of lamb, as well as baklava and yogurt to die for. There may be a line around lunchtime, but it moves quickly. The deli is closed on weekends. ⊠ *1120 19th St. NW* ⊕ *greekdelidc.com* Ⓜ *Farragut W.*

■ **Teaism Dupont Circle.** A few blocks northeast of Dupont Circle and closer to the neighborhood's galleries, take a break in the tranquil surroundings of D.C.'s favorite tea salon, which offers not only a variety of teas, but also intriguing sweets and Asian-inspired comfort food. ⊠ *2009 R St. NW* ⊕ *www.teaism.com* Ⓜ *Dupont Circle.*

■ **Un Je Ne Sais Quoi Patisserie Française.** This French bakery specializes in "les merveilleux" (towers of meringue, cream, and ganache), which are a specialty in the owners' native region of northern France. The bakery also serves more conventional French sweets. Its small space is charming, with framed prints, an elegant antique loveseat, and bistro-sized chairs and tables. ⊠ *1361 Connecticut Ave. NW* ⊕ *unjenesaisquoi-pastry.com* Ⓜ *Dupont Circle.*

Dupont Circle, named for Civil War hero Admiral Samuel F. Dupont, is the grand hub of D.C., literally. This traffic circle is essentially the intersection of the main thoroughfares of Connecticut, New Hampshire, and Massachusetts Avenues. More important though, the area around the circle is a vibrant center for urban and cultural life in the District.

Along with wealthy tenants and basement-dwelling young adults, several museums and art galleries call this upscale neighborhood home. Offbeat shops, bookstores, coffeehouses, and varied restaurants help the area stay funky and diverse. Nearby, the Kalorama neighborhood's mansions welcome powerful movers and shakers from both political parties. Embassies enhance the elegance.

Add to the mix stores and clubs catering to the neighborhood's gay community, and this area becomes a big draw for nearly everyone. Perhaps that's why the fountain at the center of the Dupont traffic island is such a great spot for people-watching.

⊙ Sights

When you think of sightseeing in Washington, D.C., the Dupont Circle neighborhood does not leap to mind immediately. This is an area made for strolling, people-watching, drinking, dancing, eating, and shopping. Nevertheless, there are definitely a few Dupont landmarks worth visiting. Unlike D.C.'s major museums and monuments, which are operated by the federal government, some of these sites charge an admission fee.

Anderson House
LIBRARY | The palatial, Gilded Age Anderson House is the headquarters of the Society of the Cincinnati, the nation's oldest historical organization promoting knowledge and appreciation of America's independence. The society was founded by Revolutionary War veterans in 1783—George Washington was its first president general—and this has been its home since 1938. Guided tours of the first and second floors reveal the history of the society, the significance of the American Revolution, and the lives and collections of the home's first owners, Larz and Isabel Anderson. Built in 1905, the home was the Andersons' winter residence and retains much of its original contents—an eclectic mix of furniture, tapestries, paintings, sculpture, and Asian art. Larz, a U.S. diplomat from 1891 to 1913, and his wife, Isabel, an author and benefactress, assembled their collection as they traveled the world during diplomatic postings. Today, the house also features an exhibition gallery and research library, and it hosts concerts and lectures. ✉ 2118 Massachusetts

Dupont Circle and Kalorama

Ave. NW, Dupont Circle ☎ 202/785–2040 ⊕ www.societyofthecincinnati.org ✉ Free ☾ Closed Mon. Ⓜ Dupont Circle.

Dupont Underground

ARTS VENUE | The former streetcar station, located alongside Dupont Circle, has consistently reinvented itself—from nuclear-era fallout shelter to a short-lived food court in the early '90s. The latest incarnation, a funky arts space, has survived since 2016. It hosts a diverse range of changing art exhibitions, social gatherings, and concerts. Here, you might catch an exhibit of works by D.C.'s up-and-coming photographers or an underground (literally) jazz performance. The space is only open for events, so check the website to see what's scheduled. ✉ *19 Dupont Circle NW, Dupont Circle* ⚓ *Entrance looks like a red Metro sign that says "Dupont Underground"* ⊕ *www.dupontunderground.org.*

Heurich House Museum

HOUSE | This opulent, Romanesque Revival mansion, also known as the Brewmaster's Castle, was the home of Christian Heurich, a German immigrant who made his fortune in the beer business. Heurich's brewery was in Foggy Bottom, where the Kennedy Center stands today. The building, a National Register of Historic Places landmark, is considered one of the most intact Victorian houses in the country, and all the furnishings were owned and used by the Heurichs. The interior is an eclectic mix of plaster detailing, carved wooden doors, and painted ceilings. The downstairs Breakfast Room, which also served as Heurich's *bierstube* (or beer hall), is decorated like a Rathskeller with the German motto "A good drink makes old people young." Heurich must have taken the proverb seriously. He drank beer daily, had three wives, and lived to be 102. Head to the website to see the latest programming, which includes guided tours, a holiday market, and outdoor happy hours. ✉ *1307 New Hampshire Ave. NW, Dupont Circle*

☎ 202/429–1894 ⊕ www.heurichhouse.org ✉ $10 ☾ Closed Sun.–Wed. Ⓜ Dupont Circle.

The Mansion on O Street Museum

HOUSE | FAMILY | This is D.C.'s funkiest museum. A reimagining of your grandma's attic by surreal filmmaker Federico Fellini, it has dozens of secret doors and passageways, as well as rooms overflowing with antiques, pictures, figures of medieval angels, and memorabilia, including 60 signed Gibson guitars, stuffed animals, chandeliers, and books. The museum, housed in five interconnecting town houses, also doubles as an inn, where rooms pay homage to notables such as John Lennon, Winston Churchill, and Rosa Parks, once a frequent visitor. You can get a peek at the themed rooms when not they're occupied by rock stars or CEOs, who value the mansion's privacy and security. ✉ *2020 O St. NW, Dupont Circle* ☎ *202/496–2020* ⊕ *www.omuseum.org* ✉ *Varies depending on exhibition and tour.*

★ The Phillips Collection

MUSEUM | With its setting on a quiet residential street and its low-key elegance, the Phillips Collection offers unhurried access to its first-rate collection of masterpieces from the 19th century and later. At the heart of the collection are works by distinguished Impressionist and Modern artists, including Pierre-Auguste Renoir, Vincent van Gogh, Paul Cézanne, Edgar Degas, Pablo Picasso, Paul Klee, and Henri Matisse. A stunning quartet of Mark Rothko works merits its own room. The museum opened in 1921 in the Georgian Revival mansion of collector Duncan Phillips, who wanted to showcase his art in a museum that would stand as a memorial to his father and brother. In the intervening years, the museum expanded, and now includes much more gallery space, a café, a gift shop, and an auditorium. ✉ *1600 21st St. NW, Dupont Circle* ☎ *202/387–2151*

The many fountains in Dupont Circle make it a nice place for a walk.

⊕ www.phillipscollection.org ✉ Free weekdays; from $10 ⊙ Closed Mon. Ⓜ Dupont Circle.

Spanish Steps
NEIGHBORHOOD | Named for the Spanish Steps in Rome, D.C.'s Spanish Steps aren't quite as grand as their European counterparts, but they do provide a tranquil reprieve from the hustle and bustle of the city. Located next to Embassy Row, the steps offer a view of the Dupont Circle neighborhood. A lion-head fountain at the top is a good place to relax with a book or make a wish in the fountain with pennies. The steps are near the Woodrow Wilson House. ✉ 1725 22nd St. NW, Dupont Circle Ⓜ Dupont Circle.

The Whittemore House
HOUSE | You don't have to be a Democrat to enjoy this historic building, which became the headquarters for the Women's National Democratic Club in 1927. The exquisitely decorated mansion, built in the 1890s and designed by D.C. architect Harvey Page for opera singer Sarah Adams Whittemore, has housed senators and cabinet members over the years. Now it's best known for its library, where Eleanor Roosevelt did her radio broadcasts, and its full-length portraits of first ladies, painted in a whimsical style by folk artist April Newhouse. ✉ 1526 New Hampshire Ave. NW, Dupont Circle ☎ 202/232–7363 ⊕ democraticwoman. org/art-exhibitsmuseum ⊙ Closed Fri.– Mon. in Aug. Ⓜ Dupont Circle (Q St. exit).

Woodrow Wilson House
HOUSE | President Wilson and his second wife, Edith Bolling Wilson, retired in 1921 to this Georgian Revival house designed by Washington architect Waddy B. Wood. It was on this quiet street that Wilson lived out the last few years of his life. It is the only presidential museum in the nation's capital. Wilson died in 1924— Edith survived him by 37 years—and bequeathed the house and its contents to the National Trust for Historic Preservation. Tours of the home provide a wonderful glimpse into the lives of this couple and the dignitaries who visited

them here. Items on display include his cane collection, a Gobelin tapestry, a mosaic from Pope Benedict XV, the pen used by Wilson to sign the declaration that launched the United States into World War I, and the shell casing from the first shot fired by U.S. forces in the war. The house also contains memorabilia related to the history of the short-lived but influential League of Nations, including the colorful flag Wilson hoped would be adopted by that organization. ✉ 2340 S St. NW, Dupont Circle ☎ 202/387–4062 ⊕ www.woodrowwilsonhouse.org 🎫 $10 ⊘ Closed Mon., also Tues.–Thurs. in Jan. and Feb. Ⓜ Dupont Circle.

🍴 Restaurants

Diners who want to spend $200 per person for an exquisite meal as well as those looking for something memorable yet more affordable will be happy in this neighborhood. Connecticut Avenue alone offers blocks and blocks of interesting restaurants. Throughout the neighborhood, happy hours—often with creative small bites—abound, even at many upscale venues. Greek, Italian, French, Asian, Russian, Latin American, and Middle Eastern cuisines are represented, as is distinctive American regional cooking.

Annabelle
$$$ | AMERICAN | The latest creation by famed D.C. restaurateur Ashok Bajaj is located where the legendary Restaurant Nora used to sit. This modern American eatery focuses on locally sourced ingredients, handmade pasta, and whimsical desserts. **Known for:** extensive wine list; beautiful decor; led by former White House chef Frank Ruta. ⑤ Average main: $30 ✉ 2132 Florida Ave. NW, Washington ☎ 202/916–5675 ⊕ www.annabelledc.com.

Anju
$$ | KOREAN | Anju, the reinvention of chef Danny Lee's Mandu, serves unique takes on Korean classics with mainstays

such as succulent seared galbi (short rib) with bib lettuce and perilla leaves, as well as—in an homage to its old name —mandu (dumplings). Many of Anju's recipes come from Lee's mom, chef Yesoon Lee, who you can sometimes spot on-site, and, since opening in 2019, it has dominated the best restaurant lists of local publications and bloggers. **Known for:** modern Korean food; creative tasting menu; creative cocktails. ⑤ Average main: $20 ✉ 1805 18th St. NW, Dupont Circle ☎ 202/845–8936 ⊕ www.anjurestaurant.com.

Bistrot du Coin
$$ | FRENCH | A well-established local favorite, this cozy bistro has a monumental zinc bar and a menu of moderately priced French classics, including onion soup, duck breast, cassoulet, and steaks garnished with a pile of crisp fries. Enjoy your meal with a glass of the house Beaujolais, a Côtes du Rhône, or an Alsatian white. **Known for:** many varieties of mussels; a big party every July 14, Bastille Day; fun local hangout. ⑤ Average main: $26 ✉ 1738 Connecticut Ave. NW, Dupont Circle ☎ 202/234–6969 ⊕ www.bistrotducoin.com Ⓜ Dupont Circle.

CHIKO
$ | ASIAN FUSION | CHIKO (a hybrid of Chinese and Korean, as is the food) Dupont Circle is the second outpost of this revered restaurant, featured in many of the city's "Best of" lists. Although the model is fast-casual, there's nothing fast or casual about the quality of food presented at the restaurant. **Known for:** award-winning D.C. dining; upscale fast casual; modern Korean food. ⑤ Average main: $15 ✉ 2029 P St. NW, Dupont Circle ☎ 202/331–3040 ⊕ www.chikodc.com.

Glen's Garden Market
$ | AMERICAN | Tucked away on picturesque S Street NW, Glen's Garden Market is a hybrid grocery store and coffee shop–café. With a focus on locally sourced ingredients, the cafe offers

delicious sandwiches like a grilled bahn mi, freshly made pizzas, and hearty soups. **Known for:** community-focused; tasty sandwiches; market space. $ *Average main: $10* ⊠ *2001 S St. NW, Dupont Circle* ☎ *202/588–5698* ⊕ *www. glensgardenmarket.com.*

★ Hank's Oyster Bar Dupont Circle

$$ | **SEAFOOD** | The watchword is simplicity at this chic take on the shellfish shacks of New England. Daily offerings include a half-dozen varieties of oyster on the half shell, both from the West Coast and local Virginia waters, as well as fish dishes and a "meat-and-two" special for those who prefer turf to surf. **Known for:** a bittersweet chocolate chunk at the end of the meal; half-price oyster bar happy hours; no desserts. $ *Average main: $26* ⊠ *1624 Q St. NW, Dupont Circle* ☎ *202/462–4265* ⊕ *www.hanksdc.com* Ⓜ *Dupont Circle.*

HipCityVeg

$ | **VEGETARIAN** | Vegans and carnivores alike will rejoice over HipCityVeg's creative, plant-based, fast-casual menu. The Philadelphia-born company serves a popular vegan cheesesteak, accompanied by sweet potato fries, of course. **Known for:** vegan Philly cheesesteak; vegan milk shakes; one of the few plant-based fast foods spots in the city. $ *Average main: $12* ⊠ *1300 Connecticut Ave. NW, Dupont Circle* ☎ *202/318–6010* ⊕ *www. hipcityveg.com.*

Iron Gate

$$ | **MEDITERRANEAN** | In the former carriageway and stable house of a Dupont Circle town house, Iron Gate's romantic setting compliments its upscale Mediterranean fare, served either à la carte or via a tasting menu with optional wine pairings. The menu changes but always includes a seasonal variation on the house focaccia, buratta and feta dip, and staples like the mixed grill and whole fish for two. **Known for:** five-course and multicourse "family" table tasting menus; patio adorned with fairy lights

and wisteria vines; eclectic cocktails. $ *Average main: $25* ⊠ *1734 N St. NW, Dupont Circle* ☎ *202/524–5202* ⊕ *www. irongaterestaurantdc.com* Ⓜ *Dupont Circle.*

★ Komi

$$$$ | **MEDITERRANEAN** | Young, energetic chef-owner Johnny Monis offers one of the city's most adventurous dining experiences in this tiny space. The multicourse, prix-fixe menu, which changes daily, showcases contemporary fare with distinct Mediterranean influences. **Known for:** intimate ambience; impressive wine list (but no cocktails); reservations that book up very quickly. $ *Average main: $165* ⊠ *1509 17th St. NW, Dupont Circle* ☎ *202/332–9200* ⊕ *www.komirestaurant. com* ⊘ *Closed Sun. and Mon. No lunch* Ⓜ *Dupont Circle.*

Kramerbooks & Afterwords

$$ | **CAFÉ** | **FAMILY** | From early morning until after midnight (even later on weekends), you'll find chatty diners at this bookstore café. Breakfast fare is popular, as are the many crab-inflected dishes and spicy pastas. **Known for:** crave-worthy desserts; full bar; popular patio. $ *Average main: $21* ⊠ *1517 Connecticut Ave. NW, Dupont Circle* ☎ *202/387–3825* ⊕ *kramers.com* Ⓜ *Dupont Circle.*

★ Little Serow

$$$$ | **THAI** | Guests start lining up as early as at 4:30 pm with the hope of getting a hard-to-score table at this cozy restaurant in the basement of a row house. Chef Johnny Monis brings the magic of Komi to his creative, seven-course menus featuring unique northern Thai dishes (say, crispy rice salad or shrimp curry) that bring on the heat—literally. **Known for:** walk-in only, no reservations; strict no-substitutions or special-requests policy; Mekhong whiskey–marinated pork ribs. $ *Average main:* ⊠ *1511 17th St. NW, Dupont Circle* ⊕ *www.littleserow. com* ⊘ *Closed Sun. and Mon.* Ⓜ *Dupont Circle.*

Little Sesame

$ | ISRAELI | For those craving the flavors of Israel, Little Sesame is the place. This fast-casual spot in the Golden Triangle serves bowls of creamy hummus topped with colorful veggies and savory proteins. **Known for:** hummus bowls; vanilla tahini soft serve; Israeli cuisine. ⑤ *Average main: $11* ✉ *1828 L St. NW, Dupont Circle* ☎ *202/975–1971* ⊕ *www.eatlittlesesame.com.*

Mission Dupont

$$ | MEXICAN | Mission Dupont serves tacos, burritos, nachos, and other Tex-Mex fare in a casual setting. It's a popular hangout for young professionals, graduate students, and interns. **Known for:** fairly priced cocktails; casual atmosphere; close to the Metro. ⑤ *Average main: $20* ✉ *1606 20th St. NW, Dupont Circle* ☎ *202/525–2010* ⊕ *www.missiondupont.com.*

Nazca Mochica

$$ | PERUVIAN | Many people think of seviche when they hear "Peruvian cuisine," but diners at Nazca Mochica will lose out if they don't look beyond that. The restaurant, owned by native Peruvian Walter Lopez, offers an array of Peruvian classics such as *lomo saltado* (marinated, stir-fried beef), *ají de gallina* (chicken stew), and *anticuchos* (beef skewers). **Known for:** authentic Peruvian food; seviches; Michelin Bib Gourmand. ⑤ *Average main: $20* ✉ *1633 P St. NW, Dupont Circle* ☎ *202/733–3170* ⊕ *www.nazcamochica.com.*

Obelisk

$$$$ | ITALIAN | Despite its tiny dining room, this Italian stalwart, under the helm of veteran chef Esther Lee, has maintained a pull on special-occasion diners since the late 1980s, offering a pricey, five-course, prix-fixe dinner that changes nightly. A sample menu—with its mouthwatering delicacies—is posted on the website to give diners an idea of what to expect. **Known for:** standout burrata; attentive service; accommodating many dietary restrictions (except for vegan) with advance notice. ⑤ *Average main: $80* ✉ *2029 P St. NW, Dupont Circle* ☎ *202/872–1180* ⊕ *www.obeliskdc.com* ⊗ *Closed Sun. and Mon. No lunch* ☞ *Doesn't take American Express* Ⓜ *Dupont Circle.*

The Pembroke

$$ | AMERICAN | The Pembroke at the Dupont Circle Hotel is one of the most beautifully designed D.C. hotel restaurants, and it's not unusual to see an influencer posing in the newly renovated space. A wraparound porch allows for tons of natural light, and a coral leather booth is the perfect place to be seen while eating a colorful salad, hearty steak, or delicate seafood dish from the American-focused menu. **Known for:** Instagram-worthy setting; steak and seafood dishes; incredible key lime pie. ⑤ *Average main: $25* ✉ *1500 New Hampshire Ave. NW, Dupont Circle* ☎ *202/448–4302* ⊕ *www.theprembrokedc.com.*

★ Pisco y Nazca Ceviche Gastrobar

$$ | PERUVIAN | Visit South America without leaving the Golden Triangle at Pisco y Nazca, a modern Peruvian restaurant known for its authentic food (indeed, the team here travels to Peru at least once a year to learn about new dishes and techniques). Start with a pisco sour—the bar makes the traditional version of Peru's national cocktail as well as creative, tropically flavored varieties—and then choose from dishes that include colorful seviche plates, mini *causa rellenas* (a potato dish), and *lomo saltado* (stir-fried beef). **Known for:** fun and affordable happy hour; traditional piso sour and other cocktails; authentic Peruvian cuisine. ⑤ *Average main: $22* ✉ *1823 L St. NW, Dupont Circle* ☎ *202/559–3726* ⊕ *www.piscoynazca.com.*

Tabard Inn Restaurant

$$$ | AMERICAN | The inn is historical, with its fireplaces and antique furnishings, but the restaurant's culinary sensibilities are thoroughly modern. The menu changes

seasonally but consistently offers excellent seafood and vegetarian options. **Known for:** D.C. landmark where movers and shakers sometimes breakfast; great brunch (complete with homemade doughnuts); attractive patio. $ *Average main: $30 ⊠ Hotel Tabard Inn, 1739 N St. NW, Dupont Circle* ☎ *202/331–8528* ⊕ *www.tabardinn.com* Ⓜ *Dupont Circle.*

Teaism Dupont Circle

$ | **ASIAN FUSION** | The imposing exterior belies the spare yet serene two-story space offering breakfast specialties, healthy Japanese and Thai-style entrées, and desserts. There's a lovely street view from the second level. **Known for:** large variety of teas; Japanese bento boxes; salty oat cookies. $ *Average main: $12 ⊠ 2009 R St. NW, Dupont Circle ⊕ 2 blocks north of Dupont Circle Metro* ☎ *202/667–3827* ⊕ *www.teaism.com* Ⓜ *Dupont Circle.*

Hotels

Around the Dupont traffic circle you'll find everything that makes D.C. what it is: embassies from all over the world with their ethnically diverse communities, vibrant Connecticut Avenue, and an assortment of theaters, museums, and galleries—seemingly on every block. This rich Washington neighborhood has something for everyone. And, of course, the Circle is also known for its fabulously eclectic gatherings of people. The posh Kalorama neighborhood, immediately to the northwest, includes gorgeous mansions.

Akwaaba DC

$$ | **B&B/INN** | The brainchild of former *Essence* editor Monique Greenwood, this 1890s town house turned guesthouse—one of three inns Greenwood has opened—celebrates the richness of African American literature. **Pros:** lovely neighborhood location; applause-worthy breakfast; afternoon refreshments. **Cons:** $50 nonrefundable deposit to reserve a room; two-night minimum stay required for advance reservations; no elevator. $ *Rooms from: $225 ⊠ 1708 16th St. NW, Dupont Circle* ☎ *877/893–3233* ⊕ *www.dcakwaaba.com* ↝ *8 rooms* ⫯❁⫯ *Free Breakfast* Ⓜ *Dupont Circle.*

★ The Dupont Circle Hotel

$$ | **HOTEL** | This newly renovated hotel has a stylish lobby; a sleek bar, The Doyle, where dapper bartenders serve craft cocktails; and modern, minimalist rooms done in neutral colors with splashes of orange or purple. **Pros:** right on Dupont Circle; free Wi-Fi; fitness center. **Cons:** traffic and noise on Dupont Circle; pretty busy on the weekends; limited storage space in some rooms. $ *Rooms from: $228 ⊠ 1500 New Hampshire Ave. NW, Dupont Circle* ☎ *202/483–6000* ⊕ *www.doylecollection.com/dupont* ↝ *312 rooms* ⫯❁⫯ *No meals* Ⓜ *Dupont Circle.*

The Embassy Row Hotel

$ | **HOTEL** | Just steps from Dupont Circle, this modern boutique hotel has a stylish, playful lobby in subdued colors and rooms designed for a young, hip crowd. **Pros:** yoga classes offered on the rooftop in good weather; central location; business center. **Cons:** pricey valet parking; smallish baths and closets; rooftop pool area can get crowded. $ *Rooms from: $149 ⊠ 2015 Massachusetts Ave. NW, Dupont Circle* ☎ *202/265–1600* ⊕ *www. destinationhotels.com/embassy-row-hotel* ↝ *231 rooms* ⫯❁⫯ *No meals* Ⓜ *Dupont Circle.*

The Fairfax at Embassy Row

$ | **HOTEL** | Rooms at this grande dame, a longtime favorite for many travelers, are spacious and elegant, albeit a tad old-fashioned, but the lobby, bar, and restaurant area were extensively renovated in 2018. **Pros:** ample lobby seating area; imposing building complete with chandeliers and a sweeping staircase; great location. **Cons:** expensive valet parking; rooms can be a bit old-fashioned. $ *Rooms from: $99 ⊠ 2100*

Massachusetts Ave. NW, Dupont Circle
☎ 202/293–2100, 888/625–5144 ⊕ www.
fairfaxwashingtondc.com ⟳ 279 rooms
†⊙† No meals Ⓜ Dupont Circle.

★ Kimpton Hotel Palomar Washington DC

$ | HOTEL | Draws here include a hard-to-beat location and modern rooms that are not only some of the largest in town, but are also decorated with cool abstract art, accessories in rich jewel tones, and plush purple-and-fuchsia furnishings. **Pros:** complimentary coffee and tea and free wine during nightly happy hour; free bikes on loan; heated outdoor pool. **Cons:** even in suites, baths are smallish; expensive valet parking and amenity fee; shampoos and soaps in large dispensers rather than hotel size. Ⓢ Rooms from: $174 ✉ 2121 P St. NW, Dupont Circle ☎ 202/448–1800 ⊕ www.hotelpalomar-dc.com ⟳ 335 rooms †⊙† No meals Ⓜ Dupont Circle.

The Mansion on O Street

$$$$ | HOTEL | FAMILY | Rock 'n' roll palace meets thrift shop in this guesthouse, a funky D.C. landmark that draws celebrities and notables. **Pros:** also doubles as a museum that can be toured; fun ambience; nearly all the items are on sale. **Cons:** claustrophobic for those who like uncluttered decor; a few rooms are close to the catering kitchen; nonrefundable reservation deposit of one-night's lodging. Ⓢ Rooms from: $450 ✉ 2020 O St. NW, Dupont Circle ☎ 202/496–2020 ⊕ www.omansion.com ⟳ 23 rooms †⊙† No meals Ⓜ Dupont Circle.

Residence Inn Washington, D.C./Dupont Circle

$ | HOTEL | FAMILY | This hotel is not posh, but it is ideal for families or business travelers staying for a few days, and all rooms have kitchen facilities, including a full-size refrigerator. **Pros:** free hot breakfast daily in very attractive dining area; two blocks from Metro; clean and comfortable. **Cons:** small gym and business center; no pool; corporate, uninspiring decor. Ⓢ Rooms from: $125 ✉ 2120 P St. NW, Dupont Circle ☎ 202/466–6800,

800/331–3131 ⊕ www.marriott.com ⟳ 107 suites †⊙† Free Breakfast Ⓜ Dupont Circle.

★ Swann House

$ | B&B/INN | Whether you are eating breakfast in the formal dining room or unwinding with a glass of sherry in the parlor, everything is lovely at this elegant urban retreat. **Pros:** guest computer and free Wi-Fi; fireplaces in some rooms; most rooms have tubs, and a few have whirlpool baths. **Cons:** have to carry your own luggage; no elevator; many rooms have two-night minimums in spring and fall. Ⓢ Rooms from: $201 ✉ 1808 New Hampshire Ave. NW, Dupont Circle ☎ 202/265–4414 ⊕ www.swannhouse.com ⟳ 12 rooms †⊙† Free Breakfast Ⓜ Dupont Circle.

🍸 Nightlife

Bars and nightclubs dot Connecticut Ave, where, after 10 pm most nights, Café Citron brings out the bongos and pulses to a Latin rhythm. Close by, you'll find Dupont's gay scene (or what's left of it), concentrated mainly on 17th Street. A variety of gay-friendly, lively, and offbeat bars and restaurants stretch between P and R Streets, many with outdoor seating. JR's Bar & Grill and Cobalt are favorites. D.I.K. Bar is the place to be on Tuesday, Friday, and Saturday for the always-popular karaoke nights. On the Tuesday before Halloween, the annual High Heel Drag Race proceeds down 17th Street; elaborately costumed drag queens and other revelers strut their stuff along the route from Church to R Streets and then race to the finish line.

BARS AND LOUNGES
The Admiral

BREWPUBS/BEER GARDENS | The Admiral, which is just steps from Dupont Circle, has one of the largest outdoor spaces in D.C., namely a 2,000-plus-square-foot patio. Although it serves pub food such as burgers, pulled pork sliders, and quesadillas, it's an upgrade from the typical sports bar thanks to rich wood paneling and hip, Navy-themed, neon art. On the weekends, it serves as a late-night hangout with drinks and food served until last call. ⊠ *1 Dupont Circle NW, Dupont Circle* ☎ *202/506–6696* ⊕ *www.theadmiraldc.com.*

Board Room

BARS/PUBS | "Put down your smart phone and interact!" is the motto at this pub, with 20-plus beers on tap, a full bar, and many board games to rent—from tried-and-true classics to vintage oddities. To enhance the fun, you can bring in your own food or have it delivered. Just don't bring in booze or other beverages; you are expected to buy them on the premises. Kids are welcome on occasion, but the rule is 21 and older. Reservations are accepted. ⊠ *1737 Connecticut Ave. NW, Dupont Circle* ☎ *202/518–7666* ⊕ *www. boardroomdc.com* Ⓜ *Dupont Circle.*

Hank's Oyster Bar

BARS/PUBS | A small, sleek, and unpretentious nautical-themed bar offers a half-price raw bar after 10 pm every night of the week, here and at its locations on Capitol Hill, the Wharf, and Old Town Alexandria. The bartenders are friendly, giving you tastes of different wines or drinks to try, along with recommendations on the daily catch and other food options, including one of the best lobster rolls around. ⊠ *1624 Q St. NW, Dupont Circle* ☎ *202/462–4265* ⊕ *www.hank-soysterbar.com* Ⓜ *Dupont Circle.*

JR's Bar & Grill

BARS/PUBS | A popular institution on the 17th Street strip, this narrow, window-lined space packs in a mostly male, mostly professional, gay crowd. Various nights offer show-tune singalongs, trivia contests, and a "Sunday Funday" daylong happy hour. ⊠ *1519 17th St. NW, Dupont Circle* ☎ *202/328–0090* ⊕ *www. jrsbar-dc.com* Ⓜ *Dupont Circle.*

Larry's Lounge

BARS/PUBS | Opened for almost 10 years, Larry's Lounge is a popular gay bar known for its colorful stained-glass entrance and friendly atmosphere. Be prepared to wait for one of the coveted patio seats, especially on nice spring or fall days. Bonus: dogs are welcome on their patio, so you will see plenty of furry friends hanging out. ⊠ *1840 18th St. NW, Dupont Circle* ☎ *202/483–1483* ⊕ *m.mainstreethub.com/index.php/ larryslounge.*

Russia House Restaurant and Lounge

BARS/PUBS | The Russia House has an old-world feel to it. Mount the steep stone steps, and you'll find yourself in a cozy bar and lounge with red damask wallpaper, comfortable leather chairs, and understated chandeliers. You may be listening to Russian rappers as you drink a wide assortment of vodkas and indulge in happy hour plates of Russian favorites. The dinner menu also offers traditional Russian dishes. ⊠ *1800 Connecticut Ave. NW, Dupont Circle* ☎ *202/234–9433* ⊕ *www.russiahouselounge.com* Ⓜ *Dupont Circle.*

St. Arnold's Mussel Bar on Jefferson

BARS/PUBS | This unassuming space in the basement of a Dupont town house is named after the patron saint of brewing, and it's certainly blessed with its choice of hard-to-find Belgian beers. The Belgian theme continues on the menu, and mussels (available in essentially half-price pots during happy hour) are prepared in numerous ways. There's an additional location in Cleveland Park. ⊠ *1827 Jefferson Pl. NW, Dupont Circle* ☎ *202/833–1321* ⊕ *www.starnoldsdc. com* Ⓜ *Dupont Circle.*

DANCE CLUBS

Cafe Citron

BARS/PUBS | One of the longest-running Latin clubs in D.C., Cafe Citron maintains its relevance with the salsa-dancing set. After 10 pm Monday through Saturday, the café becomes a nightclub featuring

DJs who play primarily Latin music, spiced with Euro dance and techno. The café also offers daily happy hours until 8 and late-night happy hours after 9 on Friday and Saturday. (It's closed Sunday.) Work up an appetite, and indulge in Latin American snacks such as Bolivian salteñas. ⊠ *1343 Connecticut Ave. NW, Dupont Circle* ☎ *202/422–3005* ⊕ *www. cafecitrondc.com* Ⓜ *Dupont Circle.*

🎭 Performing Arts

Talented troupes perform in unique venues that are sprinkled throughout the Dupont Circle neighborhood, among them the Keegan Theatre on Church Street, which aims to present classic and modern plays and musicals at affordable ticket prices. Sunday chamber concerts also are performed at the Phillips Collection, providing an exquisite venue for both eyes and ears.

MUSIC
Phillips Collection
MUSIC | Duncan Phillips's mansion is more than an art museum. On Sunday afternoon from October through May, chamber groups from around the world perform in the elegant Music Room. Plus, on the first Thursday of the month, from 5 to 8:30 pm, the museum offers Phillips After 5, treating visitors to musical performances, food and drink, gallery talks, films, and more. ⊠ *1600 21st St. NW, Dupont Circle* ☎ *202/387–2151* ⊕ *www.phillipscollection.org* Ⓜ *Dupont Circle.*

THEATER
The Keegan Theatre
THEATER | A hidden gem in Dupont Circle, this 120-seat theater offers a rich variety of classic and modern plays and musicals, with a focus on powerful storytelling in an intimate setting. ⊠ *1742 Church St. NW, Dupont Circle* ☎ *703/892–0202* ⊕ *keegantheatre.com* Ⓜ *Dupont Circle.*

Theater J
THEATER | One of the country's most distinguished Jewish performance venues offers an ambitious range of programming that includes work by noted playwrights, directors, designers, and actors. Past performances have included one-person shows featuring Sandra Bernhard and Judy Gold as well as edgier political pieces. ⊠ *1529 16th St. NW, Dupont Circle* ☎ *202/518–9400* ⊕ *www. theaterj.org* Ⓜ *Dupont Circle.*

👜 Shopping

You might call Dupont Circle a younger, less staid version of Georgetown—almost as pricey, but with more apartment buildings than houses. Its many restaurants, offbeat shops, and specialty stores give it a cosmopolitan air. The street scene here is more urban than Georgetown's, with bike messengers and chess aficionados filling up the park. The Sunday farmers' market attracts shoppers with organic food, artisanal cheeses, homemade soap, and hand-spun wool. Browsing is an adventure in this neighborhood. Several boutiques offer designer clothing for women, and Dupont shops also include exquisite jewelry from Turkey as well as inexpensive bling and well-designed products for home and baby.

ART GALLERIES
IA&A at Hillyer
ART GALLERIES | Around the corner from the Phillips Collection, this art space features works from local, regional, and international contemporary artists, and also regularly hosts artist talks and other events. With a mission to support emerging artists and to encourage artistic collaboration across the globe, Hillyer offers intellectually stimulating exhibits that provoke and intrigue. ⊠ *9 Hillyer Ct. NW, Dupont Circle* ☎ *202/338–0325* ⊕ *athillyer.org* Ⓜ *Dupont Circle.*

Marsha Mateyka Gallery

ART GALLERIES | Just around the corner from the Phillips Collection sits this gallery that showcases the work of nearly 20 contemporary artists. You'll find paintings, sculptures, photography, drawings, and prints by international artists including Athena Tacha, Jae Ko, William T. Wiley, Nathan Oliveira, and the estate of Gene Davis. ⊠ 2012 R St. NW, Dupont Circle ☏ 202/328–0088 ⊕ www.marshamateykagallery.com ⊘ Closed Sun.–Wed. Ⓜ Dupont Circle.

★ Studio Gallery

ART GALLERIES | Founded in 1956 by Jennie Lea Knight (whose work is in the collections of many D.C. museums), Studio exhibits contemporary work by local artists, some of whom have also received international acclaim. The spacious gallery occupies two floors in an elegant town house, and exhibitions change frequently. Don't miss the sculpture garden in back of the house. ⊠ 2108 R St. NW, Dupont Circle ☏ 202/232–8734 ⊕ www.studiogallerydc.com ⊘ Closed Sun.–Thurs. Ⓜ Dupont Circle.

BOOKS

★ Kramerbooks & Afterwords Café

BOOKS/STATIONERY | One of Washington's best-loved independent bookstores has a choice selection of fiction and nonfiction. It also hosts many author talks and panel discussions throughout the year. Kramerbooks shares space with Afterwords Café, which is open from early morning until late at night. ⊠ 1517 Connecticut Ave. NW, Dupont Circle ☏ 202/387–1400 ⊕ www.kramers.com Ⓜ Dupont Circle.

Second Story Books

BOOKS/STATIONERY | One of the largest used and rare book stores in the country, Second Story Books has grown along with its neighborhood, and its orderly and classy space houses rare books, signed first editions, maps, posters, manuscripts, CDs, prints, and DVDs.

(There are often bargain books for sale, usually outside the store.) A knowledgeable staff is always on hand to help you shop. ⊠ 2000 P St. NW, Dupont Circle ☏ 202/659–8884 ⊕ www.secondstorybooks.com Ⓜ Dupont Circle.

CLOTHING

★ Betsy Fisher

CLOTHING | Catering to women of all ages and sizes in search of contemporary and trendy styles, this elegant shop offers one-of-a-kind accessories, clothes, shoes, and jewelry by American, Canadian, and European designers, including popular Montréal designers Marie Saint Pierre, Iris Setlakwe, and Judith & Charles. ⊠ 1224 Connecticut Ave. NW, Dupont Circle ☏ 202/785–1975 ⊕ www.betsyfisher.com Ⓜ Dupont Circle.

★ Secondi

CLOTHING | One of the city's finest consignment stores carries a well-chosen selection of women's designer and casual clothing, accessories, and shoes. Its airy and well-curated second-story space offers Isabel Marant, Louis Vuitton, Donna Karan, Prada, Chanel, and Marchesa labels. ⊠ 1702 Connecticut Ave. NW, 2nd fl., Dupont Circle ☏ 202/667–1122 ⊕ www.secondi.com Ⓜ Dupont Circle.

CRAFTS AND GIFTS

The Chocolate Moose

CRAFTS | This store is simple, sheer fun for adults and kids alike. Looking for clacking, windup teeth? You can find them here, along with unusual greeting cards, whimsical and colorful socks, and unique housewares and handicrafts. If playing with all those fun toys makes you hungry, you can pick up a select line of premium European chocolates. ⊠ 1743 L St., NW, Dupont Circle ☏ 202/463–0992 ⊕ www.chocolatemoosedc.com ⊘ Closed Sun. Ⓜ Farragut N.

★ **Shop Made in DC**

GIFTS/SOUVENIRS | This Dupont Circle shop offers a rotating selection of strictly locally made goods. Find art, books, T-shirts, and even baby onesies made by area designers and artists. An on-site café sells local coffees, teas, beers, and spirits to accompany a rotating selection of fast-casual food. The gift boxes are highly prized. ✉ *1330 19th St. NW, Dupont Circle* ⊕ *www.shopmadeindc.com.*

HOME FURNISHINGS
★ **Tabletop**

HOUSEHOLD ITEMS/FURNITURE | This is a delightful place to find distinctive gold earrings by Daphne Olive, the designer and store owner, as well as wooden bookends, bento boxes, and game sets from Wolfum of California. Orla Kiely bags and kitchenware feature bold floral designs. A baby and children's section displays adorable clothing as well as books for the smallest feminist. Walls are adorned with Chive ceramic flowers. ✉ *1608 20th St. NW, Dupont Circle* ☎ *202/387–7117* ⊕ *www.tabletopdc.com* Ⓜ *Dupont Circle.*

JEWELRY
lou lou

JEWELRY/ACCESSORIES | This "blingful" boutique, jam-packed with costume jewelry and bags at price points that please the purse, draws lots of ladies looking for the latest trendy item. You'll also find lou lou boutiques in Georgetown, the U Street Corridor, and two Downtown locations. ✉ *1601 Connecticut Ave. NW, Dupont Circle* ☎ *202/588–0027* ⊕ *www.loulouboutiques.com* Ⓜ *Dupont Circle.*

Chapter 9

ADAMS MORGAN

Updated by
Sabrina Medora

👁 Sights
★☆☆☆☆

🍴 Restaurants
★★★★★

🛏 Hotels
☆☆☆☆☆

🛍 Shopping
★★★☆☆

🍸 Nightlife
★★★★★

NEIGHBORHOOD SNAPSHOT

TOP EXPERIENCES

■ **Eat ethnic food:** Take a culinary trip around the world in Adams Morgan. From Ethiopia to El Salvador to Japan to Turkey, there is a vast selection of nations represented within the restaurant scene.

■ **Hang out like a local:** Adams Morgan, with its quirky shops and international restaurants, seems like a world away from conservative Capitol Hill. Work up a sweat running up the hills of Meridian Hill Park to catch a glorious view of Washington, D.C. Afterward, grab a latte and browse through rare vinyl at Songbyrd Record Cafe and Music bar.

■ **Move and connect:** Meridian Hill Park brings the community together through different events. You can catch drumming circles, meditation, and yoga at the park.

■ **Stay out all night:** If you want to party on until the break of dawn, this is the place to do it. Don't miss the live blues music at Madam's Organ, the salsa dancing at Habana Village, and craft cocktails at Jack Rose Dining Saloon and The Green Zone.

GETTING HERE

Adams Morgan has two Metro stops that are a pleasant 10-minute walk away. From the Woodley Park–Zoo/Adams Morgan Metro station, take a short walk south on Connecticut, then turn left on Calvert Street, and cross over Rock Creek Park on the Duke Ellington Bridge. If you get off at the Dupont Circle Metro stop, walk east, turning left on 18th Street.

The heart of Adams Morgan is at the intersection of Columbia Road and 18th Street. Don't even dream about finding parking here on weekend evenings.

If you are taking the Metro, make sure to check the DC Metro website (wmata.com) to confirm the weekend hours. You can also get there quickly by cab or rideshare.

Several buses such as the 90, 96, 42, 43 also take you to Adams Morgan.

PLANNING YOUR TIME

■ Start your day with a walk around the neighborhood. After the few sights, be sure to stop in at the Line Hotel for a coffee at Café Spoken or cheesy *pupusas* (flatbreads) at El Tamarindo. Keep moving on to 18th Street for some window-shopping, cocktails, small plates, and live music. Dance the night away at the various clubs and bars, then grab some late-night pizza or empanadas.

QUICK BITES

■ **Brothers and Sisters.** The restaurant in the Line Hotel takes a quirky and award-winning approach to multicultural cuisines. ✉ *1770 Euclid St. NW* ⊕ *www.thelinehotel.com* Ⓜ *Woodley Park–Zoo/Adams Morgan.*

■ **El Tamarindo.** This Adams Morgan favorite is famous for their authentic El Salvadorean pupusas but you can also sit at their patio and have a margarita and people watch. ✉ *1785 Florida Ave. NW* ⊕ *www. eltamarindodc.com* Ⓜ *Dupont Circle.*

■ **Sakuramen.** Get your ramen fix at Sakuramen ramen bar with a wide selection of broths and flavor combinations. ✉ *2441 18th St. NW* ⊕ *sakuramen. net* Ⓜ *Woodley Park–Zoo/ Adams Morgan.*

To the urban and hip, Adams Morgan is like a beacon in an otherwise stuffy landscape. D.C. may have a reputation for being staid and traditional, but drab suits, classical tastes, and bland food make no appearance here.

Adams Morgan

Adams Morgan takes its name from two elementary schools that came together in 1958 after desegregation. It remains an ethnically diverse neighborhood with a blend of cuisines, offbeat shops, and funky bars and clubs.

Adams Morgan and its neighboring Columbia Heights comprise the city's Latin Quarter. The area wakes up as the sun goes down, and young Washingtonians in their weekend best congregate along the sidewalks, crowding the doors of this week's hot bar or nightclub. Typical tourist attractions are sparse, but the scene on a Saturday night has its own appeal. If you're here on the second Saturday in September, sample the vibrant neighborhood culture at the Adams Morgan Day Festival, which happens to be D.C.'s largest neighborhood festival.

◉ Sights

Less touristy and more community-based, Adams Morgan is great for a day of light sightseeing followed by window-shopping and heavy eating. Known for its bustling food and live music scene, there's always a place to pop into and lose track of time.

Meridian Hill Park

CITY PARK | Landscape architect Horace Peaslee created Meridian Hill Park, a noncontiguous section of Rock Creek Park, after a 1917 study of the parks of Europe. As a result, it contains elements of gardens in France, Italy, and Switzerland. John Quincy Adams lived in a mansion here after his presidency, and the park later served as an encampment for Union soldiers during the Civil War. All 50 states are represented by a state tree or flower. Meridian Hill is unofficially known as **Malcolm X Park** in honor of the civil rights leader. Weekends bring a mix of pickup soccer games, yoga, joggers running the stairs, and a weekly (weather permitting) drum circle. A statue of **Joan of Arc** poised for battle on horseback stands above the terrace, and a statue of **Dante** is on a pedestal below. Cell-phone tours illuminate the history of the landmarks inside the park. ⊠ *Meridian Hill Park, 16th St. NW and W St. NW, Adams Morgan* ⊕ *www.nps.gov/mehi* Ⓜ *U St./African-Amer Civil War Memorial/Cardozo or Columbia Heights.*

🍴 Restaurants

In Adams Morgan, find everything from greasy spoons and jumbo-slice pizza joints to exquisite fine-dining options. The next culinary frontier lies just east along Columbia Road, where immigrant communities dine, and young families flock to increasingly upscale bistros for refined takes on comfort-food favorites.

Adams Morgan

KEY
- Exploring Sights
- Restaurants
- Hotels

Sights ▼
1 Meridian Hill Park E4

Restaurants ▼
1 Brothers and Sisters C3
2 El Tamarindo C5
3 The Imperial............. C5
4 Jack Rose
  Dining Saloon C5
5 Keren Cafe
  & Restaurant............. C5
6 Lapis........................ C4
7 Lucky Buns C5
8 Mezè C4
9 Mintwood Place C3
10 Roofers Union C3
11 Sakuramen C4
12 Spoken English........... C3
13 Tail Up Goat............. C3
14 Tryst C3

Hotels ▼
1 Adam's Inn............... C2
2 Churchill Hotel Near
  Embassy Row B5
3 Generator Hotel
  Washington, DC......... B6
4 The Line DC............... C3
5 The Normandy Hotel ... B5
6 Washington Hilton...... B5

Brothers and Sisters

$ | **AMERICAN** | The lobby of the Line Hotel in D.C. is vibrant unlike any other, entirely on account of this restaurant, which celebrates the multicultural nature of the city. Enjoy twists on American classics with Asian flavors (cavatelli pasta seasoned with miso), a simple but compelling cocktail menu, and an extensive selection of cakes and pastries. **Known for:** creative Asian inspired menu; late-night bar menu; fresh-baked goods. $ Average main: $13 ⊠ The Line DC, 1770 Euclid St. NW, Adams Morgan ☎ 202/588–0525 ⊕ www.brothersandsistersdc.com Ⓜ Woodley Park–Zoo/Adams Morgan.

El Tamarindo

$ | **LATIN AMERICAN** | With almost 40 years in operation, El Tamarindo, an El Salvadorean and Mexican restaurant, has weathered the neighborhood's many changes. Guests come for their savory pupusas (a thick corn tortilla) with various fillings to satisfy every taste from a vegan to a carnivore. **Known for:** pupusas; late-night bites; lively brunch. $ Average main: $15 ⊠ 1785 Florida Ave. NW, Adams Morgan ☎ 202/328–3660 ⊕ https://eltamarindodc.com/ Ⓜ Dupont Circle.

The Imperial

$$ | **AMERICAN** | This design-forward restaurant has a stunning, two-tier, see-and-be-seen rooftop, as well as plenty of other Instagrammable spots. It also offers colorful cocktails and an eclectic menu of Mid-Atlantic staples such as crab cakes and Virginia oysters—not to mention decadent seafood towers (and towering burgers) that are in keeping with its name. **Known for:** beautiful design; happening patio area; creative cocktail program. $ Average main: $18 ⊠ 2001 18th St. NW, Adams Morgan ☎ 202/299–0334 ⊕ www.imperialdc.com ⊘ Closed Mon. and Tues.

★ Jack Rose Dining Saloon

$$ | **AMERICAN** | With an extensive collection of whiskey bottles currently on the wall (your experience may vary),

the food sometimes gets overshadowed here. But Southern-inspired dishes like smoked whiskey wings, lump crab cakes, pickled-corn hush puppies, and buttermilk biscuits make the menu much more than just something to accompany all the booze. **Known for:** small plates of modern Southern cuisine; fun rooftop tiki bar; immense selection of whiskeys. $ Average main: $27 ⊠ 2007 18th St. NW, Adams Morgan ☎ 202/588–7388 ⊕ www.jackrosediningsaloon.com ⊘ Closed Mon. and Tues. Ⓜ U St./African-Amer Civil War Memorial/Cardozo.

Keren Cafe & Restaurant

$ | **AFRICAN** | The Washington, D.C. metro area is home to one of the largest Eritrean populations in the United States, and many in the community get their taste of home at this well-established restaurant. Try the shiro, an aromatic Eritrean chickpea stew served in a clay pot along with spongy injera bread. **Known for:** Eritrean food; American and Eritrean breakfast; late-night dining. $ Average main: $14 ⊠ 1780 Florida Ave. NW, Adams Morgan ☎ 202/265–5764 ⊕ www.orderkerencafeandrestaurant.com.

★ Lapis

$$ | **AFGHAN** | The modern Afghan cuisine shines at this chic yet comfortable—and well-priced—Adams Morgan spot. Seven different varieties of kebabs (prepared via a secret recipe "known only to our mom and the NSA") are the stars of the menu, but you'll also want to try the dumplings. **Known for:** different types of kebabs prepared with top-secret family recipe; carefully crafted cocktails; excellent bottomless brunch. $ Average main: $18 ⊠ 1847 Columbia Rd. NW, Adams Morgan ☎ 202/299–9630 ⊕ www.lapisdc.com Ⓜ Dupont Circle.

Lucky Buns

$ | **BURGER** | As the name suggests, Lucky Buns focuses on burgers and sandwiches. Indulge in a decadent double-patty burger or a spicy chicken sandwich, a favorite with D.C. food writers. **Known for:**

juicy burgers; cocktails; outdoor dining on the patio. $ *Average main: $15* ⊠ *2000 18th St. NW, Adams Morgan* ☎ *202/506–1713* ⊕ *luckybunsdc.com* Ⓜ *Woodley Park–Zoo/Adams Morgan.*

Mezè

$$ | TURKISH | A fixture in the neighborhood dining scene, this authentic Turkish restaurant and wine bar with a patio serves dishes such as *doner* kebabs, *manti* , and *dolmas.* If cocktails are more your thing, take advantage of the mojito bar, offering a wide selection of the drink in flavors like watermelon and blueberry. **Known for:** Turkish kebabs and dolmas; mojito bar; extensive wine selection. $ *Average main: $17* ⊠ *2437 18th St. NW, Adams Morgan* ☎ *292/797–0017* ⊕ *www.mezedc.com* ⊘ *Closed Mon.* Ⓜ *Woodley Park–Zoo/Adams Morgan.*

Mintwood Place

$$$ | FRENCH | At this saloon-inspired venue, European and American flavors come together with seasonal ingredients. The menu changes weekly, with dishes like a half-roasted chicken with truffle butter or seared sea scallops with roasted eggplant. **Known for:** European meets American cuisine; great happy-hour deals; seasonal menu that changes every week. $ *Average main: $29* ⊠ *1813 Columbia Rd. NW, Adams Morgan* ☎ *202/234–6732* ⊕ *www.mintwoodplace.com* ⊘ *Closed Mon. No lunch weekdays.*

Roofers Union

$$ | CONTEMPORARY | The cavernous space that once hosted one of the capital's most notoriously crazy bars is now a symbol of the area's maturation, thanks to a slick makeover and classy comfort-food lineup. The hearty but well-designed fare includes four types of house-made sausage and a fried-chicken sandwich redolent of sriracha sauce that will rock a spice-lover's world. **Known for:** comfort food with great sausage options; hip, youthful vibe; excellent rooftop deck and bar. $ *Average main:*

$23 ⊠ *2446 18th St. NW, Adams Morgan* ☎ *202/232–7663* ⊕ *www.roofersuniondc. com* ⊘ *No lunch* Ⓜ *Woodley Park–Zoo/Adams Morgan.*

Sakuramen

$ | RAMEN | Gourmet versions of Japanese ramen soup have become the latest trend to storm the city, and this hole-in-the-wall gem strikes the perfect balance between keep-it-simple affordability and adventurous flair. Embodying both of those traits in one bowl is the D.C. Miso, which pairs traditional fish cake and seaweed with a shot of Monterey Jack cheese. **Known for:** innovative ramen; casual basement vibe; beef buns and crispy dumplings. $ *Average main: $14* ⊠ *2441 18th St. NW, Adams Morgan* ☎ *202/656–5285* ⊕ *www.sakuramen.net* ⊘ *Closed Mon. No lunch Tues.–Fri.*

★ Spoken English

$ | ASIAN | A restaurant unlike any other in D.C., Spoken English is tucked away within the kitchen of Brothers and Sisters. The *tachinomiya*-style (standing only) setup encourages adventurous eating and conversation among friends and strangers. **Known for:** small plates of Asian street food; standing room only; exclusive sake selections. $ *Average main: $13* ⊠ *The Line DC, 1770 Euclid St. NW, Adams Morgan* ✛ *Ask hostess at Brothers and Sisters to direct you* ☎ *202/588–0525* ⊕ *www.thelinehotel. com/dc* ⊘ *Closed Sun. and Mon. No lunch* Ⓜ *Woodley Park–Zoo/Adams Morgan.*

★ Tail Up Goat

$$ | CONTEMPORARY | Standouts on the carb-heavy menu—bread gets its own section—include cavatelli with a spicy pork-belly ragù and seaweed sourdough bread. The menu changes regularly, but the lamb ribs are a sure thing (when available). **Known for:** lots and lots of carbs; constantly changing menu; small groups only (five people or less). $ *Average main: $25* ⊠ *1827 Adams Mill*

The stairs in Meridian Hill Park are popular with joggers: run up and down 10 times, and you've covered almost a mile.

Rd. NW, Adams Morgan ✛ Entrance on Lanier Pl. side of building ☎ 202/986–9600 ⊕ www.tailupgoat.com ⊘ No lunch Ⓜ Woodley Park–Zoo/Adams Morgan.

Tryst

$ | **AMERICAN** | **FAMILY** | Bohemian and unpretentious, this coffeehouse–bar serves fancy sandwiches and exotic coffee creations. Comfy chairs and couches fill the big open space, where you can sit for hours sipping a cup of tea—or a martini—while chatting or clacking away at your laptop. **Known for:** excellent coffee; all-day brunch menu; premium sandwiches and design-your-own salads. $ Average main: $11 ⊠ 2459 18th St. NW, Adams Morgan ☎ 202/232–5500 ⊕ www.trystdc.com Ⓜ Woodley Park–Zoo/Adams Morgan.

 Hotels

This thriving multiethnic community is the place to be for a fabulous assortment of aromas, languages, tastes, and late-night entertainments. A short walk from a nearby hotel or Metro stop rewards you with salsa, hip-hop, jazz, or the latest in experimental performance art. Its neighborhoods of 19th- and early-20th-century homes and row houses and its proximity to Rock Creek Park provide this bustling area with a tranquil shell.

Adam's Inn

$ | **B&B/INN** | Live like a local at this cozy and affordable Victorian-style bed-and-breakfast set in three residential town houses near Adams Morgan, the zoo, and Dupont Circle. **Pros:** near Metro; lively neighborhood; backyard garden is a Certified Wildlife Habitat by the National Wildlife Federation. **Cons:** some shared baths; steps to climb; some guests complain of noise between rooms. $ Rooms from: $174 ⊠ 1746 Lanier Pl. NW, Woodley Park, Adams Morgan ☎ 202/745–3600, 800/578–6807 ⊕ www.adamsinn.com ⇌ 27 rooms ⏁⏃ Free Breakfast Ⓜ Woodley Park–Zoo/Adams Morgan.

Churchill Hotel Near Embassy Row

$$ | HOTEL | One of the Historic Hotels of America, this Beaux Arts landmark built in 1906 has spacious guest rooms that are comfortable, elegant, and include small work and sitting areas; many also have excellent views. **Pros:** good-size rooms; relaxed and quiet; comfortable walking distance to Adams Morgan and northern Dupont Circle. **Cons:** older building; some rooms very small; limited room-service hours. Ⓢ *Rooms from: $289* ✉ *1914 Connecticut Ave. NW, Adams Morgan* ☎ *202/797–2000, 800/424–2464* ⊕ *www.thechurchillhotel.com* ⤳ *173 rooms* ⦿ *No meals* Ⓜ *Dupont Circle.*

Generator Hotel Washington, DC

$ | HOTEL | Within walking distance of Adam's Morgan, this hip, new, modern lodging concept offers everything from shared dorm rooms to luxurious suites, as well as a sleek co-working space for travelers and locals alike. **Pros:** amazing views from some rooms; modern rooms at affordable prices; cozy pool area. **Cons:** a busy location on Connecticut Avenue; some rooms are dorm style; hard to find parking around the area. Ⓢ *Rooms from: $100* ✉ *1900 Connecticut Ave. NW, Dupont Circle* ☎ *202/332–9300* ⊕ *www.staygenerator.com* ⤳ *148 rooms* ⦿ *No meals* Ⓜ *Dupont Circle.*

★ The Line DC

$$ | HOTEL | A former church, The Line Hotel DC was made for those who want to stay among the locals. **Pros:** uniquely designed rooms; excellent restaurants; pets (dogs, cats, large, small) stay free. **Cons:** can be loud; lots of stairs to climb; rooms are on the small side. Ⓢ *Rooms from: $268* ✉ *1770 Euclid St. NW, Adams Morgan* ☎ *202/588–0525* ⊕ *www.thelinehotel.com/dc* ⤳ *220 rooms* ⦿ *No meals.*

The Normandy Hotel

$ | HOTEL | On a quiet street in the embassy area of Connecticut Avenue stands this small Irish chain hotel. **Pros:** quiet location; intimate setting; walking distance to restaurants. **Cons:** smallish rooms; no room service; no restaurant. Ⓢ *Rooms from: $129* ✉ *2118 Wyoming Ave. NW, Adams Morgan* ☎ *202/483–1350, 202/483–1350* ⊕ *www.thenormandydc.com* ⤳ *75 rooms* ⦿ *No meals* Ⓜ *Dupont Circle.*

Washington Hilton

$$$ | HOTEL | Yes, it's a fairly large hotel and can be busy at times, but this historic 1965 hotel, at the intersection of Dupont Circle, Adams Morgan, and U and 14th Streets, has a great location and is a perfect spot to unwind after a day of business or seeing the sights. **Pros:** great lobby; plenty of services; lots of restaurants and shops within walking distance. **Cons:** corporate feel; busy, noisy location; fee for Wi-Fi. Ⓢ *Rooms from: $348* ✉ *1919 Connecticut Ave. NW, Adams Morgan* ☎ *202/328–2080* ⊕ *www.washington.hilton.com* ⤳ *1117 rooms* ⦿ *No meals* Ⓜ *Dupont Circle.*

🍸 Nightlife

Adams Morgan is Washington's version (albeit much smaller) of New Orleans' French Quarter. The streets are often jammed with people of all ages and descriptions. Bars and restaurants of all types line the streets, making it easy to find one that will suit your tastes. Be prepared for crowds on the weekends and a much tamer vibe on weeknights. Getting here is easy, with four nearby Metro stops: Woodley Park–Zoo/Adams Morgan (Red Line), Dupont Circle (Red Line), Columbia Heights (Green and Yellow lines), and U Street/African-Amer Civil War Memorial/Cardozo (Green and Yellow lines). Taxis also are easy to find, except after last call, when the crowds pour out of bars.

BARS AND LOUNGES
Green Zone

BARS/PUBS | Named after Baghdad's Green Zone, the theme of the bar is bringing people together. Popular ever since it opened, it's now a fixture on the "best cocktails" lists compiled by D.C. publications and blogs. The creative drinks combine Middle Eastern spices such as saffron and za'atar with Western spirits like rum and whiskey. Pair your beverage with Lebanese olives, creamy hummus, and savory falafel. ⊠ *2226 18th St. NW, Adams Morgan* ⊕ *www. thegreenzonedc.com.*

Madam's Organ

BARS/PUBS | Neon lights behind the bar and walls covered in kitsch and works by local artists add to the gritty feel of this trilevel place that's hard to miss and hard not to like. An eclectic clientele listens to the live music that's performed every night (open-mike night is Tuesday) and soaks up rays on the roof deck by day. ⊠ *2461 18th St. NW, Adams Morgan* ☎ *202/667–5370* ⊕ *www.madamsorgan.com* Ⓜ *Woodley Park–Zoo/Adams Morgan.*

DANCE CLUBS

Habana Village

DANCE CLUBS | No matter what the temperature is outside, it's always balmy inside this unpretentious Cuban oasis. The tiny dance floors are packed nightly with couples moving to the latest live salsa and merengue music. When it's time to cool down, you can head to one of several lounges and sip the house specialty: a mojito garnished with sugarcane. ⊠ *1834 Columbia Rd. NW, Adams Morgan* ☎ *202/462–6310* ⊕ *www.habanavillage.com* Ⓜ *Woodley Park–Zoo.*

 Performing Arts

Adams Morgan has long been the hub of the city's best avant-garde performances, primarily offered by the District of Columbia Arts Center. You can enjoy an incredible meal at one of many nearby ethnic restaurants, see a performance at the Gala Hispanic Theatre, and then head to one of the neighborhood's colorful bars after the show.

THEATER AND PERFORMANCE ART

District of Columbia Arts Center

ARTS CENTERS | Known by area artists as DCAC, this cross-genre space shows changing exhibits in its gallery and presents avant-garde performance art, improv, and experimental plays in its tiny, funky black-box theater. DCAC is the home of Washington's oldest experimental theater group, Theatre Du Jour. ⊠ *2438 18th St. NW, Adams Morgan* ☎ *202/462–7833* ⊕ *www.dcartscenter. org* Ⓜ *Woodley Park–Zoo/Adams Morgan.*

Gala Hispanic Theatre

THEATER | This company attracts outstanding Hispanic actors from around the world, performing works by such leading dramatists as Federico García Lorca and Mario Vargas Llosa. Plays are presented in English or in Spanish with projected subtitles. The company performs in the Tivoli Theatre in Columbia Heights, a hot spot for Latino culture and cuisine. ⊠ *Tivoli Sq., 3333 14th St. NW and Park Rd., Columbia Heights, Adams Morgan* ☎ *202/234–7174* ⊕ *www.galatheatre.org* Ⓜ *Columbia Heights.*

🛍 Shopping

Scattered among the dozens of Latin, Ethiopian, and international restaurants in this most bohemian of Washington neighborhoods is a score of eccentric shops. If quality is what you seek, Adams Morgan and nearby Woodley Park can be a minefield; tread cautiously. Still, this is good turf for the bargain hunter. ■ **TIP→ If bound for a specific shop, you may wish to call ahead to verify hours.** The evening hours bring scores of revelers to the row, so plan to go before dark unless you want to couple your shopping with a party pit stop.

How to get there is another question. Though the Woodley Park–Zoo/Adams Morgan Metro stop is relatively close to the 18th Street strip (where the interesting shops are), getting off here means that you will have to walk over the bridge on Calvert Street. Five minutes longer, the walk from the Dupont Circle Metro stop is more scenic; you cruise north on 18th Street through tree-lined streets of row houses and embassies. You can also easily catch Metrobus No. 42 or a cab from Dupont to Adams Morgan.

BOOKS

Lost City Books

BOOKS/STATIONERY | FAMILY | Since 1981, this multilevel used-book store has been selling "rare to medium rare" books with plenty of meaty titles in all genres, especially out-of-print literature. Formerly called Idle Time Books, Lost City Books retains all the charm that has kept it in business for over four decades. ⊠ 2467 18th St. NW, Adams Morgan ☎ 202/232–4774 ⊕ lostcitybookstore.com Ⓜ Woodley Park–Zoo/Adams Morgan.

CHOCOLATE

The Chocolate House

FOOD/CANDY | FAMILY | For chocoholics with a gourmet palate, this is one-stop shopping. Offerings are both foreign (Michel Cluizel from France and Amedei from Italy) and domestic (Askinosie from Missouri and Amano from Utah). Selections from D.C.-area chocolatiers make for tasty souvenirs. If you can, attend one of the classes. ⊠ 1904 18th St. NW, Adams Morgan ☎ 202/903–0346 ⊕ www.thechocolatehousedc.com Ⓜ Dupont Circle.

CLOTHING

Le Bustiere Boutique

CLOTHING | Tucked away on the second floor of a building on busy Columbia Road, this local- and woman-owned boutique offers high-end lingerie, swimwear, and sleepwear. The staff provides the kind of personal service that enables you to find just the right piece to suit your needs. ⊠ 1744 Columbia Rd., #2, Adams Morgan ☎ 202/745–8080 ⊕ lebustiere.com Ⓜ Woodley Park–Zoo/Adams Morgan.

Meeps

CLOTHING | Catering to fans of retro glamour and low prices, this shop near the bottom of the Adams Morgan strip stocks vintage clothes and costumes (from the '60s through the '90s) for women and men. ⊠ 2104 18th St. NW, Adams Morgan ☎ 202/265–6546 ⊕ www.meepsdc.com Ⓜ Dupont Circle.

Mercedes Bien Vintage

CLOTHING | The carefully selected vintage clothing and shoes sold here include everything from cocktail dresses to cowboy boots. You will also find jewelry and belts, all handpicked by the owner, Mercedes, who has been in the vintage business since the early '80s. This small shop offers exceptional, personal service and is only open on weekends. ⊠ 2423 18th St. NW, Adams Morgan ☎ 202/360–8481 ⊙ Closed weekdays Ⓜ Woodley Park–Zoo/Adams Morgan.

SHOES

Fleet Feet Sports Shop

SPECIALTY STORES | The expert staff at this friendly shop will assess your feet and your training schedule before recommending the perfect shoes, apparel, or accessories for running, swimming, soccer, or cycling. The shop also hosts running events, a great way to explore the city. ⊠ 1841 Columbia Rd. NW, Adams Morgan ☎ 202/387–3888 ⊕ www.fleetfeetdc.com Ⓜ Woodley Park–Zoo/Adams Morgan.

Chapter 10

U STREET CORRIDOR AND SHAW

10

WITH LOGAN CIRCLE AND COLUMBIA HEIGHTS

Updated by
Jessica van Dop DeJesús

 Sights
★★☆☆☆

 Restaurants
★★★★★

 Hotels
★☆☆☆☆

 Shopping
★★★★☆

 Nightlife
★★★★★

NEIGHBORHOOD SNAPSHOT

TOP EXPERIENCES

■ **African American Civil War Memorial and Museum:** Learn about the lives of slaves and freedmen, and discover whether your ancestors fought in black Civil War regiments.

■ **Ben's Chili Bowl:** This D.C. institution has perfected its recipe over the last 50 years.

■ **Street art:** Keep your eyes open for colorful murals throughout the neighborhood. From the famous murals of Ben's Chili Bowl to Blagden Alley, there's plenty of street art to take in.

■ **International food:** From Ghana to El Salvador to Italy, you can take a culinary trip around the world in this neighborhood.

■ **Live music:** Music greats like Duke Ellington made this neighborhood famous back in the 1920s. Dance at El Techo, or rock out at the 9:30 Club or Black Cat.

GETTING HERE

The Green Line Metro stops at 13th and U. To get to the African American Civil War Memorial, exit onto 10th Street. There's limited street parking, but you are better off taking a cab or other ride service since the area is popular, though the area is also walkable.

The Shaw–Howard University metro station is at 8th and S.

Buses 90 and 92 travel from Woodley Park through Adams Morgan to 14th and U, while Buses 52, 53, and 54 travel north from several downtown Metro stops up 14th Street.

PLANNING YOUR TIME

You can spend a good day eating your way through the many international restaurants in the area, admiring the colorful row houses, and taking pictures of the intricately designed murals. You can fill an evening with a traditional theater experience or a live music show. U Street is a nightlife destination for the city, with its many clubs and bars, while Shaw is a good bet for craft cocktail bars and unique dining.

QUICK BITES

■ **Mi Casita Bakery & Deli.** Mi Casita is an excellent spot for a fast but authentic Mexican food fix from Mexican conchas (sweet bread) to quesadillas to tacos. ✉ 3429 14th St. NW ⊕ www.busboysandpoets.com Ⓜ U St/African-Amer Civil War Memorial/Cardozo.

■ **Roaming Rooster.** One of Northeast D.C.'s favorite chicken sandwich spot opened an outpost on U Street. Try its famous hot Nashville chicken sandwich. ✉ 1301 U St. NW ⊕ www.roamingroosterdc.com Ⓜ U St./African-Amer Civil War Memorial/Cardozo.

■ **Seylou Bakery and Mill.** Forego the chains and head to Seylou for phenomenal coffees and teas, as well as whole-grain and naturally sourced baked goods, snacks, and even bread to go. ✉ 926 N St. NW, Suite A ⊕ www.seylou.com Ⓜ Mt. Vernon Sq. 7th St.–Convention Center.

Home-style Ethiopian food, offbeat boutiques, and live music are fueling the revival of the U Street, Logan Circle, and Shaw areas. This part of the District once survived on memories of its heyday as a center of Black culture and jazz music in the first half of the 20th century; now it's a vibrant, food-savvy restaurant and nightlife destination.

The area was especially vibrant from the 1920s to the 1950s, when it was home to jazz genius Duke Ellington, social activist Mary McLeod Bethune, and poets Langston Hughes and Georgia Douglas Johnson. In the 1950s, Supreme Court Justice Thurgood Marshall, then still a lawyer, organized the landmark *Brown v. Board of Education* case at the 12th Street YMCA. Now, murals and artwork speckled across the Shaw neighborhood reflect the art and artists that added to the town's vibrancy, among a lively resurgence of culture, cuisine, and nightlife.

U Street has become a nightlife destination with music venues and theaters, but Shaw and Logan Circle have emerged as the new restaurants strips for fantastic and niche culinary experiences.

◉ Sights

This area of the District is not one for sightseers, but there's one noteworthy museum you may wish to visit.

African American Civil War Memorial and Museum

MUSEUM | This museum highlights and commemorates the contributions of the 209,145 members of the United States Colored Troops, who have long been ignored in the history of the Civil War. It also sets out to serve the educational needs of the local, national, and international community through learning and experiences within the interpretation on the history of the USCT. The museum is free to visitors. Give yourself an hour to explore the main exhibit, *Glorious March to Liberty, Civil War to Civil Rights*. Tours are available by appointment only. ✉ *1925 Vermont Ave. NW, Logan Circle* ☎ *202/667–2667* ⊕ *www.afroamcivilwar. org* ▦ *Free* Ⓜ *Shaw–Howard U.*

D.C. Alley Museum

LOCAL INTEREST | If you love street art, take a stroll along the D.C. Alley Museum, funded by the DC Commission on the Arts and Humanities Public Art Building Communities Program. Local artists take turns creating art in the many garages surrounding Blagden Alley in Shaw. The murals take on local issues, social justice, and women's rights. The museum is open-air, and you can go whenever you choose as there are no admission charges. You can find more details about the artists and the art on the website.

Did You Know?

Ben's Chili Bowl never closed its doors during the riots that followed the 1968 assassination of Dr. Martin Luther King Jr. Instead, the culinary king of the neighborhood fed both policemen and activists alike.

✉ *Blagden Alley, Shaw* ☎ *No phone* ⊕ *www.dcalleymuseum.com* Ⓜ *Convention Center.*

Mary McCloud Bethune Council House National Historic Site

HOUSE | The site of the first headquarters for the National Council of Negro Women, the Mary McLeod Bethune Council House celebrates the life and legacy of Bethune, who founded the council and also served as president of the National Association of Colored Women. It was the council's headquarters from 1943 to 1966, and Bethune herself lived here from 1943 to 1949. The archives of the history of African American women in the United States and Bethune's legacy are housed here as well. After a lengthy construction project to update the archival research areas and to stabilize the physical foundations, the site reopened to the public in December 2018. ✉ *1318 Vermont Ave. NW, Shaw* ☎ *202/426–5961* ⊕ *www.nps.gov/mamc* Ⓜ *Dupont Circle.*

🍴 Restaurants

U Street links Shaw, centered near Howard University's campus, to Adams Morgan, and is known for indie rock clubs, edgy bars, and trendy restaurants. Although the urban hipster vibe is being threatened by skyrocketing rents and the intrusion of chain stores, you'll still find more tattoos and sneakers than pinstripes and pearls here. Logan Circle is southwest from both of Shaw's Metro stations: U Street/African-American Civil War Memorial/Cardozo and Shaw–Howard University (both on the Green and Yellow lines).

All Purpose Pizzeria

$ | **ITALIAN** | You can get nearly any pizza you might want, from a classic Margherita style with the standard mozzarella, tomato, and oregano toppings to more elaborate pizzas like Enzo the Baker with smoked bacon, Calabrian chilies, and red

onion. For lighter fare, try some of the hand-selected meats off the salumi menu or one of the *spuntini* ("little snacks") that include braised octopus and squash "hummus." There are no shortages of antipasti and salad offerings, either. **Known for:** seasonally inspired pizzas; delicious antipasti; pickup and delivery. Ⓢ *Average main: $16* ✉ *1250 9th St. NW, Shaw* ☎ *202/849–6174* ⊕ *allpurposedc.com* Ⓜ *Mt. Vernon Sq. 7th St.–Convention Center.*

★ Anafre

$$ | **MEXICAN** | At this celebrated restaurant, whose name means "clay oven," chef Antonio Solis infuses his creative dishes with the regional flavors of his native Mexico. The *queso fundido* (savory melted cheese) served in a banana leaf is one of the most requested starters. **Known for:** authentic Mexican food; lively space; extensive cocktail list. Ⓢ *Average main: $18* ✉ *3704 14th St. NW, Columbia Heights* ☎ *202/758–2127* ⊕ *www.anafredc.com.*

Appioo

$$ | **AFRICAN** | Washington, D.C. is a hub for the African diaspora, with many different countries represented in the city's culinary scene. Appioo, a well-established Ghanaian restaurant owned by chef Prince Matey, is set in the basement of a row house and has an intimate dining room decorated with intricate African wood sculptures. **Known for:** authentic Ghanian food; live music; intimate dining room. Ⓢ *Average main: $18* ✉ *1924 9th St. NW, Shaw* ☎ *202/588–7366* ⊕ *www.appiooafricanbargrill.com* Ⓜ *Shaw.*

★ Ben's Chili Bowl

$ | **AMERICAN** | **FAMILY** | A U Street fixture for decades, Ben's serves chili—on hot dogs, on Polish-style sausages, on burgers, and on its own—to Washingtonians and visitors alike. The shiny, red-vinyl stools give the impression that little has changed since the 1950s (the original location still doesn't accept credit

Sights ▼

1 African American Civil War Memorial and Museum E3
2 D.C. Alley Museum E8
3 Mary McLeod Bethune Council House National Historic Site.... C7

Restaurants ▼

1 All-Purpose Pizzeria..... F8
2 Anafre..................... B1
3 Appioo F3
4 Ben's Chili Bowl.......... D2
5 Calabash Tea & Tonic .. G3
6 Chaplin's F6
7 Chercher Ethiopian Restaurant............... F7
8 Colada Shop............. B3
9 Compass Rose C3
10 Convivial F6
11 Cork Wine Bar & Market................. O4
12 The Dabney............... F8
13 DCity Smokehouse I4
14 Doi Moi................... B4
15 Dukem................... D2
16 El Rinconcito Cafe E8
17 Espita Mezcaleria F7
18 Estadio B6
19 Haikan................... F2
20 Hazel F2
21 Izakaya Seki............. D2
22 Le Diplomate C5
23 Los Hermanos........... B1
24 Maydan.................. C1
25 Mezcalero............... B1
26 Milk Bar Flagship @ Logan Circle.......... B6
27 Napoli Pasta Bar......... E1
28 Oohhs & Aahhs E2
29 Pearl Dive Oyster Palace................... B5
30 the pig................... B7
31 The Red Hen............... I4
32 Room 11.................. E1
33 The Royal H3
34 San Lorenzo Ristorante + Bar F7
35 Seven Reasons B1
36 Seylou Bakery and Mill F7
37 Thip Khao................ B1
38 Tico...................... B3
39 Tiger Fork F7
40 Unconventional Diner F8

Hotels ▼

1 The Darcy Washington DC, Curio Collection by Hilton A7
2 Hotel Zena................ C9

KEY

1 Exploring Sights
1 Restaurants
1 Hotels

cards), but don't be fooled: this favorite of former President Barack Obama has rocketed into the 21st century with an iPhone app, an upscale Southern cuisine restaurant next door, and menu additions like turkey burgers and meatless chili that nod to modern times. **Known for:** legendary half-smoke chili bowls; Southern-style breakfast; cheese fries and milk shakes. ⑤ *Average main: $7* ✉ *1213 U St. NW, U Street* ☎ *202/667–0058* ⊕ *www. benschilibowl.com* ▭ *No credit cards* Ⓜ *U St./African-Amer Civil War Memorial/ Cardozo.*

Calabash Tea & Tonic

$ | CAFÉ | This award-winning teahouse, named Yelp's "Most Loved Business in D.C." in 2019, features over 80 teas, tonics, and body products based on founder Dr. Sunyatta Amen's Jamaican Maroon and Native American great-grandmothers' time-tested formulas. After you're greeted at the counter, one of Calabash's skilled staff will craft a concoction based on your needs or desires. **Known for:** custom teas to cure ailments; vegan desserts and pastries; bohemian decor. ⑤ *Average main: $7* ✉ *1847 7th St. NW, Shaw* ☎ *202/525–5386* ⊕ *www. calabashtea.com* Ⓜ *Shaw.*

Chaplin's

$ | ASIAN | Inspired by the 1930s star Charlie Chaplin, this is the first ramen house–cocktail bar in Shaw. Burmese chef Myo Htun transports you with his take on traditional gyoza, shumai, and any number of ramen combinations, while Ari and Micah Wilder offer carefully curated cocktails. **Known for:** delicious ramen and gyoza; house-made cocktails; 1930s film theme. ⑤ *Average main: $14* ✉ *1501 9th St. NW, Shaw* ☎ *202/644–8806* ⊕ *www. chaplinsdc.com* Ⓜ *Mt. Vernon Sq. 7th St.–Convention Center.*

Chercher Ethiopian Restaurant

$ | ETHIOPIAN | In Shaw, a neighborhood known for its traditional Ethiopian food, this celebrated spot offers both authentic flavor and great prices. Named for the

West Hararghe zone of Ethiopia, the restaurant celebrates the traditional cuisine that is eaten mostly utensil-free, using a special spongy bread, injera, to scoop up food that's laid out on a large platter. **Known for:** authentic and delicious injera; plenty of vegan options; great value. ⑤ *Average main: $14* ✉ *1334 9th St. NW, Shaw* ☎ *202/299–9703* ⊕ *www. chercherrestaurant.com.*

★ Colada Shop

$ | CUBAN | Escape to Cuba via a *cafesito* at this spot, which has a two-floor patio and is situated just off lively 14th Street. If you'd like something more potent than a coffee, there are plenty of cocktails, from piña coladas to guava frosé. **Known for:** Cuban-style coffee; stylish decor; Latin pastries. ⑤ *Average main: $12* ✉ *1405 T St. NW, U Street* ☎ *202/931–4947* ⊕ *www.coladashop.com.*

Compass Rose

$$ | FUSION | Take a trip around the world at Compass Rose, a restaurant celebrating global cuisine. Inspired by her travels, owner Rose Previte features many of her favorite dishes, from seviches to kebabs to the signature *khachapuri* (Georgian cheese-filled bread). **Known for:** eclectic decor; creative menu; extensive wine list. ⑤ *Average main: $20* ✉ *1346 T St. NW, U Street* ☎ *202/506–4765* ⊕ *www. compassrosedc.com* ⊘ *Closed Mon. and Tues.*

Convivial

$$ | FRENCH | This cozy French restaurant serves classics such as ratatouille, steak frites, and coq au vin. The extensive wine list focuses on French varieties, guaranteeing perfect pairings. **Known for:** French plates meant for sharing; lots of local regulars; lively patio. ⑤ *Average main: $25* ✉ *801 O St. NW, Logan Circle* ☎ *202/525–2870* ⊕ *www.convivialdc. com* ⊘ *No lunch* Ⓜ *Mt. Vernon Sq. 7th St.–Convention Center.*

★ Cork Wine Bar & Market

$$ | **WINE BAR** | This rustic, dimly lit wine bar brings chic cuisine to the city's hippest neighborhood. The wine list features rare varietals—with a dozen still under $11 per glass—but even teetotalers will be enchanted by the menu's classic dishes. **Known for:** more than 50 wines by the glass; relaxing patio; favorite small plates to share. $ *Average main: $24* ⊠ *1805 14th St. NW, U Street* ☎ *202/265–2675* ⊕ *www.corkdc.com* ⊙ *Closed Mon.* Ⓜ *U St./African-Amer Civil War Memorial/ Cardozo.*

★ The Dabney

$$ | **AMERICAN** | While many of D.C.'s standout restaurants earn their accolades for takes on cuisine from far-flung corners of the globe, at the Dabney, Virginia-born chef Jeremiah Langhorne draws rave reviews for his commitment to Mid-Atlantic cuisine. Larger plates might include whole lacquered quail stuffed with cornbread or a family-style serving of chicken and dumplings, but small plates predominate, and waiters will help you balance out your meal. **Known for:** creative cocktails; low-key farmhouse vibe; handcrafted desserts. $ *Average main: $21* ⊠ *122 Blagden Alley NW, Shaw* ☎ *202/450–1015* ⊕ *www.thedabney.com* ⊙ *Closed Mon.* Ⓜ *Mt. Vernon Sq. 7th St.– Convention Center.*

DCity Smokehouse

$ | **BARBECUE** | **FAMILY** | DCity Smokehouse continues to be a beloved neighborhood barbecue spot. Located in residential Bloomingdale, the restaurant serves a variety of meats smoked in-house. **Known for:** barbecue; neighborhood staple; affordable eats. $ *Average main: $15* ⊠ *203 Florida Ave. NW, Bloomingdale* ☎ *202/733–1919* ⊕ *www.dcitysmokehouse.com.*

Doi Moi

$$ | **MODERN ASIAN** | The rise of foodie culture can leave adventurous diners feeling like they've turned over every culinary stone, but this pilgrimage into the Southeast Asian unknown will wow even the most jaded eater. Doi Moi (Vietnamese for "new changes") puts a new spin on several traditional Southeast Asian cuisines: fried beef jerky with shark sriracha, wok-tossed mussels, and crispy-fried snapper are leading lights. **Known for:** adventurous Asian cuisine spanning several regions; bright and modern interior; special vegetarian and gluten-free menus. $ *Average main: $25* ⊠ *1800 14th St. NW, U Street* ☎ *202/733–5131* ⊕ *www.doimoidc.com* ⊙ *No lunch* Ⓜ *U St./African-Amer Civil War Memorial/ Cardozo.*

Dukem

$ | **ETHIOPIAN** | For more than 20 years, Dukem has been a favorite of those seeking authentic Ethiopian food. Guests come for the injera, a spongy flatbread topped with tibs, a dish with cubed tender lamb or beef fried with onion, rosemary jalapeño pepper served with injera, and salad and spicy awazie sauce. **Known for:** well-established restaurant; vegetarian- and vegan-friendly options; occasional live Ethiopian music on weekends. $ *Average main: $18* ⊠ *1114–1118 U St. NW, U Street* ☎ *202/667–8735* Ⓜ *U St.*

El Rinconcito Cafe

$ | **LATIN AMERICAN** | A trip to D.C. is not complete without tasting *pupusas,* the El Salvadoran tortillas filled with chorizo, cheese, and chicharrón. El Rinconcito Cafe, a fixture in Shaw for El Salvadoran and Mexican cuisine, specializes in pupusas and also serves quesadillas, tacos, and enchiladas—all at affordable prices. **Known for:** pupusas; affordable meals; neighborhood spot for El Salvadoran food. $ *Average main: $10* ⊠ *1129 11th St. NW, Shaw* ☎ *202/789–4110* ⊕ *www. rinconcitocafe.com* Ⓜ *Convention Center.*

Espita Mezcaleria

$$$ | **MEXICAN** | *Maíz* (corn) and agave are the cornerstones of the food and drink menus at Espita, which serves authentic Mexican small plates, mains, and desserts. The award-winning tortillas,

house-made using recipes brought from Mexico by the sous-chef, are the most popular items on the menu. **Known for:** popular weekend happy hour; extensive mezcal list and themed cocktails; authentic Mexican flavor. ⑤ *Average main: $28* ⊠ *1250 9th St. NW, Logan Circle* ☎ *202/621–9695* ⊕ *espitadc.com* ⊘ *No lunch weekdays* Ⓜ *Shaw–Howard U.*

★ Estadio

$$$ | SPANISH | The name of this polished palace means "stadium," and its gorgeously Baroque interior, which surrounds a high-wire open kitchen, makes a perfect stage for energetic and flavorful uses of top-notch ingredients. The menu, developed during research jaunts throughout Spain, is a master class in tapas, with smoky grilled scallions punched up by garlicky romesco sauce and *tortilla española* smoother than any served in Barcelona. **Known for:** classic Spanish tapas with new flavors; boozy slushies; beautiful dining room. ⑤ *Average main: $28* ⊠ *1520 14th St. NW, Logan Circle* ☎ *202/319–1404* ⊕ *www.estadio-dc.com* ⊘ *No lunch Mon.–Thurs.* Ⓜ *U St./African-Amer Civil War Memorial/ Cardozo.*

Haikan

$ | JAPANESE | Located on a lively block, Haikan is a recent addition from the popular Daikaya Group, famous for its ramen restaurants throughout the city. The restaurant serves different types of ramen, featuring pork-based, Sapporo-style dishes. **Known for:** Sapporo-style ramen; lively dining room ; rotating selection of Japanese appetizers. ⑤ *Average main: $15* ⊠ *805 V St. NW, Shaw* ☎ *202/299–1000* ⊕ *www.haikandc.com* ⊘ *Closed Mon. and Tues. except for takeout* Ⓜ *Shaw.*

★ Hazel

$$ | CHIU CHOW | The Mediterranean- and Middle Eastern–influenced medium-size plates like eggplant with cucumber, sumac, and hummus fries are favorites at this popular restaurant. With heated lamps, whimsical decor, and firepits, the patio is a coveted spot, even in winter. **Known for:** cozy patio; small plates; great cocktails. ⑤ *Average main: $25* ⊠ *808 V St. NW, U Street* ☎ *202/847–4980* ⊕ *www.hazelrestaurant.com* ⊘ *No lunch Mon.–Sat.* Ⓜ *U St./African-Amer Civil War Memorial/Cardozo.*

Izakaya Seki

$$ | JAPANESE | The only crowd-pleasing flourishes here are the freshness of the scallop carpaccio and the perfect sear on the grilled yellowtail jaw, and that's all adventurous foodies will need to make the most of a quiet evening at this family-owned, off-the-beaten-path spot marked by little more than a red Japanese lantern outside the door. Dare to try some beef tongue or cured squid off the sake accompaniments menu of smaller plates. **Known for:** authentic, non-Americanized Japanese cuisine; timed reservations for large groups; small, adventurous plates like beef tongue. ⑤ *Average main: $22* ⊠ *1117 V St. NW, U Street* ☎ *202/588–5841* ⊕ *www.sekidc.com* ⊘ *Closed Mon. No lunch* Ⓜ *U St./African-Amer Civil War Memorial/Cardozo.*

★ Le Diplomate

$$$ | BRASSERIE | In this faithful re-creation of a convivial Parisian bistro, the attention to detail makes a night here into more than just a meal. This excellent spot prizes quality above all, from graceful martinis and hand-stuffed ricotta ravioli to succulent, textbook-worthy steak frites and roasted chicken. **Known for:** Parisian-bistro vibe; juicy steak frites; popular brunch menu. ⑤ *Average main: $30* ⊠ *1610 14th St. NW, U Street* ☎ *202/332–3333* ⊕ *www.lediplomatedc.com.*

Los Hermanos

$ | LATIN AMERICAN | The owners of Los Hermanos (meaning "brothers" in Spanish), which was initially a bodega, began offering home cooked–style Dominican food after customers began asking about the smells that were coming from the back of the store. A must-order is *mangú*, the national dish of the Dominican Republic made with mashed plantains and accompanied by salami, fried cheese, and egg. **Known for:** authentic Dominican food; affordable prices; casual neighborhood restaurant. $ *Average main: $12* ⊠ *1428 Park Rd. NW, Columbia Heights* ☎ *202/483–8235* ⊕ *www.loshermanosfordc.com* Ⓜ *Columbia Heights.*

Maydan

$$$$ | **MIDDLE EASTERN** | Michelin-starred Maydan is an idyllic culinary journey of the Middle East with an intricate entrance, wood fire taking center stage, and a colorful bar. Maydan transformed their outdoor seating into a Middle-Eastern dining experience called "Tawle." Guests must order from the prix-fixe menu, which includes a variety of family-style dishes inspired by the Middle-East, Northern Africa, and the Caucuses. **Known for:** Michelin starred; Middle Eastern wood-fired kebabs; craft cocktails. $ *Average main: $65* ⊠ *1346 Florida Ave. NW, U Street* ⊕ *www.maydandc.com* ⊘ *Closed Mon. and Tues.*

Mezcalero

$ | **MEXICAN** | Mezcalero, the more casual sister restaurant to Anafre by chef Antonio Solis, serves a variety of appetizers such as Mexican-style ceviche, guacamole, and grilled oysters. The authentic burritos are generously filled with carne asada, chorizo, or mixed vegetables, and, as the restaurant's name implies, mezcal plays a big role on the cocktail list. **Known for:** authentic Mexican food; great happy hour specials; mezcal cocktails. $ *Average main: $12* ⊠ *3714 14th St. NW, Columbia Heights* ☎ *202/803–2114* ⊕ *www.mezcalerodc.com* Ⓜ *Columbia Heights.*

Milk Bar Flagship @ Logan Circle

$ | **AMERICAN** | If you're a fan of sprinkles, pie, ice cream, and birthday cake, then this is the place for you to eat in or grab something to go. But don't expect

run-of-the-mill pastries: founder Christina Tosi has created an empire of modernized American confections, including soft serve made with cereal-infused milk, cakes shrunken into truffles, and favorites like the Compost Cookie and Crack Pie. **Known for:** American desserts with a modern twist; signature birthday layer cake and cereal-milk soft serve; baking classes on site. $ *Average main: $6* ⊠ *1525 15th St. NW, Logan Circle* ⊹ *Corner of 15th St. and Church St. NW* ☎ *202/506–1357* ⊕ *milkbarstore.com* Ⓜ *Dupont Circle or Mt. Vernon Sq. 7th St.–Convention Center.*

★ Napoli Pasta Bar

$$ | **ITALIAN** | Located on a residential street, this restaurant offers an authentic Italian dining experience. Chef and owner Antonio Ferraro brings the flavors of his native Napoli to Washington, D.C., with fresh, house-made pasta dishes, such as fusilli with crab meat or decadent gnocchi, served on colorful, hand-painted plates. **Known for:** Vespa table; house-made pasta; Italian wine list. $ *Average main: $18* ⊠ *2737 Sherman Ave. NW, Columbia Heights* ☎ *202/588–8752* ⊕ *www.napolipastabar.com* Ⓜ *Columbia Heights.*

Oohhs & Aahhs

$ | **SOUTHERN** | No-frills soul food is what you'll find at this friendly eat-in or takeout place, where the price is right, and the food is delicious. Ultrarich macaroni and cheese, succulent chicken and waffles, and teriyaki salmon just beg to be devoured, and collard greens are cooked with vinegar and sugar rather than the traditional salt pork. **Known for:** home-style soul cooking; mac and cheese, collard greens, and hummingbird cake; late-night weekend hours. $ *Average main: $15* ⊠ *1005 U St. NW, U Street* ☎ *202/667–7142* ⊕ *www.oohhsnaahhs. com* Ⓜ *U St./African-Amer Civil War Memorial/Cardozo.*

Pearl Dive Oyster Palace

$$ | SEAFOOD | Chef Jeff Black does serve three kinds of po'boys, but that's about as working-class as it gets at this dazzlingly decorated homage to the bivalve. East and West Coast oysters come raw, with perfect dipping sauces—at half-price all day on Monday and during happy hour every other day—or warm in five irresistible guises, from bacon wrapped to crusted in cornmeal and sprinkled with sweet-potato hash. **Known for:** upscale oysters (both raw and warm); steak options for nonoyster lovers; classy cocktails. $ *Average main: $24* ⊠ *1612 14th St. NW, U Street* ☏ *202/319–1612* ⊕ *www.pearldivedc.com* ☾ *No lunch Mon.–Thurs.* Ⓜ *U St./African-Amer Civil War Memorial/Cardozo.*

the pig

$$ | AMERICAN | As the name implies, this restaurant celebrates pork—from patties to barbecue ribs to pulled-pork sandwiches, all made with meat sourced from a Maryland farm. Enjoy signature cocktails such as the Three Little Pigs—8 Weeks 'til the Slaughter (a Manhattan), the Pegroni (a Negroni), and the Swine Boulevard (a Boulevardier). **Known for:** pork-themed menu; craft cocktails; both small and large plates. $ *Average main: $20* ⊠ *1320 14th St. NW, Logan Circle* ☏ *202/290–2821* ⊕ *www.thepigdc.com* Ⓜ *Mt. Vernon Sq. 7th St.–Convention Center.*

★ The Red Hen

$$$ | AMERICAN | The cozy farmhouselike setting helped make the Red Hen a must-try for Italian-influenced takes on American dishes. If the name and giant hen on the facade have you thinking poultry, you'd be right to follow your instincts and order the pan-roasted half chicken. **Known for:** savvy wine list; pan-roasted half chicken; delicious pasta options. $ *Average main: $28* ⊠ *1822 1st St. NW, U Street* ☏ *202/525–3021* ⊕ *www. theredhendc.com* ☾ *No lunch* Ⓜ *Shaw–Howard U.*

★ Room 11

$ | WINE BAR | You're invited to the coolest house party in the city, where deft hands in a tiny kitchen turn out urbane plates that go down like a designer outfit hidden on the sale rack. From the roasted mushroom risotto at dinner to the perfectly assembled breakfast sandwich on a biscuit for brunch, this small wonder has a dish for every mood. **Known for:** intimate (read: tiny) hip space; brunch-time biscuit sandwich; outdoor patio with heating lamps in winter. $ *Average main: $15* ⊠ *3234 11th St. NW, U Street* ☏ *202/332–3234* ⊕ *www.room11dc.com* ☾ *No lunch weekdays* Ⓜ *Columbia Heights.*

The Royal

$ | LATIN AMERICAN | The Royal is both a Michelin-recognized Bib Gourmand restaurant and a well-priced, local favorite for breakfast, lunch, dinner, or just for a matcha latte while working on your laptop at the bar. The second concept by owner Paul Carlson, it's a celebration of his family's international roots, with a strong emphasis on vegetarian and gluten-free options. **Known for:** Colombian-inspired food; small plates and house-made cocktails; neighborhood favorite. $ *Average main: $15* ⊠ *501 Florida Ave. NW, Shaw* ☏ *202/332–7777* ⊕ *www. theroyaldc.com* Ⓜ *Shaw–Howard U.*

San Lorenzo Ristorante + Bar

$$ | ITALIAN | Chef and owner Massimo Fabbri, previously of Tosca and Posto, opened the first restaurant of his own to highlight the tastes of Tuscany and pay homage to his roots. Named for the patron saint of chefs, this soothing restaurant reminds you of Italy itself with a cream and golden palette, wooden beams, distressed plaster, and Italian art. **Known for:** sophisticated yet casual style; classic Tuscan dishes like rosticciana and pappardelle with rabbit ragù; house-made pastas. $ *Average main: $25* ⊠ *1316 9th St. NW, Shaw* ☏ *202/588–8954* ⊕ *www. sanlorenzodc.com* Ⓜ *Mt. Vernon Sq. 7th St.–Convention Center.*

★ Seven Reasons

$$$ | LATIN AMERICAN | At Seven Reasons, one of D.C.'s most talked-about restaurants in the past two years, chef Enrique Limardo honors his native Venezuela with creative versions of *arepas* (stuffed cornmeal cakes) and *arroz bomba* (rice with seafood). The restaurant also takes you on a Latin American tour with offerings such as Argentinean-style steak or Peruvian-style seviche. **Known for:** picturesque rooftop patio; high-end Latin American cuisine; open kitchen plan. $ *Average main: $35 ⊠ 2208 14th St. NW, U Street ☎ 202/417–8563 ⊕ www.sevenreasons-dc.com ☉ Closed Mon.* Ⓜ *U St.*

★ Seylou Bakery and Mill

$ | AMERICAN | Skip the chains, and head to this beloved local coffee shop and whole-grain bakery offering fresh sourdough creations, whole wheat almond croissants, and seasonal veggie frittatas. Grab a specialty coffee, a yerba-maté or nettle tea, and a 100% whole-wheat chocolate croissant or buckwheat muffin on your way to tour the city. **Known for:** freshly made breads and whole wheat pastries; specialty coffees and teas; locally sourced ingredients. $ *Average main: $7 ⊠ 926 N St. NW, Suite A, Shaw ☎ 202/842–1122 ⊕ www.seylou.com ☉ Closed Mon.–Thurs.* Ⓜ *Mt. Vernon Sq. 7th St.–Convention Center.*

Thip Khao

$ | LAO | FAMILY | Chef-owner Seng Luangrath learned to cook as a young girl in a refugee camp and later brought the cuisine of Laos and Thailand to northern Virginia and then D.C. The atmosphere at her Columbia Heights outpost might be casual, but the flavors of its food are complex. **Known for:** deep menu of authentic Laotian cuisine; minced-meat salads known as laab; bourbon and ginger cider drinks. $ *Average main: $16 ⊠ 3462 14th St. NW, Logan Circle ☎ 202/387–5426 ⊕ thipkhao.com ☉ Closed Mon.* Ⓜ *Columbia Heights.*

Tico

$$ | LATIN AMERICAN | One of Boston's celebrity chefs, Michael Schlow, scored prime real estate for this fast-paced parade of small Latin and South American plates with big personalities. The half-dozen seviches add witty touches like pressed watermelon and crispy rice, while the tacos thrill with inventive ingredients from shrimp to duck-skin "cracklings." **Known for:** exciting (and tasty) vegetarian options; very small plates (so ordering several is a must); all-night happy hour on Monday. $ *Average main: $25 ⊠ 1926 14th St. NW, U Street ☎ 202/319–1400 ⊕ www.ticodc.com ☉ No lunch* Ⓜ *U St./African-Amer Civil War Memorial/Cardozo.*

Tiger Fork

$ | CHINESE FUSION | Come here if you're looking for edgier Hong Kong cuisine, perhaps pork ribs slathered in soy-and-ginger sauce, a tofu claypot, *cheung fun* with shrimp and flowering chives, or chili wontons. Finish your meal with a traditional street dessert: a bubble waffle topped with "fun stuff" (sprinkles, lychee, Pocky sticks, and *dulce de leche*). **Known for:** Asian street-style food; late-night menu; bubble waffles. $ *Average main: $16 ⊠ 922 N St. NW, Shaw ⊹ Enter in rear, off Blagden Alley ☎ 202/733–1152 ⊕ www.tigerforkdc.com* Ⓜ *Mt. Vernon Sq. 7th St.–Convention Center.*

Unconventional Diner

$$ | AMERICAN | All of the typical diner and Southern favorites on the menu here have an unusual twist, befitting the name of this restaurant. Start with the kale nachos or potpie poppers, then, if you're really hungry, dive into a plate of fried chicken or the "French Dip" pappardelle. **Known for:** modernized American diner food; potpie poppers (bite-size chicken potpies); good daily breakfast and weekend brunch. $ *Average main: $20 ⊠ 1207 9th St. NW, Shaw ☎ 202/847–0122 ⊕ unconventionaldiner.com* Ⓜ *Mt. Vernon Sq. 7th St.–Convention Center.*

Hotels

A stay in this hip neighborhood affords a cooler, more-local District experience. Hotels here are right in the mix of some of the city's most unique restaurants and bars, and the area is just a Metro or car ride away from the major sites and museums.

The Darcy Washington DC, Curio Collection by Hilton

$$$ | HOTEL | FAMILY | One of the city's latest hotel triumphs, this stylish treasure just around the corner from the buzzy 14th Street Corridor aims to bring a sophisticated European touch to the cosmopolitan capital city. **Pros:** sophisticated style and lobby; central location; pet-friendly. **Cons:** no spa or pool; only expensive valet parking available; closest Metro is a 10-minute walk. $ *Rooms from: $300* ✉ *1515 Rhode Island Ave. NW, Logan Circle* ☎ *202/232–7000* ⊕ *www.thedarcyhotel.com* ➥ *226 rooms* ⟊ *No meals* Ⓜ *Dupont Circle.*

Hotel Zena

$ | HOTEL | Located in Thomas Circle, Hotel Zena (which stands out with a towering mural of two stunning women in warrior regalia) is an homage to women; guests are welcomed with a massive art installation of the late feminist icon, Ruth Bader Ginsburg, made of handpainted tampons. **Pros:** centrally located; creative, woman-focused theme; rooftop pool and bar. **Cons:** open lobby restaurant with no private dining area; message many be too partisan for some; expensive parking. $ *Rooms from: $151* ✉ *1155 14th St. NW, Logan Circle* ☎ *202/737–1200* ⊕ *www.viceroyhotelsandresorts.com/zena* ➥ *191 rooms* Ⓜ *Mt. Vernon Sq.*

ⓨ Nightlife

Decades ago, the U Street corridor was famous as D.C.'s Black Broadway. After many dormant years, the neighborhood has come roaring back with a lively bar,

club, and music scene that's expanding both north and south along 14th Street. The U Street corridor is easily accessible from the U Street/African-American Civil War Memorial/Cardozo Metro stop, on the Green and Yellow lines. Taxis also are easy to find.

In the last couple of years, nearby Shaw has become the most revitalized downtown neighborhood in the capital. But any night out in Shaw almost by default includes spending time in the U Street corridor to the north and west—especially because some destinations, like the Howard Theatre and the 9:30 Club, straddle both increasingly diverse urban neighborhoods. Shaw is centered on 7th Street, with Howard University and Hospital to the north and the Washington Convention Center at the very southern edge.

BARS AND LOUNGES
All Souls

BARS/PUBS | All Souls feels like the perfect dive, a great place to meet up with friends and chat away in a booth, fresh drink or craft beer in hand. The simple yet refined cocktails are described in loving detail, alongside interesting wines and craft brews, on signs at the bar. You can order snacks, but you can also bring food in or have it delivered, making this feel even more like a friendly, neighborhood hangout. ✉ *725 T St. NW, Shaw* ☎ *202/733–5929* ⊕ *allsoulsbar.com* Ⓜ *Shaw–Howard U.*

Anxo Cidery

BREWPUBS/BEER GARDENS | Take a trip to Spain at Anxo (an-cho) Cidery. Here you can sample a multitude of ciders, a drink tied to the culture of the Basque country, and explore the unusual combinations produced from apples: from bright or fruit-forward to structured or rustic. Try one of the many flights, a dessert ice cider, and even some obscure, rare ciders. The bar also serves beer, wine, and cocktails for those who want something more familiar, and there's a menu of *pintxos* (small bites) as well. ⊠ *300 Florida Ave. NW, Shaw* ☎ *202/986–3795* ⊕ *www.anxodc.com* Ⓜ *Shaw–Howard U.*

Black Jack

BARS/PUBS | A red-velvet, almost vaude-ville-like interior around the bar offers a saucy experience upstairs from the high-ly rated Pearl Dive Oyster Palace. In the back, you'll find a bocce court surrounded by stadium-style seats so onlookers can recline, imbibe, and cheer simultaneous-ly. Though the most exquisite cocktail confections can be pricey, there's also an impressive beer lineup and a worthwhile menu ranging from mussels to pizza. There's a happy hour every day; it runs all day on Sunday. ⊠ *1612 14th St. NW, Logan Circle* ☎ *202/319–1612* ⊕ *www. blackjackdc.com* Ⓜ *U St./African-Amer Civil War Memorial/Cardozo.*

Busboys and Poets

BARS/PUBS | Part eatery, part bookstore, and part event space, this popular local hangout draws a diverse crowd and hosts a wide range of entertainment, from poetry open mics to music to guest authors and activist speakers. The name is an homage to Langston Hughes, who worked as a busboy in D.C. before becoming a famous poet. This original location is open until 1 am on Friday and Saturday—there's another Downtown (at 1025 5th Street NW), as well as outposts in upper D.C., Maryland, and Virginia. ⊠ *2021 14th St. NW, U Street* ☎ *202/387–7638* ⊕ *www.busboysandpo-ets.com* Ⓜ *U St./African-Amer Civil War Memorial/Cardozo.*

Café Saint-Ex

BARS/PUBS | Named for Antoine de Saint-Exupéry, French pilot and author of *The Little Prince,* this bi-level bar has two distinct atmospheres. The upstairs brasserie has pressed-tin ceilings and a propeller hanging over the polished wooden bar. Downstairs is the Gate

54 nightclub, designed to resemble an airplane hangar, with dropped corru-gated-metal ceilings and backlit aerial photographs. The downstairs DJs draw a fairly young crowd, while the upstairs menu attracts a more subdued clientele for dinner. ⊠ *1847 14th St. NW, U Street* ☎ *202/265–7839* ⊕ *www.saint-ex.com* Ⓜ *U St./African-Amer Civil War Memorial/ Cardozo.*

Calico

BARS/PUBS | Tucked away in Blagden Alley in the heart of Shaw, this hipster's dream offers kitschy decor made modern and an ethereal garden backyard. Take a boozy adult juice box to the urban backyard, featuring a 3,000-square-foot patio with farmhouse tables, string lights, plants, and a vintage greenhouse. Formerly a boxing gym and art studio, the restaurant offers a menu with elevated takes on cookout classics like crab cakes, short ribs, and hoagies. ⊠ *50 Blagden Alley NW, Shaw* ☎ *202/791–0134* Ⓜ *Mt. Vernon Sq. 7th St.–Convention Center.*

Chi-Cha Lounge

BARS/PUBS | Groups of young profession-als relax on sofas and armchairs in this hip hangout modeled after an Ecuado-rian hacienda, while Latin jazz mingles with pop music in the background and old movies run silently behind the bar. The place gets packed on weekends, so come early to get a coveted sofa along the back wall. Pair your cocktails with a Cocina Nikkei (Japanese Peruvian) menu, including ceviches and gyozas (Japanese dumplings).Or try a hookah filled with a range of flavored tobaccos, from apple to watermelon. A dress-to-impress dress code is strictly enforced. ⊠ *1624 U St. NW, U Street* ☎ *202/234–8400* ⊕ *www. chichaloungedc.com* Ⓜ *U St./African-Am-er Civil War Memorial/Cardozo.*

ChurchKey

BARS/PUBS | There's an astounding selection of beers at ChurchKey—555 varieties from more than 30 countries, including 50 beers on tap and exclusive draft and cask ales. If you have trouble making a choice, bartenders will offer you 4-ounce tasters. The urban-vintage vibe balances unassuming and pretentious in pretty much equal measure, reflected in a menu that ranges from tater tots to Caesar salads to rotating flatbread options. ✉ 1337 14th St. NW, Logan Circle ☎ 202/567–2576 ⊕ www.churchkey-dc.com Ⓜ McPherson Sq.

★ Columbia Room

BARS/PUBS | Derek Brown's two-time James Beard–nominated ode to the American cocktail is tucked away on Blagden Alley in D.C.'s hippest neighborhood for gourmands. Perhaps the coolest and chicest cocktail bar in Shaw, the Columbia Room features a curated drinks list that changes seasonally and includes combinations that dazzle and surprise. Head up a flight of stairs to the outdoor Punch Garden, offering a special seasonal menu, or step into the Spirits Library for one of the many featured, or even no-proof, cocktails. An even grander experience awaits in the Tasting Room, where you can sample cocktails accompanied by small bites that enhance the flavors. ✉ 124 Blagden Alley NW, Shaw ☎ 202/316–9396 ⊕ www.columbiaroom-dc.com Ⓜ Mt. Vernon Sq. 7th St.–Convention Center.

★ Cork Wine Bar

WINE BARS—NIGHTLIFE | On weekends, the crowds can spill onto 14th Street—but one of the best wine bars in D.C. is worth the wait. An outstanding wine list (mainly French and Italian) is matched with delectable small plates, perfect for sharing. ✉ 1805 14th St. NW, U Street ☎ 202/265–2675 ⊕ www.corkdc.com Ⓜ U St./African-Amer Civil War Memorial/ Cardozo.

The Dabney Cellar

BARS/PUBS | A separate concept from The Dabney restaurant, the Cellar is hidden down a set of stone steps in the restaurant's basement. The dim lighting and small size make you feel as if you stumbled on a D.C. speakeasy, but the bar itself shares a lot of the same open, earthy tones of the larger restaurant. The Cellar riffs off classic cocktails for its specialty list and has a large selection of wines, cider, and beer. If you feel peckish, try some of the specialty bar snacks, written on the blackboard nightly. You can't go wrong with the raw bar or the carefully selected cheeses and charcuterie. ✉ The Dabney, 1222 9th St. NW, Shaw ✛ Basement entrance ☎ 202/450–1015 ⊕ thedabney.com Ⓜ Mt. Vernon Sq. 7th St.–Convention Center.

Dacha Beer Garden

BREWPUBS/BEER GARDENS | Set off by a three-story mural of Elizabeth Taylor, Dacha has become the go-to outdoor drinking venue in midtown D.C., with lines of people (and their dogs) waiting to get in most evenings anytime of year whenever the weather isn't bitterly cold or inclement. (A windscreen wall and heaters further help keep patrons toasty during the winter.) The beer garden serves drafts of craft beers from Germany, Belgium, and the United States as well as Bavarian-inspired nosh, while the adjoining café serves hot coffee and bagels and sandwiches during the day. ✉ 1600 7th St. NW, Shaw ☎ 202/350–9888 ⊕ www.dachadc.com Ⓜ Shaw–Howard U.

El Techo

CAFES—NIGHTLIFE | Sip margaritas under the palm trees at El Techo, a unique rooftop ba, where the scene is tropical thanks to a canopy of plants and whimsical flowers. The bar also offers an extensive menu of small bites and tacos, as well as heavier dishes such as carne asada and paella for two. A DJ spins upbeat Latin dance music, and there are plenty of seating areas for those who do not feel like dancing. The retractable roof allows for year-round fun. ✉ 606 Florida Ave. NW, Shaw ☎ 202/836–4270 ⊕ www.eltechodc.com Ⓜ Shaw.

La Jambe

WINE BARS—NIGHTLIFE | Named both for
the legs of a wine and a leg of ham,
this is the place to fill your metaphori-
cal hollow leg with wine, cheese, and
charcuterie. Choose from a variety of
reds, whites, and everything in between
(even a few French cider styles), or go
for a flight of brandy and whisky. All of
the cocktails and spirits here are either
from France or the District. Happy hour
runs from 5 to 7 Tuesday through Friday,
and brunch is served from 11 to 3 on
weekends. ⊠ *1550 7th St. NW, Shaw*
☎ *202/627–2988* ⊕ *www.lajambedc.com*
Ⓜ *Shaw–Howard U.*

Lulu's Winegarden

WINE BARS—NIGHTLIFE | The owner of
The Royal and his wife transformed the
former Vinoteca into Lulu's Winegarden.
The drink menu focuses on wine, offering
rare finds and keeping them at under
$50 a bottle. Named after the owner's
daughter, the bar–restaurant has three
lush outdoor dining spaces: the 24-seat,
ivy-lined front patio; the charming,
plant-filled, 40-seat back courtyard; and
the 16-seat, terracotta-hued "streatery"
outfitted with tropical fauna and lounge
seating. The menu offers savory dips
like whipped feta and smoked whitefish
paired with a bottle of wine from the
long list. ⊠ *1940 11th St. NW, U Street*
☎ *202/332–9463* ⊕ *www.vinotecadc.com*
Ⓜ *U St./African-Amer Civil War Memorial/
Cardozo.*

Maxwell Park

WINE BARS—NIGHTLIFE | At Maxwell Park,
dinner and dessert are both a glass of
wine. The themed menu, which changes
monthly, offers more than 50 wines by
the glass. Try a sweet wine or aperitif for
dessert, or mix things up with a cocktail,
perhaps a seasonal gin and house-made
tonic. If you don't know what you want,
ask one of the trained sommeliers about
the 500 labels on the bottle list, or have
a 2.5-ounce tasting glass (just watch
the prices because there are some rare

wines here). Enjoy the outdoor patio,
which is heated in the winter, or cozy
into the bar, open nightly at 5. ⊠ *1336 9th
St. NW, Shaw* ☎ *202/792–9522* ⊕ *max-
welldcwine.com* Ⓜ *Mt. Vernon Sq. 7th
St.–Convention Center.*

★ Morris American Bar

BARS/PUBS | Founded by *Top Chef* alum
Spike Mendelsohn and D.C. nightlife
entrepreneur Vinoda Basnayake, this
Shaw bar serves spectacular cocktails.
You'll feel like you're simultaneously at
a 1950s-era diner, sitting on a backyard
patio, and in a Wes Anderson film.
The happy-hour menu features slightly
cheaper cocktail options, wine, and beer,
while the full menu offers cleverly crafted
cocktails. Both menus change monthly,
so make sure you return to see what's
new, and if you're unsure of what to
order, just ask a bartender. The bar menu
includes cheese and charcuterie boards,
dips, and salads. ⊠ *1020 7th St. NW,
Shaw* ☎ *833/366–7747* ⊕ *morrisbardc.
com* Ⓜ *Mt. Vernon Sq. 7th St.–Convention Center.*

Nellie's Sports Bar

BARS/PUBS | This popular sports bar with
a gay following makes everyone feel
welcome. Catch the games on multiple
screens, or try your luck with "drag
bingo" or trivia games. Spaces in this
eclectic two-story venue range from roof
deck to cozy pub room to a dining area
serving all-American pub grub meets
Venezuelan specialties—from empanadas to arepas. And every weekend brings
a reservations-required brunch buffet
with drag queens as servers. ⊠ *900 U St.
NW, U Street* ☎ *202/332–6355* ⊕ *www.
nelliessportsbar.com* Ⓜ *U St./African-Am-
er Civil War Memorial/Cardozo.*

Number Nine

BARS/PUBS | The heart of Logan Circle
nightlife is this predominantly male
gay bar attracting guests of all ages.
The downstairs lounge offers plush
banquettes and street views, while big-
screen viewing is offered upstairs at the

9½ video bar. The daily happy hour (5–9 pm) offers two-for-one drinks. At any time this is a great place for a cocktail and some good conversation in a bustling neighborhood that includes, a block away on 14th Street, Trade, which is another popular, no-frills gay bar from the same owners as Number Nine. ⊠ *1435 P St. NW, Logan Circle* ☎ *202/986–0999* ⊕ *www.numberninedc.com* Ⓜ *Dupont Circle.*

The Passenger

BARS/PUBS | If you're looking for Chartreuse on tap, a handwritten crafted cocktail list, and a laid-back vibe, this is the place for you. It has the feeling of a local dive bar but with the cocktail menu and bar bites of a funky D.C. bar. Be dazzled by the seemingly hundreds of bottles lining the bar, and enjoy the occasional band upstairs on weekends. ⊠ *1539 7th St. NW, Shaw* ☎ *202/853–3588* ⊕ *www.passengerdc.com* Ⓜ *Mt. Vernon Sq. 7th St.–Convention Center.*

The Saloon

BARS/PUBS | This classic watering hole has no TVs, no light beer, and no martinis. What it does have are locals engaged in conversation—a stated goal of the owner—and some of the world's best beers, including the rare Urbock 23, an Austrian brew that is rated one of the tastiest and strongest in the world, with 9.6% alcohol content (limit one per customer). The Saloon also offers a broader bar menu, too. ⊠ *1205 U St. NW, U Street* ☎ *202/462–2640* Ⓜ *U St./African-Amer Civil War Memorial/Cardozo.*

Service Bar

$ | |BARS/PUBS | At one of the city's most creative cocktail bars, the space is cozy, the vibe is casual, and the crowd is artsy. Interestingly named cocktails include the Griselda Blanco, which is served in a tiki glass and made with tequila, mezcal, coconut, lime, grapefruit, and cardamom bitters. Bring your appetite as the bar also serves food, including a popular fried-chicken sandwich—or skip the bun, and order a full fried-chicken dinner. ⊠ *926–928 U St. NW, U Street* ☎ *202/462–7232* ⊕ *www.servicebardc.com* ☉ *Closed Mon.*

DANCE CLUBS
★ Flash

DANCE CLUBS | The decline of megaclubs in D.C. has coincided with a rise in more intimate and inviting venues for those serious about dancing. This photography-themed jewel near the Howard Theatre replaced a pawnshop—a telling sign of this changing neighborhood. An operational photo booth is an entry point to the main upstairs dance floor, which envelops you in walls lined with 10,000 LED lights and a best-in-the-business Funktion One sound system. Pioneering underground DJs—Carl Craig, Chus & Ceballos—move their flocks of a couple hundred fans while intermittently flashing them from the rigged 24 parabolic reflectors behind them. ⊠ *645 Florida Ave. NW, Washington* ☎ *202/827–8791* ⊕ *www.flashdc.com* Ⓜ *Shaw–Howard U.*

Local 16

BARS/PUBS | When they have to remove all the chairs in the joint to make more room for dancing, you know you've picked a good spot. Locals and out-of-towners alike pack in on weekends to enjoy the joyful pop music, multiple dance rooms, and the outdoor-deck bar perched one story above 16th Street. Luxe couches, chandeliers, vintage pieces, and winding staircases enhance the atmosphere of a Victorian house party with a modern twist. There's an outstanding happy hour and brunch on weekends. ⊠ *1602 U St. NW, U Street* ☎ *202/265–2828* ⊕ *www.localsixteen.com* Ⓜ *U St./African-Amer Civil War Memorial/Cardozo.*

JAZZ AND BLUES
New Vegas Lounge

MUSIC CLUBS | The New Vegas Lounge may be a vestige from a grittier, less affluent era, but the Logan Circle club is in its nearly fifth decade of offering live blues every weekend. Vegas Lounge is run by the wife and sons of its late founder, known as Dr. Blues. Friday- and Saturday-night performances by the house ensemble, the Out of Town Blues Band, attract an eclectic crowd, from veteran blues fans to newer residents who don't know from Muddy Waters—drawn to the club out of sheer curiosity, or because it's a refreshing cultural and historical diversion in the neighborhood. ⊠ *1415 P St. NW, Logan Circle* ☎ *202/483–3971* ⊕ *www.newvegasloungedc.com* Ⓜ *Dupont Circle.*

ROCK AND POP
★ Black Cat
MUSIC CLUBS | Way before its stretch of 14th Street became the trendiest few blocks in town, the Black Cat was a destination for alternative music and quirky nostalgic dance parties. The venue is a host for midsize rock concerts and smaller, local acts focused on indie, alternative, and underground music, with favorites such as the Dandy Warhols, the Ravonettes, and Ex Hex. The Black Cat also regularly hosts artistic events, including comedy, edgy burlesque, and independent film nights. The postpunk crowd whiles away the time in the ground floor's Red Room, a side bar with pool tables, an eclectic jukebox, and no cover charge. The club is also home to Food for Thought, a legendary vegetarian café. ⊠ *1811 14th St. NW, U Street* ☎ *202/667–4490* ⊕ *www.blackcatdc.com* Ⓜ *U St./African-Amer Civil War Memorial/ Cardozo.*

DC9
MUSIC CLUBS | With live music most days of the week, this small two-story rock club with an upper deck hosts fledgling indie bands and the occasional nationally known act. There's a narrow bar on the ground floor, a sizable concert space on the second floor, and an enclosed roof deck on top. DJs take the controls for weekend-night dance parties. Concertgoers can enjoy snacks, sandwiches, and burgers every night and until 1 am on weekends. ⊠ *1940 9th St. NW, U Street* ☎ *202/483–5000* ⊕ *www.dcnine.com* Ⓜ *U St./African-Amer Civil War Memorial/ Cardozo.*

★ 9:30 Club
MUSIC CLUBS | The inimitable 9:30 Club is consistently ranked as one of the best concert venues in the country—as much a place in which bands aspire to play as it is a place that music fans love to patronize. The best indie and up-and-coming performers are the main attractions, though every now and then a bigger act such as Adele, Drake, Ed Sheeran, or Leon Bridges stop by to soak up the vibe of this large but cozy space wrapped by balconies on three sides. Once graced by legends such as Nirvana, Bob Dylan, and Johnny Cash, the venue is now a great spot for big labels looking for an intimate vibe. For its various music genres from country to pop, this venue has become one of the most attended clubs of its size. ■**TIP→ There are no bad views here, and the excellent sound system means you can stand anywhere for a great show experience.** ⊠ *815 V St. NW, U Street* ☎ *202/265–0930* ⊕ *www.930.com* Ⓜ *U St./African-Amer Civil War Memorial/ Cardozo.*

Velvet Lounge
MUSIC CLUBS | Squeeze up the narrow stairway, and check out the eclectic local and national bands that play at this unassuming, tiny neighborhood joint. In addition to performers ranging from indie mainstays to critically touted up-and-comers, the venue regularly hosts comedy and variety shows. ⊠ *915 U St. NW, U Street* ☎ *202/462–3213* ⊕ *www.velvet-loungedc.com* Ⓜ *U St./African-Amer Civil War Memorial/Cardozo.*

🎭 Performing Arts

With unique plays and intimate venues, the U Street corridor, Shaw, and Logan Circle have plenty of cultural experiences to choose from.

In the 1930s and 1940s, U Street was known for its classy theaters and jazz clubs. Throughout its history, U Street, known as the "Black Broadway," has witnessed iconic musicians such as Duke Ellington and Ella Fitzgerald perform in historic venues like the Howard Theatre. After decades of decline following the 1968 riots, the neighborhood has been revitalized, gentrifying at lightning speed while retaining a diverse mix of multi-ethnic young professionals and older, working-class African Americans. U Street resident and Associate Justice of the Supreme Court Sonia Sotomayor has said, "U Street is the East Village." At night, the neighborhood's club, bar, and restaurant scene comes alive. During the day the street scene is more laid-back, with more locals than tourists occupying the distinctive shops.

MAJOR VENUES
★ The Howard Theatre

MUSIC | Opened in 1910, the Howard Theatre continues to be a draw in Washington, D.C. Initially a venue to highlight African American artists, the Howard Theatre now hosts diverse performances, from '80s hard rock by Sebastian Bach of Skid Row to old-school hip-hop by Slick Rick to Puerto Rican reggae by Cultura Profética. Listed on the National Register of Historic Places in 1974, it has also hosted many American musical icons, from Duke Ellington to Ella Fitzgerald, in its intimate space. The theater closed in 1970 and reopened in 2012 after an extensive remodel. ✉ 620 T St. NW, U Street ☎ 202/803–2899 ⊕ thehowardtheatre.com Ⓜ Shaw–Howard U.

Lincoln Theatre

MUSIC | The Lincoln Theatre is a historical venue from 1922, back when Washington

natives Duke Ellington and Pearl Baily were joined by the likes of Ella Fitzgerald, Billie Holiday, Nat King Cole, and Louis Armstrong. Today, the 1,200-seat theater presents modern musical artists, including Kendrick Lamar, Hozier, and Billy Idol, as well as comedic performers like Demetri Martin, Tig Notaro, and Ilana Glazer. ✉ 1215 U St. NW, U Street ☎ 202/328–6000 ⊕ www.thelincolndc.com Ⓜ U St./African-Amer Civil War Memorial/Cardozo.

THEATER
★ Studio Theatre

THEATER | This multifaceted theater company, one of the city's busiest, produces an eclectic season of contemporary European and offbeat American plays in four spaces: the original Mead and Milton theaters, the newer 200-seat Metheny Theatre, and the experimental Stage 4. ✉ 1501 14th St. NW, Dupont Circle ☎ 202/332–3300 ⊕ www.studiotheatre.org Ⓜ Dupont Circle.

The In Series

MUSIC | Cabaret, experimental chamber opera, and Spanish musical theater (also known as zarzuela) are among the hallmarks of this company founded in 1982. Performances are held at Source, GALA Hispanic Theater, and the Atlas Performing Arts Center. ✉ 1835 14th St. NW, U Street ☎ 202/204–7763 ⊕ www.inseries.org.

Washington Stage Guild

THEATER | This company performs neglected classics as well as contemporary literary plays in the Undercroft Theatre of Mount Vernon Place United Methodist Church. In recent years, they have produced lesser-known works by Oscar Wilde and George Bernard Shaw. Contemporary plays such as Tryst by Karoline Leach and David Marshall Grant's Pen are also offered. ✉ 900 Massachusetts Ave. NW, Logan Circle ☎ 240/582–0050 ⊕ www.stageguild.org Ⓜ Dupont Circle.

🛍 Shopping

ANTIQUES AND COLLECTIBLES
★ GoodWood

ANTIQUES/COLLECTIBLES | It's described by its owners as an American mercantile and dry goods store, but when you open the door, you'll feel as if you've been invited into a friend's warm and inviting loft. Displays throughout the store beautifully showcase 19th-century antique furniture. You'll also discover leather goods; vintage mirrors and other decorative home items; men's and women's grooming products and perfumes from around the world; Peruvian alpaca and wool scarves; Swedish clogs; and comfortable dresses, sweaters, and tops from American and international designers. ⊠ 1428 U St. NW, U Street ☎ 202/986–3640 ⊕ www.goodwooddc.com Ⓜ U St./African-Amer Civil War Memorial/Cardozo.

BEAUTY/COSMETICS
Aesop Skincare

PERFUME/COSMETICS | Stop by the signature store, the first in the District, of this Australian skin-care company for effective and unique skin, hair, and fragrance products created using the finest-quality plant-based and laboratory-made ingredients. ⊠ 1924 8th St. NW, Space 110, Shaw ☎ 202/299–9435 ⊕ www.aesop.com Ⓜ Shaw–Howard U.

Le Labo

PERFUME/COSMETICS | In both its design and its products, the first D.C. brick-and-mortar location of this French-influenced New York perfumerie reflects the cool, indie vibe of the Shaw neighborhood. Preferring "soulful fragrances" to everyday perfumes, Le Labo's manifesto is to create luxurious, handcrafted, non-animal-tested scents for "passionate souls." Visit this unique shop, and take a whiff of best-sellers like Santal 33, Rose 31, Bergemote 22, and Thé Noir 29. ⊠ 1924 8th St. NW, No. 120, Shaw ☎ 202/986–0600 ⊕ www.lelabofragrances.com Ⓜ Shaw–Howard U.

CLOTHING
Bonobos

CLOTHING | This signature men's shop achieved its fame with comfortable, stylish pants. Shopping and shipping are made easy here: simply go into the guideshop, find your style and fit, and then have your finds shipped directly to you. You can make a one-hour appointment (with a complimentary beer), walk out without bags, and enjoy free shipping and returns. ⊠ 1924 8th St. NW, No. 123, Shaw ☎ 202/868–1210 ⊕ bonobos.com/guideshop Ⓜ Shaw–Howard U.

Current Boutique

CLOTHING | Don't be fooled by the new dresses in the front—this shop is a consignment shopper's dream. "Current" styles from brands such as Tory Burch, BCBG, Marc Jacobs, and Diane Von Furstenberg just might fit better when you buy them at a third of their original price. ⊠ 1809 14th St. NW, U Street ☎ 202/588–7311 ⊕ www.currentboutique.com Ⓜ U St./African-Amer Civil War Memorial/Cardozo.

Marine Layer

CLOTHING | This San Francisco–based retailer is known for its soft, eco-friendly, and durable T-shirts. The company's signature fabric, MicroModal, is made from beechwood pulp and woven into the product line for men and women. In addition to T-shirts, you'll find equally comfortable dresses, pants, outerwear, loungewear, sweaters, and hats. ⊠ 1627 14th St. NW, Logan Circle ☎ 202/864–6686 ⊕ www.marinelayer.com Ⓜ U St./African-Amer Civil War Memorial/Cardozo.

GIFTS
Cherry Blossom Creativei

BOOKS/STATIONERY | Although you can find modern, upscale stationery brands and office products here, what you should come for are the company's unique neighborhood maps, which are as colorful and creative as they are decorative and beautiful—certainly suitable for framing. In addition to maps of trendy District neighborhoods, look for those of New York, San Francisco, Chicago, and Baltimore. ✉ 2128 8th St. NW, Shaw ☎ 202/319–2979 ⊕ www.cherryblossomworkshop.com Ⓜ Shaw–Howard U.

★ Grand Cata

WINE/SPIRITS | Best friends Julio Robledo and Pedro Rodriguez teamed up to open this wine and spirits store focusing on small Latin American producers. You can find a rare Uruguayan Tannat or a fine Mexican sparkling wine. Not a wine drinker? Grand Cata also offers a wide selection of spirits, mostly from small-batch producers in Mexico and Spain, as well as craft beers. Don't forget the snacks: the selection here includes those from Rodriguez's native Puerto Rico. Wine- and food-centered books, cocktail bar accessories, and other musings make unique gifts. Check the shop's calendar for details on free wine tastings. ✉ 1550 7th St. NW, Shaw ☎ 202/525–5702 ⊕ www.grandcata.com.

Lee's Flower and Card Shop

FLOWERS | Sisters Stacie and Kristie Lee own the beloved U Street flower and card shop initially opened by their paternal grandparents in 1945. Aside from preparing flower arrangements for the District's many social events, they also provide cards and small potted plants, making it an ideal spot to grab a green gift for a local friend. ✉ 1026 U St. NW, U Street ☎ 202/265–4965 ⊕ www.leesflowerandcard.com.

Shinola

SPECIALTY STORES | Once a Studebaker showroom in the 1920s, this gorgeous shop is now one of Michigan-based Shinola's nationwide flagship stores. You'll find leather-band watches; supple leather bags, coats, and journals; elegant and classic silver, gold, and rose-gold jewelry designed by Pamela Love; home accessories; and yes, even bicycles. ✉ 1631 14th St. NW, U Street ☎ 202/470–0200

⊕ www.shinola.com ⊗ Closed Sun. and Mon. Ⓜ U St./African-Amer Civil War Memorial/Cardozo.

HOME FURNISHINGS
★ Miss Pixie's

HOUSEHOLD ITEMS/FURNITURE | The well-chosen collectibles—handpicked by Miss Pixie herself—include gorgeous textiles, antique home furnishings, lamps, mirrors, glass- and silverware, and artwork. The reasonable prices will grab your attention, as will the location, in an old car-dealer showroom. ✉ 1626 14th St NW, U Street ☎ 202/232–8171 ⊕ www.misspixies.com Ⓜ U St./African-Amer Civil War Memorial/Cardozo or Dupont Circle.

Zawadi

HOUSEHOLD ITEMS/FURNITURE | The name means "gifts" in Swahili, but you may want to buy the beautiful African art, textiles, home accessories, and jewelry for yourself. ✉ 1524 U St. NW, Suite 1, U Street ☎ 202/232–2214 ⊕ www.zawadiarts.com ⊗ Closed Mon. and Tues. Ⓜ U St./African-Amer Civil War Memorial/Cardozo.

Chapter 11

UPPER NORTHWEST

Updated by
Bob Carden

👁 Sights	🍴 Restaurants	🛏 Hotels	🛍 Shopping	🍸 Nightlife
★★★★☆	★★☆☆☆	★★☆☆☆	★★★★☆	★☆☆☆☆

NEIGHBORHOOD SNAPSHOT

TOP EXPERIENCES

■ **House Museums:** The Hillwood Estate, Museum and Gardens showcase cereal heiress Marjorie Merriweather Post's collection of Imperial Russian art and Fabergé eggs, as well as 25 gorgeous acres of formal French and Japanese gardens. Chagalls, Picassos, and Monets inside contrast with the architecture at the modernist Kreeger Museum.

■ **National Zoo:** Visit the giant pandas, lions, and other members of the animal kingdom while you enjoy a stroll outdoors.

■ **Shopping in Friendship Heights:** Once the closest thing D.C. had to Rodeo Drive, this area is still a great shopping destination but isn't as high-end anymore; sure, there are still loads of big names, including Cartier, Tiffany, and Saks Fifth Avenue, but now those upscale retailers are sharing equal billing with T.J. Maxx and H&M.

■ **U.S. Naval Observatory:** View the heavens through one of the world's most powerful telescopes (on Monday evening with a reservation).

■ **Washington National Cathedral:** Look for the Darth Vader gargoyle on the soaring towers of this landmark, then relax among the rosebushes in the Bishop's Garden. Concerts are held here, too.

GETTING HERE

Connecticut Avenue attractions, such as the zoo, are accessible from the Red Line Metro stops between Woodley Park–Zoo/Adams Morgan and Van Ness–UDC. The Friendship Heights bus travels north from Georgetown along Wisconsin Avenue and takes you to the National Cathedral.

Parking can be tricky along Massachusetts Avenue. It is more practical for good walkers to hoof it up the street or take Bus N2, N3, N4, or N6 between Dupont Circle and Friendship Heights. For more-outlying sights, driving or cabbing it may be the best way to visit.

PLANNING YOUR TIME

■ The area has plenty of restaurants and some sights but limited nightlife compared to other parts of the city. You may want to plan your zoo trip around daily programs, such as the small-mammal feeding. Animals are most active in the early morning and late afternoon. Sights can be far apart, so leave time for travel and parking, if necessary.

QUICK BITES

■ **Cava.** This fast-casual restaurant offers a variety of Greek and Mediterranean bowls and is open until 10. ✉ *4237 Wisconsin Ave. NW* ⊕ *www.cava.com* Ⓜ *Tenleytown–AU.*

■ **Rocklands Barbeque.** Stop in here for great barbecue that's tasty, fast, and reasonably priced (though not near a Metro station). ✉ *2418 Wisconsin Ave. NW* ⊕ *www.rocklands.com* Ⓜ *Woodley Park–Zoo/Adams Morgan.*

■ **Vace Italian Deli.** Great pizza (whole or by the slice) and subs are all fast and good. It's open most nights until 9. ✉ *3433 Connecticut Ave. NW* ⊕ *www.vaceitaliandeli.com* Ⓜ *Cleveland Park.*

The Upper Northwest corner of D.C. is predominantly residential and in many places practically suburban. There are several good reasons, however, to visit the leafy streets, including the National Zoo and National Cathedral.

If the weather is fine, spend an afternoon strolling through Hillwood Gardens or tromping through Rock Creek Park's many acres. You'll have to travel some distance to see multiple attractions in one day, but many sights are accessible on foot from local Metro stops.

Sights

Fort Reno Park

CITY PARK | At 429 feet above sea level, the highest point in Washington has been used in different eras as a Civil War fort, the site of telegraph and radio towers, and a reservoir. In 1864, Abraham Lincoln watched nearby as outnumbered Union troops defended the capital from a formidable Confederate advance led by General Early, in the only battle to take place in the capital. Today, the park is enjoyed by soccer players, dog-park regulars, and picnickers. Most of the Civil War–era earthworks are gone, and two curious faux-medieval towers, built in 1929, mark the reservoir site, which is not accessible to the public. Nonetheless, the park has an appealing city view and plenty of room to run around. A popular, free outdoor concert series takes place every summer featuring many of the area's most esteemed indie-rock acts, from Fugazi to Dismemberment Plan to Priests. ⊠ *Chesapeake St. NW at Nebraska Ave. NW, Upper Northwest* ☎ *202/895–6070 visitor information, 202/521–1493 summer concert info only* ⊕ *www.fortreno.com* Ⓜ *Tenleytown–AU.*

Glover-Archbold Park

NATIONAL/STATE PARK | Groves of beeches, elms, and oaks flourish at this 183-acre park, part of the Rock Creek system, which begins just west of Georgetown and ends, 3½ miles later, near Van Ness Street. Along the way you'll experience a stream valley with ancient trees and possible bird sightings. And chances are you'll have the trail mostly to yourself. ⊠ *Wisconsin Ave. at Van Ness St. NW, Upper Northwest* ⊕ *www.nps.gov/pohe/index.htm* Ⓜ *Tenleytown–AU.*

Hillwood Estate, Museum and Gardens

HOUSE | Long before the age of Paris Hilton, cereal heiress Marjorie Merriweather Post was the most celebrated socialite of the 20th century, famous for her fabulous wealth and beauty, as well as her passion for collecting art and creating some of the world's most lavish homes. Of these, the 25-acre Hillwood Estate, which Merriweather Post bought in 1955, is the only one now open to the public. The 36-room Georgian mansion, where she regularly hosted presidents, diplomats, and royalty, is sumptuously appointed, with a formal Louis XVI drawing room, private movie theater and ballroom, and magnificent libraries filled with portraits of the glamorous hostess and her family and acquaintances, as well as works from her rich art collection.

KEY
- Exploring Sights
- Restaurants
- Hotels

Upper Northwest

Sights ▼

1. Fort Reno Park E1
2. Glover-Archbold Park C6
3. Hillwood Estate, Museum and Gardens.........................J1
4. Kahlil Gibran Memorial Garden.................H7
5. The Kreeger Museum.............B7
6. President Lincoln's Cottage J1
7. Rock Creek Park J7
8. Smithsonian National Zoological Park J5
9. Washington National Cathedral F5

Restaurants ▼

1. The Avenue........................ G1
2. BlackSalt Fish Market & Restaurant...........................A8
3. Cafe of India E1
4. Comet Ping Pong G1
5. District Kitchen J6
6. Duke's Counter.....................I5
7. Le Chat Noir E1
8. Millie's................................A1
9. Parthenon Restaurant.............G1
10. Pete's New Haven Style Apizza E1
11. RNF..................................E1
12. St. Arnold's Mussel Bar............I3
13. Sushiko Chevy Chase E1
14. 2 Amys F4

Hotels ▼

1. Kimpton Glover Park Hotel F6
2. Omni Shoreham Hotel..............I6
3. Washington Marriott Wardman Park......................I6
4. Woodley Park Guest House I6

She was especially fascinated with Russian art, and her collection of Russian icons, tapestries, gold and silver work, and Fabergé eggs is considered to be the largest and most significant outside Russia. She devoted equal attention to her gardens; you can wander through 13 acres of them. Allow two to three hours to tour. ⊠ *4155 Linnean Ave. NW, Upper Northwest* ☎ *202/686–5807, 202/686–8500* ⊕ *www.hillwoodmuseum. org* 🎟 *$18 ($15 weekdays if purchased online)* ⊘ *Closed Mon.* Ⓜ *Van Ness–UDC.*

Kahlil Gibran Memorial Garden

CITY PARK | In a town known for political combat, this tiny urban park is a wonderful place to find some peace. The shady park combines Western and Arab symbols and is perfect for contemplation. From the Massachusetts Avenue entrance, a stone walk bridges a grassy swale. Farther on are limestone benches that are engraved with sayings from Gibran and that curve around a fountain and a bust of the namesake Lebanese-born poet, who emigrated to the United States at the turn of the 20th century and remains one of the best-selling poets of all time. The garden is near the grounds of the United States Naval Observatory and across from the British Embassy. ⊠ *3100 block of Massachusetts Ave. NW, Upper Northwest* ☎ *202/895–6000* 🎟 *Free* Ⓜ *Woodley Park–Zoo/ Adams Morgan or Dupont Circle.*

The Kreeger Museum

MUSEUM | The cool white domes and elegant lines of this Postmodern landmark stand in stark contrast to the traditional feel of the rest of the Foxhall Road neighborhood. Designed in 1963 by iconic architect Philip Johnson, the building was once the home of GEICO executive David Lloyd Kreeger and his wife, Carmen. Music is a central theme of the art and the space: the Kreegers wanted a showpiece residence that would also function as a gallery and recital hall. The art collection includes works by Renoir,

Degas, Cézanne, and Munch; African artifacts; and outstanding examples of Asian art. Especially stunning are the outdoor sculptures by Henry Moore, Leonardo Nierman, and others, including John L. Dreyfuss—six of his large-scale pieces surround the museum's reflecting pool. The domed rooms also have wonderful acoustics, and serve as an excellent venue for the classical concerts that are regularly performed here. The museum is not reachable by Metro; you need to take a car or taxi to get here. ⊠ *2401 Foxhall Rd. NW, Upper Northwest* ☎ *202/338–3552* ⊕ *www.kreegermuseum.org* 🎟 *$10, Sculpture Garden free* ⊘ *Closed Sun. and Mon.*

President Lincoln's Cottage

HOUSE | In June 1862, President Lincoln moved from the White House to this Gothic Revival cottage on the grounds of the Soldiers' Home to escape the oppressive heat of Washington and to grieve for the loss of his son Willie. Lincoln and his wife, Mary, lived in the cottage until November of that year, and because they found it to be a welcome respite from wartime tensions, they returned again during the summers of 1863 and 1864. Lincoln ultimately spent a quarter of his presidency at this quiet retreat; he was here just one day before he was assassinated. Considered the most significant historic site of Lincoln's presidency outside the White House, it was here that he developed the Emancipation Proclamation. Visitors may picnic on the cottage grounds, which have been landscaped to look as they did when Lincoln lived here. ∎TIP➔ **As you go up the hill toward the Cottage, there's a panoramic view of the city, including the Capitol dome. The 251-acre Soldier's Home sits atop the third-tallest point in D.C.** ⊠ *Armed Forces Retirement Home, 140 Rock Creek Church Rd. and Upshur St. NW, Petworth* ☎ *202/829–0436* ⊕ *www.lincolncottage. org* 🎟 *$15* Ⓜ *Georgia Ave.–Petworth.*

★ Rock Creek Park

NATIONAL/STATE PARK | FAMILY | The 1,800 acres surrounding Rock Creek have provided a cool oasis for visitors and D.C. residents ever since Congress set them aside for recreational use in 1890. The bubbling, rocky stream draws nature lovers to the miles of paved walkways. Bicycle routes, jogging and hiking paths, and equestrian trails wind through the groves of dogwoods, beeches, oaks, and cedars, and 30 picnic areas are scattered about. An asphalt bike path running through the park has a few challenging hills but is mostly flat, and it's possible to bike several miles without having to stop for cars (the roadway is closed entirely to cars on weekends). The most popular run in Rock Creek Park is along a trail that follows the creek from Georgetown to the National Zoo, about 4 miles round-trip. Rangers at the Nature Center and Planetarium introduce visitors to the park and keep track of daily events; guided nature walks leave from the center on weekends at 2. The park is open only during daylight hours. ⊠ *5200 Glover Rd. NW, Nature Center and Planetarium, Upper Northwest* ☎ *202/895–6070* ⊕ *www.nps.gov/rocr.*

★ Smithsonian National Zoological Park

ZOO | FAMILY | The Smithsonian's National Zoo features 1,800 animals, representing 300 species, in as close as you can get to their native surroundings. Arrive between 11 and 2 (weather permitting), and you can catch orangutans traversing the "O" line, a series of cables and towers near the Great Ape House that allow the primates to swing hand over hand about 35 feet above your head. The giant pandas, Tian Tian and Mei Xiang, have been the zoo's most famous residents since 2000; one of their cubs also resides here, and another was just born this past summer. They delight visitors of all ages. The zoo was designed by famed landscape architect Frederick Law Olmsted, who also designed New York's Central Park. Try visiting early morning or late afternoon, since many animals sleep midday. Nighttime visits are especially fun during the Thanksgiving and Christmas holidays as the zoo sparkles with the annual Zoo-Lights event. ⊠ *3001 Connecticut Ave. NW, Upper Northwest* ☎ *202/673–4800, 202/673–4717* ⊕ *nationalzoo.si.edu* ⊠ *Free* Ⓜ *Cleveland Park or Woodley Park–Zoo/Adams Morgan.*

★ Washington National Cathedral

RELIGIOUS SITE | Construction of the sixth-largest cathedral in the world began in 1907 with a rock from the village of Bethlehem and the structure has been the spiritual symbol of Washington ever since. Like its 14th-century Gothic counterparts, it has a nave, flying buttresses, transepts, and vaults, all built stone by stone. The stunning cathedral is Episcopalian, but it's the site of frequent interfaith services. State funerals for presidents Eisenhower, Reagan, and Ford as well as Senator John McCain were held here, and the tomb of Woodrow Wilson is on the south side of the grounds. The Pilgrim Observation Gallery provides a wonderful view of the city, and the cathedral is blessed with the lovely Bishop's Garden, with boxwoods, ivy, yew trees, and stone work from European ruins. In 2011, the cathedral sustained earthquake damage; restoration work is expected to continue for several years, but the cathedral remains open during the process. ⊠ *Wisconsin and Massachusetts Aves. NW, Upper Northwest* ☎ *202/537–6200, 202/537–6207 tour information* ⊕ *www.nationalcathedral.org* ⊠ *From $12* Ⓜ *Cleveland Park or Tenleytown–AU, then take any 30 series bus.*

🍴 Restaurants

After the requisite cooing over the pandas and other cuddly creatures at the National Zoo, consider wandering around this popular neighborhood, where you'll see plenty of locals eating, drinking, and playing. Many Hill staffers, journalists, and other inside-the-Beltway types live along this hilly stretch of Connecticut Avenue. Eateries and shops line the few blocks near each of the Red Line Metro stops. Eateries in Cleveland Park range from tiny takeout spots to upscale restaurants where you stand a good chance of spying your favorite Sunday-morning talk-show guests at a nearby table. International cuisines are abundant here, especially in Cleveland Park. Lined up along the stately stretch of modern row houses are diverse dining options ranging from Afghan to Thai.

The Avenue

$$ | AMERICAN | FAMILY | This inviting, all-American bar and restaurant is right near the D.C./Maryland border; brick and wood make the space feel cozy and warm. Seafood, sandwiches, and hefty salads highlight the menu. **Known for:** large outdoor patio; food truck with crab delicacies; multilevel establishment. ⑤ *Average main: $21* ✉ *5540 Connecticut Ave., Northwest* ✛ *A hike from Metro, if driving street parking is usually available* ☎ *202/244–4567* ⊕ *www.theavenuedc.com.*

BlackSalt Fish Market & Restaurant

$$$ | SEAFOOD | Just beyond Georgetown in the residential neighborhood of Palisades, BlackSalt is part fish market, part gossipy neighborhood hangout, part swanky restaurant. Fish offerings dominate, and vary from classics like oysters Rockefeller and fried Ipswich clams to more-offbeat fixings like cocoa-spiced big-eye tuna and a butterscotch *pot de crème* for dessert. **Known for:** fresh fish dishes; one of the best brunches in D.C.; brioche French toast. ⑤ *Average main: $33* ✉ *4883 MacArthur Blvd., Upper Northwest* ☎ *202/342–9101* ⊕ *www.blacksaltrestaurant.com* ⊗ *No lunch Mon.–Sat.*

Cafe of India

$$ | INDIAN | FAMILY | The menu at this traditional Indian restaurant features a few surprises, including an inventive shrimp and coconut masala, a local favorite. The dining room has an elegant feel, with long drapes, white tablecloths, and fine crystal. **Known for:** crackling spinach, shrimp, and coconut masala; extensive Indian beer and wine list; authentic Indian cuisine. ⑤ *Average main: $25* ✉ *4909 Wisconsin Ave., Tenleytown* ✛ *Tenleytown* ☎ *202/244–1395* ⊕ *www.cafeofindiadc.com* Ⓜ *Tenleytown.*

Comet Ping Pong

$ | PIZZA | FAMILY | Pizza (and beer) in the front, Ping-Pong (and foosball) in the back make this pizza joint a neighborhood favorite for folks of all ages. While you can make your own pizza (including one with a gluten-free crust) from almost three dozen toppings, you'll be well served opting for one of the kitchen's specialty pies. **Known for:** make-your-own pizzas with dozens of toppings; live music; sunrise pizza for brunch. ⑤ *Average main: $12* ✉ *5037 Connecticut Ave. NW, Upper Northwest* ☎ *202/364–0404* ⊕ *www.cometpingpong.com* ⊗ *No lunch Mon.–Thurs.* Ⓜ *Cleveland Park.*

District Kitchen

$$ | AMERICAN | FAMILY | The exposed brick and warm woods may signal upscale saloon, but District Kitchen is much more, offering an eclectic, farm-to-table menu featuring the restaurant's signature dish, a large and tasty bowl of paella. Sure, there are burgers, steaks, and the like, but also charcuterie, cheese plates, mussel plates, seared shrimp, and a load of fish dishes. **Known for:** monster signature paella dish; good seafood; nice beer selection. ⑤ *Average main: $20* ✉ *2606 Wisconsin Ave. NW, Woodley Park* ☎ *202/238–9408* ⊕ *www.districtkitchen.com* ⊗ *No lunch Mon.–Thurs.* Ⓜ *Woodley Park–Adams Morgan/Zoo.*

Duke's Counter

$ | BRITISH | FAMILY | A shabby-chic bar-restaurant directly across the street from the National Zoo has been deemed by one local paper to have the best burger in D.C. If it's not the best, it's close: a big, tasty patty made from charbroiled Angus beef that's on a pub menu with other continental options, including British breakfasts offered all day. **Known for:** excellent burgers; wide-ranging menu of sandwiches and small plates; small and busy (so get there early or wait). $ *Average main: $14* ⊠ *3000 Connecticut Ave., Northwest* ☎ *202/733–4808* ⊕ *www.dukescounter.com* Ⓜ *Woodley Park–Zoo/Adams Morgan.*

★ **Le Chat Noir**

$$$ | FRENCH | This unpretentious but intimate and stylish bistro recalls a Parisian café, with dark woods, white table cloths, and cozy tables—not to mention the owner himself is from Paris. The main floor has two dining rooms, one of which has floor-to-ceiling windows that open to the street when weather permits. **Known for:** classic French bistro; great date spot; alfresco dining feel. $ *Average main: $30* ⊠ *4907 Wisconsin Ave., Tenleytown* ☎ *202/244–2404* ⊕ *www.lechatnoirrestaurant.com* Ⓜ *Tenleytown.*

Millie's

$$ | AMERICAN | FAMILY | The menu at this classic neighborhood bar–restaurant concentrates on seafood, with both Cape Cod and Baja influences, bringing a coastal dining experience to the city with a winning formula. Look for cod, lobster rolls, fish tacos, and even panfried trout. **Known for:** inventive seafood; casual coastal atmosphere; takeout ice-cream counter. $ *Average main: $21* ⊠ *4866 Massachusetts Ave. NW, Northwest* ☎ *202/733–5789* ⊕ *www.milliesdc.com* Ⓜ *Tenleytown–AU.*

★ **Parthenon Restaurant**

$$ | GREEK | You can never have enough Greek restaurants, and Parthenon is among the best in town. This traditional Greek food, including great moussaka, pastitsio, salads, and grilled fish. **Known for:** traditional Greek cooking in a blue-and-white taverna setting; large portions; attached to Chevy Chase Lounge. $ *Average main: $25* ⊠ *5510 Connecticut Ave. NW, Upper Northwest* ☎ *202/966–7600*

⊕ *www.parthenon-restaurant.com* Ⓜ *Friendship Heights.*

★ **Pete's New Haven Style Apizza**

$ | PIZZA | FAMILY | Pete's is a Friendship Heights landmark, serving "New Haven-style" (thin crust, coal-fired) pizzas and offering an extensive toppings list. The spacious patio gives you enough room to spread out. **Known for:** white-clam pizza; chef-driven; locally owned. $ *Average main: $12* ⊠ *4940 Wisconsin Ave., Friendship Heights* ☎ *202/237–7383* ⊕ *www.petespizza.com* Ⓜ *Friendship Heights.*

RNF

$$ | FUSION | FAMILY | A new addition to the neighborhood, RNF (real nutritious food) went brick and mortar after two years as a catering company. Look for modern American fare, with dishes like crab cakes, wood-fired pizzas, and massive sea-bass fish sandwiches. **Known for:** inventive and healthy seafood; vegetarian options; sunny dining room. $ *Average main: $20* ⊠ *5534 Connecticut Ave., Northwest* ☎ *202/244–1208.*

St. Arnold's Mussel Bar

$$ | BELGIAN | FAMILY | A casual spot near the zoo, this Belgian restaurant offers loads of Belgian beers on tap, large plates of mussels and fries, and Belgian waffles for dessert. The restaurant has two levels, but the street level is much more inviting. **Known for:** great mussels and beer; outdoor dining in the summer; fun happy hour. $ *Average main: $18* ⊠ *3433 Connecticut Ave. NW, Cleveland Park* ☎ *202/621–6719* ⊕ *starnoldsmusselbar.com* Ⓜ *Cleveland Park.*

Sushiko Chevy Chase

$$ | JAPANESE | At the city's self-touted first raw-fish restaurant, the cuts are always ocean fresh, the cocktails fruity, and the presentations classic. Think blue crab topped with avocado and tuna crowned by jalapeño, while hot delicacies like melt-on-the-tongue fried tempura are always reliable. **Known for:** pioneer of the D.C. sushi scene; classic sushi

presentations; bread pudding with green tea mousse for dessert. $ *Average main: $24* ✉ *5455 Wisconsin Ave. NW, Chevy Chase* ☎ *301/961–1644* ⊕ *www.sushiko-restaurants.com* Ⓜ *Friendship Heights.*

★ 2 Amys

$$ | PIZZA | FAMILY | Call it the Brando of D.C. pizzerias, because this Neapolitan sensation has played godfather to a number of throne-stealing wood ovens elsewhere in town since it opened more than a decade ago. Simple recipes allow the ingredients to shine through and make the "wine bar" menu of small Italian plates as exemplary as the pies. **Known for:** authentic Neapolitan wood-fired pizza with a chewy crust; pancetta happy hour on Saturday; family-friendly (read: noisy) atmosphere. $ *Average main: $20* ✉ *3715 Macomb St. NW, Upper Northwest* ☎ *202/885–5700* ⊕ *2amyspizza. com* ▭ *No credit cards* ☉ *No lunch Mon.*

 # Hotels

Whether you travel north through Rock Creek Park on a scenic jaunt, head up Connecticut Avenue past the National Zoo, or take Wisconsin Avenue starting at the Washington National Cathedral, you see a diverse collection of prosperous neighborhoods with single-family homes, apartment high-rises, and shopping districts. These Upper Northwest communities won't have as many museums or as much history as the other parts of D.C., but they still have plenty of sights, movie theaters, and minimalls.

Kimpton Glover Park Hotel

$$ | HOTEL | In the heart of Embassy Row (and near Washington Cathedral and Dumbarton Oaks) is this Kimpton hotel and its beautifully decorated rooms with lovely views of the city. **Pros:** classic Kimpton service, charm, and extras; spacious rooms; great Italian restaurant. **Cons:** distance from Metro and Downtown; valet parking is $35 per day; hefty daily amenity fee. $ *Rooms from: $289*

✉ *2505 Wisconsin Ave. NW, Upper Northwest* ☎ *202/337–9700* ⊕ *www. gloverparkhotel.com* ᴥ *150 rooms* ⦿ *No meals* Ⓜ *Woodley Park–Zoo/Adams Morgan.*

★ Omni Shoreham Hotel

$$$$ | HOTEL | FAMILY | Since its opening in 1930, this elegant landmark overlooking Rock Creek Park, a Historic Hotel of America, has welcomed heads of state, U.S. politicians, and celebs like the Beatles, Judy Garland, and Bob Hope. **Pros:** historic property with gorgeous grounds and good views from many rooms; great pool and sundeck; walking/jogging trails through Rock Creek Park. **Cons:** not near major sights; noisy at times; extremely large. $ *Rooms from: $409* ✉ *2500 Calvert St. NW, Woodley Park, Upper Northwest* ☎ *202/234–0700, 800/834–6664* ⊕ *www.omnihotels.com* ᴥ *834 rooms* ⦿ *No meals* Ⓜ *Woodley Park–Zoo/Adams Morgan.*

Washington Marriott Wardman Park

$$$ | HOTEL | FAMILY | In a pleasant neighborhood, this is a good choice for families—kids will love the outdoor pool and the proximity to the pandas at the zoo—and is popular with groups. **Pros:** right next to Metro stop; light-filled sundeck and pool; pretty residential neighborhood with lots of restaurants. **Cons:** busy and hectic public areas; massive size; fee for in-room Wi-Fi. $ *Rooms from: $379* ✉ *2660 Woodley Rd. NW, Woodley Park, Upper Northwest* ☎ *202/328–2000, 800/228–9290* ⊕ *www.marriott.com* ᴥ *1152 rooms* ⦿ *No meals* Ⓜ *Woodley Park–Zoo/Adams Morgan.*

★ Woodley Park Guest House

$$ | B&B/INN | Experience the height of hospitality at this charming bed-and-breakfast on a quiet residential street near the zoo. **Pros:** close to Metro; excellent breakfast; friendly and welcoming hosts. **Cons:** some shared baths; limited privacy; no television. $ *Rooms from: $260* ✉ *2647 Woodley Rd. NW, Woodley Park, Upper Northwest* ☎ *202/667–0218,*

866/667–0218 ⊕ *www.dcinns.com* ⇦ *15 rooms* ⱺ *Free Breakfast* Ⓜ *Woodley Park–Zoo/Adams Morgan.*

 Performing Arts

Summer is when the performing arts come alive in Upper Northwest D.C. One of the city's gems is Carter Barron, an outdoor amphitheater in Rock Creek Park that offers a variety of musical and cinema events during August. Other venues include the refurbished Avalon Theatre, which features outstanding documentaries and hard-to-find independent films.

FILM
Avalon Theatre
FILM | FAMILY | This classic movie house from 1923 is D.C.'s only nonprofit film center. The theater offers a wide array of studio films and independent and foreign films, plus monthly showcases of the best in French, Israeli, Czech, and Greek cinema. The theater also offers programming for families and children. ✉ *5612 Connecticut Ave. NW, Upper Northwest* ☎ *202/966–6000 info line, 202/966–3464 box office* ⊕ *www.theavalon.org* Ⓜ *Friendship Heights.*

MUSIC
Washington National Cathedral
MUSIC | Concerts and recitals by visiting musicians augment the choral and church groups that frequently perform in this breathtaking cathedral. Recitals on the massive pipe organ are offered every Sunday afternoon, and the choir sings Evensong most weekdays around 5:30. Admission is frequently free. ✉ *Massachusetts and Wisconsin Aves. NW, Cathedral Heights, Upper Northwest* ⊹ *From Tenleytown–AU Metro station, take any 30 series bus south* ☎ *202/537–6207* ⊕ *www.nationalcathedral.org* Ⓜ *Tenleytown–AU.*

 Shopping

The major thoroughfare, Wisconsin Avenue, runs northwest through the city from Georgetown toward Maryland. It crosses the border in the midst of the Friendship Heights shopping district, which is also near Chevy Chase. It's at this border where you'll find the Chevy Chase Pavilion with retailers, including H&M, J.Crew, Marshalls, Nordstrom Rack, Old Navy, and World Market. Other chains like Anthropologie, Saks Fifth Avenue, and Bloomingdale's can be found at The Shops at Wisconsin Avenue and at Mazza Gallerie. This neighborhood also boasts stand-alone designer stores like Christian Dior, Jimmy Choo, Ralph Lauren, and Tiffany and Co. There are a few local gems in the surrounding area. Other neighborhoods in the District yield more interesting finds and offer more enjoyable shopping and sightseeing, but it's hard to beat Friendship Heights/Upper Northwest for sheer convenience and selection.

BOOKS
★ Politics and Prose
BOOKS/STATIONERY | After being bought by two former *Washington Post* reporters in 2011, this legendary independent continues the tradition of jam-packed author events and signings. In the downstairs coffee shop and wine bar, The Den, you can debate the issues of the day or read a book while enjoying a casual meal or snack. ✉ *5015 Connecticut Ave. NW, Upper Northwest* ☎ *202/364–1919* ⊕ *www.politics-prose.com* Ⓜ *Van Ness–UDC.*

CLOTHING
★ Catch Can
CLOTHING | Bright and breezy clothes made of mostly natural fibers, plus comfortable but playful shoes and funky rain boots, make casual wear as fun as it is practical. The owners' love of color continues with a sizeable collection of jewelry, greeting cards, housewares,

and soaps. ✉ *5516 Connecticut Ave. NW, Upper Northwest* ☎ *202/686–5316* ⊕ *www.catchcan.com* Ⓜ *Friendship Heights.*

Everett Hall

CLOTHING | D.C.'s own Everett Hall designs men's suits that are richly classic in their material and cutting-edge in their design, color, and sensibility. Starting at around $1,500, the suits appeal to professionals who want something unique. ✉ *Chevy Chase Pavilion, 5301 Wisconsin Ave. NW, Friendship Heights* ☎ *202/362–0191* ⊕ *www.everetthallboutique.com* Ⓜ *Friendship Heights.*

Julia Farr

CLOTHING | Women who lobby on Capitol Hill and lunch at the country club look to Julia for a professional and polished look. Decorated in soothing sea shades, her boutique carries classic styles from emerging and established designers. Farr also has her own fashion line of classic and elegant wardrobe staples including skirts, blouses, jackets, and dresses inspired by D.C.'s historical and cultural landmarks. And, since they're named after these landmarks, any item would make a beautifully practical souvenir. Appointments are welcomed. ✉ *5232 44th St. NW, Upper Northwest* ☎ *202/364–3277* ⊕ *www.juliafarrdc.com* Ⓜ *Friendship Heights.*

Tabandeh

CLOTHING | Located in the Mazza Gallerie, this avant-garde women's collection includes an expertly selected cache of Rick Owens tops and Ann Demeule-meester clothing, along with accessories including stunning leather belts and handbags. The jewelry pieces in the store are dazzling—rings, necklaces, earrings, and pendants made with precious and semiprecious stones from designers like Samiar 13 and Erickson Beamon—and are sure to add panache to your ward-robe. ✉ *5300 Wisconsin Ave. NW, Upper*

Northwest ☎ *202/966–5080* ⊕ *www. tabandehjewelry.com* Ⓜ *Friendship Heights.*

FOOD AND WINE

Calvert Woodley Fine Wines and Spirits

FOOD/CANDY | In addition to the excellent selection of wine and hard liquor, 200 kinds of cheese and other picnic and cocktail-party fare is on hand. The international offerings have made this a favorite pantry for embassy parties. ✉ *4339 Connecticut Ave. NW, Upper Northwest* ☎ *202/966–4400* ⊕ *www.calvertwoodley. com* Ⓜ *Van Ness–UDC.*

Rodman's Discount Foods and Drugstore

FOOD/CANDY | The rare store that carries wine, cheese, and space heaters, Rodman's is a fascinating hybrid of Target and Dean & DeLuca. The appliances are downstairs, the imported peppers and chocolates upstairs. ✉ *5100 Wisconsin Ave. NW, Upper Northwest* ☎ *202/363–3466* ⊕ *www.rodmans.com* Ⓜ *Friendship Heights.*

GIFTS

Le Village Marche

GIFTS/SOUVENIRS | This eclectic gift and home decor shop offers unique trinkets, soaps, cocktail napkins, and French cookware. Perfect for any Francophile, it has the feel of an upscale Parisian flea market. ✉ *3318 Wisconsin Ave., Northwest* ☎ *202/362–4444* ⊕ *www. levillagemarche.com* Ⓜ *Cleveland Park Station.*

Chapter 12

D.C. WATERFRONT

SOUTHWEST WATERFRONT, THE WHARF, SOUTHEAST, AND ANACOSTIA

Updated by
Claire Handscombe

 Sights
★★★★☆

 Restaurants
★★★★★

 Hotels
★★★★★

 Shopping
★★★★☆

 Nightlife
★★★★★

NEIGHBORHOOD SNAPSHOT

TOP EXPERIENCES

■ **The Wharf:** The newest spot on the District's waterfront offers many dining options at all price points, live music, seasonal events, and waterfront recreation.

■ **Pier at The Wharf:** From bench swings and boardwalks to paddleboards and a kids' park, the piers at The Wharf are the best places to experience the waterfront in D.C.

■ **The Yards:** The Yards offer miles of walking track along D.C.'s waterfront, a grassy area for picnics and concerts, first-class restaurants, D.C.'s first winery, and a wading pool for the kids.

■ **Music Venues:** The Anthem is the District's newest music venue and great for a night out, with its 6,000-person-capacity industrial space packed with the newest performers. Also, check out Union Stage and Pearl Street Warehouse at The Wharf.

■ **Dining:** Waterfront restaurants are among the best and newest in the District, with tons of different cuisines, styles, and price options. Be sure to reserve: they're also popular.

GETTING HERE

By road, Metro, or via the Potomac River, the Waterfront has many options for transportation. Take the Green Line directly to the Navy Yard–Ballpark station to put you right by The Yards and Nationals Stadium. The Waterfront station will put you a 10- to 15-minute walk from The Wharf. The round-trip SW Neighborhood Shuttle also runs daily between The Wharf and L'Enfant Plaza/VRE station, the National Mall, and L'Enfant Retail on 10th Street SW. The Wharf also has water-taxi service from Transit Pier, connecting to stops in Georgetown, Maryland's National Harbor, and Old Town Alexandria in Virginia. Check out The Wharf's website for hours of operation. Parking at the Waterfront can be limited and expensive, so keep that in mind before going, and expect heavy traffic on weekends. The Green Line continues on to Anacostia, but you can also reach the area by bicycle, bus, or even boat.

PLANNING YOUR TIME

■ Allow extra time if exploring any of the museums. If you are in the mood for a concert, check out the many venues. All the restaurants here are popular and busy, so make reservations. Most of the shops in the Waterfront are open daily and great if you have time to kill before a meal. If you want a sportier day, pack accordingly for getting in the Potomac or pool.

QUICK BITES

■ **Dolcezza.** When in need of coffee on The Wharf, pick up an Italian espresso and perhaps a gelato or pastry as well. ⊠ *99 District Sq. SW* ⊕ *dolcezzagelato.com* Ⓜ *Waterfront.*

■ **Milk Bar.** Stop in for delicious and unique desserts like "crack pie," cereal milk soft serve, or birthday cake like you've never seen. ⊠ *49 District Sq. SW* ⊕ *milkbarstore.com* Ⓜ *Waterfront.*

■ **Shake Shack.** The famous one-stop shop for all things burgers, fries, and shakes. ⊠ *975 Wharf St. SW* ⊕ *www.shakeshack.com* Ⓜ *Waterfront.*

The District has finally expanded the Waterfront with the Navy Yard and The Wharf, the two newest areas along the water.

World-class parks, waterfront recreation, convenient shopping, one-of-a-kind dining, two sports stadiums, and premier events are all part of Capitol Riverfront, a 500-acre neighborhood along the Anacostia River in Southeast D.C. that encompasses the Navy's oldest onshore outpost.

The Naval Yard is where you'll find the National Museum of the U.S. Navy; its west side is flanked by a waterfront boardwalk that is part of the Anacostia Riverwalk Trail, which is popular with cyclists, runners, and walkers. Watersports opportunities are also abundant along the boardwalk thanks to a 52-slip marina where you can rent kayaks, canoes, and paddleboards.

Sights

Some of the sights in this area are actually in the Navy Yard. To gain entrance, you'll need a government-issued photo ID (driver's license, passport card, or passport) if you are over 18.

Audi Field

SPORTS VENUE | Soccer is incredibly popular in the nation's capital, finding a major following among the international residents who miss the big matches of home, as well as families whose kids play the sport. In 2018, fans of Washington's Major League Soccer team, D.C. United, were wowed with the opening of Audi Field, an innovative, 20,000-seat stadium near the revitalized Southwest waterfront and just a few blocks from Nationals Park. In addition to 31 luxury suites, the facility boasts 500,000 square feet of on-site retail, office, and residential space. The team's 2018 acquisition of the international superstar Wayne Rooney has only fueled the excitement. ⊠ 100 Potomac Ave. SW, Southwest ☎ 202/587–5000 ⊕ www.dcunited.com/audi-field Ⓜ Navy Yard–Ballpark.

Congressional Cemetery

CEMETERY | Established in 1807 "for all denominations of people," this cemetery is the final resting place for such notables as U.S. Capitol architect William Thornton, Marine Corps march composer John Philip Sousa, Civil War photographer Mathew Brady, FBI director J. Edgar Hoover, and many members of Congress. Air Force veteran and gay rights activist Leonard Matlovich is also buried here under a tombstone that reads "When I was in the military, they gave me a medal for killing two men, and a discharge for loving one." The cemetery is about a 20-minute walk from the Capitol. You can take a self-guided tour year-round during daylight hours; pick up a map at the gatehouse or download one from the cemetery website. On Saturday from April through October, you can join a one-hour docent-led tour at 11 am; no reservations are required. Additionally, on the third Saturday of the month at 1 pm, there are often Civil War–themed tours. ⊠ 1801 E St. SE, Capitol Hill ☎ 202/543–0539 ⊕ www.congressionalcemetery.org Ⓜ Stadium–Armory or Potomac Ave.

D.C. Waterfront

KEY

- ● Exploring Sights
- ● Restaurants
- ● Quick Bites
- ● Hotels

0		1,000 ft
0		200 m

Frederick Douglass National Historic Site

GARDEN | Cedar Hill, the Anacostia home of abolitionist Frederick Douglass, was one of the first Black National Historic Sites that Congress designated. Douglass, a former slave born in 1818 who escaped to freedom and delivered rousing abolitionist speeches at home and abroad, resided here from 1877 until his death in 1895. The house, which has been meticulously restored and has a wonderful view of Washington across the Anacostia River, contains many of Douglass's belongings, including hundreds of books displayed on his custom-built bookshelves and Limoges china set on the family dining table. A short film on Douglass's life is shown at a nearby visitor center. Entry to the home requires participation in a 30-minute ranger-led tour, for which you must arrive 30 minutes in advance; reserve by phone or online (⊕ *www.recreation.gov*). ✉ *1411 W St. SE, Anacostia* ☎ *202/426–5961, 202/444–6777 museum tours* ⊕ *www. nps.gov/frdo* ⛴ *House $2; garden and visitor center free* Ⓜ *Anacostia*.

Kenilworth Park and Aquatic Gardens

GARDEN | Exotic water lilies, lotuses, hyacinths, and other water-loving plants thrive in this 8-acre sanctuary of quiet ponds, protected wetlands, and marshy flats, listed on the National Register of Historic Places. The gardens' wetland animals include turtles, frogs, beavers, spring azure butterflies, and dozens of species of birds, which may be seen along the 1.5-miles of walking trails.
■ TIP➜ **Visit in July for the peak lily bloom; 9 am is the best time to see early morning blossoms.** There's a tiny, child-friendly museum in the visitor center. Dogs are welcome but must be on a leash. The nearest Metro stop is a 10-minute walk away, but there is ample free parking. Exit gates are locked promptly at 4. ✉ *1550 Anacostia Ave., Anacostia* ⚓ *At Douglas St. NE* ☎ *202/692–6080* ⊕ *www. nps.gov/keaq* ⛴ *Free* Ⓜ *Deanwood*.

Nationals Park

SPORTS VENUE | Just over a decade ago, Nationals Park opened and brought new life to the Navy Yard area, where new bars and restaurants are constantly springing to life. The ballpark hosts 81 games per season, and while Nats fans come out in droves, the park isn't just for lovers of the game. Nationals Park was created to bring high-quality entertainment to the District and now has a reputation for some of the best outdoor concerts in the area, with past performances by Billy Joel, Bruce Springsteen, Elton John, Taylor Swift, the Eagles, and James Taylor. Whether you come for a game or concert, there are plenty of retail spaces and food-service venues like the Budweiser Terrace with its happy hour, a Ben's Chili Bowl, and Shake Shack. There are also activities and areas for children and families with the brand-new Kids Play Area and the state-of-the-art Nursing Mothers Lounge. ✉ *1500 S. Capitol St. SE, Southeast* ☎ *202/675–6287* ⊕ *www. mlb.com/was/ballpark/information* ⛴ *Tours $15 ($10 concessions)* Ⓜ *Navy Yard–Ballpark*.

Smithsonian Anacostia Community Museum

MUSEUM | FAMILY | A pioneer in the community museum movement, in a historically Black neighborhood in Southeast Washington, this museum examines the impact of contemporary social issues on urban communities, including environment, urban life, and encounters with other cultures. The engaging exhibitions employ video, art, crafts, and photography, along with dynamic public programs including musical performances, crafts workshops, and storytellers. The museum's striking facade features traditional African design elements: brickwork patterns evoke West African kente cloth, the concrete cylinders reference the stone towers of Zimbabwe, and diamond patterned adornments resemble those found on the adobe houses of Mali. The museum is near the Frederick Douglass

The District has more than one botanical garden. Kenilworth Park and Aquatic Gardens focuses on wetland flora and fauna and is on the National Register of Historic Places.

National Historic Site and Kenilworth Aquatic Gardens. There's free on-site parking. ⊠ *1901 Fort Pl. SE, Anacostia* ☎ *202/633–4820, 202/633–4844 group tours* ⊕ *anacostia.si.edu* 🚇 *Free* Ⓜ *Anacostia, then Bus W2/W3.*

U.S. Navy Museum

MUSEUM | The history of the U.S. Navy, from the Revolution to the present, is chronicled here, with exhibits ranging from the fully rigged foremast of the USS *Constitution* (better known as *Old Ironsides*) to a U.S. Navy Corsair fighter plane hanging from the ceiling. All around are models of fighting ships, a real Vietnam-era Swift boat, working periscopes, and displays on famous naval battles along with portraits of the sailors who fought in them. In front of the museum is a collection of guns, cannons, and missiles. The **Navy Art Collection,** including many works by Navy artists, is also housed in the museum. Explore the **Cold War Gallery** in Building 70 with

exhibits that explore the Navy's response to the threat of Soviet military power and communist ideology. ⚠ **All visitors to the museum must have a valid photo ID and report to the Visitor Control Center (VCC) at the Washington Navy Yard's primary access gate at 11th and O Streets. The VCC is only open weekdays until 3:30 pm. If you're planning to visit the museum on the weekend, you must be prevetted. A Base Access Pass Registration must be submitted at least seven days before your visit. Call 202/433–3018 for access-related questions.** ⊠ *Navy Yard, 805 Kidder Breese St. SE , Bldg. 76, Southeast* ⊹ *Enter through visitor gate at 11th and O Sts. SE and show valid photo ID; you'll receive a pass and map of surroundings* ☎ *202/685–0589 museum, 202/433–4882 USS Barry* ⊕ *www.history. navy.mil* 🚇 *Free* Ⓜ *Eastern Market or Navy Yard–Ballpark.*

🍴 Restaurants

Some great new restaurants have opened in The Wharf to supplement the area's other dining spots. Many of these eateries are particularly popular on game days.

Agua 301 Restaurant

$$ | **MEXICAN** | You'll be impressed by the modern approaches to traditional Mexican food at this restaurant, which aims to be more than a simple neighborhood Tex-Mex joint. More-conventional tacos and empanadas stand beside an innovative Mexican-inflected take on paella, and lighter options include ceviche, soups, salads, and *bocaditos* (little bites to accompany your drinks). **Known for:** modern Mexican cuisine; great empanadas and tacos; extensive mezcal and tequila list. ⑤ *Average main: $20* ✉ *Yards Park, 301 Water St. SE, Southeast* ☎ *202/484–0301* ⊕ *www.agua301. com* Ⓜ *Navy Yard–Ballpark.*

★ All-Purpose Pizzeria

$$ | **ITALIAN** | "Best pizza in DC" is a hotly contested title, but All-Purpose Pizzeria down on the Capitol Riverfront is a strong contender. Its whole wheat dough is carefully made with high-quality ingredients, and you'll find a mix of classic and intriguing choices like chili-roasted corn, chili-lime aioli, or truffle honey. **Known for:** riverfront rooftop; Italian antipasti dishes; Italian-style cocktails. ⑤ *Average main: $20* ✉ *79 Potomac Ave. SE, D.C. Waterfront* ☎ *202/629–1894* ⊕ *allpurposedc. com* Ⓜ *Navy Yard–Ballpark.*

The Arsenal at Bluejacket

$$ | **CONTEMPORARY** | Most restaurants pair beer with food, but here you'll find the opposite: the refined but hearty new American fare is designed to complement the ten brews on tap. If you're not sure whether an herbal saison or the spicy fruit of a Scotch ale would go best with a bone-in beef short rib in a Kansas City rub, don't be afraid to ask the gracious cast of servers. **Known for:** in-house brewery that produces excellent speciality beer; industrial vibe; fantastic Sunday brunch. ⑤ *Average main: $25* ✉ *300 Tingey St. SE, D.C. Waterfront* ☎ *202/524–2862* ⊕ *www.bluejacketdc. com.*

★ Chloe

$$ | **INTERNATIONAL** | Successfully balancing casual with sophisticated and local with upscale, this is the perfect neighborhood restaurant, and its inclusion in the Michelin Guide is further proof. Chef Haidar Karoum, previously at Proof, Estadio, and Doi Moi, traces a delicious personal culinary journey at Chloe, with dishes from across the globe that are served with noteworthy flair. **Known for:** seasonal, internationally inspired small plates; superb desserts; sophisticated yet casual dining experience. ⑤ *Average main: $25* ✉ *1331 4th St. SE, D.C. Waterfront* ☎ *202/313–7007* ⊕ *restaurantchloe. com* 🕐 *No lunch weekdays* Ⓜ *Navy Yard–Ballpark.*

Colada Shop

$ | **CUBAN** | There was great excitement in summer 2020, when the second Colada Shop opened, an extension of its very popular first branch in Northwest D.C. Its breakfast menu, in particular, is extensive and appealing, bringing a Cuban twist to familiar sounding offerings and offering a wide variety of coffees, including café con leche and café bonbon, made with condensed milk. **Known for:** wide range of great coffee; Cuban twist on breakfast; great empanadas. ⑤ *Average main: $12* ✉ *10 Pearl St. SW, D.C. Waterfront* ☎ *202/932–2980* ⊕ *coladashop.com* Ⓜ *Waterfront.*

Del Mar

$$$$ | **SPANISH** | The newest concept by celebrated chef Fabio Trabocchi celebrates coastal Spain with authentic seafood, tapas, paella, aged charcuterie, and fresh meats. Start your meal in this elegant yet fun restaurant with a

seasonal gin and tonic made with house-mixed tonics and additions. **Known for:** traditional Spanish cuisine emphasizing seafood; large menu of mostly shareable plates; elegant dining experience. $ *Average main: $36* ⊠ *791 Wharf St. SW, D.C. Waterfront* ☎ *202/525–1402* ⊕ *www.delmardc.com* ⊗ *Closed Mon. and Tues.* Ⓜ *Waterfront.*

Due South

$$ | **AMERICAN** | If you are looking for good renditions of Southern cuisine with flavorful, modernist twists, you'll feel at home here. You can't go wrong with the blackened catfish po-boy and a side of stewed tomato and okra, and definitely don't skip out on dessert, often served with handmade ice cream from the shop next door. **Known for:** buttermilk fried chicken; shrimp and grits; frosé. $ *Average main: $22* ⊠ *301 Water St. SE, Southeast* ☎ *202/479–4616* ⊕ *duesouthdc.com* Ⓜ *Navy Yard–Ballpark.*

Hank's Oyster Bar

$$ | **AMERICAN** | The decor and the "urban beach food," with such classics as fried oysters and delicious crab cakes, will transport you to New England; for those who don't like fish, there is tropical jerk chicken, molasses-braised short ribs, or Mediterranean couscous. One of several locations in the metro area created by chef Jamie Leeds, The Wharf location is the biggest Hank's yet and offers both indoor and outdoor seating for the full waterfront effect. **Known for:** New England seafood and decor; waterfront views for happy hour; seasonal seafood and cocktails. $ *Average main: $21* ⊠ *701 Wharf St. SW, D.C. Waterfront* ☎ *202/817–3055* ⊕ *hanksoysterbar.com* Ⓜ *Waterfront.*

Kaliwa

$$ | **ASIAN FUSION** | One of the more unique culinary experiences at The Wharf, Kaliwa offers an Asian-fusion style incorporating tastes from the Philippines, Korea, and Thailand, all cooked in an open kitchen that may make you feel like you're in an Asian street market. The menu includes everything from cold, sushi-type small plates to full-on spicy Thai-style curries. **Known for:** Asian-style street food; dishes drawing from three distinct Asian cuisines; fun drinks. $ *Average main: $25* ⊠ *751 Wharf St. SW, D.C. Waterfront* ☎ *202/516–4739* ⊕ *www.kaliwadc.com* Ⓜ *Waterfront.*

Kith/Kin

$$ | **CARIBBEAN** | If you want great waterfront views while enjoying unique food, you won't do better than Kith/Kin, a hot spot of recent years inspired by Afro-Caribbean culture and located within the upscale InterContinental hotel. Don't let the simplified menu fool you: it boasts such disparate dishes as Trinidadian goat curry or Brussels suya cooked in West African spices. **Known for:** Afro-Caribbean food; great outdoor seating arrangement; handcrafted cocktails. $ *Average main: $18* ⊠ *801 Wharf St. SW, D.C. Waterfront* ☎ *202/878–8600* ⊕ *kithandkindc.com* Ⓜ *Waterfront.*

Mi Vida

$$ | **MEXICAN** | Spanning two floors and with waterfront patio seating, Mi Vida is good whether you are looking for a popular happy hour or a full meal in the heart of The Wharf. The menu is Mexican, focusing on home cooking and street food, prepared in a more modern style and served alongside an expansive list of mezcals and tequilas, as well as the signature mango margarita with ginger, agave, lime, and passion fruit. **Known for:** frozen mango margarita; great happy hour; fantastic views. $ *Average main: $24* ⊠ *98 District Sq. SW, D.C. Waterfront* ☎ *202/516–4656* ⊕ *mividamexico.com* Ⓜ *Waterfront.*

★ Osteria Morini

$$$ | **ITALIAN** | The stylish design and superlative pastas of this take on cuisine from northern Italy's Emilia-Romagna region might seem like an unexpected

match for the sports fans flocking to Nationals Park. But you can't ask for a better way to cap off a day at the ballpark than the wood-grilled meats here. **Known for:** prosciutto, mortadella, and wood-grilled meats; pleasant patio location close to the water; proximity to the baseball stadium. $ *Average main: $32* ⊠ *301 Water St. SE, Southeast* ☎ *202/484–0660* ⊕ *osteriamorini.com* Ⓜ *Navy Yard–Ballpark.*

★ Shilling Canning Company

$$$ | AMERICAN | Shilling Canning takes pride in the quality of its fresh, locally sourced ingredients, and it shows. The Shilling family hails from Baltimore, where they were known for their positive values and respect for the community, as well as their excellent food products—chef Shilling and his team are clearly devoted to honoring the family legacy with a similar ethos. **Known for:** great customer service; a pleasant patio; upscale, locally sourced food. $ *Average main: $35* ⊠ *360 Water St. SE, D.C. Waterfront* ☎ *202/554–7474* ⊕ *shillingcanning.com* Ⓜ *Navy Yard–Ballpark.*

Toastique

$ | AMERICAN | Aptly named, this little spot serves all things on toast, including an avocado smash (with marinated tomatoes and radishes, it's the hands-down favorite), the PB Crunch (with bananas, strawberries, and granola), and a tomato burrata (also with herbed ricotta, basil, and a balsamic glaze). But the restaurant is not created from bread alone; you'll also find a variety of juices, smoothies, and fruit bowls. **Known for:** gourmet toasts; cold-pressed juices; refreshing smoothies. $ *Average main: $12* ⊠ *764 Main Ave. SW, D.C. Waterfront* ☎ *202/484–5200* ⊕ *www.toastique.com* Ⓜ *Waterfront.*

Coffee and Quick Bites

Dolcezza

$ | ITALIAN | With nearly 10 locations, plus the original factory near Gallaudet University, this local chain has become a District favorite for gelato. The new Wharf branch is one of the largest, with full-fledged breakfast offerings in addition to award-winning gelato and ample seating outside in a great people-watching spot. **Known for:** Italian gelato; great coffee; Southern-style breakfast. $ *Average main: $10* ⊠ *99 District Sq. SW, D.C. Waterfront* ☎ *202/414–7595* ⊕ *dolcezzagelato.com/locations/wharf* Ⓜ *Waterfront.*

Hotels

The Waterfront is by far one of the most interesting areas in which to stay right now, with spectacular views, unique and sophisticated dining, and plenty of water and outdoor activities to keep you busy. There is also great nightlife here, with lots of bars and hip music venues. All of the hotels are very new and chic, as well as conveniently located for the Waterfront and National Mall.

Canopy by Hilton Washington DC The Wharf

$$ | HOTEL | FAMILY | At the forefront of the Wharf's revitalized hospitality scene, this new concept hotel by Hilton offers stylish rooms with rustic barn doors, a cool tan-and-beige palette, and plenty of extras. **Pros:** most rooms have water views; fun rooftop bar; convenient location. **Cons:** no pool; shared space with Hyatt House; can be loud at night. $ *Rooms from: $250* ⊠ *975 7th St. SW, D.C. Waterfront* ☎ *202/488–2500* ⊕ *canopy3.hilton.com* ⇥ *175 rooms* ⏐⏐ *Free Breakfast* Ⓜ *Waterfront.*

Courtyard Washington Capitol Hill/Navy Yard

$$ | HOTEL | Just a block from a Metro station and within walking distance to Nationals Park, this is a smart choice for

budget-savvy travelers. **Pros:** good value; popular bar; close to Metro. **Cons:** popular with groups, so some nights may be noisy; parking in nearby garage is expensive; restaurants in area can be busy. ⑤ *Rooms from: $199 ⊠ 140 L St. SE, Navy Yard, D.C. Waterfront ☎ 202/479–0027 ⊕ www.marriott.com ⇄ 204 rooms* ⑽ *No meals* Ⓜ *Navy Yard–Ballpark.*

Hyatt House Washington DC/The Wharf

$$$ | **HOTEL** | Just above the hubbub of The Wharf waterfront, the new Hyatt House offers a convenient location with some welcome amenities, including a pool and family-sized suites with kitchenettes. **Pros:** family-friendly setup; convenient location; outdoor pool. **Cons:** the area can be noisy; shared spaces with Canopy Hotel; restaurants can be very busy. ⑤ *Rooms from: $339 ⊠ 725 Wharf St. SW, D.C. Waterfront ☎ 202/554–1234 ⊕ hyatt.com ⇄ 237 rooms* ⑽ *Free Breakfast* Ⓜ *Waterfront.*

InterContinental Washington D.C.–The Wharf

$$$ | **HOTEL** | Styling itself as an urban resort, D.C.'s new InterContinental offers spacious, modern rooms and a dazzling, soaring, wood-and-stone. open-atrium lobby with floor-to-ceiling windows looking out over the river. **Pros:** fantastic rooms with great views; central location; unique spa and pool. **Cons:** area can be loud at night; restaurants in area can be very busy; no meals included. ⑤ *Rooms from: $329 ⊠ 801 Wharf St. SW, D.C. Waterfront ☎ 202/800–0844 ⊕ www.intercontinental.com ⇄ 284 rooms* ⑽ *No meals* Ⓜ *Waterfront.*

Ⓨ Nightlife

This increasingly busy area is starting to become a place to go after dark.

BARS AND LOUNGES
The Brighton SW1

BARS/PUBS | The Brighton is like a bigger and more modern version of your local neighborhood pub. Offering a massive British footprint on The Wharf, this sprawling space has a huge bar, outside seating, and even a second floor called the Lookout Lounge. Next door to the Anthem, it's particularly popular on weekends and after a show. Sip any of the dozen beers on draft, from sours to darks, feel free to ask the server for a cocktail, or have a glass of frosé or another of the myriad frozen drinks. The pub-theme food menu is chockablock full of British classics like chicken curry and fish-and-chips. ⊠ *949 Wharf St. SW, D.C. Waterfront ☎ 202/735–5398 ⊕ www.brighton-dc.com* Ⓜ *Waterfront.*

Cantina Bambina

BARS/PUBS | Above the Anthem's box office and Water Taxi's ticket office—and just across from the music venue—this ultracasual bar and snack bar has become a favorite of Wharf area concert-goers as well as those just looking for a drink and some spectacular views. Feast your eyes on the long margarita and cocktail list, and grab some small bites at the bar stand downstairs. It gets busy here, so expect to stand during your visit, but that just makes it easier to take in the waterfront views. ⊠ *960 Wharf St. SW, D.C. Waterfront ⊕ www.cantinabambina.com* Ⓜ *Waterfront.*

District Winery

WINE BARS—NIGHTLIFE | D.C.'s first-ever winery is a unique spot in the heart of The Yards, serving all locally made, small-batch wines that can be paired with dishes in its new full-service restaurant, Ana. Tour the winery to learn how head winemaker Conor McCormack produces his vintages, enjoy a tasting, and then indulge in a meal overlooking the Anacostia River. The menu at Ana consists of tapas-style small bites, with dinner on weekdays and brunch on weekends. The winery also hosts weddings and offers a date-night package for the romantically inclined. ⊠ *The Yards, 385 Water St. SE, Southeast ☎ 202/484–9210 ⊕ districtwinery.com* Ⓜ *Navy Yard–Ballpark.*

Kirwan's Irish Pub

BARS/PUBS | With authentic decor, music, and booze, this pub is about as Irish as it gets in the District. Started by a former Guinness employee, Kirwan's is the place to bask in live traditional music with a good pint on real Irish furniture or at the carved bar. There is plenty of space here with two floors and a full restaurant if you want a good Irish meal before the nightlife takes over. ⊠ *Canopy by Hilton Washington DC The Wharf, 749 Wharf St. SW, D.C. Waterfront* ✛ *Below hotel, which sits above ground level* ☎ *202/554–3818* ⊕ *www.kirwansonthewharf.com* Ⓜ *Waterfront.*

Mission

BARS/PUBS | With two floors, a gigantic 150-foot bar, and 600 feet of outdoor balconies, Mission is easily the city's roomiest spot for pregame or post-work get-togethers. There's both a daily happy hour as well as a late-night happy hour from 10 to close Thursday through Sunday. Stop in for a glass of wine, beer, Tito's, or even a house margarita, all on tap, and some traditional Mexican mixed with Tex-Mex food. Weekends feature bottomless margaritas and guacamole. ⊠ *1221 Van St. SE, Southeast* ☎ *202/810–7010* ⊕ *missionnavyyard.com* Ⓜ *Navy Yard–Ballpark.*

Whiskey Charlie

BARS/PUBS | You may have to search a bit to find this bar, but walk through the lobby of the Canopy by Hilton, head up to the roof in the special elevator, and you'll find a waterfront vista like no other in the city. Munch on some light bites, and choose from the well-curated menu of craft cocktails (go for the Mermaid margarita), all while enjoying a view that stretches from the Capitol building to the Pentagon, or sit inside with floor-to-ceiling windows and sophisticated decor. ⊠ *975 7th St. SW, D.C. Waterfront* ☎ *202/488–2500* ⊕ *whiskeycharliewharf.com* Ⓜ *Waterfront.*

MUSIC CLUBS

The Anthem

MUSIC CLUBS | The coolest new music venue in D.C. made its home at the helm of The Wharf—and made a splash with the music world's biggest indie and alternative rock acts, even presenting Foo Fighters on opening night. The first midsize venue of its kind in the District (there's a max of 6,000) feels vast and industrial but has elegant design touches, as well as specially angled seats that preclude bad sightlines. Enjoy beer on tap or in the can, cocktails, and homemade Belgian waffles ("Wharfles") before or during the show in the open-air Marquee Bar upstairs (it's also open when there's no performer). ⊠ *901 Wharf St. SW, D.C. Waterfront* ☎ *202/888–0020* ⊕ *www.theanthemdc.com* Ⓜ *Waterfront.*

Pearl Street Warehouse

MUSIC CLUBS | The 1950s diner-inspired space may make you feel as if you were in New Orleans or Nashville, but walk through a garage door, and you'll find an intimate, modern (there are plugs under the bar to recharge your phone), and lively entertainment space for small bands. The diner serves breakfast on weekends and stays open even if shows are going on. A bar links the performance space to the outside alleyway. You don't always have to buy a ticket to enjoy the music and drinks offered here; some nights, you can just sit at the bar and bask in the musical glory. All seating is first-come, first-served, and some shows sell out. The restaurant is open Monday through Wednesday from 3 to midnight and Thursday through Sunday from 8:30 to midnight. ⊠ *33 Pearl St. SW, D.C. Waterfront* ☎ *202/380–9620* ⊕ *www.pearlstreetwarehouse.com* Ⓜ *Waterfront.*

Union Stage

MUSIC CLUBS | This unique live music venue is also a popular spot in the neighborhood for pizza, beer, and seasonal cocktails. The Tap Room bar serves 16 beers on tap and 16 in cans, as well as good cocktails, wine, and soft drinks. Downstairs is the music and another bar. Performances here may be by emerging or established talent, but it's an intimate space with exceptional sound and lighting. Even when there's no show, people come in to grab a now-famous Jersey-style pizza with a variety of toppings. Another pizza takeout window is across from the Anthem on Wharf Street. ⊠ *740 Water St. SW, D.C. Waterfront* ☎ *877/987–6487* ⊕ *www.unionstage. com* Ⓜ *Waterfront.*

🎫 Performing Arts

★ Arena Stage

THEATER | The first regional theater company to win a Tony Award performs innovative American theater, reviving such classic plays as *Oklahoma* and also showcasing the country's best new playwrights. The architecturally magnificent Mead Center for American Theatre houses three stages and, after the Kennedy Center, is the second-largest performing arts complex in Washington. Near the Waterfront neighborhood in Southwest D.C., the Mead Center features the Fichandler Stage, a theater-in-the-round seating 680; the Kreeger Theater, a modified thrust seating 514; and the Kogod Cradle, a 200-seat black-box theater for new or experimental productions. ■TIP➔ **Inside the Mead, the Richard's Place Café serves meals inspired by the shows playing that evening.** ⊠ *1101 6th St. SW, Southwest* ☎ *202/554–9066* ⊕ *www.arenastage.org* Ⓜ *Waterfront.*

🛍 Shopping

BOOKS
Politics and Prose

BOOKS/STATIONERY | The second of three locations of this well-loved local institution is a go-to shop for travelers staying at nearby hotels or for anyone, really, who wants something good to read while seated on one of The Wharf's many piers. This branch has all the books you could need, as well as ample room to browse or listen to a speaker at an event. It's also a great place to pick up classy D.C.-themed gifts and notecards. Store hours are 10–8 Tuesday through Sunday and 11–7 on Monday. ⊠ *70 District Sq. SW, D.C. Waterfront* ☎ *202/488–3867* ⊕ *www.politics-prose.com/wharf* Ⓜ *Waterfront.*

CLOTHING
A Beautiful Closet

CLOTHING | Step into A Beautiful Closet for fair-trade international goods, including jewelry, clothing, home decor, and accessories. All items here are curated by former World Bank staff member Pamela Sofola. If you're in a rush or just can't decide what to buy, request a personalized styling consultation. ⊠ *20 District Sq. SW, D.C. Waterfront* ☎ *202/488–1809* ⊕ *abeautifulclosetdc.com* Ⓜ *Waterfront.*

GIFTS
Steadfast Supply

JEWELRY/ACCESSORIES | Steadfast is the place to get small, unique District gifts. The store carefully curates its inventory from local small businesses and displays each designer's name and story so you know who you're buying from. It's a fun, lively spot filled with items from over 100 brands, and there's also classroom space for calligraphy and other creative workshops, as well as areas and gifts geared to children. ⊠ *301 Tingey St. SE, #140, Washington* ⊹ *Entrance on Water St.* ☎ *202/308–4441* ⊕ *www.steadfast-supplydc.com* Ⓜ *Navy Yard–Ballpark.*

Willow

JEWELRY/ACCESSORIES | Willow is just across the waterfront and a perfect spot to shop before a meal or ballgame with its boutique clothing, jewelry, and gifts. Willow designs its own glassware and a few other small items in-house, while other cards, gifts, and plants are sourced through local companies. There's a great collection of baby items here, too. ✉ *1331 4th St. SE, Southeast* ☎ *202/643–2323* ⊕ *www.willowstores. com* Ⓜ *Navy Yard–Ballpark.*

HOME FURNISHINGS
Patrick's Fine Linens & Home Décor
HOUSEHOLD ITEMS/FURNITURE | Patrick's is a well-known source in Alexandria for upscale furniture, home decor, dishes, and perfumes; its first branch is now open at The Wharf. Complement your home with top-notch dinnerware and other designer goods from Hermès China, Juliska, Vista Alegre, and Ralph Lauren, among others. Pick up a bottle of perfume or cologne by Carthusia, C.O. Bigelow, or Santa Maria Novella, or take home a luxury candle from LAFCO, NEST, or Thymes. ✉ *771 Wharf St. SW, D.C. Waterfront* ☎ *202/601–7296* ⊕ *www. patricksdesigns.com* Ⓜ *Waterfront.*

JEWELRY
Diament Jewelry
JEWELRY/ACCESSORIES | Diament Jewelry is a unique treasure trove of vintage and handmade jewelry, along with gifts and accessories from local makers. The neatly displayed clothing, candles, paper goods, and accessories lend a high-class feel to this neat, floral-inspired boutique. A large inventory of vintage rings, bracelets, and necklaces invites you to dig for your next favorite treasure, with options ranging from inexpensive bracelets to pricey, one-of-a-kind diamond rings. Follow the shop on Instagram for the owner's latest finds. ✉ *33 District Sq. SW, D.C. Waterfront* ☎ *347/868–7150* ⊕ *www.diament-jewelry.com* Ⓜ *Waterfront.*

SPORTING GOODS
Pacers Running
SPORTING GOODS | Pacers Running is a perfect fit for the Navy Yard, selling sports and running gear to the Yard's ever-active, outdoorsy clientele. You can get specialty footwear, running togs, and lifestyle gear, as well as active and injury-prevention accessories. ✉ *300 Tingey St. SE , No. 160, Southeast* ☎ *202/554–1216* ⊕ *www. runpacers.com* Ⓜ *Navy Yard–Ballpark.*

Chapter 13

ARLINGTON

WITH NORTHERN VIRGINIA

Updated by
Delesia Watson

⊙ Sights
★★★★☆

🍽 Restaurants
★★☆☆☆

🛏 Hotels
★★☆☆☆

👜 Shopping
★★★★☆

🍸 Nightlife
★☆☆☆☆

NEIGHBORHOOD SNAPSHOT

TOP EXPERIENCES

■ **Arlington National Cemetery:** The most visited cemetery in the country is the final resting place for more than 400,000 Americans, from unknown soldiers, 4,000 Black Americans who were former slaves, to John F. Kennedy and his wife, Jacqueline Kennedy Onassis.

■ **Udvar-Hazy Center (National Air and Space Museum):** See the Boeing B-29 *Enola Gay,* space shuttle *Discovery,* and hundreds of other aviation and space artifacts in these immense hangars near Dulles International Airport.

■ **United States Air Force Memorial:** Just south of Arlington Cemetery, this memorial honors members of the Air Force who've given their lives in service to the country.

■ **United States Marine Corps War Memorial:** Commonly called the Iwo Jima Memorial, it's located just north of Arlington cemetery and is a powerful tribute to all of the marines who have lost their lives in battle since 1775.

GETTING HERE

You can reach Arlington National Cemetery and the U.S. Air Force and Marine Corps memorials by Metro (Arlington Cemetery on the Blue Line, Pentagon City on the Blue or Yellow lines, Rosslyn on the Orange, Blue, or Silver lines) or Metrobus, although there will be some walking involved. You can also get to these sites with a car or via Big Bus and Old Town Trolley tours. Your best bet is to use Metro to visit the Pentagon and 9/11 Memorial (Pentagon stop via Blue or Yellow line). You'll need a car to visit the Udvar-Hazy Center.

PLANNING YOUR TIME

You can easily combine a visit to Arlington cemetery with visits to the DEA Museum, the Pentagon and 9/11 Memorial, and U.S. Air Force and Marine Corps memorials; it will be a full day and require advance planning for the Pentagon tour.

VISITING THE UDVAR-HAZY CENTER

■ A visit to the Udvar-Hazy Center (National Air and Space Museum) will require a good part of a day due to its location; a car is needed, and you'll probably encounter some traffic. If you're flying out of nearby Dulles Airport, you can combine a morning visit to the center with a late afternoon or evening departure.

QUICK BITES

■ **Cheesetique.** The menu is focused on sandwiches as well as mac 'n' cheese, fondues, and other cheesy delights at this cheese and wine store that's also a full-service restaurant. ✉ *800 N. Glebe Rd., Arlington* ⊕ *www.cheesetique.com* Ⓜ *Ballston–MU.*

■ **Good Stuff Eatery.** *Top Chef* Spike Mendelsohn's burger joint is perfect for a quick, hearty bite. This location is in Arlington's busiest area—Crystal City. ✉ *2110 Crystal Dr., Arlington* ⊕ *www.goodstuffeatery.com* Ⓜ *Crystal City.*

■ **Kabob Palace.** This spot is widely known to have Arlington's best kebabs. ✉ *2315 S. Eads St., Arlington* ⊕ *www.kabobpalaceusa.com* Ⓜ *Crystal City.*

Discover American treasures, historical attractions, diverse dining, first-class shopping, and eclectic arts and entertainment in the northern Virginia city of Arlington.

Just across the Potomac River from D.C. (complete with easy Metro access), this area offers a great blend of history and urban excitement. Some other noteworthy spots are farther out in northern Virginia, without the Metro access, including some good restaurants in Falls Church.

Spend a day or two visiting Arlington National Cemetery, the Marine Corps War Memorial, the Air Force Memorial, and the National 9/11 Pentagon Memorial. If you're traveling with kids or just want to ooh and aah over very cool planes and rockets, don't miss the Udvar-Hazy Center in Chantilly near Dulles International Airport. This companion facility to the National Air and Space Museum on the National Mall displays thousands of aviation and space artifacts in huge hangars; you can even watch restoration projects in progress.

⊙ Sights

★ Arlington National Cemetery
CEMETERY | Nearly 400,000 Americans who died during wartime, as well as many notable Americans (among them Presidents William Howard Taft and John F. Kennedy, General John Pershing, and Admiral Robert E. Peary), are interred in these 624 acres across the Potomac River from Washington, established as the nation's cemetery in 1864. Prior to 1857, the land was a plantation owned by George Washington Parke

Custis, grandson of Martha Washington. Enslaved people built Arlington House, which became the country's first memorial to Custis's step-grandfather, George Washington; the house and plantation were later passed down to Custis's daughter, Mary Anna Custis Lee, the wife of Confederate general Robert E. Lee. Arlington was very much a typical working plantation before it was a cemetery, with 196 slaves living and working on the property the Lees inherited it. By the third year of the Civil War, with Lee decamped to the south and leading Confederate forces, the land was seized by Union forces and set aside for military burials to accommodate the rising death toll.

Today, it's the most famous national cemetery in the country, with an average of 30 funerals held every weekday and another six to eight funerals on Saturday for people who did not require or request military honors. You can visit dozens of notable gravesites, monuments, and even an arboretum. Section 27, one of the oldest parts of the cemetery, is a particular must for modern-day visitors. Fifteen-hundred African American soldiers who fought in the Civil War and the ensuing Indian Wars are buried here, as are over 3,800 nonmilitary African Americans (including many who were formerly enslaved); they are buried in graves marked only as "citizen" or "civilian." You should also visit the section of the cemetery called Freedman's Village, which

Did You Know?

The Pentagon's 9/11 Memorial was the first to be completed, having been dedicated on September 11, 2008, and is dedicated to the 184 people who lost their lives at the Pentagon that day (59 aboard American Airlines Flight 77 and 125 inside the Pentagon). The youngest victim was 3, the oldest 71, and their memorial benches are presented in order of age.

existed from 1863 to 1900. The area was originally designed by the government as a short-term refugee camp for runaway slaves; it quickly became a robust community, complete with schools, hospitals, and churches (interestingly, records indicate no residents of this village are buried at Arlington).

Tour bus services are provided for a fee every 15 to 25 minutes (buy tickets in the Welcome Center). Wheelchairs and strollers are not allowed. For a map of the cemetery or help finding a grave, download the cemetery's app, ANC Explorer, or use the computers at the Welcome Center. ⊠ *1 Memorial Ave., Arlington* ✛ *West end of Memorial Bridge* ☎ *877/907–8585 for general information and to locate a grave* ⊕ *www.arlingtoncemetery.mil* ⊠ *Free; parking from $2 per hr; Arlington National Cemetery tours $15* Ⓜ *Arlington Cemetery.*

Pentagon

GOVERNMENT BUILDING | The headquarters of the United States Department of Defense is the largest low-rise office building in the world. Approximately 24,000 military and civilian workers arrive daily. Astonishingly, the mammoth structure, completed in 1943, took less than two years to construct. Following the September 11, 2001, crash of hijacked American Airlines Flight 77 into the northwest side of the building, the damaged area was removed in just over a month and repaired in a year. In this same area is the America's Heroes Memorial and Chapel, which pays tribute to the civilians and military members killed in the attack. South of the building is the 2-acre outdoor Pentagon Memorial, with its 184 benches commemorating the lives lost on 9/11. Tours of the Pentagon are free and last about 60 minutes, including a presentation and approximately 1½ miles of walking. They must be reserved online through the Pentagon Tour Office at least two weeks, but no more than three

months, in advance. ⊠ *Arlington* ✛ *I–395 at Columbia Pike and Rte. 27* ☎ *703/697–1776* ⊕ *pentagontours.osd.mil* ⊠ *Free* ☉ *No tours on weekends* Ⓜ *Pentagon.*

Pentagon Memorial

MEMORIAL | Washington's own 9/11 memorial honors the 184 people who perished when the hijacked American Airlines Flight 77 crashed into the northwest side of the Pentagon. Stainless-steel-and-granite benches engraved with the victims' names are arranged in order by date of birth and where they were when they died. The names of the victims who were inside the Pentagon are situated so that visitors reading their names face the Pentagon, and names of the victims on the plane are arranged so that visitors reading their names face skyward. At each bench is a lighted pool of flowing water. Designed by Julie Beckman and Keith Kaseman, the memorial opened to the public on September 11, 2008, the seventh anniversary of the attacks. Volunteer docents periodically stand near the entrance and answer questions. There is no public parking, with the exception of five stalls for handicap-permitted vehicles. ⊠ *1 Rotary Rd., Pentagon, Arlington* ☎ *301/740–3388* ⊕ *www.pentagonmemorial.org* ⊠ *Free* Ⓜ *Pentagon.*

Udvar-Hazy Center (National Air and Space Museum)

MUSEUM | **FAMILY** | Unlike the museum on the Mall, which is divided into smaller galleries with dense history and science exhibits, the Udvar-Hazy Center displays large aircraft and spacecraft, hung as though in flight throughout two vast, multilevel hangars. This focus makes the center more appealing for families with kids who may not be old enough to take in detailed historical narratives, but will certainly ooh and aah over the marvelous planes. It is also much less crowded than the Mall museum, with room to move. Gaze upon historic aircraft like the Lockheed SR-71 Blackbird, the fastest

Arlington and
Northern Virginia

jet in the world; the sleek, supersonic Concorde; and the *Enola Gay,* which, in 1945, dropped the first atomic bomb to be used in war on Hiroshima, Japan. Walk alongside space shuttle *Discovery,* and browse displays of astronaut paraphernalia, including space food and space underwear! If you want to visit the museum while you are waiting for a flight or connection at Dulles, the Fairfax Connector Bus 983 runs daily between the museum and airport for $1.75 (SmarTrip card or cash); the trip takes 15 minutes. ⊠ *14390 Air and Space Museum Pkwy., Chantilly* ☎ *703/572–4118, 866/868–7774 IMAX information* ⊕ *www.airandspace. si.edu* ⊠ *Free; IMAX film from $9; flight simulators from $8; parking $15.*

United States Air Force Memorial

MEMORIAL | On a beautiful hillside in Arlington, the Air Force Memorial honors the service and sacrifice of America's airmen. Three stainless-steel, asymmetrical spires slice through the skyline up to 270 feet, representing flight, the precision of the "bomb burst" maneuver performed by the Air Force Thunderbirds, and the three core values of the Air Force: Integrity first, Service before self, and Excellence in all we do. The spires are adjacent to the southern portion of Arlington National Cemetery and visible from the Tidal Basin and Interstate 395 near Washington. At the base of the spires is an 8-foot statue of the honor guard, a glass wall engraved with the missing man formation, and granite walls inscribed with Air Force values and accomplishments. On Friday evenings throughout the summer, the United States Air Force Band performs concerts on the memorial lawn. ⊠ *1 Air Force Memorial Dr., Arlington* ⊹ *Off Columbia Pike* ☎ *703/979–0674* ⊕ *www.airforce-memorial.org* ⊠ *Free* Ⓜ *Pentagon City or Pentagon.*

United States Marine Corps War Memorial

MEMORIAL | **FAMILY** | Also known as the Iwo Jima memorial, it is inspired by

the iconic photograph taken during the Battle of Iwo Jima in World War II. The memorial depicts six marines raising the current U.S. flag and honors all U.S. Marine Corps personnel whose lives were lost since 1775. It's a 15-minute walk from the Metro station at Arlington National Cemetery, much of it uphill. ⊠ *U.S. Marine Corps War Memorial, U.S. Marine Memorial Circle, Arlington* ⊕ *www.nps.gov/gwmp* ⊠ *Free* Ⓜ *Arlington Cemetery.*

Restaurants

Ashby Inn

$$$$ | **AMERICAN** | If there's a recipe for a perfect country inn restaurant, chef Tom Whitaker and sommelier Stuart Brennen have it. Head about an hour west of D.C., and your reward is extraordinary comfort food. À la carte menu items— like smoked duck with pickles and rye or monkfish with leeks and truffles—are made with fresh local ingredients and presented in an intimate setting. **Known for:** intimate country inn dining; views of the Blue Ridge Mountains; prix-fixe menus with local ingredients. ⑤ *Average main: $45* ⊠ *692 Federal St., Paris* ☎ *540/592–3900* ⊕ *www.ashbyinn.com* ⊘ *Closed Mon. and Tues.*

Fyve Restaurant Lounge

$$$ | **MODERN AMERICAN** | Chefs cycle in and out as often as guests breeze through the adjoining Ritz-Carlton, so this dining room is anything but staid or predictable despite its shopping-mall environs. Warm tones of red and orange accentuate the autumnal notes of butternut squash soup or the unexpected duo of roasted beets and crisped chickpeas. **Known for:** inside Ritz-Carlton hotel; lounge serves smaller bites; healthful meals. ⑤ *Average main: $30* ⊠ *Ritz-Carlton, 1250 S. Hayes St., Pentagon City* ☎ *703/415–5000* ⊕ *www.ritzcarlton.com* ⊟ *No credit cards* Ⓜ *Pentagon City.*

Continued on page 266

ARLINGTON, THE NATION'S CEMETERY

The most famous, most visited cemetery in the country is the final resting place for close to 400,000 Americans, from unknown soldiers to John F. Kennedy. With its tombs, monuments, and "sea of stones," Arlington is a place of ritual and remembrance, where even the most cynical observer of Washington politics may find a lump in their throat or a tear in their eye.

EXPERIENCING THE SEA OF STONES

In 1864, a 200-acre plot directly across the Potomac from Washington, part of the former plantation of Robert E. Lee, was designated America's national cemetery. Today, the cemetery covers 624 acres.

Today, Arlington's major monuments and memorials are impressive, but the most striking experience is simply looking out over the thousands upon thousands of headstones aligned across the cemetery's hills.

Most of those buried here served in the military—from reinterred Revolutionary War soldiers to troops killed in Iraq and Afghanistan. As you walk through the cemetery, you're likely to hear a trumpet playing taps or the report of a gun salute. An average of 27 funerals a day are held here, Monday through Friday. There currently are nearly 400,000 graves in Arlington; it's projected that the cemetery will be filled by 2060.

FINDING A GRAVE
At the Welcome Center, staff members and computers can help you find the location of a specific grave. You need to provide the deceased's full name and, if possible, the branch of service and year of death.

WHO GETS BURIED WHERE
With few exceptions, interment at Arlington is limited to active-duty members of the armed forces, veterans, and their spouses and minor children. In Arlington's early years as a cemetery, burial location was determined by rank (as well as, initially, by race), with separate sections for enlisted soldiers and officers. Beginning in 1947, this distinction was abandoned. Grave sites are assigned on the day before burial; when possible, requests are honored to be buried near the graves of family members.

ABOUT THE HEADSTONES
Following the Civil War, Arlington's first graves were marked by simple whitewashed boards. When these decayed, they were replaced by cast-iron markers covered with zinc to prevent rusting. Only one iron marker remains, for the grave of Captain Daniel Keys (Section 13, Lot 13615, Grid G-29/30).

In 1873, Congress voted in the use of marble headstones, which continues to be the practice today. The government provides the standard-issue stones free of charge. Next of kin may supply their own headstones, though these can only be used if space is available in one of the sections where individualized stones already exist.

THE SAME, BUT DIFFERENT
Regulation headstones can be engraved with one of 54 symbols indicating religious affiliation. In section 60, the headstones of soldiers killed in Afghanistan and Iraq reflect the multicultural makeup of 21st-century America. Along with a variety of crosses and the Star of David, you see the nine-pointed star of the Baha'i; a tepee and three feathers representing the Native American faiths; the Muslim crescent and star; and other signs of faith. (Or lack of it. Atheism is represented by a stylized atom.)

Opposite: Sea of Stones; Upper left: Burial ceremony; Bottom left: A soldier placing flags for Memorial Day. Right: Coast Guard headstone.

PLANNING YOUR VISIT TO ARLINGTON

ARLINGTON BASICS

Getting Here: You can reach Arlington on the Metro, by foot over Arlington Memorial Bridge (southwest of the Lincoln Memorial), or by car—there's a large parking lot by the Visitors Center on Memorial Drive. Also, the Big Bus Tours (☎ 877/332–8689 ⊕ www.bigbustours.com) and Old Town Trolley (☎ 202/832–9800 ⊕ www.oldtowntrolley.com) both have Arlington National Cemetery stops in their loops. But only Old Town Trolley offers 7 stops within the cemetary (🎟 $13.50).

🕙 Apr.–Sept., daily 8–7; Oct.–Mar., daily 8–5.

🎟 Cemetery free, parking $2 per hr.

☎ 877/907–8585 for general information and to locate a grave.

⊕ www.arlingtoncemetery.mil

✗ No food or drink is allowed at the cemetery. There are water fountains in the Welcome Center, and from fall through spring a water fountain operates near the amphitheater at the Tomb of the Unknowns. You can also purchase bottled water at the Women's Memorial.

TOURING OPTIONS

Your first stop at the cemetery should be the Welcome Center, where you can pick up a free brochure with a detailed map. Once there you have a choice: tour by bus or walk.

Arlington by Bus. Arlington National Cemetery Tours leave every 15 to 25 minutes from just outside the Welcome Center April through September, daily 8:30–6, and October through March, daily 8:30–4. The 45 to 60-minute tour includes stops at the Kennedy grave sites, The Tomb of the Unknown Soldier, and Arlington House. Your bus driver will provide basic facts about the cemetery.

Arlington on Foot. Walking the cemetery requires some stamina, but it allows you to take in the thousands of graves at your own pace. On the facing page is a walking tour that includes the major points of interest. Audio tours are available in the Welcome Center.

Above: 3rd Infantry Honor Guard

A WALKING TOUR

■ Head west from the Welcome Center on Roosevelt Drive and turn right on Weeks Drive to reach the **Kennedy graves;** just to the west is **Arlington House.** (1/4 mile)

■ Take Crook Walk south, following the signs, to the **Tomb of the Unknowns**; a few steps from the tomb is **Section 7A**, where many distinguished veterans are buried. (3/10 mile)

■ To visit the graves of soldiers killed in Afghanistan and Iraq, take Roosevelt Drive past Section 7 and turn right on McClellan Drive, turn right when you get to Eisenhower Drive, then go left onto York Drive. The graves will be on your right. (6/10 mile)

■ Walk north along Eisenhower Drive, which becomes Schley Drive; turn right onto Custis Walk, which brings you to **Section 27,** where 3,800 former slaves are buried. (3/4 mile)

■ Leave the cemetery through the Ord and Weitzel Gate, cross Marshall Drive carefully, and walk to the 50-bell **Netherlands Carillon,** where there's a good vista of Washington. To the north is the **United States Marine Corps War Memorial,** better known as the **Iwo Jima Memorial**. (1/4 mile)

ARLINGTON'S MAIN ATTRACTIONS

The Kennedy Graves

Once while taking in the view of Washington from Arlington National Cemetery, President John F. Kennedy commented, "I could stay here forever." Seeing Kennedy's grave is a top priority for most visitors. He's buried beneath an eternal flame, next to graves of two of his children who died in infancy, and of his wife, Jacqueline Kennedy Onassis. Across from them is a low wall engraved with quotations from Kennedy's inaugural address. Nearby, marked by simple white crosses, are the graves of Robert F. Kennedy and Ted Kennedy.

The gas-fueled flame at the head of John F. Kennedy's grave was lit by Jacqueline Kennedy during his funeral. A continuously flashing electric spark reignites the gas if the flame is extinguished by rain, wind, or any other cause.

Many visitors ask where Kennedy's son John F. Kennedy Jr. is buried. His ashes were scattered in the Atlantic Ocean, near the location where his plane went down in 1999.

Arlington House

Long before Arlington was a cemetery, it was part of the 1,100-acre plantation of George Washington Parke Custis, a grandchild of Martha and (by marriage) George Washington. Enslaved people built Arlington House between 1802 and 1818. After Custis's death, the property and its slaves were given to his daughter, Mary Anna Randolph Custis, who wed Robert E. Lee in 1831. The couple made Arlington House their home for the next 30 years.

In 1861 Lee turned down the position of commander of the Union forces and left Arlington House, never to return. Union troops turned the house into an Army headquarters, and 200 acres were set aside as a national cemetery. By the end of the Civil War headstones dotted the estate's hills.

The house looks much as it did in the 19th century and a quick tour takes you past objects once owned by the Custises, the Lees, and the Washingtons. The views from Arlington House remain spectacular. ☎ *703/235–1530* ⊕ *www.nps. gov/arho* 🎟 *Free* ⏰ *Daily 9:30–4:30.*

The Tomb of the Unknown Soldier

The first burial at the Tomb of the Unknowns, one of the cemetery's most imposing monuments, took place on November 11, 1921. In what was part of a world-wide trend to honor the dead after the unparalleled devastation of World War I, an unidentified soldier was interred under the large white-marble sarcophagus. Unknown servicemen killed in World War II and Korea joined him in 1958.

The Memorial Amphitheater west of the tomb is used for ceremonies on Veterans Day, Memorial Day, and Easter. Decorations awarded to the unknowns are displayed in an indoor trophy room.

One of the most striking activities at Arlington is the precision and pageantry of the changing of the guard at the Tomb of the Unknowns. From April through September, soldiers from the Army's U.S. Third Infantry (known as the Old Guard) change guard every half hour during the day. For the rest of the year, and at night all year long, the guard changes every hour.

The Iwo Jima Memorial

Ask the tour bus driver at Arlington where the Iwo Jima is, and you might get back the quip "very far away." The memorial commonly called the Iwo Jima is officially named the United States Marine Corps War Memorial, and it's actually located just north of the cemetery. Its bronze sculpture is based on one of the most famous photos in American military history, Joe Rosenthal's February 23, 1945, shot of five marines and a navy corpsman raising a flag atop Mt. Suribachi on the Japanese island of Iwo Jima. By executive order, a real flag flies 24 hours a day from the 78-foot-high memorial. P703/289–2500

On Tuesday evening at 7 pm from early June to mid-August there's a Marine Corps sunset parade on the grounds of the Iwo Jima Memorial. On parade nights a free shuttle bus runs from the Arlington Cemetery visitors' parking lot.

The Old Guard are not making a fashion statement in their sunglasses—they're protecting their eyes from the sun's glare off the white marble of the tomb.

★ Inn at Little Washington

$$$$ | FRENCH | A 90-minute drive from the District takes you past hills and farms to the English-style country manor that is the site of this well-regarded hotel restaurant. The service matches the setting, and diners can choose items from two menus: Gastronauts (contemporary endeavors) or Good Earth (vegetarian), both of which have dishes that rotate daily. **Known for:** themed (and pricey) tasting menus; special-occasion dining destination; old English manor vibe. ⑤ *Average main: $265* ✉ *309 Middle St., Washington* ✛ *At Main St.* ☎ *540/675– 3800* ⊕ *www.theinnatlittlewashington. com* ⊘ *Closed Tues.*

★ Kabob Palace

$ | AFGHAN | FAMILY | The sign out front says parking is reserved for taxis, but it's not so they can pick up passengers— it's so the drivers can duck into this fast-casual restaurant for the area's top kebabs. It's open 24 hours a day, seven days a week, and its chicken, lamb, and spicy beef kabobs are cooked to perfection and best dipped in chutney sauce and chased with a bite of naan. **Known for:** authentic kebabs; crispy, chewy naan; open 24/7. ⑤ *Average main: $15* ✉ *2315 S. Eads St., Arlington* ☎ *703/486–3535* Ⓜ *Crystal City.*

★ 2941 Restaurant

$$$ | FRENCH FUSION | Soaring ceilings, a woodsy lakeside location, and a koi pond make this one of the most striking dining rooms in the area. Executive chef Bertrand Chemel's introduction to cooking began with an apprenticeship at a French bakery, and his flair for rising dough shows. **Known for:** romantic date-night dining; peanut butter baked Alaska; gorgeous decor. ⑤ *Average main: $35* ✉ *2941 Fairview Park Dr., Falls Church* ☎ *703/270–1500* ⊕ *www.2941.com* ⊘ *No lunch. Closed Sun.*

Yong Kang Street

$ | TAIWANESE | FAMILY | With a name inspired by an actual street in Taipei, this dumpling house is in Pentagon City's famous Fashion Centre Mall. In addition to its signature dumplings, it's also known for noodles and shrimp fried rice. **Known for:** great dumplings; fast service; cheap prices. ⑤ *Average main: $6* ✉ *Fashion Centre at Pentagon City, 1100 S. Hayes St., Arlington* ☎ *571/982–4718* Ⓜ *Pentagon City.*

🛏 Hotels

Across the Potomac, with excellent Metro access and views of D.C., you'll find Arlington County, one of the largest districts in the Washington metro area. Its neighborhoods include Pentagon City with its three popular malls: Pentagon Row, Fashion Centre, and Pentagon Centre; Crystal City with its underground network of corridors linking offices and shops to high-rise apartments; Ballston, home to the Washington Capitals National Hockey League training facility; and Rosslyn, a former ferry landing turned transportation hub for rail, car, and bike. These thriving communities might not offer as much as D.C. proper, but they have everything the weary traveler might need in terms of accommodations, cuisine, and entertainment, sometimes at a more affordable price point.

Hyatt Centric Arlington

$$ | HOTEL | If you're feeling energetic, it's just a 15-minute walk to Georgetown over Key Bridge from this solid, over-the-Potomac choice, but if energy is lacking, the hotel is just across from the Rosslyn Metro station. **Pros:** across from a Metro station; runners and walkers can receive trail maps and GPS watches; nice-size rooms. **Cons:** dull neighborhood; not great for kids; not close to any major sights. ⑤ *Rooms from: $289* ✉ *1325 Wilson Blvd., Arlington* ☎ *703/525–1234* ⊕ *www.*

hyatt.com 🛏 318 rooms ℗ No meals
Ⓜ Rosslyn.

Le Méridien Arlington

$$ | **HOTEL** | This modern gem, just over
the bridge from Georgetown and steps
from the Metro, offers stylish and com-
fortable rooms, many with great views
of the Potomac River. **Pros:** convenient
to Metro and Arlington cemetery; nice
artwork throughout; great views of the
skyline. **Cons:** fee for in-room Wi-Fi unless
you're an SPG member; some rooms
are small. ⓢ *Rooms from: $293* ✉ *1121
N. 19th St., Arlington* ☎ *703/351–9170*
⊕ *www.lemeridienarlingtonhotel.com*
🛏 *154 rooms* ℗ *No meals* Ⓜ *Rosslyn.*

Renaissance Arlington Capital View Hotel

$ | **HOTEL** | Spacious rooms, excellent
service, and a good on-site contemporary
Italian restaurant all add up to an excel-
lent hotel choice outside the city. **Pros:**
nice-size fitness center; stunning lobby
with dramatic artwork; delightful coffee
shop. **Cons:** fee for in-room Wi-Fi; noise
from trains on one side of hotel; a bit of
a walk to restaurants. ⓢ *Rooms from:
$200* ✉ *2800 Potomac Ave., Arlington*
☎ *703/413–1300* ⊕ *www.marriott.com*
🛏 *300 rooms* ℗ *No meals* Ⓜ *Crystal City
or Ronald Reagan Washington National
Airport.*

The Ritz-Carlton Pentagon City

$$$ | **HOTEL** | **FAMILY** | The feel is more
contemporary and casual-chic than what
is generally associated with this luxury
chain, and it's convenient for both downtown D.C. and Ronald Reagan Washington National Airport, with direct access
to the Metro. **Pros:** connected to shops
and restaurants; welcome amenity kit for
children; 24-hour fitness center. **Cons:** daily fee for Wi-Fi; less luxurious than other
Ritz properties; expensive, given the
location. ⓢ *Rooms from: $319* ✉ *1250
S. Hayes St., Arlington* ☎ *703/415–5000,
800/241–3333* ⊕ *www.ritzcarlton.com/
pentagoncity* 🛏 *366 rooms* ℗ *No meals*
Ⓜ *Pentagon City.*

🍸 Nightlife

Just across the Potomac, Arlington and
Alexandria boast some top-notch bars
and lounges—with considerably more
parking and less hectic traffic than D.C.
Also accessible by the Metro, revitalized
Ballston and Clarendon are interesting
and enjoyable, though more laid-back,
even quiet, places to visit at night.

MUSIC CLUBS
State Theatre

MUSIC CLUBS | This is the place to go to
see concerts by aging hit makers from
the past such as the Smithereens or
tribute bands to the likes of Led Zeppelin,
Pink Floyd, and Bon Jovi. Attendees have
the choice of sitting or standing in this
renovated movie theater, which is about
10 miles south of D.C. The popular 1980s
retro dance parties, featuring the Leg-
warmers tribute band, draw locals who
like to dress the part. ✉ *220 N. Washington St., Falls Church* ☎ *703/237–0300*
⊕ *www.thestatetheatre.com* Ⓜ *E. Falls
Church.*

🎭 Performing Arts

Suburban Virginia is home to a number
of outstanding performance venues
offering Shakespeare, opera, dance,
popular music, and more. Arlington's
Signature Theatre stages some of the
best musical productions in the area
and is only a short trip from downtown
Washington, while Synetic Theatre, made
nationally famous by its production of
Silent Hamlet, is but a Metro stop away
in Crystal City.

MAJOR VENUES
George Mason University Center for the Arts

ARTS CENTERS | This state-of-the-art
performance complex on the suburban Virginia campus of George Mason
University satisfies music, ballet, and
drama patrons with regular performances
in its 2,000-seat concert hall, the 467-
seat proscenium Harris Theater, and an

intimate 200-seat black-box theater. The 10,000-seat Patriot Center, a venue for pop acts and sporting events, is also on campus. ✉ *George Mason University, 4400 University Dr., MS 2F5, Fairfax* ☎ *703/993–2787, 888/945–2468* ⊕ *cfa. gmu.edu.*

Wolf Trap National Park for the Performing Arts

ARTS CENTERS | At the only national park dedicated to the performing arts, the 7,000-seat outdoor Filene Center hosts more than 80 performances from June through September. They range from pop and jazz concerts to dance and musical theater productions. The National Symphony Orchestra is based here in summer, and the Children's Theatre-in-the-Woods delivers 70 free performances. In colder months, the intimate, indoor Barns at Wolf Trap fill with the sounds of musicians playing folk, country, and chamber music, along with many other styles. The park is just off the Dulles Toll Road, about 20 miles from downtown Washington. Wolf Trap provides round-trip bus service from the West Falls Church Metro stop during events. ✉ *1645 Trap Rd., Vienna* ☎ *703/255–1900, 703/255–1868* ⊕ *www.wolftrap.org* Ⓜ *W. Falls Church–VT/UVA.*

THEATER
Signature Theatre

THEATER | The Tony Award–winning Signature Theatre company has earned national acclaim for its presentation of contemporary plays and groundbreaking American musicals, especially those of Stephen Sondheim. The company performs in a dramatic facility with two black-box performance spaces, the 299-seat MAX and the 99-seat ARK. ✉ *4200 Campbell Ave., Arlington* ☎ *703/820–9771* ⊕ *www.sigtheatre.org.*

Synetic Theatre

THEATER | **FAMILY** | One of the most distinctive performing arts groups in the Washington area uses music, dance, high energy, acting, and athleticism to transform the works of Shakespeare, Dante, Edgar Allan Poe, and Robert Louis Stevenson into visual theatrics that are guaranteed to leave audiences fascinated. The award-winning theater is tucked away in Virginia's Crystal City, a short Metro ride away from downtown Washington. ✉ *1800 S. Bell St., Arlington* ☎ *703/824–8060* ⊕ *synetictheater.org* Ⓜ *Crystal City.*

Chapter 14

SIDE TRIPS FROM WASHINGTON, D.C.

Updated by Sabrina Medora
and Delesia Watson

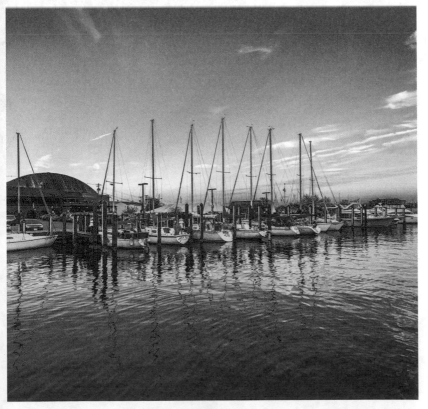

⊙ Sights	🍸 Restaurants	🧳 Hotels	🛍 Shopping	🍸 Nightlife
★★★★★	★★★★☆	★★★★☆	★★★☆☆	★★★☆☆

WELCOME TO SIDE TRIPS FROM WASHINGTON, D.C.

TOP REASONS TO GO

★ **Get a history lesson:** The sprawling Mount Vernon, the plantation and home of George and Martha Washington, serves as a reminder of the power and complex legacy of our first president—a Founding Father and leader in the American Revolution, and, simultaneously, an enslaver of hundreds of people.

★ **Travel back in time:** Delve into Colonial history in Old Town Alexandria, then fast-forward to the 21st century with funky shops, artists' galleries, hot restaurants, boutiques, and bars. Don't miss Alexandria's farmers' market, held every Saturday year-round from 7 am to noon. Believe it or not, it has been around since George Washington's produce was sold here.

★ **Feast on some crabs:** Head east to Annapolis on the Chesapeake Bay, and enjoy a Maryland specialty: blue crabs by the bushel (the bib is optional).

With just a bit of planning, any one of these trips can be done in a day or even an afternoon.

1 Alexandria, Virginia. Alexandria is across the Potomac and 7 miles downstream from Washington. In the 18th century it was a notable commercial port; it's now a big small town loaded with historic homes, shops, and restaurants.

2 Mount Vernon, Virginia. Sixteen miles south of D.C. is George Washington's beautifully preserved Mount Vernon, the most visited historic house in America.

3 Woodlawn, Virginia. Woodlawn was the estate of Martha Washington's granddaughter.

4 Gunston Hall, Virginia. Gunston Hall was the residence of George Mason, a patriot and author of the document on which the Bill of Rights was based.

5 C&O Canal National Historic Park, Maryland. The Maryland side of the Potomac River offers dramatic waterfalls, picnic areas, and bike paths. The dramatic and beautiful Great Falls are on the Virginia side of the Potomac.

6 National Harbor, Maryland. Washington's newest entertainment destination is just a water taxi ride away from the National Mall. The biggest draw is the new MGM National Harbor Hotel and Casino, which already accounts for more than 40% of Maryland's total gaming revenue.

7 Annapolis, Maryland.
Maryland's capital is a
popular destination for
seafood lovers and boating
fans. The city's nautical
reputation is enhanced by
the presence of the U.S.
Naval Academy. It also has
one of the country's
largest assemblages of
18th-century architecture.

8 Baltimore, Maryland.
Thirty-nine miles north of
Washington—a trip made
easy by the MARC
commuter rail's weekend
Penn Line service ($7 each
way)—Baltimore's
burgeoning restaurant
scene has earned national
acclaim. But crabs and Old
Bay aren't the only things
on the menu. A world of
fine flavors—Afghan,

Indian, Italian, Japanese,
Korean, and Spanish,
among others—makes it a
choice destination for
foodies, especially given
the outside-the-Beltway
prices.

The District of Columbia was carved out of Maryland and Virginia in July 1790 and borders both states, with Virginia to the west and southwest, and Maryland to the north, east, and southeast. The entire region is very historic, and within an hour of D.C. are getaway destinations connected to the nation's first president, naval history, and Colonial events.

In Virginia, Alexandria was once a bustling Colonial port, and its Old Town preserves this flavor with cobblestone streets, historic taverns, and a busy waterfront. Cycle 7 miles downriver along the banks of the Potomac to get here, or hop on the Metro for a quick 30-minute ride. Mount Vernon, George Washington's plantation, is 8 miles south of Alexandria. Make a day of it, and visit two other historic homes—Woodlawn and Gunston Hall—that are nearby.

In Maryland, you can visit a historic canal that was begun in the early 18th century to connect Washington, D.C., to Cumberland, MD. Another option is to get out on the water in Annapolis, a major center for boating and home to the U.S. Naval Academy. Feast on Chesapeake Bay's famous crabs, then watch the midshipmen parade on campus at the academy. Or you can visit the booming city of Baltimore.

Getting Here and Around

All of these side-trips can be reached within an hour from D.C. if you have a car. Just be aware that parking can be difficult in some places.

Most of these destinations can be reached by public transportation (though in the case of Annapolis, not easily). But Gunston Hall and the sections of the C&O Canal outside of Georgetown are only reachable by car.

To Get To:	By Car:	By Public Transit:
Alexandria	George Washington Memorial Pkwy. or Jefferson Davis Hwy. (Rte. 1) south from Arlington (10 mins)	The Blue or Yellow Line to the King St.–Old Town Metro stop (25 mins from Metro Center)
Mount Vernon	Exit 1 off the Beltway; follow signs to George Washington Memorial Pkwy. southbound (30 mins)	The Yellow Line to the Huntington Metro stop, then Fairfax County Connector Bus No. 101, 151, or 159 (45–50 mins); ferry from Pier 4 (90 minutes)
Woodlawn	Rte. 1 southwest to the second Rte. 235 intersection; entrance is on the right at the traffic light (40 mins)	Bus No. 101, 151, or 159 from Huntington Metro station (45–50 mins)
Gunston Hall	Rte. 1 south to Rte. 242; turn left and go 3½ miles to entrance (30 mins)	No Metro or bus
Annapolis	U.S. 50 east to the Rowe Blvd. Exit (35–45 mins, except during weekday rush hour when it may take twice as long)	Amtrak from Union Station to BWI; MTA Light Rail from BWI to Patapsco Light Rail Station; transfer to Bus No. 14 (2 hrs)
C&O Canal	George Washington Memorial Pkwy. northwest 15.1 miles (30 mins)	No Metro or bus
National Harbor	I–295 South 10 miles (30 mins)	Water taxi from The Wharf (45 mins)
Baltimore	Baltimore–Washington Pkwy. 39 miles (1 hr)	MARC Penn Line or Amtrak train from Union Station (28–60 mins)

Alexandria, Virginia

A short drive (or bike ride) from Washington, Alexandria provides a welcome break from the monuments and hustle and bustle of the District. Here you encounter America's Colonial heritage. Founded in 1749 by Scottish merchants eager to capitalize on the booming tobacco trade, Alexandria became one of the most important Colonial ports and has been associated with the most significant personages of the Colonial, Revolutionary, and Civil War periods. In Old Town, this colorful past is revived through restored 18th- and 19th-century homes, churches, and taverns; on the cobblestone streets; and on the revitalized waterfront, where clipper ships docked and artisans displayed their wares. Alexandria also has a wide variety of small- to medium-size restaurants and pubs, plus a wealth of boutiques and antiques dealers vying for your time and money.

GETTING HERE AND AROUND

Take either the George Washington Memorial Parkway or Jefferson Davis Highway (Route 1) south from Arlington to reach Alexandria. ■TIP→ Stop at the Alexandria Visitor Center at Ramsay House (221 King Street) to get oriented.

The King Street–Old Town Metro stop (about 25 minutes from Metro Center) is

Alexandria, Virginia

Sights ▼

1 Alexandria Black History Museum **C1**
2 Athenaeum **E4**
3 Captain's Row **E4**
4 Carlyle House Historic Park **E3**
5 Christ Church **D3**
6 Friendship Firehouse **C3**
7 Gadsby's Tavern Museum **D3**
8 George Washington Masonic National Memorial **A3**
9 Lee-Fendall House Museum and Garden... **D2**
10 The Lyceum: Alexandria's History Museum **C4**
11 National Inventors Hall of Fame and Museum **A5**
12 Old Presbyterian Meeting House.......... **D5**
13 Old Town Farmers Market......... **D3**
14 Stabler-Leadbeater Apothecary Museum... **D4**
15 Torpedo Factory Art Center................. **E4**

Restaurants ▼

1 Cheesetique.............. **A1**
2 Columbia Firehouse.... **D4**
3 Don Taco **C3**
4 Hank's Oyster Bar Old Town.................. **C3**
5 Le Refuge................ **D3**
6 Mason Social **C1**
7 Nasime.................. **B3**
8 Sweet Fire Donna's..... **A4**
9 Taverna Cretekou........ **C3**
10 Tequila & Taco **A4**
11 Vermilion.................. **C3**
12 Virtue Feed & Grain **E4**
13 Warehouse Bar and Grille **E4**
14 Whiskey & Oyster **A4**

Hotels ▼

1 The Alexandrian, Autograph Collection ... **D4**
2 Embassy Suites Alexandria— Old Town.................. **A3**
3 Hotel Indigo Old Town Alexandria.... **E4**
4 Kimpton Lorien Hotel & Spa **B3**
5 Morrison House, Autograph Collection ... **C4**
6 The Westin Alexandria............... **A4**

right next to the Masonic Memorial and a 10-block walk on King Street from the center of Old Town. ■TIP→ **A free King Street trolley runs daily between the King Street Metrorail station and the Potomac River Waterfront. Hours are 10 am to 10:15 pm Sunday–Wednesday and 10 am to midnight Thursday–Saturday.**

TOURS

A great way to learn more about Alexandria's fascinating history is on a walking tour with Alexandria Colonial Tours or Old Town Experience. All tours depart from the Alexandria Visitor Center at Ramsay House.

Alexandria Colonial Tours

WALKING TOURS | FAMILY | Some of America's most historic moments have happened on the streets of Alexandria. Relive and explore them through historical tours or—for the more adventurous—ghost tours. One tour option focuses on Black history including enslaved Black people and freedmen in the post-Civil War era. You can opt for private tours or group tours for up to 20 people. ⊠ *201 King St., No. 3, Old Town* ☎ *703/519–1749* ⊕ *www.alexcolonialtours.com* ☑ *$13.*

Courageous Journey: Alexandria's Black History Driving Tour

DRIVING TOURS | FAMILY | This eight-site, self-guided tour offers a deep look at how Black history has shaped both Alexandria and the United States. Visitors can begin at Barrett Branch Library, where 26-year-old attorney, Samuel Tucker, joined five other African American men in staging a sit-in in 1939. Blocks away is Alfred Street Baptist Church, the oldest active historically Black congregation. The tour also suggest ways to explore more at nearly every stop. ⊠ *Visitor Center, 221 King St., Old Town* ☎ *703/838–5005* ⊕ *www.visitalexandriava.com.*

Old Town Experience

WALKING TOURS | FAMILY | Explore the history, legends, and folklore of Alexandria on a 90-minute walking tour. You'll visit the Carlyle House, Gadsby's Tavern, Christ Church, Captain's Row, and Old Presbyterian Meeting House, among others. ⊠ *507 Prince St., Old Town* ☎ *703/836–0694* ⊕ *www.oldtowntour-alexandriava.com* ☑ *$15* Ⓜ *King St.–Old Town.*

VISITOR INFORMATION

CONTACTS Alexandria Visitor Center. ⊠ *Ramsay House, 221 King St., Old Town* ☎ *703/838–5005* ⊕ *www.visitalexandriava.com.*

Sights

Founded in 1749, Alexandria is known for well-preserved architecture dating back to before George Washington considered it his "adopted' home town. Alexandria, now a nationally designated historic district, is easily walkable, with historic attractions to discover on every street. Most of the sights are free, though some have a nominal fee. Alexandria is a warm and welcoming place, ideal for anyone from solo travelers to families with small children and pets.

Alexandria Black History Museum

MUSEUM | This collection, devoted to the history of African Americans in Alexandria and Virginia, is housed in part in the Robert H. Robinson Library, a building constructed in the wake of a landmark 1939 sit-in protesting the segregation of Alexandria libraries. The Watson Reading Room, next to the museum, holds a vast collection of books, periodicals, videos, and historical documents detailing the social, economic, and cultural contributions of African Americans who helped shape the city's growth since its establishment in 1749. The federal census of 1790 recorded 52 free African Americans living in the city, but the town was one of the largest slave-exporting points in the South, with at least two highly active slave markets. ✉ *902 Wythe St., Old Town* ☎ *703/746–4356* ⊕ *www. alexblackhistory.org* 🎫 *$2* ⊗ *Closed Sun. and Mon.* Ⓜ *King St.–Old Town.*

Athenaeum

MUSEUM | One of the most noteworthy structures in Alexandria, this striking Greek Revival edifice at the corner of Prince and Lee streets stands out from its many redbrick Federal neighbors. Built in 1852 as a bank, and later used as a Union commissary headquarters, then as a talcum powder factory for the Stabler-Leadbeater Apothecary, the Athenaeum now houses the gallery of the Northern Virginia Fine Arts Association, which hosts free rotating art exhibitions, classes, and receptions throughout the year. This block of Prince Street between Fairfax and Lee streets is known as **Gentry Row,** after the 18th- and 19th-century inhabitants of its imposing three-story houses. ✉ *201 Prince St., Old Town* ☎ *703/548–0035* ⊕ *www.nvfaa. org* 🎫 *Free* ⊗ *Closed Mon.–Wed.* Ⓜ *King St.–Old Town.*

Captain's Row

NEIGHBORHOOD | Many of Alexandria's sea captains once lived on this block, which gives visitors the truest sense of what the city looked like in the 1800s. The houses are now all private residences and reflect the style of the Federal period. While the cobblestone pavement is a replica, it accurately represents the original which, according to local folklore, was laid down by Hessian soldiers taken prisoner in the Revolutionary War. Captain's Row is one of only two streets in Alexandria that is paved with cobblestones. ✉ *100–199 Prince St., Old Town* Ⓜ *King St.–Old Town.*

Carlyle House Historic Park

HOUSE | **FAMILY** | The Carlyle House offers a rich, nuanced portrait of both American and Alexandrian history. As one of the largest slaveholders in Virginia at the

Alexandria's Farmers' Market 👁

If it's Saturday and you're up early, join the locals at Alexandria's Farmers' Market, one of the oldest continually operating farmers' markets in the country—open for business since the 1700s. The market is held from 7 am to noon year-round at Market Square (*301 King St.*), a few steps away from Old Town's waterfront. In addition to incredible produce and flowers, you'll find handmade crafts and prepared foods.

time, John Carlyle established himself as a powerful merchant, city founder, and local leader. Built in 1753 by enslaved people, the house hosted many important mid-18th century figures, from a meeting between General Braddock and royal governors on the French and Indian War to the likes of George Washington, Thomas Jefferson, and Benjamin Franklin for parties and balls. Today, the house serves as a museum where visitors can get a behind-the-scenes look at Alexandria's history over the course of time. ✉ *121 N. Fairfax St., Old Town* ☎ *703/549–2997* ⊕ *www.novaparks.com/ parks/carlyle-house-historic-park* 🎫 *$5* ⊗ *Closed Mon.* Ⓜ *King St.–Old Town.*

Christ Church

RELIGIOUS SITE | **FAMILY** | George Washington was a pewholder in this Episcopal church, which remains in nearly original condition. (Washington paid quite a lot of money for pews 59 and 60.) Built in 1773, it's a fine example of an English Georgian country-style church with its Palladian window, interior balcony, and English wrought-brass-and-crystal chandelier. Docents give tours during visiting hours. ✉ *118 N. Washington St., Old Town* ☎ *703/549–1450* ⊕ *www.*

historicchristchurch.org ☒ $5 donation suggested Ⓜ King St.–Old Town.

Friendship Firehouse

MUSEUM | FAMILY | Alexandria's showcase firehouse dates from 1855 and is filled with typical 19th-century implements, but the resident Friendship Fire Company was established in 1774 and bought its first engine in 1775. Among early fire engines on display is a hand pumper built in Philadelphia in 1851. Most everything can be seen through the windows even when the firehouse is closed. ☒ 107 S. Alfred St., Old Town ☎ 703/746–3891 ⊕ www.alexandriava.gov/FriendshipFirehouse ☒ $2 ⊙ Closed weekdays Ⓜ King St.–Old Town.

Gadsby's Tavern Museum

MUSEUM | FAMILY | The museum consists of two buildings—a circa-1785 tavern and the 1792 City Hotel. These were the centers of political and social life. Notable patrons included John Adams, James Madison, Thomas Jefferson, and even George Washington (who celebrated two of his birthdays in the ballroom). The taproom, dining room, assembly room, ballroom, and communal bedrooms have been restored to their original appearances. Special events include costumed reenactments, balls, afternoon teas, and free tours on President's Day, Mother's Day, and Father's Day. Opt for a self-guided or group tour, or enjoy an after-hours lantern tour with a costumed guide. ☒ 134 N. Royal St., Old Town ⊹ Take the free King St. trolley (runs every 15 mins) to King and Royal Sts., then walk ☎ 703/746–4242 ⊕ www.gadsbystavern.org ☒ $5 ⊙ Closed Mon. and Tues. Nov.–Mar. Ⓜ King St.–Old Town.

George Washington Masonic National Memorial

MEMORIAL | FAMILY | Because Alexandria, like Washington, D.C., has no really tall buildings, the spire of this memorial dominates the surroundings and is visible for miles. The structure overlooks King and Duke Streets, Alexandria's

major east–west arteries, and reaching it requires a respectable uphill climb from the King Street Metrorail and bus stations. From the ninth-floor observation deck (reached by elevator), you get a spectacular view of Alexandria and Washington, but access above the first two floors is by guided tour only. The memorial contains furnishings from the first Masonic lodge in Alexandria. George Washington became a Mason in 1752 in Fredericksburg and then became Charter Master of the Alexandria lodge when it was chartered in 1788, remaining active in Masonic affairs during his tenure as president, from 1789 to 1797. Daily guided tours are included with admission, but you need to make a reservation. ☒ 101 Callahan Dr., Old Town ☎ 703/683–2007 ⊕ www.gwmemorial.org ☒ $18 Ⓜ King St.–Old Town.

Lee-Fendall House Museum and Garden

HOUSE | FAMILY | Built in 1785 at historic Lee Corner, the Lee-Fendall House was, over the course of the next 118 years, home to 37 members of the Lee family as well as several enslaved people; it also served as a Union hospital. The house and its furnishings, of the 1850–70 period, present an intimate study of 19th-century family life. Highlights include a splendid collection of Lee heirlooms, period pieces produced by Alexandria manufacturers, and a tour focusing on the enslaved and free servants who lived in the house (a permanent exhibition exploring their lives is currently in the works). There's also a beautifully restored, award-winning garden, which can be visited without buying a ticket for the museum. ☒ 614 Oronoco St., Old Town ☎ 703/548–1789 ⊕ www.leefendallhouse.org ☒ $7 ⊙ Closed Mon. and Tues. Ⓜ King St.–Old Town.

The Lyceum: Alexandria's History Museum

MUSEUM | FAMILY | Built in 1839 and one of Alexandria's best examples of Greek Revival design, the Lyceum is also a local history museum. Restored in the

1970s for the Bicentennial, it has an impressive collection, including examples of 18th- and 19th-century silver, tools, stoneware, and Civil War photographs taken by Mathew Brady. Over the years the building has served as the Alexandria Library, a Civil War hospital, a residence, and offices. ☒ *201 S. Washington St., Old Town* ☎ *703/838–4994* ⊕ *www.alexandri-ava.gov/Lyceum* ☒ *$3 (free for Alexandria residents)* Ⓜ *King St.–Old Town.*

Old Presbyterian Meeting House

RELIGIOUS SITE | Except from 1899 through 1949, the Old Presbyterian Meeting House has been the site of an active Presbyterian congregation since 1772. Scottish pioneers founded the church, and Scottish patriots used it as a gathering place during the Revolution. Four memorial services were held for George Washington here. The tomb of an unknown soldier of the American Revolution lies in a corner of the small churchyard, where many prominent Alexandrians—including Dr. James Craik, physician and best friend to Washington, and merchant John Carlyle—are interred. The original sanctuary was rebuilt after a lightning strike and fire in 1835. The interior is appropriately plain; if you'd like to visit the sanctuary you can borrow a key in the church office at 323 South Fairfax Street, or just peek through the many wide windows along both sides. ☒ *323 S. Fairfax St., Old Town* ☎ *703/549–6670* ⊕ *www.opmh.org* ☒ *Free* Ⓜ *King St.–Old Town.*

Old Town Farmers Market

HISTORIC SITE | **FAMILY** | One of the nation's oldest continually operating farmers markets has served Alexandria residents since 1753. On Saturday mornings, residents and visitors alike can get fresh meat, dairy, fish, fruits, and vegetables from area farmers. Local artists also sell their work in the bustling Market Square. Stop by year-round. ☒ *301 King St., Old Town* ☎ *703/746–3200* ⊕ *www.alexandri-ava.gov.*

Stabler-Leadbeater Apothecary Museum

MUSEUM | Once patronized by Martha Washington, the Stabler-Leadbeater Apothecary is one of the oldest in the country (the reputed oldest is in Bethlehem, Pennsylvania). The shop now houses a museum of memorabilia, including one of the finest collections of apothecary bottles in the country. In fact, they have so many of these original bottles that it took six years to process them all. Tours include discussions of Alexandria life and medicine, as well as the history of the family who owned and ran the shop for 141 years. ☒ *105–107 S. Fairfax St., Old Town* ☎ *703/746–3852* ⊕ *www.apothecarymuseum.org* ☒ *$5* ⊙ *Closed Mon. and Tues. Nov.–Mar.* Ⓜ *King St.–Old Town.*

National Inventors Hall of Fame and Museum

MUSEUM | **FAMILY** | Located inside the United States Patent and Trademark Office, the National Inventors Hall of Fame spotlights more than 500 inventors and the greatest technological and trademarked achievements. Browse the interactive gallery of inductees, have a seat in a 1965 Ford Mustang merged with a 2015 Ford Mustang, test your eye for authenticity, and more. The gift shop has some truly one-of-a-kind mementos and gifts. ☒ *National Inventors Hall of Fame, 600 Dulnay St., Old Town* ✣ *In atrium of United States Patent and Trademark Office's Madison Bldg., easily accessible from King St. and Eisenhower Ave. Metro stations* ☎ *571/272–8400* ⊕ *www.uspto.gov/about-us/uspto-locations/alexandria-va/national-inventors-hall-fame-and-museum* ⊙ *Closed Sun.* Ⓜ *King St. or Eisenhower Ave.*

Torpedo Factory Art Center

MUSEUM | **FAMILY** | Torpedoes were manufactured here by the U.S. Navy during World War II, but now the building houses six galleries, as well as the studios and workshops of about 160 artists and artisans. You can observe printmakers,

King Street is the heart of historic Old Town Alexandria, Virginia, with lively restaurants and shops.

jewelers, sculptors, painters, potters, textile artists, and glass makers as they create original work in their studios. The Torpedo Factory also houses the Alexandria Archaeology Museum, which displays artifacts such as plates, cups, pipes, and coins from an early tavern, as well as Civil War soldiers' equipment. If archaeological activities interest you, call to sign up for the well-attended public digs (offered monthly from June through September and occasionally in October). ✉ 105 N. Union St., Old Town ⚓ Take free King St. trolley to Old Town waterfront. The Torpedo Factory is about 100 feet from final stop (King and Union Sts.) ☎ 703/838–4565, 703/746–4399 Archaeology Museum ⊕ www.torpedofactory. org ✉ Free ⊘ Closed Mon. and Tues. Ⓜ King St.–Old Town.

🍴 Restaurants

For centuries, the founding fathers and other international dignitaries have dined in Alexandria. Today, you can choose from more than 200 restaurants in all price ranges. During Alexandria's biannual restaurant weeks in January and August, dozens of establishments offer either a $35 three-course meal or dinner for two, and several also offer lunch specials.

Cheesetique

$ | AMERICAN | Fans of cheese and wine will fall in love with this adorable retail shop and restaurant. With more than 200 cheeses from local and domestic creameries, a large selection of less available wines, and an extensive menu that covers every fan favorite from grilled cheese to mac 'n' cheese, visitors will find themselves in cheese heaven. **Known for:** wide variety of both domestic and international cheeses; great wine selections; cheese boards with wine pairings. $ Average main: $15 ✉ 2411 Mt. Vernon Ave. ☎ 703/706–5300 ⊕ www. cheesetique.com.

Columbia Firehouse

$$ | AMERICAN | FAMILY | Built in 1883 in the heart of Old Town and used as an actual firehouse, this historic building now just off bustling King Street houses a popular

brasserie with a barroom, atrium, and patio. There's a menu of comfort food, small plates, and steaks; there's also an excellent seafood selection, including a good raw bar. **Known for:** good staples like fish-and-chips, beef bourguignon, and steak frites; beautiful interior; separate bar menu of seafood and sandwiches. ⑤ *Average main: $24* ✉ *109 St. Asaph St., Old Town* ☎ *703/683–1776* ⊕ *columbiafirehouse.com.*

Don Taco

$ | **MEXICAN FUSION** | As its name suggests, tacos of every variety are the specialty at this lively spot in the heart of Alexandria's busy King Street. From tacos to rice bowls, burritos, and small plates for sharing, Don Taco's menu will make you crave more than just one item. **Known for:** late-night happy hour (until 2 am); large tequila menu; excellent desserts. ⑤ *Average main: $12* ✉ *808 King St., Old Town* ☎ *703/518–8800* ⊕ *www. dontacova.com.*

★ Hank's Oyster Bar Old Town

$$ | **AMERICAN** | **FAMILY** | This classic raw bar is consistently busy thanks to a nice mix of locals and visitors. No doubt it's because the oysters, clams, and lobster rolls are incredibly fresh, and the wine list is great. **Known for:** amazing oysters, duh; nonseafood dinner specials; daily raw bar deals. ⑤ *Average main: $25* ✉ *1026 King St., Old Town* ☎ *703/739–4265* ⊕ *www. hanksoysterbar.com.*

Le Refuge

$$$ | **FRENCH** | At this local favorite, run by Jean François Chaufour and his wife, Françoise, for more than 30 years, lovingly prepared French country fare is served with beaucoup flavor. Popular selections include trout, bouillabaisse, garlicky rack of lamb, frogs' legs, and beef Wellington. **Known for:** authentic French cuisine with no pretension; three-course prix-fixe lunch and dinner options; tasty profiteroles for dessert. ⑤ *Average main: $30* ✉ *127 N. Washington St., Old Town*

☎ *703/548–4661* ⊕ *www.lerefugealexandria.com* ⊘ *Closed Sun.* Ⓜ *King St.–Old Town.*

★ Mason Social

$$ | **CONTEMPORARY** | The depth of Mason Social's seasonal menu made it a hit right from the get-go. Adventurous eaters will relish options like the marrow burger while those happier with more traditional staples will be delighted with the fried green tomatoes or jumbo lump crab cakes. **Known for:** brunch; long list of craft cocktails; bone marrow burger. ⑤ *Average main: $24* ✉ *728 N. Henry St., Old Town* ☎ *703/548–8800* ⊕ *www. mason-social.com* Ⓜ *Braddock Rd.*

Nasime

$$$$ | **JAPANESE FUSION** | A tiny gem, Nasime serves an exquisite, five-course tasting menu of both traditional and contemporary Japanese flavors. The selections change frequently based on the season and availability of products, but it always include a wonderful blend of raw, grilled, fried, and baked dishes, plus dessert. **Known for:** stunning, artlike dishes; revolving menu of fresh sushi; intimate seating. ⑤ *Average main: $48* ✉ *1209 King St., Old Town* ☎ *703/548– 1848* ⊕ *www.nasimerestaurant.com* ⊘ *Closed Mon.*

Sweet Fire Donna's

$ | **BARBECUE** | **FAMILY** | A popular choice for locals, this barbecue joint is known for brisket, daily specials, and some of the best happy hour deals in town. Looking for a late night bite? **Known for:** barbecue; happy hour; $2 late-night tacos. ⑤ *Average main: $12* ✉ *510 John Carlyle St., Old Town* ☎ *571/312–7960* ⊕ *sweetfiredonnas.com* Ⓜ *King St.–Old Town.*

Taverna Cretekou

$$ | **MODERN GREEK** | Whitewashed stucco walls and colorful macramé tapestries bring a bit of the Mediterranean to the center of Old Town. The menu takes diners on a trip around Greece—each

dish identifies its region of origin, and the whole country is represented. **Known for:** extensive Greek-only wine list; live music on Thursday; romantic canopied garden. ⑤ *Average main: $22* ✉ *818 King St., Old Town* ☎ *703/548–8688* ⊕ *www.tavernacretekou.com* ⊗ *Closed Mon.* Ⓜ *King St.–Old Town.*

Tequila & Taco

$ | **MEXICAN FUSION** | This popular neighborhood restaurant with funky decor is known for its weekend brunches and freshly squeezed margaritas. Tacos are a mix of traditional like carnitas and al pastor, as well as fun, such as fried chicken and cauliflower. **Known for:** weekend brunch; fresh margaritas; lively atmosphere. ⑤ *Average main: $12* ✉ *540 John Carlyle St., Old Town* ☎ *703/721–3203* ⊕ *alexandriataco.com* Ⓜ *King St.–Old Town.*

★ Vermilion

$$$ | **MODERN AMERICAN** | Be sure to make reservations because foodies flock here for a taste of its award-winning modern American cuisine. Vermilion favors locally sourced, sustainable ingredients, though quality trumps local here, so you may find a Scottish salmon alongside a Shenandoah beef fillet on this Mid-Atlantic menu. **Known for:** casual, hip interior with exposed brick and gas lamps; popular weekend brunch; house-made pastas. ⑤ *Average main: $32* ✉ *1120 King St., Old Town* ☎ *703/684–9669* ⊕ *www.vermilionrestaurant.com* ⊗ *No lunch Tues.* Ⓜ *King St.–Old Town.*

Virtue Feed & Grain

$$ | **AMERICAN** | Housed in what was once a feed house in the 1800s (now beautifully restored with reclaimed wood, antique bricks, and glass panes), this lively American tavern serves an all-day menu and weekend brunch, and has a club-like feel on weekend nights. You can sample a wide variety of selections with a seasonal bent, from duck meat loaf and pasta puttanesca to a grilled chicken BLT or a gem lettuce salad. **Known for:** classic

farm-to-table cuisine with some spice; fried chicken and waffles for brunch; late-night menu. ⑤ *Average main: $20* ✉ *106 S. Union St., Old Town* ☎ *571/970–3669* ⊕ *www.virtuefeedgrain.com.*

Warehouse Bar and Grill

$$ | **SEAFOOD** | Situated in Old Town Alexandria, the casual yet elegant Warehouse specializes in prime aged steaks and seafood. The historic building that houses it features caricatures of the local gentry on the wall and an antique mahogany bar that's a great place to enjoy a drink. **Known for:** antique mahogany bar; casual elegance; great steak. ⑤ *Average main: $25* ✉ *214 King St., Old Town* ☎ *703/683–6868* ⊕ *www.warehouseoldtown.com.*

Whiskey & Oyster

$$ | **AMERICAN** | **FAMILY** | While the interior is sophisticated, the atmosphere is casual. The menu boasts, naturally, an impressive selection of whiskeys and oysters. **Known for:** classic and Maine lobster rolls (in season); dog-friendly patio; outdoor dining (weather dependent). ⑤ *Average main: $20* ✉ *301 John Carlyle St., Old Town* ☎ *703/567–1533* ⊕ *whiskeyandoyster.squarespace.com* Ⓜ *King St.–Old Town.*

Hotels

A short train-ride away from Washington, D.C., Alexandria is an excellent option for those who want a quieter stay near the District. Choose from dozens of larger chains or boutique hotels, all ranking highly for ambience and service.

The Alexandrian Autograph Collection

$$ | **HOTELHOTEL** | **FAMILY** | Both business and leisure travelers will enjoy the historic charm of The Alexandrian, just blocks from the waterfront; guests can also dine at King & Rye, its Southern-American restaurant and outdoor patio with a focus on high-quality regional ingredients, whiskeys and bourbons. **Pros:** pet-friendly; 24-hour health center; inner rooms include balconies overlooking the center

courtyard. **Cons:** can be noisy; breakfast on weekends only; guest room decor dull in comparison to lobby. ⑤ *Rooms from: $160* ⌧ *480 King St., Old Town* ⚏ *Take free trolley toward waterfront from anywhere on King St. starting at King St.–Old Town Metro* ☎ *703/549–6080* ⊕ *thealexandrian.com* ⬎ *241 rooms* ⑩ *Free breakfast* Ⓜ *King St.–Old Town.*

Embassy Suites Alexandria–Old Town
$$ | **HOTEL** | **FAMILY** | A location across from the Metro station makes this all-suites hotel a convenient base for city exploration. **Pros:** large rooms; good breakfast; complimentary fitness center. **Cons:** small indoor pool is often crowded; parking is expensive; popular with school groups. ⑤ *Rooms from: $270* ⌧ *1900 Diagonal Rd., Old Town* ☎ *703/684–5900, 800/362–2779* ⊕ *embassysuites3.hilton.com* ⬎ *288 rooms* ⑩ *Free Breakfast.*

Hotel Indigo Old Town Alexandria
$ | **HOTEL** | At Alexandria's only waterfront hotel, guests can take in views of the river from their rooms or from the restaurant after a day exploring Old Town, a neighborhood marked by cobblestone streets and 18th-century town houses. **Pros:** waterfront views; free Wi-Fi; walk-in showers. **Cons:** expensive valet parking; modern, yet lackluster room decor; poor noise insulation. ⑤ *Rooms from: $159* ⌧ *220 S. Union St., Old Town* ☎ *703/721–3800* ⊕ *www.hotelindigooldtownalexandria.com* ⬎ *120 rooms* ⑩ *No meals.*

Kimpton Lorien Hotel & Spa
$$$ | **HOTEL** | Service is top-notch at this casually elegant boutique hotel in the heart of Old Town Alexandria. **Pros:** central to Old Town sights; full-service spa (only one in town) and well-appointed fitness center; free use of bikes. **Cons:** no pool; daily fee for valet-only parking; some rooms are small. ⑤ *Rooms from: $339* ⌧ *1600 King St., Old Town* ☎ *703/894–3434* ⊕ *www.lorienhotelandspa.com* ⬎ *107 rooms* ⑩ *No meals* Ⓜ *King St.–Old Town.*

Morrison House, Autograph Collection
$$$ | **HOTEL** | **FAMILY** | Originally built in 1985 in the style of a Federalist mansion for Morrion's wife, Morrison House was later turned into a bed-and-breakfast-style boutique hotel. **Pros:** newly renovated luxury suites; delightful literary theme, including on-site library; live music Thursday–Saturday evening. **Cons:** about a 15-minute walk from Metro and train stations; daily fee for valet-only parking; fee for in-room Wi-Fi. ⑤ *Rooms from: $329* ⌧ *116 S. Alfred St., Old Town* ☎ *703/838–8000* ⊕ *morrisonhouse.com* ⬎ *45 rooms* ⑩ *No meals* Ⓜ *King St.–Old Town.*

The Westin Alexandria
$$ | **HOTEL** | **FAMILY** | The staff seems genuinely happy to see you come through the door at this hotel just 1½ miles from the cobbled streets of Old Town Alexandria, and if you don't need or want to be in D.C.—only 20–25 minutes away by Metro—you'll get more for your travel dollar here. Decorated in blues, wood tones, and imported Jerusalem stone, the lobby and public areas have something of a Frank Lloyd Wright feel. **Pros:** indoor heated pool and 24-hour gym are complimentary; free shuttle to waterfront and Old Town and close to airport (though no shuttle); pet-friendly. **Cons:** outside the city; half-hour walk to waterfront; fee for in-room Wi-Fi. ⑤ *Rooms from: $283* ⌧ *400 Courthouse Sq.* ☎ *703/253–8600* ⊕ *www.westin.com/alexandria* ⬎ *319 rooms* ⑩ *No meals* Ⓜ *Eisenhower Ave.*

Nightlife

Alexandria is not without nightlife options, including a few good bars and places to hear live music.

★ The Birchmere
MUSIC CLUBS | A legend in the D.C. area, the Birchmere is one of the best places outside the Blue Ridge Mountains to hear acoustic folk, country, and bluegrass. Enthusiastic crowds regularly enjoy table-side service while taking in

performances by artists such as Judy Collins, Don McLean, Bela Fleck, and Emmylou Harris. But the club is also a draw for some of the country's best jazz and R&B artists (Rachelle Farrell, Sheila E., Angie Stone). ✉ *3701 Mt. Vernon Ave.* ☎ *703/549–7500* ⊕ *www.birchmere.com.*

Fishmarket

BARS/PUBS | There's something different in just about every section of this multilevel, multiroom space, though the nightlife centers on the sports-focused Anchor Bar. The thirty- and fortysomething crowd watching local televised games is boisterous. If you really like beer, order a "Schooner" size; at 32 ounces, it's a glass big enough to put your face in. Or make it an innocent night out at the adjacent Pop's Old Fashioned Ice Cream Co. ✉ *105 King St., Old Town* ☎ *703/836–5676* ⊕ *www.fishmarketva.com* Ⓜ *King St.–Old Town.*

🏃 Activities

An asphalt bicycle path leads from the Virginia side of Key Bridge (across from Georgetown), past Ronald Reagan National Airport, and through Alexandria all the way to Mount Vernon. Bikers in moderately good condition can make the 16-mile trip in less than two hours. You can rent bicycles as well as sailboats, paddleboards, and kayaks in Alexandria.

Washington Sailing Marina

BOATING | FAMILY | A great place to rent a bike is the Washington Sailing Marina, which is beside the Mount Vernon Bike Trail just past the airport. A 12-mile ride south will take you right up to the front doors of Mount Vernon. Cruiser bikes rent for $11 per hour or $35 per day. You can also rent kayaks ($16 per hour), small sailboats ($17 to $25 per hour), and paddleboards ($22 per hour). The marina is open 9–5 daily. ✉ *1 Marina Dr.* ☎ *703/548–9027* ⊕ *www.washingtonsailingmarina.com.*

National Harbor

12 miles south of Downtown Washington, D.C., 2 miles west of Oxon Hill.

National Harbor sprawls across 350 acres of previously abandoned banks of the Potomac River, across from Old Town Alexandria. It's about a 25-minute water taxi ride from the National Mall and provides an alternative if you're D.C.-bound and don't mind commuting. While only one-quarter as tall as the London Eye, the Capital Wheel's 42 glass-enclosed gondolas soar 180 feet above the Potomac River, affording breathtaking views over the District.

Shopping and dining is a mix of big names and successful family-owned businesses.

The new MGM National Harbor Hotel and Casino brings Las Vegas–style entertainment inside the Beltway, while its upscale boutiques and shops, including Sarah Jessica Parker's eponymous shoe store, aim for mass appeal.

GETTING HERE AND AROUND

The easiest way to reach National Harbor is by car via Interstate 295, Interstate 95, or Interstate 495, but keep in mind that neither street nor garage parking is free. Water taxis from Old Town Alexandria, the National Mall, or Georgetown are also convenient. Once in National Harbor, the National Harbor Circulator shuttle provides easy transport along Waterfront Street and between the Tanger Outlets, Gaylord National Resort, and MGM National Harbor Hotel for a onetime cost of $5, good for all-day riding.

TOURS
★ Potomac Riverboat Company

BOAT TOURS | FAMILY | Jump aboard a cruise ship from National Harbor's dock for a water tour of Mount Vernon, Alexandria, or Washington's monuments and memorials. The trip to Mount Vernon includes admission to the grounds.

The company also operates water taxis across the Potomac to even more sight-seeing, shopping, and dining options in Alexandria, Georgetown (transfer at Alexandria), The Wharf, or the National Mall. ✉ *Commercial Pier, 145 National Plaza* ☎ *703/684–0580, 877/511–2628* ⊕ *www.potomacriverboatco.com* 🎫 *Round-trip $21.*

Sights

The Awakening
PUBLIC ART | FAMILY | This sculpture, created by J. Seward Johnson, depicts a 72-foot giant struggling to free himself from the earth and is actually five separate pieces buried in the ground. The statue was originally at Hains Point in Washington but was moved to National Harbor in 2008. Feel free to climb all over the giant; everyone else does. ✉ *National Plaza.*

★ The Capital Wheel
VIEWPOINT | FAMILY | Stunning at sunset, the nearly 200-foot ascent on this giant Ferris wheel affords views of Alexandria's Masonic Temple, the Washington Monument, and the U.S. Capitol, lasting approximately 15 minutes. Glass-enclosed gondolas are climate-controlled and wheelchair-accessible. Landlubbers can enjoy drinks and Potomac vistas from the Flight Deck bar at the base of the wheel since admission tickets are not required. ✉ *141 American Way* ☎ *301/842–8650* ⊕ *thecapitalwheel.com* 🕐 *$15.*

🍴 Restaurants

Elevation Burger
$ | BURGER | One of the few restaurants in National Harbor without waiter service, this burger joint is known for its grass-fed organic beef and heaping servings of skinny fries. The original Elevation Burger comes with two patties, while a Half-the-Guilt burger consists of one beef patty and one veggie patty. **Known for:**

organic, grass-fed, free-range burgers; french fries cooked in olive oil; thick shakes, including chocolate mixed with black cherry. ⑤ *Average main: $12* ✉ *108 Waterfront St.* ☎ *301/567–9290* ⊕ *www.elevationburger.com* ⊟ *No credit cards.*

★ Old Hickory Steakhouse
$$$$ | STEAKHOUSE | The signature restaurant of the Gaylord National Resort, Old Hickory is perfect for a romantic meal watching the sun set over the harbor or for an expense-account evening of cocktails and fine cigars out on the terrace. The signature 24-ounce porterhouse comes with four sauce choices: béarnaise, bordelaise, green peppercorn, and blue cheese. **Known for:** prime cuts of meat; waterfront views; excellent cheese courses. ⑤ *Average main: $55* ✉ *Gaylord National Resort & Convention Center, 201 Waterfront St.* ☎ *301/965–4000* ⊕ *www.oldhickoryrestaurant.com* 🕐 *No lunch.*

The Walrus Oyster & Ale House
$$$ | SEAFOOD | FAMILY | Inspired by the Lewis Carroll poem, "The Walrus and the Oyster," this restaurant is a gem for excellent seafood and views. Come here for a crab cake sandwich or select from the list of fresh, briny Chesapeake oysters in a casual, modern pub setting. **Known for:** all things oysters; patio seating; friendly service. ⑤ *Average main: $30* ✉ *152 Waterfront St.* ☎ *301/567–6100* ⊕ *www.walrusoysterandale.com.*

Hotels

AC Hotel National Harbor
$ | HOTEL | Loftlike spaces, dramatic art, and lounge seating in the second-floor lobby create a minimalistic atmosphere more like a nightclub than your standard Marriott hotel. **Pros:** outdoor patio and fantastic views of the Capital Wheel and Potomac River; free in-room Wi-Fi; more affordable than most of the other hotels in National Harbor. **Cons:** small closets; expensive valet parking on-site or cheaper off-site self-parking; small

fitness room. $ *Rooms from: $179* ✉ *156 Waterfront St.* ☎ *301/749–2299* ⊕ *www.marriott.com* ⤳ *192 rooms* ❍︎*No meals.*

Gaylord National Resort and Convention Center

$$ | HOTEL | FAMILY | Guests at this larger-than-life resort can dine, shop, get pampered, and even go clubbing without ever leaving the property, which anchors the National Harbor waterfront and, with about a 25-minute ride to the National Mall, provides an alternative to the more expensive options downtown. **Pros:** waterfront location; water taxi to Alexandria and National Mall; full-service spa, fitness center, and indoor pool. **Cons:** downtown D.C. is fairly far; extra per-day resort fee; resort might be too big for some. $ *Rooms from: $233* ✉ *201 Waterfront St.* ☎ *301/965–4000, 855/516–1090 reservations* ⊕ *www.marriott.com* ⤳ *1996 rooms* ❍︎*No meals.*

★ MGM National Harbor

$$$ | HOTEL | The newest addition to the Potomac waterfront at National Harbor is the ultramodern MGM. **Pros:** great restaurants by some of the nation's most celebrated chefs; awesome views from many of the public spaces and rooms; Maryland's most popular gambling venue. **Cons:** might be too overwhelming for some travelers; room rates are high; expensive nightly resort fee. $ *Rooms from: $370* ✉ *101 MGM National Ave.* ☎ *844/646–6847* ⊕ *www.mgmnationalharbor.com* ⤳ *308 rooms* ❍︎*No meals.*

C&O Canal National Historic Park

Extends 13 miles west from Georgetown, including Great Falls Tavern, which is 23 miles northwest of Georgetown.

Although it was a vital link with the country's western territories, rapids and waterfalls along the 185 miles between Cumberland and Washington originally made it impossible for traders to travel the entire distance by boat. Upon completion in 1850, the Chesapeake & Ohio Canal, with its 74 locks, provided an economical and practical way for traders to move goods through the Washington area to the lower Chesapeake, but floods and competition from the B&O Railroad would end traffic less than a century later. The railroad transferred ownership of the canal to the federal government in 1938 to settle a $2 million debt. Since 1971, the canal has been a national park, providing a window into the past and a marvelous place to enjoy the outdoors.

C&O Canal National Historic Park originates in Georgetown and encloses a 184.5-mile towpath that ends in Cumberland, Maryland. This relic of America's canal-building era and a few structures are still there.

GETTING HERE AND AROUND

C&O Canal National Historic Park is along the Maryland side of the Potomac and is accessible by taking Canal Road or MacArthur Boulevard from Georgetown or by taking Exit 41 off the Beltway and then following the signs to Carderock. Along the southbound lanes of Canal Road are several roadside spots where you can park and visit restored canal locks and lock houses.

To reach Great Falls Park, take the scenic and winding Route 193 (Exit 13 off Route 495, the Beltway) to Route 738 (Old Dominion Drive), and follow the signs. It takes about 25 minutes to drive to the park from the Beltway.

◉ Sights

Clara Barton National Historic Site

HOUSE | Beside Glen Echo Park's parking lot is this monument to the founder of the American Red Cross. Barton first used the structure, built by the founders of Glen Echo village, to store Red Cross supplies; later it became both her home and the organization's headquarters.

Today, the building is furnished with period artifacts and many of her possessions. Access is by a 45-minute guided tour only, typically offered only on Friday and Saturday. Check the park's website to plan your visit. ✉ *5801 Oxford Rd., Glen Echo* ☎ *301/320–1410* ⊕ *www.nps.gov/clba* 🎟 *Free* 🕙 *Closed Sun.–Thurs.*

★ Great Falls Park

NATIONAL/STATE PARK | FAMILY | Facing the C&O Canal National Historical Park across the Potomac River on the Virginia side, this is where the steep, jagged falls of the Potomac roar into the narrow Mather Gorge, the rocky narrows that make the Potomac churn. No matter the time of year, the views of the falls and river are spectacular, and more than 150 species of birds make their home in and around the 800-acre park. Great Falls Park is a favorite for outings; here you can follow trails past the old Patowmack Canal and among the boulders and forests lining the edge of the falls. There are three overlooks in the park, two of which are accessible to people with disabilities. Camping and alcoholic beverages are not allowed, but you can fish (a Virginia or Maryland license is required), climb rocks (climbers must register first at the visitor center or lower parking lot), or—if you're an experienced boater with your own equipment—go white-water kayaking (*below* the falls only). ⚠ **As is true all along this stretch of the river, the currents are deadly. Despite frequent signs and warnings, there are those who occasionally dare the water and drown.** Staff members conduct special tours and walks year-round. ✉ *9200 Old Dominion Dr., McLean* ☎ *703/757–3101* ⊕ *www.nps.gov/grfa* 🎟 *$20 per vehicle; $35 for annual pass.*

Great Falls Tavern Visitor Center

INFO CENTER | Headquarters for the Palisades area of C&O Canal National Historic Park, this visitor center has displays of canal history and photographs that show how high the river can rise. A platform on

Olmsted Island, accessible from near the tavern, provides a spectacular view of the falls. On the lock walls are grooves worn by decades of friction from boat towlines. Interpretive ranger programs are offered year-round (in winter the schedule is limited), including hikes, nature walks, demonstrations, and lectures. Themed canal-boat rides are available in spring, summer, and fall, and the schedule varies depending on the month. Ongoing efforts to repair and restore locks can result in temporary towpath closures; call the visitor center for the exact schedule on the day of your visit. ✉ *11710 MacArthur Blvd., Potomac* ☎ *301/767–3714* ⊕ *www.nps.gov/choh* 🎟 *$20 per vehicle; $35 annual pass.*

 Activities

The C&O Canal National Historic Park and its towpath are favorites of walkers, joggers, bikers, and canoeists. The path has a slight grade, which makes for a leisurely ride or hike. Most recreational bikers consider the 13 miles from Georgetown to Great Falls Tavern an easy ride; you need to carry your bike for only one short stretch of rocky ground near Great Falls. You can also take a bike path that parallels MacArthur Boulevard and runs from Georgetown to Great Falls Tavern. Storm damage has left parts of the canal dry, but many segments remain intact and navigable by canoe.

BOAT TOURS
C&O Canal Barges

BOAT TOURS | FAMILY | During one-hour rides on mule-drawn barges along the C&O Canal at Great Falls, costumed guides and volunteers explain the history of the waterway. Run by the National Park Service, the barge rides depart from its visitor center on weekends, from April through October. Check with park service about tour availability. ✉ *Great Falls Tavern Visitor Center, 11710 MacArthur Blvd., Potomac* ☎ *301/739–4200* ⊕ *www.nps.gov/choh* 🎟 *$8.*

Mount Vernon, Virginia

*16 miles southeast of Washington, D.C.,
8 miles south of Alexandria.*

Once a working plantation in the 18th century, Mount Vernon is an enduring reminder of the life and legacy of George Washington, including his lifelong status as a slaveowner. This historic site features an authentically interpreted 18th-century home, lush gardens and grounds, captivating museum galleries, and immersive educational programs.

GETTING HERE AND AROUND

To reach Mount Vernon by car from the Capital Beltway (Route 495), take Exit 1, and follow the signs to George Washington Memorial Parkway southbound. Mount Vernon is about 8½ miles south. From downtown Washington, cross into Arlington on Key Bridge, Memorial Bridge, or the 14th Street Bridge, and drive south on the George Washington Memorial Parkway past Ronald Reagan National Airport through Alexandria straight to Mount Vernon. The trip from D.C. takes about a half hour.

Getting to Mount Vernon by public transportation requires that you take both the Metro and a bus. Begin by taking the Yellow Line train to the Huntington Metro station. From here, take Fairfax County Connector Bus No. 101 ($1.75 cash or $1.25 with SmarTrip card). Buses on each route leave about once an hour—more often during rush hour—and operate weekdays from about 5 am to 9:15 pm, weekends from about 6:30 am to 7 pm.

CONTACTS Fairfax County Connector.
☏ 703/339–7200 ⊕ www.fairfaxconnector.com. **Washington Metro Area Transit Authority.** ☏ 202/637–1328 *customer relations* ⊕ www.wmata.com.

TOURS
Gray Line
BUS TOURS | Gray Line runs a nine-hour Mount Vernon and Arlington National

Cemetery tour, Friday through Sunday from January through mid-March and daily mid-March through December. Priced at $90, it includes admission to the mansion and grounds. The tour departs at 8 am from Union Station. ⊠ *Washington* ☏ *202/779–9894 weekdays 8:30 am–6:30 pm* ⊕ *www.graylinedc.com.*

Spirit of Mount Vernon
BOAT TOURS | FAMILY | You can enjoy a Potomac River cruise and explore George Washington's famous grounds in one trip. *Spirit of Mount Vernon* is the only cruise option that provides a narrated sightseeing round-trip from the Washington, D.C., Waterfront area to Mount Vernon and back. The boats dock directly at Mount Vernon, and it's a short walk up the hill to the estate. Admission to the grounds of Mount Vernon is included in the fare. Cruise goers have three hours to explore Mount Vernon grounds and gardens before embarking back to their original destination. Cruises are offered on select dates from March through October. ⊠ *580 Water St., Pier 4, Southwest* ☏ *866/302–2469 boat reservations* ⊕ *www.spiritcruises.com/washington-dc/cruises/mount-vernon* Ⓜ *Waterfront–SEU.*

◉ Sights

Whether you're visiting for the day or spending a few days in Mount Vernon, there is much to see and do. George Washington's former plantation is one of the most popular historic estates in the country, averaging over 1 million guests each year. Despite this, there is an air of consistent tranquility, between the vast grounds and a well-organized programming schedule. Take a room-by-room tour of our founding father's mansion followed by a stroll through his grounds and gardens. Explore the various outbuildings in which enslaved people ran Mount Vernon's many operations, including blacksmithing, laundry, and cooking. You can learn more about these

The exterior of the plantation house at Mount Vernon may look as if it's built of stone, but it's not. It's rusticated pine with sand thrown into the wet paint to give it the rough look of sandstone blocks.

enslaved people—who represented 90% of Mount Vernon's residents at the time of Washington's death—by visiting one of their living quarters on the property, such as Pioneer Farm. You can also explore the estate by way of interactive shows, tours, tributes, and exhibitions. Mount Vernon also provides a variety of dining options that are suitable for families, large groups, and fine dining alike.

George Washington's Gristmill and Distillery

HISTORIC SITE | Reproductions of these two operations sit near the Mount Vernon estate, on the sites of the originals. In 1799, the distillery was the largest American whiskey producer. Today, using the same recipe and processes—thanks to the excellent records kept by Washington—small batches of his whiskey are made and sold here. During guided tours, led by costumed interpreters, you'll meet an 18th-century miller and watch the water-powered wheel grind grain into cornmeal before seeing the grain being distilled. The mill and distillery are 3 miles from Mount Vernon on Route 235 toward

U.S. 1, almost to Woodlawn. General-admission tickets to Mount Vernon include the gristmill and distillery. ✉ *5429 Grist Mill Woods Way* ☎ *703/780–3383* ⊕ *www.mountvernon.org* ✉ *$20 ($18 if booked online), includes admission to Mount Vernon estate* ⊙ *Closed Nov.–Mar.*

★ George Washington's Mount Vernon

HISTORIC SITE | **FAMILY** | This plantation and the surrounding lands (some 8,000 acres with five operating farms) had been in the Washington family for nearly 70 years by the time the future president inherited it all in 1743. Washington used his wife's financial wealth and hundreds of enslaved people to transform the main house from an ordinary farm dwelling into what was, for the time, a grand mansion. The red-roof main house is elegant though understated, with quite ornate first-floor rooms, especially the formal large dining room, with a molded ceiling decorated with agricultural motifs. You can stroll around the estate's 500 acres and three gardens, visiting workshops, kitchen, carriage house, greenhouse, slave quarters, and, down the hill, the tomb of George and Martha Washington. There's also a pioneer farmer site, a 4-acre hands-on exhibit with a reconstructed barn as its centerpiece. Throughout Mount Vernon, you can learn about the over 300 enslaved people who lived here, and whose labor you see all around you. Relevant tours include "The Enslaved People of Mount Vernon" tour and the "Through My Eyes" tour, both of which explore the lives and experiences of the enslaved people who lived here and the role slavery had in the life of Washington and how he built and ran this estate.

Visitors, especially children, tend to enjoy the Museum and Education Center's interactive displays, in which actors in period dress who portray General Washington and his wife welcome visitors at special occasions throughout the year, including President's Day, Mother's and Father's Day, and July 4. ⊠ *3200 George Washington Pkwy.* ⌖ *Southern end of George Washington Pkwy.* ☎ *703/780–2000* ⊕ *www.mountvernon.org* ⊠ *$20 ($18 if booked online), includes admission to distillery and gristmill.*

Woodlawn, Virginia

3 miles west of Mount Vernon, 15 miles south of Washington, D.C.

Woodlawn was once part of the Mount Vernon estate, and from here you can still see the trees of the bowling green that fronted Washington's home. The mansion was built for Martha Washington's granddaughter, Nelly Custis, who married George Washington's nephew, Lawrence

Lewis. Also on the grounds of Woodlawn is one of Frank Lloyd Wright's "Usonian Homes," the **Pope-Leighey House.** The structure, which belongs to the National Trust for Historic Preservation, was completed in 1941 at a cost of $7,000 and is one of only three homes in Virginia designed by Wright.

GETTING HERE AND AROUND

To drive to Woodlawn, travel southwest on Route 1 to the second Route 235 intersection (the first leads to Mount Vernon). The entrance to Woodlawn is on the right at the traffic light. From Mount Vernon, travel northwest on Route 235 to the Route 1 intersection; Woodlawn is straight ahead through the intersection.

To use public transportation, take Bus No. 101, 151, or 159 ($1.75 cash or $1.25 with SmarTrip card) from Huntington Metro station. Buses returning to the station have the same numbers but are marked Huntington.

 Sights

The Woodlawn Plantation is a two-part manor that consists of a home as well as a farm complex. It was recognized on the National Register of Historic Places in 2005 and is worth the short trip from Alexandria or Washington, D.C.

Woodlawn and Pope-Leighey House
HOUSE | FAMILY | Completed in 1805, Woodlawn was designed by William Thornton, a physician and amateur architect who drew up the original plans for the U.S. Capitol. Built on a site selected by George Washington as a gift for his nephew, the mansion has commanding views of the surrounding countryside and the Potomac River. At first, it was a plantation where more than 100 people, most of them enslaved, lived and worked. Yet Woodlawn's many future owners would be active opponents of enslavement and racism, from Quaker abolitionists who subdivided the property into farmsteads for free African

Americans to Senator Oscar Underwood, one of the only anti-Ku Klux Klan southern politicians in the post-Reconstruction era. Guides and exhibitions offer insight into the architectural details of the house as well as its unique legacy.

The modest and sparsely furnished Pope-Leighey House, designed by Frank Lloyd Wright, provides a stark contrast to Woodlawn. It was moved here from Falls Church, Virginia, in 1964, to save it from destruction during the building of Route 66. Built to bring nature inside, the 1,200-square-foot, two-bedroom, one-bath home features Tidewater red cypress, brick, a flat roof, and tall glass windows and doors. Even the furniture was designed by Wright. The home was commissioned by journalist Lauren Pope and his wife, Charlotte, and they lived here for six years, selling the house in 1946 to Robert and Marjorie Leighey. ⊠ *9000 Richmond Hwy., Alexandria* ☎ *703/780–4000* ⊕ *www.woodlawn-popeleighey.org* 🖾 *From $10* ☉ *Closed Tues.–Thurs.*

Gunston Hall, Virginia

12 miles south of Woodlawn, 25 miles south of Washington, D.C.

Down the Potomac from Mount Vernon is the home of another important George. Gentleman-farmer George Mason was a colonel of the Virginia militia and author of the Virginia Declaration of Rights, the model for the U.S. Bill of Rights, which called for freedom of the press, tolerance of religion, and other fundamental democratic principles. Mason was a framer of the Constitution but refused to sign the final document because it didn't stop the importation of slaves, adequately restrain the powers of the federal government, or include a bill of rights. Mason's objections spurred the movement for the inclusion of the Bill of Rights into the Constitution. This 18th-century Georgian mansion was located at the center of a 5,500-acre plantation. You can tour the home and grounds of Gunston Hall, a National Historic Landmark.

GETTING HERE AND AROUND
You'll have to use a car to get to Gunston Hall because there is no bus stop within walking distance. Travel south on Route 1, 9 miles past Woodlawn to Route 242; turn left there and go 3½ miles to the plantation entrance.

⊙ Sights

Not far from George Washington's home lies Gunston Hall, a mansion built in the 18th century for founding father George Mason. Many well-known historical figures have set foot on this land. The mansion is now known for its association with Mason as well as its intricate, unique architecture and interior design. It serves as a museum and is open to the general public.

★ **George Mason's Gunston Hall**
HOUSE | FAMILY | The Georgian-style mansion has some of the finest hand-carved ornamented interiors in the country and is the handiwork of the 18th-century's foremost architect, William Buckland, originally an indentured servant from England. Construction of Gunston Hall took place between 1755 and 1759. Buckland went on to design several notable buildings in Virginia and Maryland, including the Hammond-Harwood and Chase-Lloyd houses in Annapolis. It is believed he worked closely with another indentured servant, William Bernard Sears, to complete the house. Unlike other Virginia colonial homes which tended to be very simple, Gunston Hall was the only house known to have had chinoiserie decoration. The interior and the outbuildings have been meticulously restored.

While one of the reasons Mason didn't sign the Declaration of Independence is allegedly because it didn't stop the

importation of enslaved people, Mason was also a slaveholder of at least 300 people in his lifetime, many of whom lived at Gunston Hall. While touring the property, you have the opportunity to learn about the lives of some of these individuals, although there is currently not a permanent exhibit focusing on them.

The formal gardens, excavated by a team of archaeologists, are famous for their boxwoods-some were planted during George Mason's time, making them among the oldest in the country. The Potomac is visible past the expansive deer park, and Mason's landing road to the river has been found. Guided tours are offered daily every half hour between 9:30 am and 4:30 pm, with longer tours on Monday morning and Thursday afternoon (see the website for specific times). ✉ 10709 Gunston Rd., Mason Neck ☎ 703/550–9220 ⊕ www.gunstonhall. org ⛏ $10.

★ **National Museum of the Marine Corps**
MUSEUM | FAMILY | The glassy atrium of this 118,000-square-foot homage to the military's finest soars into the sky next to the Marine Corps Base Quantico. The design was inspired by the iconic photograph of marines lifting the American flag on Iwo Jima. Inside the museum, visitors are able to see the flag itself, as well as experience the life of a marine. The museum is completely interactive and also has a staggering collection of tanks, aircraft, rocket launchers, and other weapons. There is even a rifle range simulator, where guests of all ages can learn how to hold a laser rifle and practice hitting targets. Family Day at the Museum is held the second Saturday of the month with activities and crafts. There also are gallery hunts for children ages 4–10 that encourage exploration of the museum. ✉ 18900 Jefferson Davis Hwy., Triangle ☎ 877/635–1775 ⊕ www. usmcmuseum.org ⛏ Free.

Annapolis, Maryland

32 miles east of Washington, D.C.

This beautiful city, the capital of Maryland, offers something for everyone. Whether you spend one or several days here, you'll discover fascinating history; exciting sporting, visual, and performing arts events; great dining, shopping, and nightlife; and dozens of recreation activities. There are more 18th-century brick homes in Annapolis than in any other city in the nation, and, because the city is so walkable, it is truly a walk down memory lane. It's also a popular boating destination, and, on warm sunny days, the waters off City Dock become center stage for boats of all sizes. If you love the water, the Chesapeake Bay, and the area's winding inlets, creeks, and rivers provide wonderful opportunities for paddleboarding, kayaking, sailing, or fishing. One of Annapolis's longest-standing institutions is the U.S. Naval Academy, which has been training officers for the U.S. Navy and Marine Corps since 1845. As you stroll through downtown, you'll often see midshipmen in their crisp white uniforms in summer and navy blue in winter. A visit to the Naval Academy campus, to learn about its lengthy and proud history and get a close-up look at what life as a midshipman is like, is a must.

GETTING HERE AND AROUND

The drive (east on U.S. 50 to the Rowe Boulevard exit) normally takes 35–45 minutes from Washington. During rush hour (weekdays 3:30–6:30 pm), however, it takes about twice as long. Also, beware of Navy football Saturdays.

Parking spots on the historic downtown streets of Annapolis are scarce, but there are some meters for $2 an hour (maximum two hours). You can park on some residential streets for free for two hours, and on Sunday morning from 6 am to 1 pm, most parking is free.. The public garage adjacent to the Annapolis Visitors Center charges $2 per hour with a daily maximum of $15. The Annapolis Circulator offers free trolley transportation within the historic area.

TOURS

Walking tours are a great way to see the historic district, and Discover Annapolis Tours and Watermark run historical and ghost tours. Watermark and Schooner *Woodwind* Cruises offer boat trips.

Discover Annapolis Tours

BUS TOURS | Narrated 40- and 50-minute trolley tours, departing from the visitor center, introduce you to the history and architecture of Annapolis. Sights include Maryland State House, WWII Memorial and water views. ✉ *26 West St.* ☎ *410/626–6000* ⊕ *www.discoverannapolis.com* 💲 *From $15.*

Schooner Woodwind Cruises

BOAT TOURS | Two 74-foot sailboats, *Woodwind* and *Woodwind II*, make daily trips and overnight excursions. Guests aboard the two-hour cruises are guaranteed to see sites like the Chesapeake Bay and United States Naval Academy. Depending on the wind direction and speed, cruisers may also see the Chesapeake Bay Bridge (perhaps even going underneath), Thomas Point Lighthouse, and the Annapolis skyline. ✉ *Annapolis Waterfront Hotel dock, 80 Compromise St.* ☎ *410/263–7837, 410/263–1981* ⊕ *www.schoonerwoodwind.com* 💲 *From $65.*

★ Watermark

WALKING TOURS | Tour guides wearing Colonial-style dress take you to the State House, St. John's College, and the Naval Academy on their very popular twice-daily, 2¼-hour "Four Centuries Walking Tour." There's also a "Historic Ghost Walk" on weekends. Watermark also runs boat tours, lasting from 40 minutes to 7½ hours, going as far as St. Michael's on the Eastern Shore, where there's a maritime museum as well as dining and boutiques. ✉ *1 Dock St.* ☎ *410/268–7601* ⊕ *www.watermarkjourney.com* 💲 *From $18.*

VISITOR INFORMATION
CONTACTS Visit Annapolis & Anne Arundel County. ✉ *26 West St.* ☎ *410/280–0445, 888/302–2852* ⊕ *www.visitannapolis. org.* **Visitor Information Booth.** ✉ *1 Dock St. ⊹ Ego Alley* ☎ *410/280–0445* ⊕ *www. visitannapolis.org.*

⊙ Sights

Banneker-Douglass Museum
MUSEUM | FAMILY | This museum of African American heritage is named in honor of abolitionist Frederick Douglass and scientist Benjamin Banneker. This former church and its next-door neighbor make up a museum that tells the stories of African Americans in Maryland through performances, lectures, educational programs, and both permanent and changing exhibits. ✉ *84 Franklin St.* ☎ *410/216–6180* ⊕ *bdmuseum.maryland. gov* ➔ *Free* ⊘ *Closed Sun. and Mon.*

Hammond-Harwood House
HOUSE | Based on the Villa Pisani in Montagnana, Italy, this 1774 home was a Colonial high-style residence. Currently, the museum is working to provide and present greater visibility and documentation about those enslaved at Hammond-Harwood House, including wills and letters. Up to seven women, men, and children were enslaved here in the 19th century, according to census records, and a slavery exhibition documents what scholars and historians have learned about them thus far. There are also exhibits of Colonial art by Charles Willson Peale and Rembrandt Peale, as well as displays of decorative arts—everything from Chinese-export porcelain to Georgian-period silver. ✉ *19 Maryland Ave.* ☎ *410/263–4683* ⊕ *www.hammond-harwoodhouse.org* ➔ *$10* ⊘ *Closed Tues. By reservation Apr.–Dec.*

Historic London Town and Gardens
HISTORIC SITE | The 17th-century tobacco port of London, on the South River a short car ride from Annapolis, was made up of 40 dwellings, shops, and taverns. London all but disappeared in the 18th century, its buildings abandoned and left to decay, but one of the few remaining original Colonial structures is a three-story brick house, built by William Brown between 1758 and 1764, with dramatic river views. Newly reconstructed buildings include a tenement for lower-class workers, a carpenter's shop, and a barn. Guests can walk around on their own or take a 30-minute docent-led tour. Allow more time to wander the house grounds, woodland gardens, and a visitor center with an interactive exhibit on the area's archaeology and history. ✉ *839 London-town Rd., Edgewater* ☎ *410/222–1919* ⊕ *www.historiclondontown.org* ➔ *$10* ⊘ *Closed Mon. and Tues.*

Kunta Kinte–Alex Haley Memorial
MEMORIAL | FAMILY | *The Story Wall,* comprising 10 plaques along the waterfront, recounts the history of African Americans in Maryland. These granite-framed markers lead to a sculpture group depicting Alex Haley, famed author of *Roots,* reading to a group of children of different ethnic backgrounds. Here you'll also see a plaque that commemorates the 1767 arrival of Kunta Kinte, who was brought from Africa, sold into slavery, and later immortalized in Haley's novel. Across the street is "The Compass Rose," a 14-foot-diameter inlaid bronze map of the world oriented to true north with Annapolis in the center. ✉ *Sidewalk at City Dock* ⊕ *www.alexhaley.com.*

St. Anne's Episcopal Church
RELIGIOUS SITE | In the center of one of the historic area's busy circles, this brick building is one of the city's most prominent places of worship. King William III donated the communion silver when the parish was founded in 1692, but the first St. Anne's Church wasn't completed until 1704. The second church burned in 1858, but parts of its walls survived and were incorporated into the present structure, which was built the following year. Free

Annapolis, Maryland

Sights ▼

1 Banneker-Douglass Museum **C3**

2 Hammond-Harwood House **D2**

3 Historic London Town and Gardens............. **A5**

4 Kunta Kinte–Alex Haley Memorial **D3**

5 St. Anne's Episcopal Church **C2**

6 St. John's College........ **C1**

7 United States Naval Academy **D1**

8 U.S. Naval Academy Museum **D1**

9 William Paca House and Garden.............. **D2**

Restaurants ▼

1 Cantler's Riverside Inn.. **E1**

2 Carrol's Creek Cafe..... **D4**

3 Chick & Ruth's Delly.... **C3**

4 49 West Coffeehouse, Winebar and Gallery.... **B2**

5 Galway Bay Irish Restaurant and Pub..... **C2**

6 Harry Browne's.......... **C2**

7 Iron Rooster............. **D2**

8 Metropolitan Kitchen & Lounge **B3**

9 Osteria 177 .... **C3**

10 Preserve................. **C2**

11 Rams Head Tavern **C2**

12 Vin 909 Winecafé....... **D5**

Quick Bites ▼

1 Old Fox Books and Coffeehouse **D2**

Hotels ▼

1 Annapolis Waterfront Hotel, Autograph Collection................. **D3**

2 Country Inn & Suites by Radisson, Annapolis, MD **B1**

3 Gibson's Lodgings of Annapolis................ **D2**

4 Historic Inns of Annapolis................. **C2**

5 Scotlaur Inn **C3**

6 The Westin Annapolis................ **A3**

guided tours are offered the first and third Monday of every month at 10 am and every Wednesday at 12:30 pm.

The churchyard contains the grave of the last Colonial governor, Sir Robert Eden. ⊠ *Church Circle* ☎ *410/267–9333* ⊕ *www.stannes-annapolis.org* ✉ *Free.*

St. John's College

COLLEGE | St. John's is the third-oldest college in the country (after Harvard and William and Mary) and adheres to a Great Books program: all students follow the same four-year, liberal-arts curriculum, which includes philosophy, mathematics, music, science, Greek, and French. Students are immersed in the classics through small classes conducted as discussions rather than lectures. Start a visit here by climbing the slope of the long, brick-paved path to the cupola of McDowell Hall.

Down King George Street toward the water is the **Carroll-Barrister House,** now the college admissions office. Once home to Charles Carroll (not the signer of the Declaration, but his cousin), the house was built in 1722 at Main and Conduit streets and moved onto campus in 1955. The **Elizabeth Myers Mitchell Art Gallery,** on the east side of Mellon Hall, presents world-class exhibits and special programs that relate to the fine arts. ⊠ *60 College Ave.* ☎ *410/263–2371* ⊕ *www.sjc.edu* ☉ *Mitchell Gallery closed Mon.*

★ United States Naval Academy

COLLEGE | Probably the most interesting and important site in Annapolis, the Naval Academy, established in 1845, occupies 338 waterfront acres along the Severn River. The midshipmen (the term used for both women and men) go to classes, conduct military drills, and practice or compete in intercollegiate and intramural sports. Your visit to "The Yard" (as the USNA grounds are nicknamed) will start at the **Armel-Leftwich Visitor Center.** The visitor center features an exhibit, *The*

Quarter Deck, which introduces visitors to the academy's mission, including a 13-minute film, *The Call to Serve,* and a well-stocked gift shop. From here you can join one of the hour-long, guided, walking tours of the academy. The centerpiece of the campus is the bright, copper-clad dome of the interdenominational **U.S. Naval Academy Chapel,** beneath which is buried Revolutionary War naval hero John Paul Jones. You can go inside Bancroft Hall (one of the world's largest dormitories) and see a sample room and the glorious Memorial Hall. ■TIP➜ **Visitors can have lunch on campus either at Drydock in Dahlgren Hall or the Naval Academy Club.** ⊠ *121 Blake Rd.* ⊹ *Enter on foot through Visitor Access Center at Gate 1* ☎ *410/293–8687* ⊕ *www.usna. edu* ✉ *Free* ☞ *All visitors 18 years and older must have government-issued photo ID to be admitted. Visitors may not park on campus.*

U.S. Naval Academy Museum

MUSEUM | FAMILY | Displays of model ships and memorabilia from naval heroes and fighting vessels tell the story of the U.S. Navy. The Rogers Ship Model Collection has nearly 80 models of sailing ships built for the British Admiralty, the largest display of 17th- and 18th-century ship models in North America. Kids of all ages will enjoy watching the restoration and building of model ships on the ground level and might even learn a few tricks of the trade should they wish to purchase a model ship kit to build when they get home. ⊠ *Preble Hall, 118 Maryland Ave.* ⊹ *On campus, so government-issued photo ID is required for visitors 18 and older* ☎ *410/293–2108* ⊕ *www.usna.edu* ✉ *Free.*

William Paca House and Garden

HOUSE | A signer of the Declaration of Independence, William Paca (pronounced "PAY-cuh") was a Maryland governor from 1782 to 1785. His house was built from 1763 through 1765, and its original garden was finished by 1772. The

Did You Know?

The Navy's Blue Angels fly over each graduating class at the U.S. Naval Academy in Annapolis to celebrate their accomplishments.

main floor (furnished with 18th-century antiques) retains its original Prussian blue and soft gray color scheme, and the second floor houses more 18th-century pieces. The adjacent 2-acre pleasure garden provides a longer perspective on the back of the house, plus worthwhile sights of its own: upper terraces, a Chinese Chippendale bridge, a pond, a wilderness area, physic garden, and formal arrangements. An inn, Carvel Hall, once stood in the gardens, now planted with 18th-century perennials. Guests can take a self-guided tour of the garden, but to see the house, take the docent-led tour. Private tours can be arranged. The last tour leaves 1½ hours before closing. ✉ 186 Prince George St. ☎ 410/990–4543 ⊕ www.annapolis.org 🎫 $15 🕙 Closed Jan. and Feb.

🍴 Restaurants

In the beginning, there was crab: crab cakes, crab soup, whole crabs to crack. This Chesapeake Bay specialty is still found in abundance, but Annapolis has broadened its horizons to include eateries—many in the historic district—that offer many sorts of cuisines. Ask for a restaurant guide at the visitor center.

★ Cantler's Riverside Inn

$$$ | SEAFOOD | Jimmy Cantler, a native Marylander who worked as a waterman on Chesapeake Bay, founded this local institution 40 years ago. The no-nonsense interior has nautical items laminated beneath tabletops, and steamed mussels, clams, and shrimp as well as a tomato-based Maryland crab soup, seafood sandwiches, crab cakes, and much more. **Known for:** seasonal outdoor dining right next to the water; steamed crabs served on a "tablecloth" of brown paper; a classic casual Maryland seafood experience. 💲 Average main: $35 ✉ 458 Forest Beach Rd. ☎ 410/757–1311 ⊕ www.cantlers.com.

Carrol's Creek Cafe

$$$ | AMERICAN | You can walk, catch a water taxi from City Dock, or drive over the Spa Creek drawbridge to this local favorite in Eastport. Whether you dine indoors or out, the view of historic Annapolis and its harbor is spectacular. **Known for:** à la carte Sunday brunch; upscale (but not too pricey) seafood specialties; amazing city and harbor views. 💲 Average main: $34 ✉ 410 Severn Ave. ☎ 410/263–8102 ⊕ www.carrolscreek.com.

Chick and Ruth's Delly

$ | AMERICAN | Deli sandwiches (many named after local politicians), burgers, subs, crab cakes, and milk shakes are the fare at this very busy counter-and-booth institution. Baltimoreans Ruth and Chick Levitt purchased the building, built in 1899, in 1965. **Known for:** giant milk shakes (including a 6-pounder); patriotic decor and a daily recitation of the Pledge of Allegiance; homemade pies and breads. 💲 Average main: $9 ✉ 165 Main St. ☎ 410/269–6737 ⊕ www.chickandruths.com.

49 West Coffeehouse, Winebar and Gallery

$$ | ECLECTIC | In what was once a hardware store, this casual eatery has one interior wall of exposed brick and another of exposed plaster; both are used to hang art for sale by local artists. Daily specials are chalked on a blackboard and include a large cheese-and-pâté plate, flatbread pizzas, deli sandwiches, espresso, waffles, soups, and salads. **Known for:** live music every night; eclectic coffeehouse vibe; flatbread pizzas, deli sandwiches, and coffee galore. 💲 Average main: $17 ✉ 49 West St. ☎ 410/626–9796 ⊕ 49westcoffeehouse.com.

★ Galway Bay Irish Restaurant and Pub

$ | IRISH | Step inside this Irish pub, and you'll be welcomed like a member of the family. As would be expected, the corned beef and cabbage and other traditional Irish menu items (along with classic Annapolis bar food like crab and oysters) are fantastic. **Known for:** traditional Irish grub and hospitality; authentic house-made corned-beef hash; Sunday brunch with live music. $ *Average main: $12* ✉ *63 Maryland Ave.* ☎ *301/263–8333* ⊕ *www.galwaybaymd.com.*

Harry Browne's

$$$ | **AMERICAN** | In the shadow of the state house, this understated establishment has long held a reputation for quality food and attentive service that ensures bustle year-round, especially during the busy days of the legislative session (early January into early April) and special weekend events at the Naval Academy. The menu clearly reflects the city's maritime culture, but also has seasonal specialties. **Known for:** political clientele; tasty homemade desserts, such as Oreo cheesecake; champagne brunch on Sunday. $ *Average main: $35* ✉ *66 State Circle* ☎ *410/263–4332* ⊕ *www.harrybrownes.com.*

★ Iron Rooster

$ | **AMERICAN** | There's often a line of hungry diners waiting for a table at this comfort-food haven located on the city dock, where the portions are generous, and the service is first-rate. You can enjoy breakfast all day—Benedicts and omelets are top sellers, as are the chicken and waffles and the shrimp and grits. **Known for:** daily homemade pop-tart specials; Southern-inspired all-day breakfast (including amazingly light and fluffy biscuits); long lines. $ *Average main: $15* ✉ *12 Market Space* ☎ *410/990–1600* ⊕ *www.ironroosterallday.com.*

Metropolitan Kitchen & Lounge

$$ | **MEDITERRANEAN** | One of the few restaurants in the city with a rooftop, this establishment co-owned by Annapolis mayor Gavin Buckley, takes full advantage of its lovely perch and features live music most evenings. The menu satisfies global palates in a town otherwise known for Old Bay and crab cakes, bringing in a bit of Australia flair from the mayor's homeland. **Known for:** lamb burgers and

traditional Greek salad; one of the few rooftop bars in town; craft cocktails. $ *Average main: $24* ✉ *175 West St.* ☎ *410/280–5160.*

★ Osteria 177

$$$$ | **MODERN ITALIAN** | This might be the only local Italian restaurant that doesn't offer pizza or spaghetti. Instead, Osteria serves seafood from all over the world, meat, and pasta made on the premises. **Known for:** politicians and lobbyists at lunchtime; authentic coastal Italian cuisine; unique pastas. $ *Average main: $38* ✉ *177 Main St.* ☎ *410/267–7700* ⊕ *www.osteria177.com.*

Preserve

$$$ | **AMERICAN** | Jars of pickled chard stems and radishes, preserved lemons, and pepper jelly line the shelves at this lively spot on Main Street run by a husband-and-wife team who both have impressive culinary resumes and a shared passion for pickling, fermenting, and preserving. The chef's roots in the Pennsylvania Dutch country shine through with chicken potpie, pork and sauerkraut, and a Dutch hash and liverwurst sandwich. **Known for:** varied dishes that highlight unique preservation methods; kimchi and sauerkraut galore; lots of seasonal veggies. $ *Average main: $29* ✉ *164 Main St.* ☎ *443/598–6920* ⊕ *www.preserve-eats.com* ⊗ *Closed Mon. and Tues.*

Rams Head Tavern

$ | **BRITISH** | This traditional English-style pub serves better-than-usual tavern fare, as well as more than 100 beers—30 on tap—including five Fordham beers and others from around the world. Brunch is served on Sunday, and nationally known folk, rock, jazz, country, and bluegrass artists perform most nights. **Known for:** Maryland cream of crab soup; massive beer menu; live music. $ *Average main: $15* ✉ *33 West St.* ☎ *410/268–4545* ⊕ *www.ramsheadtavern.com.*

Vin 909 Winecafé

$ | **AMERICAN** | If it wasn't for the sign out front, you might think you're at someone's Eastport home, given the charming front porch and well-tended gardens. But walk through the doors, and you'll discover a casually hip and always crowded restaurant serving organic, sustainable, and seasonally focused food that's simply fantastic. **Known for:** crispy pizza with farm-to-table toppings; huge wine menu by the glass and bottle; diverse selection of beers. $ *Average main: $16* ⊠ *909 Bay Ridge Ave.* ☎ *410/990–1846* ⊕ *www. vin909.com* ⊘ *Closed Mon.*

☕ Coffee and Quick Bites

Old Fox Books and Coffeehouse

$ | **BAKERY** | With a carefully selected collection of new and used titles, this store is an oasis from the ubiquitous chains, and its café is a local favorite spot for an espresso drink or freshly baked pastry. After a bite, head outside to see the charming Fairy Garden and book house, which is literally made of books. **Known for:** popular meeting spot for locals; coffee drinks made with beans from local roaster, Ceremony Coffee; annual Harry Potter birthday party. $ *Average main: $7* ⊠ *35 Maryland Ave.* ☎ *410/626–2020* ⊕ *oldfoxbooks.com.*

Hotels

There are many places to stay near the heart of the city, as well as bed-and-breakfasts and chain motels a few miles outside town. Prices vary considerably. They rise astronomically for "Commissioning Week" at the Naval Academy (late May), the week of July 4, and during the sailboat and powerboat shows in October.

Annapolis Waterfront Hotel, Autograph Collection

$$$ | **HOTEL** | **FAMILY** | You can practically fish from your room at the city's only waterfront hotel (now part of Marriott's Autograph Collection), where rooms have either balconies over the water or large windows with views of the harbor or the historic district. **Pros:** "feather free room" available for the allergy sensitive upon request; accessible for travelers with disabilities; complimentary Wi-Fi throughout. **Cons:** some rooms have no waterfront view, some have only partial views; chain hotel lacks charm; parking is pricey. $ *Rooms from: $299* ⊠ *80 Compromise St.* ☎ *410/268–7555* ⊕ *www. annapoliswaterfront.com* ⤳ *150 rooms* ⦿ *No meals.*

Country Inn & Suites by Radisson, Annapolis, MD

$ | **HOTEL** | Although this hotel is 5 miles from the historic Annapolis waterfront, there's a free shuttle, and the two-room suites with pullout sofas are perfect for families. **Pros:** reliable and inexpensive option; free shuttle services; complimentary Wi-Fi. **Cons:** distance from the dock; tiny gym; small indoor heated pool can be crowded at times. $ *Rooms from: $145* ⊠ *2600 Housely Rd.* ☎ *410/571–6700, 800/456–4000* ⊕ *www. countryinns.com* ⤳ *100 rooms* ⦿ *Free Breakfast.*

Gibson's Lodgings of Annapolis

$$$ | **HOTEL** | Just half a block from the water, the three detached houses that form this hotel come from three centuries—the years 1780, 1890, and 1980, to be exact—and all the guest rooms are furnished with pre-1900 antiques. **Pros:** conveniently located between the Naval Academy and downtown; free parking in the courtyards; free continental breakfast. **Cons:** cannot accommodate children under the age of eight; two of the rooms share a bathroom; no elevator, although three rooms are on the ground floor. $ *Rooms from: $280* ⊠ *110 Prince George St.* ☎ *410/268-5555, 877/330-0057* ⊕ *www.gibsonslodgings.com* ⤳ *20 rooms* ⦿ *Free Breakfast.*

★ Historic Inns of Annapolis

$ | **B&B/INN** | Three 18th-century proper-ties in the historic district—the Governor Calvert House, Robert Johnson House, and Maryland Inn—are grouped as one inn, all offering guest rooms individually decorated with antiques and reproduc-tions. **Pros:** beautifully renovated historic properties; within walking distance of activities; lemonade or spiced cider served daily in the Calvert House. **Cons:** prices vary greatly; some rooms are small; $30 valet parking. $ *Rooms from: $159 ⊠ 58 State Circle ☎ 410/263–2641, 800/847–8882 ⊕ www.historicinnsofan-napolis.com ⬆ 124 rooms ⦶ No meals.*

Scotlaur Inn

$ | **B&B/INN** | On the two floors above Chick and Ruth's Delly in the heart of the historic district, this family-owned B&B is cozy and characterful. **Pros:** a chance to stay above one of Annapolis's landmarks; half off in nearby parking garage; literally in the heart of town. **Cons:** not for those who prefer modern style; rooms are on the small side; no elevator. $ *Rooms from: $100 ⊠ 165 Main St. ☎ 410/268–5665 ⊕ www.scotlaurinn.com ⬆ 10 rooms ⦶ Free Breakfast.*

The Westin Annapolis

$$ | **HOTEL** | **FAMILY** | About 1½ miles from City Dock, in a rapidly gentrifying neighborhood, this hotel is the center-piece of a European-themed planned community, complete with restaurants, shops, and condominiums. **Pros:** comfy "heavenly beds"; modern hotel with many amenities; spacious guest rooms. **Cons:** distance from the City Dock; Wi-Fi only free in public areas; lacking charm found in other historic properties. $ *Rooms from: $249 ⊠ 100 Westgate Circle ☎ 410/972–4300 ⊕ www.marriott.com ⬆ 225 rooms ⦶ No meals.*

Baltimore, Maryland

39 miles northeast of Washington, D.C.

Baltimore is a city of distinct neighbor-hoods. While stellar downtown attrac-tions such as the National Aquarium and the Inner Harbor draw torrents of tourists each year, much of the city's character can be found in districts like Hampden (the "p" is silent) and Federal Hill. Bal-timore was of the largest cities in early America, thanks to a protected harbor, which gave it a strategic advantage. Tour-ism grew dramatically in the early 1980s with the completion of the Harborplace shopping plaza and its crown jewel, the National Aquarium. Further development of the Inner Harbor, including Oriole Park at Camden Yards and M&T Bank Stadium, continued to fuel the city's resurgence.

GETTING HERE AND AROUND

If you are going to Baltimore by car, it's about an hour from Washington, D.C. Parking in the Inner Harbor area, where most tourist attractions are, can be expensive. Fell's Point is usually cheaper.

It's generally easier and faster (and cheaper, considering the cost of parking) to get to Baltimore from D.C. by train. MARC Penn Line trains run from Union Station to Baltimore's Penn Station several times a day, including weekends, taking about 45 minutes and costing $7. You can also take Amtrak from Union Station to Baltimore Penn Station, but it's about twice as expensive. The Camden Line runs only during commuting hours on weekdays and takes a bit longer, but takes you to Camden Station, which is more convenient to the Inner Harbor sights. You can also take a bus from Union Station, but it generally takes longer.

Once in Baltimore, you can take the free Charm City Circulator shuttle (four bus lines plus a harbor ferry), or, if you are in a hurry, jump in a taxi or ride-share.

CONTACTS **Charm City Circulator.** ✉ *1700 Cherry Hill Rd., Baltimore* 🕿 *410/545–1956* ⊕ *www.charmcitycirculator.com.* **Maryland Transit Administration.** 🕿 *800/325–7245, 410/539–5000* ⊕ *www.mta.maryland.gov.*

VISITOR INFORMATION
CONTACTS **Baltimore Visitor Center.** ✉ *401 Light St., Inner Harbor* 🕿 *877/225–8466* ⊕ *www.baltimore.org.*

👁 Sights

Most of the major sights in Baltimore are in the Inner Harbor area or nearby, but you may also want to visit some sights that are farther out, all of which are on one of the Charm City Connector routes.

★ American Visionary Art Museum
MUSEUM | The nation's primary museum and education center for self-taught or "outsider" art has won great acclaim by both museum experts and those who don't even consider themselves art aficionados. Seven galleries exhibit the quirky creations—paintings, sculptures, relief works, and pieces that defy easy classification—of untrained "visionary" artists working outside the mainstream art world. In addition to the visual stimulation of amazingly intricate or refreshingly inventive works, reading the short bios of artists will give you insight to their often-moving spiritual and expressive motivations. The museum's unusual, playful philosophy extends outside its walls, with large exhibits installed in a former whiskey warehouse, an outdoor movie theater, and a 55-foot whirligig twirling in the museum's plaza. ✉ *800 Key Hwy., Federal Hill* 🕿 *410/244–1900* ⊕ *www.avam.org* 💲 *$16* 🕑 *Closed Mon. and Tues.*

★ Baltimore Museum of Art
MUSEUM | Works by Matisse, Picasso, Cézanne, Gauguin, van Gogh, and Monet are among the 90,000 paintings, sculptures, and decorative arts on exhibit at this impressive museum near Johns Hopkins University. Particular strengths include an encyclopedic collection of Postimpressionist paintings donated to the museum by the Cone sisters, Baltimore natives who were pioneer collectors of early-20th-century art. The museum also owns the world's second-largest collection of Andy Warhol works and many pieces of 18th- and 19th-century American painting and decorative arts. The museum's Neoclassical main building was designed by John Russell Pope, the architect of the National Gallery in Washington. A $28-million renovation resulted in a new, interactive exhibition space, a renovated visitor's entrance, and a completely reworked contemporary wing. From Gertrude's, the museum restaurant, you can look out at 20th-century sculpture displayed in two landscaped gardens. ✉ *10 Art Museum Dr., Charles Village* 🕿 *443/573–1700* ⊕ *www.artbma.org* 💲 *Free* 🕑 *Closed Mon. and Tues.*

★ Fort McHenry National Monument and Historic Shrine
MILITARY SITE | This star-shaped brick fort is forever associated with Francis Scott Key and "The Star-Spangled Banner," which Key penned while watching the British bombardment of Baltimore during the War of 1812. Through the next day and night, as the battle raged, Key strained to be sure, through the smoke and haze, that the flag still flew above Fort McHenry—indicating that Baltimore's defenders held firm. "By the dawn's early light" of September 14, 1814, he saw the 30- by 42-foot "Star-Spangled Banner" still aloft and was inspired to pen the words to a poem (set to the tune of an old English drinking song). A visit to the fort includes a 15-minute history film, guided tour, and frequent living-history displays on summer weekends. To see how the formidable fortifications might have appeared to the bombarding British, catch a water taxi from the Inner Harbor to the fort

301

14

Side Trips from Washington, D.C. **BALTIMORE, MARYLAND**

303

Sights ▼

1 American Visionary
   Art Museum **F9**
2 Baltimore Museum of Art......... **D1**
3 Fort McHenry National Monument
   and Historic Shrine **G9**
4 George Peabody Library.......... **D3**
5 The National Great Blacks
   In Wax Museum **J1**
6 Oriole Park at Camden Yards..... **G8**
7 Walters Art Museum............... **C3**
8 Washington Monument........... **D3**
9 Westminster Burying
   Ground and Catacombs........... **A5**

Restaurants ▼

1   Ambassador Dining Room........ **D1**
2   Azumi............................... **G8**
3   Charleston **H8**
4   Cinghiale........................... **G8**
5   The Food Market.................. **D1**
6   Gertrude's **D1**
7   The Helmand **C2**
8   La Cuchara **D1**
9   Ouzo Bay........................... **H8**
10 The Prime Rib **E1**
11 Rye Street Tavern................. **B9**
12 Woodberry Kitchen............... **D1**

Hotels ▼

1 1840s Carrollton Inn **G6**
2 Four Seasons Baltimore **G9**
3 Hilton Baltimore Inner Harbor.... **B7**
4 Hotel Monaco Baltimore........... **C6**
5 Hotel Revival **C3**
6 The Ivy Hotel **E1**
7 Marriott Baltimore Waterfront... **G8**
8 Sagamore Pendry Baltimore......**J9**

instead of driving. ⊠ *E. Fort Ave., Locust Point* ⊹ *From Light St., take Key Hwy. for 1½ miles and follow signs* ☎ *410/962–4290* ⊕ *www.nps.gov/fomc* 💲 *$15.*

George Peabody Library

LIBRARY | Known as a "cathedral of books," the five-story reading room is consistently listed among the world's most beautiful libraries. Designed by Edmund Lind, it opened to the public in 1878. Its gilded framework of cast iron and gold showcases more than 300,000 volumes printed from the 15th to the 19th centuries in the areas of archaeology, architecture, history, literature, travel, and art. ⊠ *17 E. Mt. Vernon Pl., Mount Vernon* ☎ *410/234–4943* ⊕ *peabodyevents.library.jhu.edu.*

The National Great Blacks in Wax Museum

MUSEUM | **FAMILY** | More than 100 wax figures on display recount the triumphs and trials of Africans and African Americans. The wax figures are accompanied by text and audio. Baltimoreans honored include Frederick Douglass, who as a youth lived and worked in Fells Point; singer Billie Holiday; and jazz composer Eubie Blake. To get here from Mount Vernon, take Charles Street north and turn left at North Avenue. ⊠ *1601 E. North Ave., East Baltimore* ☎ *410/563–3404* ⊕ *www.greatblacksinwax.org* 💲 *$15* ⊙ *Closed Mon.*

★ Oriole Park at Camden Yards

SPORTS VENUE | **FAMILY** | Home of the Baltimore Orioles, Camden Yards and the nearby area bustle on game days. Since it opened in 1992, this nostalgically designed baseball stadium has inspired other cities to emulate its neotraditional architecture and amenities. The Eutaw Street promenade, between the warehouse and the field, has a view of the stadium. Look for the brass baseballs embedded in the sidewalk that mark where home runs have cleared the fence, or visit the Orioles Hall of Fame display and the monuments to retired Orioles. Daily 90-minute tours take you to nearly every section of the ballpark, from the massive JumboTron scoreboard to the dugout to the state-of-the-art beer-delivery system. ⊠ *333 W. Camden St., Downtown* ☎ *410/685–9800 general info, 410/547–6234 tour info, 888/848–2473 tickets to Orioles home games* ⊕ *www.orioles.com* 💲 *Eutaw St. promenade free, tour $15.*

★ Walters Art Museum

MUSEUM | The Walters' prodigious collection of more than 30,000 artworks provides an organized overview of human history over 5,500 years, from the 3rd millennium BC to the early 20th century. The museum houses major collections of Renaissance, Baroque, and Asian art as well as one of the nation's best collections of Egyptian, Greek, Roman, Byzantine, and Ethiopian works. It also houses Medieval armor and artifacts, jewelry and decorative works, a gift shop, a family activities and arts center on the lower-level, and a café. ⊠ *600 N. Charles St., Mount Vernon* ☎ *410/547–9000* ⊕ *www.thewalters.org* 💲 *Free* ⊙ *Closed Mon. and Tues.*

★ Washington Monument

MEMORIAL | **FAMILY** | Completed on July 4, 1829, the impressive monument was the first one dedicated to the nation's first president. An 18-foot statue depicting Washington caps the 160-foot white marble tower. The tower was designed and built by Robert Mills, the first architect born and educated in the United States; 19 years after completing Baltimore's Washington Monument, Mills designed and erected the national Washington Monument in D.C. After extensive restorations, the monument's lower-level museum has reopened; visitors can climb the 227-step circular staircase to the top and enjoy stunning bird's-eye vistas over downtown. ⊠ *Mt. Vernon Pl., Mount Vernon* ☎ *202/426-6841* ⊕ *mvpconservancy.org/the-monument* 💲 *$6* ⊙ *Closed Mon. and Tues.*

Westminster Burying Ground and Catacombs

CEMETERY | The city's oldest cemetery is the final resting place of Edgar Allan Poe and other famous Marylanders, including 15 generals from the American Revolution and the War of 1812. Dating from 1786, the cemetery was originally known as the Old Western Burying Grounds. In the early 1850s, a city ordinance demanded that burial grounds be part of a church, so a building was constructed above the cemetery, creating catacombs beneath it. In the 1930s, the schoolchildren of Baltimore collected pennies to raise the necessary funds for Poe's monument. Tours of Westminster Hall (which include the Burying Ground and Catacombs) are offered from April through November every first and third Friday at 6:30 pm and every Saturday at 10 am. ⊠ *University of Maryland, Westminster Hall, 519 W. Fayette St., Downtown* ☎ *410/706–2072 tour information and reservations* ⊕ *baltimore.org/listings/historic-sites/westminster-hall-burying-ground* 🚶 *Cemetery free; tours $5.*

🍴 Restaurants

Ambassador Dining Room

$$ | INDIAN | A Tudor-style dining room in a 1930s apartment building is the setting for superb Indian fare. Go for the classics such as chicken *tikka masala* (grilled chicken in a sauce of red pepper, ginger, garlic, and yogurt) or *alu gobi* (spicy potatoes and cauliflower). **Known for:** outdoor dining in the lovely garden; excellent service; traditional Indian desserts. $ *Average main: $26* ⊠ *3811 Canterbury Rd., Tuscany-Canterbury* ☎ *410/366–1484* ⊕ *www.ambassadordining.com* ☾ *Closed Mon.*

Azumi

$$$ | JAPANESE | In a town known for its local catch, Azumi's chef flies his fish in daily from Tokyo's famous fish market. Creative takes on Maryland specialties

are sure to delight, such as the crab starter, made with tiny Sawagani crabs, which are fried whole and pop in your mouth like buttered popcorn. **Known for:** excellent sashimi, including fresh hamachi; extensive list of Japanese whiskeys; beautiful waterfront views in a luxury hotel setting. $ *Average main: $35* ⊠ *Four Seasons Hotel Baltimore, 725 Aliceanna St., Harbor East* ☎ *443/220–0477* ⊕ *www.azumirestaurant.com.*

★ Charleston

$$$$ | SOUTHERN | Chef-owner Cindy Wolf's cuisine has a South Carolina Low Country accent with French roots—and the results are unparalleled. Inside the glowingly lit dining room, classics like she-crab soup and shrimp and grits complement more elegant fare, such as a lobster bisque spiced with curry or wild salmon with avocado. **Known for:** decadent desserts; excellent service; the city's most elegant dining room. $ *Average main: $79* ⊠ *1000 Lancaster St., Harbor East* ☎ *410/332–7373* ⊕ *www.charlestonrestaurant.com* ☾ *Closed Sun.* 🧥 *Jacket and tie.*

Cinghiale

$$ | ITALIAN | The spotlight is on wine at Cinghiale (pronounced *ching-GYAH-lay*), an open, inviting space with tall, wide windows. Enjoy hand-cut pastas such as tagliatelle with tender chicken, greens, and walnuts or lasagna with veal ragù. **Known for:** northern Italian fare; vast wine list of more than 600 bottles; sharp and unpretentious service. $ *Average main: $22* ⊠ *822 Lancaster St., Harbor East* ☎ *410/547–8282* ⊕ *www.cgeno.com* ☾ *No lunch.*

The Food Market

$$ | FUSION | FAMILY | In the heart of Hampden, on "The Avenue" (36th Street), chef Chad Gauss presents some of Baltimore's most consistently excellent dining with a global reach. Try the Amish soft pretzels with cheddar-cheese dipping sauce as a starter, then move on

to coconut green curry or the lamb with spaetzle. **Known for:** convivial atmosphere; popular Saturday and Sunday brunch with huge pours; desserts like Heath bar bread pudding. $ *Average main: $26* ✉ *1017 W. 36th St., Hampden* ☎ *410/366–0606* ⊕ *www.thefoodmarket-baltimore.com* ⊗ *No lunch weekdays.*

Gertrude's

$$ | **AMERICAN** | In the Baltimore Museum of Art, this casual yet classy spot cooks up creative Maryland specialties. Crab cakes, served with a variety of tasty sauces, are one option, Parmesan-crusted salmon is another. **Known for:** lovely outdoor terrace overlooking the sculpture garden; a commitment to sustainable Chesapeake cuisine; Sunday jazz brunch. $ *Average main: $25* ✉ *Baltimore Museum of Art, 10 Art Museum Dr., Charles Village* ☎ *410/889–3399* ⊕ *www.gertrudesbaltimore.com* ⊗ *Closed Mon.*

The Helmand

$ | **AFGHAN** | Owned by Hamid Kharzai's brother, Qayum Karzai, Helmand serves outstanding Afghan fare in a casual yet elegant space. Beautiful woven textiles and traditional dresses adorn the walls, adding color to the simple white table settings. **Known for:** outstanding lamb dishes; vegetarian; the unforgettable appetizer. $ *Average main: $13* ✉ *806 N. Charles St., Mount Vernon* ☎ *410/752–0311* ⊕ *www.helmand.com* ⊗ *Closed Mon.*

La Cuchara

$$$$ | **BASQUE** | Authentic Basque cuisine is on full display at this lovely restaurant located in the Meadow Mill building: *pinxtos* like ham croquettes with Gruyère cheese, sardines in oil, and fingerling potatoes with garlic aioli are perfect for sharing. The vast space is anchored by a 40-foot chestnut bar, behind which sits a wood-fired grill. **Known for:** duck breast with a honey-Banyuis reduction; house-made breads; friendly service. $ *Average main: $38* ✉ *3600 Clipper Mill*

Rd., Hampden ✛ *Turn into mill complex, crossing wooden bridge, which spans Jones Falls (expressway is overhead). Note: only one car can cross bridge at a time* ☎ *443/708–3838* ⊕ *www.lacuchara-baltimore.com* ⊗ *No lunch weekdays.*

Ouzo Bay

$$$ | **MEDITERRANEAN** | Blink, and you may think you're in South Beach: this trendy restaurant has quickly become the city's most popular, where the suit-and-tie crowd sidles up to the elevated bar or takes a seat on the cushy outdoor terrace. Try the grilled octopus starter, tossed with lemon juice and capers, or the charcoal-grilled whole fish, be it wild sea bass, sole, or snapper. **Known for:** laid-back, sexy vibe; Mediterranean-style seafood; grilled lamp chops. $ *Average main: $35* ✉ *1000 Lancaster St., Harbor East* ☎ *443/708–5818* ⊕ *www.ouzobay.com.*

The Prime Rib

$$$$ | **STEAKHOUSE** | Bustling and crowded, this luxuriously dark dining room is just north of Mount Vernon Square and a five-minute drive from the Inner Harbor. The leopard-print carpet and live pianist lend a swanky 1960s feel to a place that seems untouched by time, including the meat-heavy menu of steak-house classics. **Known for:** superb prime rib and an even better filet mignon; jumbo lump crab cakes; good but predominately U.S. wine list. $ *Average main: $60* ✉ *1101 N. Calvert St., Mount Vernon* ☎ *410/539–1804* ⊕ *www.theprimerib.com* ⊗ *No lunch.*

★ Rye Street Tavern

$$$ | **SOUTHERN** | Baltimore's best new restaurant is located in the rapidly developing—and hotly contested—Port Covington neighborhood, a waterfront destination just south of Federal Hill off Interstate 95. Here, New York celebrity-chef Andrew Carmellini spotlights Southern flavors, such as whiskey grilled ribs, AC's Famous Fried Chicken,

and crab-stuffed deviled eggs. **Known for:** local seafood; gorgeous Tidewater-style construction with waterfront views; craft cocktails made with locally distilled Sagamore Spirit rye. $ *Average main: $33* ⊠ *13 Rye St., Federal Hill* ☎ *443/662–8000* ⊕ *www.ryestreettavern. com* ⊗ *Closed Mon.*

★ Woodberry Kitchen

$$$$ | **AMERICAN** | In an old flour mill, Woodberry Kitchen has a cozy, relaxed atmosphere and a menu that harkens back to a simpler era. The best items are often the most basic since chef and owner Spike Gjerde is committed to sourcing the finest local ingredients. **Known for:** cast-iron chicken and biscuits with carrots and string beans; homemade ice cream with hot fudge and peanuts; lovely outdoor garden terrace. $ *Average main: $36* ⊠ *2010 Clipper Park Rd., Suite 126, Hampden* ☎ *410/464–8000* ⊕ *www. woodberrykitchen.com* ⊗ *No lunch weekdays.*

 Hotels

★ 1840s Carrollton Inn

$$ | **B&B/INN** | This boutique hotel is a series of interconnected row homes that date from the early 19th century. **Pros:** gourmet made-to-order breakfast; complimentary Wi-Fi; impeccable service. **Cons:** free parking is first come, first served; neighborhood can be noisy after hours; small elevators. $ *Rooms from: $275* ⊠ *50 Albemarle St., Baltimore* ☎ *410/385–1840* ⊕ *www.1840splaza.com* ⊃ *13 rooms* ⊚ *Free Breakfast.*

★ Four Seasons Baltimore

$$$$ | **HOTEL** | The 18-story glass tower rises above the harbor, commanding prime views from each plush and comfortable (albeit minimalist) guest room. **Pros:** hands down, Baltimore's most luxurious hotel; impeccable service; within walking distance to the Inner Harbor and Fells Point. **Cons:** room rates are steep, even in the off-season; expensive valet parking;

ongoing construction around Harbor East can be noisy. $ *Rooms from: $499* ⊠ *200 International Dr., Harbor East* ☎ *410/576–5800* ⊕ *www.fourseasons.com/baltimore* ⊃ *256 rooms* ⊚ *No meals.*

Hilton Baltimore Inner Harbor

$ | **HOTEL** | The towering Hilton has an unparalleled view of Camden Yards and a skywalk that connects to the city's convention center. **Pros:** connected to the convention center; excellent ballpark views; on-site Coffee Bean & Tea Leaf. **Cons:** rooms are considerably smaller than those at similarly priced hotels in town; it's a chain hotel, albeit a nice one; busy convention hotel generates crowds. $ *Rooms from: $194* ⊠ *401 W. Pratt St., Inner Harbor* ☎ *443/573–8700* ⊕ *www. hilton.com* ⊃ *757 rooms* ⊚ *No meals.*

Hotel Monaco Baltimore

$ | **HOTEL** | **FAMILY** | This boutique hotel is in the historic headquarters of the B&O Railroad—just 2½ blocks from the Inner Harbor and within easy walking distance of Oriole Park at Camden Yards. **Pros:** a posh downtown hotel at family-friendly prices; amenities include rooms with bunk beds, Xbox consoles; free bike-share program complete with a map of the best downtown routes. **Cons:** the reception area is on the building's second floor; ongoing construction project across the street (former Mechanic Theater); expensive valet parking. $ *Rooms from: $203* ⊠ *2 N. Charles St., Downtown* ☎ *410/692–6170* ⊕ *www.monaco-baltimore.com* ⊃ *202 rooms* ⊚ *No meals.*

Hotel Revival

$ | **HOTEL** | **FAMILY** | Joie de Vivre hotel group has made a splash in town with its rehab of a historic apartment building, right across from the Washington Monument, offering rooms with wood-laminate floors, brightly colored fabrics, and art reflecting the surrounding neighborhood. **Pros:** free Wi-Fi throughout; historical accents that instill a sense of place; location near the BSO and the

Walters Art Museum. **Cons:** area can feel forlorn at night; expensive valet parking; residential-style guest rooms curiously lack desks. ⑤ *Rooms from: $159* ✉ *101 W. Monument St., Mount Vernon* ☎ *410/727–7101* ⊕ *www.jdvhotels.com* ⇆ *107 rooms* ⊠ *No meals.*

★ The Ivy Hotel

$$$$ | **HOTEL** | Nestled in a century-old brownstone, just a few blocks from Penn Station, this boutique hotel features luxurious appointments such as original art and antiques, a library, billiards room and private interior courtyard, Frette linens atop the beds, en suite gas fireplaces, and heated floors and large soaking tubs in the bathrooms. **Pros:** small but noteworthy spa on-site; attentive staff ensures every need is met; each layout is different; some suites feature multiple levels. **Cons:** very expensive; limited privacy in a historic home setting. ⑤ *Rooms from: $595* ✉ *205 E. Biddle St., Mount Vernon* ☎ *410/514–6500* ⊕ *www. theivybaltimore.com* ⇆ *18 rooms* ⊠ *Free Breakfast.*

Marriott Baltimore Waterfront

$$ | **HOTEL** | The city's tallest hotel and one of a handful directly on the Inner Harbor, this 32-story Marriott has a Neoclassical interior that uses multihued marble, rich jewel-tone walls, and photographs of Baltimore architectural landmarks. **Pros:** newly renovated rooms; great location and view; water taxi stop right out front. **Cons:** pricey compared to nearby hotels in the same category; expensive valet parking; staff can be rude. ⑤ *Rooms from: $239* ✉ *700 Aliceanna St., Harbor East* ☎ *410/385–3000* ⊕ *www.marriott. com* ⇆ *751 rooms* ⊠ *No meals.*

Sagamore Pendry Baltimore

$$$ | **HOTEL** | **FAMILY** | The cornerstone of Fells Point has long been the Rec Pier building, once an immigration hub, then later the setting for the TV series *Homicide: Life on the Street,* and now a 128-room boutique gem that has inspired a neighborhood-wide renaissance. **Pros:** stunning infinity pool overlooking the harbor and Domino Sugar Factory; gorgeous circa-1914 ballroom with original windows and state-of-the-art technology; free Wi-Fi throughout. **Cons:** expensive valet parking; no spa; service can be pretentious. ⑤ *Rooms from: $500* ✉ *1715 Thames St., Fells Point* ☎ *443/552–1400* ⊕ *www.pendryhotels.com* ⇆ *128 rooms* ⊠ *No meals.*

Index

310

2 Amys

Fodor's WASHINGTON, D.C.

WITHDRAWN

Publisher: Stephen Horowitz, *General Manager*

Editorial: Douglas Stallings, *Editorial Director;* Jill Fergus, Jacinta O'Halloran, Amanda Sadlowski, *Senior Editors;* Kayla Becker, Alexis Kelly, *Editors*

Design: Tina Malaney, *Director of Design and Production;* Jessica Gonzalez, *Graphic Designer;* Mariana Tabares, *Design and Production Intern*

Production: Jennifer DePrima, *Editorial Production Manager;* Elyse Rozelle, *Senior Production Editor;* Monica White, *Production Editor*

Maps: Rebecca Baer, *Senior Map Editor;* Mark Stroud (Moon Street Cartography); David Lindroth, *Cartographers*

Photography: Viviane Teles, *Senior Photo Editor;* Namrata Aggarwal, Ashok Kumar, Carl Yu, *Photo Editors;* Rebecca Rimmer, *Photo Intern*

Business and Operations: Chuck Hoover, *Chief Marketing Officer;* Robert Ames, *Group General Manager;* Devin Duckworth, *Director of Print Publishing;* Victor Bernal, *Business Analyst*

Public Relations and Marketing: Joe Ewaskiw, *Senior Director Communications and Public Relations*

Fodors.com: Jeremy Tarr, *Editorial Director;* Rachael Levitt, *Managing Editor*

Technology: Jon Atkinson, *Director of Technology;* Rudresh Teotia, *Lead Developer;* Jacob Ashpis, *Content Operations Manager*

Writers: Bob Carden, Claire Handscombe, Barbara Noe Kennedy, Sabrina Medora, Jessica van Dop DeJesus, Delesia Watson

Editors: Rachael Roth, Douglas Stallings

Production Editor: Monica White

25th Edition

ISBN 978-1-64097-354-1

ISSN 0743–9741

Library of Congress Control Number 2018914616

SPECIAL SALES
This book is available at special discounts for bulk purchases for sales promotions or premiums. For more information, e-mail SpecialMarkets@fodors.com.

PRINTED IN CANADA

10 9 8 7 6 5 4 3 2 1

MIX
Paper from responsible sources
FSC
www.fsc.org   FSC® C016245

About Our Writers

Bob Carden is a business and travel writer whose work appears frequently in the *Washington Post, Philadelphia Inquirer, Chicago Tribune,* and others. He has had a long journalism career and has worked as a correspondent for CNN in Washington, D.C., PBS in Tokyo, and as a writer for the *Philadelphia Daily News.* Bob has produced four PBS documentaries dealing with international business and investment fraud. He lives in Bethesda, MD, with his wife. He updated Downtown, Penn Quarter and Chinatown, and Upper Northwest.

Claire Handscombe is a British writer who moved to Washington, D.C., in 2012 to study for an MFA in Creative Writing, but also because of an obsession with *The West Wing.* She is the host of the Brit Lit Podcast, the author of the novel *Unscripted,* and the editor of *Walk With Us: How The West Wing Changed Our Lives,;* when she's away from books, she's probably checking out a new favorite restaurant with a friend. She updated The National Mall and Federal Triangle; and The Waterfront and Southeast.

After many years as senior editor with NatGeo Travel Publishing, **Barbara Noe Kennedy** left in 2015 to fly solo as a freelance travel writer and editor, focusing on destinations, art, culture, food, and adventure around the world. She's watched D.C. grow up into a global city, though her favorite activity remains running on its leafy paths. Her website is ⊕ *barbaranoekennedy.com*. She updated Foggy Bottom, the West End, and the White House; Experience Washington, D.C.; and Travel Smart.

Sabrina Medora is considered one of the most multifaceted voices in the culinary industry. Her writing has been featured in publications such as *Bon Appetit, Plate Magazine,* the James Beard Foundation, *Heated, The Kitchn, Modern Luxury, Eater D.C., Washington City Paper,* and more. In 2018, she launched Un-Plated, a multimedia platform that celebrates the little-known stories and unsung heroes of the restaurant industry. She updated Side Trips, Georgetown, Capitol Hill, and Northeast D.C.

Jessica van Dop DeJesús is a widely published travel content creator. She's the founder of the popular foodie travel website, The Dining Traveler, and the author of the coffee-table book, *The Dining Traveler Guide to Puerto Rico.* Her writing has been featured in *Travel Channel, Modern Luxury, Washington City Paper, Southern Living,* and *Telemundo.* She was raised in Guayama, Puerto Rico. Jessica began traveling over 20 years ago as a young Marine and has traveled to more than 50 countries and lived in six. When she's not traveling, she's at home with her family in Washington, D.C. Follow her on Instagram, Facebook, Twitter, Pinterest, and YouTube @DiningTraveler. She updated U Street Corridor, Logan Circle, and Columbia Heights; Dupont Circle and Kalorama; and Adams Morgan.

Delesia Watson is a New York City–based writer, editor, and motivational speaker. Through her brand, Life is Deleesh, Delesia empowers women of all ages to live more abundantly, especially focusing on instilling self-esteem in young girls. She is writing a book to empower women to end toxic, unhealthy, and dead-end relationships, and pursuing a fresh start. When she's not writing, Delesia enjoys serving her community, thrift shopping, and watching cheesy rom-coms. She updated Arlington, Annapolis, and Baltimore.